UNDERSTANDING ORGANIZED CRIME IN GLOBAL PERSPECTIVE

This work is dedicated by
Patrick J. Ryan
to Maureen and Colm Patrick Ryan,

and

by George E. Rush
to his children Susan and Michael
and their children Sarah, Chelsea, and Chad.

Edited by
Patrick J. Ryan / George E. Rush

UNDERSTANDING ORGANIZED CRIME IN GLOBAL PERSPECTIVE
A Reader

SAGE Publications
International Educational and Professional Publisher
Thousand Oaks London New Delhi

For information:

SAGE Publications, Inc.
2455 Teller Road
Thousand Oaks, California 91320
E-mail: order@sagepub.com

SAGE Publications Ltd.
6 Bonhill Street
London EC2A 4PU
United Kingdom

SAGE Publications India Pvt. Ltd.
M-32 Market
Greater Kailash I
New Delhi 110 048 India

Printed in the United States of America

Library of Congress Cataloging-in-Publication Data

Main entry under title:

Understanding organized crime in global perspective: A reader /
 edited by Patrick J. Ryan,
   George E. Rush.
     p. cm.
   Includes bibliographical references and index.
   ISBN 0-7619-0981-8 (cloth: acid-free paper). —
   ISBN 0-7619-0982-6 (pbk.: acid-free paper)
   1. Organized crime—United States. I. Ryan, Patrick J., 1941-
   II. Rush, George E. (George Eugene), 1932-
   HV6446.U53 1997
   364.1′06′0973—dc21   97-21083

97 98 99 00 01 02 03 10 9 8 7 6 5 4 3 2 1

Acquiring Editor:	C. Terry Hendrix
Editorial Assistant:	Dale Mary Grenfell
Production Editor:	Diana E. Axelsen
Production Assistant:	Lynn Miyata
Typesetter:	Danielle Dillahunt
Indexer:	Virgil Diodato
Cover Designer:	Candice Harman

CONTENTS

ACKNOWLEDGMENTS

The editors must first recognize and gratefully acknowledge the research of the authors who made this work possible. Comparatively, editors do little; the authors make a text such as this what it is. From Cressey to Rogovin to Yasmann, from 1967 to 1997, those who study organized crime and write about it have developed a huge literature, of which this text will be a part. Most of the contributors are active members of the International Association for the Study of Organized Crime (IASOC). The membership list of this organization reads like a "Who's Who" in the study, reporting, researching, and interdiction of organized crime. Professors, news reporters, social scientists, law enforcement personnel, indeed, anyone interested in the study of organized crime can be found among the membership. For nearly 12 years, the unnamed members of IASOC have contributed to the growth of our knowledge of organized crime. You will read the work of their representatives here. Were it possible, a standing ovation would be in order for them all, for they have each indirectly enabled this text to see print.

All but two of the works in this book have previously appeared in issues of the *Journal of Contemporary Criminal Justice.* The journal would not have come into existence 12 years ago were it not for the tangible contributions of those whom the journal affectionately calls its "Founders Circle." At the midpoint of the lives of the *Journal of Contemporary Criminal Justice* and the International Association for the Study of Organized Crime, a joint venture was undertaken to devote an annual issue of the journal to organized crime. So, coming full circle, the members of IASOC who further the study of organized crime and the members of the Founders Circle who support the study of contemporary criminal justice are joined in an effort that sees no end. The more we learn of organized crime, the more we become aware of what is yet to be learned. Yet, however long such people as these continue to offer their good services, the task will be less daunting. We thank each one.

No text is finalized without the yeoman efforts of the publication staff. We thank Terry Hendrix at Sage for his open-mindedness when first approached about a reader in organized crime. With rejection notices enough to paper the wall, Terry's receptiveness to a novel idea was the impetus that put the project into the "doable" stage. His colleague, Dale Grenfell, is every author's wish for a compatible publisher's representative. Her support, gentle reminders about overdue items, and just plain being nice, moved the work apace. We owe Dale a special note of thanks. Linda Poderski copyedited the manuscript as only one truly dedicated to that task might. Thank you, Linda. The Senior Production Editor at Sage, Diana Axelsen, put the icing on the cake, taking the work of all those mentioned above and banging it into final form. Matter-of-factly, we must thank the entire staff at Sage Publications for their assistance. None could be better.

The task of saying thank you is made more difficult, given the geographic distance between the editors. Both Rush and Ryan enjoy support from their respective universities, California State University at Long Beach and Long Island University. The thank you for those colleagues, students, staff, and friends who played a part in putting this work together must be a collective one.

As usual, leaving the most valued contributors until last, we gratefully thank the many folks who volunteer to serve as manuscript reviewers for the *Journal of Contemporary Criminal Justice*. The real editors are those who say yea or nay regarding the quality of an author's work. They have made our work less burdensome for first gleaning only the best in the field for inclusion in the publication from which we gathered the material you are about to read.

INTRODUCTION

The works in this book are mainly the effort of members of the International Association for the Study of Organized Crime—either in their authorship or by editorial input. Except for the first two, all the chapters were published first as articles in the *Journal of Contemporary Criminal Justice*; all were designed for an academic audience. For that kind of audience, authors assume that a fair amount of prior reading on the subject has been done. The material is weighty, and you may be put off by the style or perhaps the absence of sex, blood, and gore. Nevertheless, if you have this book in hand, we assume that you are a serious student of organized crime and are willing to do some serious thinking about the way "this thing" developed into what many now believe is the most serious threat facing the global economy.

Meyer Lansky once said, "This thing [American organized crime] is bigger than US Steel." When Lansky issued that profundity, US Steel was America; if US Steel went belly-up, America was done for. Well, US Steel is no longer the epitome of American industry and is relegated to just another company fighting to stay alive in a much different, international market than was around prior to World War II. In the same way,

organized crime has changed to meet changing demands for service. Hard drugs are now a major source of income, a commodity rarely seen when the U.S. Mafia was "bigger than US Steel." Accordingly, we who study organized crime must continually revise strategies, methods, data collection, and whatever else is brought to bear on learning about it. Organized crime is not static, as if once known, one never need study it again. The challenge of this text, and your challenge, is to stay current, to keep up with the latest happenings in the world arena. So, if you are not the serious student of organized crime, stop reading and take this book back to the dealer for a refund. If you choose to continue, be prepared for some very serious study, some rereading of passages, some note taking, and, a requirement, some exchange of information with others studying about organized crime. Your editors believe that the materials presented here are important, indeed, required reading for those who wish to learn more or to stay current about organized crime. We believe that the material deserves a wider audience than those who read academic journals, so we have gleaned from the five issues of the *Journal* dedicated to organized crime generally, those articles that provide a fairly extensive coverage of international aspects of organized crime.

Understand that this material is but the tip of the iceberg. Parts 1 and 2 provide a historical introduction to some theorizing about what organized crime is, and that, in turn, provides a basis for understanding the more concrete, practical experiences described in the later chapters. Donald Cressey's work is the foundation, the cornerstone of the study of organized crime. This is the most often cited piece of research on the topic and lays out the hierarchical structure and organization for the "Mob." If you do not have a firm grasp of Cressey, further study is most difficult. When studying Chapter 1, "The Functions and Structure of Criminal Syndicates," understand that it was written in 1967, when the collected knowledge of organized crime could be found on a single shelf in a library. Today, that collection would fill a section, and every book on those shelves would probably mention Cressey's work. This is an important contribution to the literature. For example, Cressey's description of "a bill to outlaw the Mafia and other organized crime syndicates," authored by Senators John L. McClellan and Frank J. Lausche, was codified as the Racketeer Influenced and Corrupt Organizations Act (RICO) in 1971 and has become the most used and powerful legal weapon in the arsenal of federal prosecutors. One of Cressey's colleagues, Robert Blakley, a lawyer, actually wrote RICO, but Cressey's influence is evident. This is but one small example of the powerful influence this research had on law enforcement, the research community, and the public perception of organized crime.

The lists of works cited for the 17 chapters in this book have been collected in a separate reference list for the sake of convenience. You would be well served to scan for the parenthetical citations before reading (or as you cover) a chapter. They provide some sense of the context in which the author(s) couch their arguments. They give a hint of where the author is "coming from." Thumb through the book, pausing to note the names of authors cited. You will find the same names reappearing. Don't think this a redundancy, as if having read one author and finding that a second author used similar sources, the second chapter is a rehashing of the first. Nothing is farther from the truth. In studying the literature on any topic, you'll find a core of solid material that lays the basis, the logical starting points, for further research. Organized crime is no exception. This is research, the orderly development of a paradigm. It is a continuous process, and after you finish this text, you will have been part of it.

A little-publicized adage in academia says: If you steal from one work, that's plagiarism; if you steal from many, that's research. Feel free to do your research. Use the reference list to broaden your personal base of knowledge. If you are composing your own article as a course requirement or perhaps for publication, pay particular attention to those passages cited in the chapter you are reading. Often, parenthetical citations are signposts that say the author assumes that you, the reader, are familiar with the works cited. For other than casual reading, then, you would be well served to take a look at the works cited.

The introductory commentaries for each part of the book will guide you through the material. The commentaries draw comparisons about points of agreement, highlight disagreements, and if nothing else, let you know what to expect from each part. Certainly, you can pick and choose the order in which you study the pieces, depending on your goal. If you have no research agenda, we recommend reading the chapters as presented; each one builds on or complements the one preceding it.

Starting with the early work of Donald Cressey, this collection first provides a look at the structure and workings of the Italian version of organized crime, aka the Mafia, Cosa Nostra, the Outfit (Chicago), the Mob, or the family. Cressey's model has stood the test of time, but not without criticism. Accordingly, you will find a critique of Cressey by one of his students (Joseph Albini, Chapter 2) and a retort by two other colleagues (Charles Rogovin and Frederick Martens, Chapter 3). Part 2 provides a more dispassionate account of the debate sketched in Part 1. Robert Kelly (Chapter 4) praises Cressey's contribution, chooses not to spend time arguing about it, and offers instead his ideas about organized crime that grew out of theorizing about the underworld vis-à-vis Cressey's bureaucratic model. Similarly, Mark Haller (Chapter 5) finds some flaws in that version of organized crime and provides an alternative solution. When reading Parts 1 and 2, pay special attention to these two chapters that provide alternative views of Cressey's bureaucratic model of Cosa Nostra. This assumes, of course, that you paid particular attention to Chapter 1, by Cressey; Chapter 2, Albini's critique of Cressey; and Chapter 3, the rejoinder by Rogovin and Martens. You can skip ahead to Part 3 and learn what the Mafia and the Devil have in common, but to put your knowledge of organized crime on a really solid foundation, the Cressey piece is a must read, first. Once you get through the theoretical sections, it's all downhill.

Part 3 is somewhat different. Here, you'll find Satan and true-life stories. It serves as a nexus of the purely academic and the more earthy (or ethereal) material. In Chapter 6, Albini argues that Americans' belief in the presence of organized crime is akin to a belief in the Devil. Next time someone says something like, "This is the Devil's work," or, "The Devil made him do it," ask whether that person has ever seen the Devil. You get the message: There are things we "know" that have as much empirical support as our knowledge of hell. Mythological beliefs are not, per se, bad, but according to Albini and others (e.g., Hawkins, 1969), when similar belief systems justify the existence of both Devil and Mafia, we might want to review the latter.

In Chapter 7, Thomas Firestone takes a more prosaic approach. He examines the biographies, the memoirs, of organized crime figures to discern what gets these people into organized crime in the first place, to discover any common ground that may breed Mob Bosses. He then looks to the structure of the organization as described in the members' own words and concludes that the breaking of the code of silence

by so many Mafiosi is the death knell for the Mob.

Part 4 moves to the product of field research. In Chapter 8, Robert Lombardo, in Chicago, looks at the social organization of the Outfit. In Chapter 9, Robert Davidson does the same in the same city regarding Asian organized crime groups. Davidson does not, and neither should you, fall into the trap of labeling Asian (or Colombian, or Nigerian, or Russian) organized crime, "emerging." These groups emerged only in the sense that policymakers and law enforcement recognized them as threats. The tongs and triads were alive and well in the 19th century. The Nigerians were dealing drugs 30 years ago, and what we know about the Russian version suggests that organized crime flourished in that country under every regime and is not a novel product of the post-breakup era.

A caveat: Be wary of generalizing to the nation what you read about organized crime in Chicago. We included these two chapters because they are, in one sense, complementary. Their authors talk about the same geographic area, and each looks at criminal organizations and the reasons for their existence. But, as both Kelly (in Chapter 4) and Haller (in Chapter 5) suggest, the serious student of organized crime must look to the entire environment, must examine the social context in which the Mob operates. Thus, however good a starting point Chicago is, you should include in your database other pieces of research if you are studying groups located elsewhere. Chicago was selected for this text because that is where it all began and because we thought a look at organized crime "around the world" should include some mention of the United States. The study of organized crime surely began here (e.g., see Landesco, 1929/1968), and so these chapters provide a comparative basis for studying Russia and Asia, Europe or the Pacific Rim, or wherever else your research takes you.

Keep in mind that we now know organized crime is more than the Italian or Italian American version of it. Whatever the epidemiologists might say about the etiology, the root causes of criminal behavior, there are no delimiters based on national, racial, or ethic characteristics. It seems that where people are, organized crime is. No country is free from its influence. Consider that, at the same time that the legitimate government of Bosnia could not successfully elect a president in 1996, the illegitimate enterprise, organized crime, like the Phoenix, had grown from the ashes of war's devastation to put in place a well-oiled network of brothels and gaming houses. It was business as usual for the bad guys, a struggle for the white hats. Russia, all of Asia, South America (the subject of our next book), the emerging nations of Europe and Africa, as well as the "traditional" bastions of organized crime, each has its own version of criminality, and when the criminals band together for mutual benefit, the phenomenon is usually called *organized crime.*

No entity is safe from its influence. In Chapter 10, Maurice Punch documents the involvement of no less than the Vatican in a worldwide banking swindle. Should we condemn the Roman Catholic Church as organized crime? We think not. Punch explores the participation of church members in the precursor to the BCCI scandal, to be sure, but keep in mind that any individual in all organizations can be corrupted. He describes the connections among the Vatican, politicians, businesspeople, and the secret services in "a range of dubious and even criminal practices." A clue to why such a diverse cross section of society would become involved in organized crime activities is found in the last sentence of the chapter, which quotes banker and mastermind Roberto Calvi: "For that amount of money, people will kill." We should not be surprised at the disclosures in Punch's chapter. The scam is neither unique to, nor emblematic of, Italy.

Organized crime enterprises in Europe and Asia were around probably as long as their Mediterranean and U.S. cousins, but we just didn't study them or even know of their existence. The final chapter in Part 4 covers changing trends in international organized crime, paying particular attention to Eastern Europe. David Carter went to Europe and interviewed mainly law enforcement and intelligence gathering personnel to collect data for this research. His conclusions in Chapter 11 are quite sobering. The growth in short-term criminal alliances, the diversity of products delivered, and the transnational nature of the new criminal enterprises in Eastern Europe bode ill for the entire world. The level of violence used by these organizations to maximize profits is especially worrisome. Carter notes that denial of its existence played a historical role in the typical American reaction to organized crime. J. Edgar Hoover steadfastly refused to acknowledge that organized crime existed until the evidence for it became overwhelming and a posture of denial, patently absurd. History is a good teacher, so Carter's analysis of Eastern Europe moves us toward not repeating the errors of the past, toward not looking at organized crime as would an ostrich.

Part 5 provides a picture of organized crime in Russia, newly discovered since the breakup of the republic, but apparently as old as any other version of organized crime; its history, structure, and function are covered in Chapter 12 by Joseph Albini, Roy E. Rogers, Victor Shabalin, Valery Kutushev, Vladimir Moiseev, and Julie Anderson. "Russia as a Racket," the subtitle of Chapter 13, is a "neat" way of calling attention to similarities between Russian and Sicilian organized crime groups. The political environment in Sicily that allowed the Mafia to develop its extortion schemes and like rackets is disconcertingly similar to the cultural climate currently existent in Russia. For sure, the latter is more volatile, still changing to accommodate the prerogatives of social democracy. At the same time, say Kelly, Schatzberg, and Ryan in Chapter 13, the social changes accommodate a version of Russian organized crime with striking congruity to its older cousin in the Mediterranean.

Equally "neat" is J. Michael Waller and Victor Yasmann's entitling their look at the role of law enforcement in Russia "Russia's Great Criminal Revolution" (Chapter 14). Need we call your attention to the analogy with its cultural counterpart? This chapter suggests the thesis of the prior one, that the cultural revolution, whatever its characteristics and elements, is not without a forceful criminal element. These authors see criminality, organized or not, as part and parcel of the Russian culture. This synergism and beneficial symbiosis with the larger society are nothing new, but it is intriguing that the same cultural ties that foster the better-known organized crime groups seem to be equally effective in Russia. As Russia grows and changes to meet the demands of increased global intercourse, so too does the Russian Mob. One characteristic of organized crime is the ability to penetrate law enforcement for purpose of co-optation. Bribery opens the door to servitude. Police, once on the take, can hardly extricate themselves from the demands of the criminals who pay them. A nation is in serious trouble when corruption becomes institutionalized, as Waller and Yasmann demonstrate is a fact of Russian life. Indeed, they say that crime has become an "instrument of state policy" in that great bear of a country.

Globe-trot to the other side of the world in Part 5, and we find James McKenna arguing (in Chapter 15) that organized crime in the Royal Colony of Hong Kong is every bit as viable as in Russia, Italy, or the United States. The author of this piece spent almost a year living in the "Suzie Wong" atmosphere of Hong Kong to gather research material for this chapter. This is "get the seat of your pants dirty" research that, being firsthand, lends a heightened level of credibility to the author's commentary. Too, it's interesting reading.

The logical extension of a descriptive piece is a predictive one, so in Chapter 16, John Dombrink and John Song talk about the future of Hong Kong vis-à-vis its criminal element. Hong Kong politically returned to the People's Republic of China on July 1, 1997. Comparisons between America's Mafia and organized crime in China frequently equate the triads with the families found in the Italian version. Dombrink and Song argue that just as the Mafia is not the sum total of U.S. organized crime, the triads, as much involved as they are, cannot be considered all of Asian organized crime. Once again, the environmental/contextual bogeyman

rears its head. Although not explicitly stated, one notion pervades this chapter: If we are to understand organized crime operations in any particular place or time, the entire picture must be examined; we cannot focus on one element as being the entire phenomena.

The final chapter bridges the globe. Starting in Southeast Asia, Ken Sanz and Ira Silverman (Chapter 17) predict the globalization of Southeast Asian organized crime. The authors say this ethnic group will forge alliances with both U.S. and European Mobs, will use the immigrant enclaves in the United States for recruitment and facilitation of their activities, and poses an economic threat as dangerous as that of any other criminal group. Of particular interest is the anticipated growth in the slave trade, the adoption "industry," and the trade in human body parts. The nightly newscasts already report on the latter. When a ship runs aground in Brooklyn, New York, with a cargo of illegal immigrants, can we be expected to believe the "cargo" was destined for the legal employment market? Sanz and Silverman call our attention to the common actors who devise such criminal schemes and to their novelty. For example, they say a "unique feature" of Vietnamese criminal activity is the full enfranchisement of females. For Vietnamese criminals, the song is the same as that sung by all organized crime; however, the lyric is a bit different. Gender is not an issue when it comes to membership in a Vietnamese Mob. Reliance on loosely organized street gangs for enforcement agents also differentiates these groups from the others (although the Chinese criminals avail themselves similarly). Their ties to Southeast Asia facilitate commodity and currency exchanges with a potential that challenges the older, more sophisticated groups. Sanz and Silverman provide a fitting conclusion to this reader in arguing that the Southeast Asian Mob will form mutual assistance "pacts with other ethnic criminal groups," especially those in the United States and Europe. Can we expect otherwise in this fast-shrinking world?

The more we know about organized crime, it seems, the less we know. Every day, new groups are chronicled, new criminal schemes reported.

Such is the nature of research and study of all phenomena, yet as this reader demonstrates, our knowledge of organized crime has gone global. It's a quantum leap from understanding the parochial sphere of control of "traditional" families to recognizing the sophistication required to form intercontinental allegiances to do crime. It's safe to conclude that international organized crime is a happening whose time has come.

If you have not read extensively about organized crime, use this text as a starting point. If you are up on the topic, use the book as supplemental material to increase your store of knowledge. In both cases, the editors wish you fair sailing through this international look at organized crime, past, present, and future.

PART I

COMMENTARY

More than two decades after the first "model" of organized crime was published, a lively and sometimes heated debate surrounds the issue of who and what is considered organized crime. Equally moot is the issue of who does organized crime, who are the cast of characters in this drama that is attractive from a distance but a frighteningly real threat when seen firsthand.

In 1967, Donald Ray Cressey proposed a "bureaucratic model" (Cressey, 1967a) of organized crime that focuses attention almost exclusively on the Italian version of organized crime. He later expanded on this government report to offer a neatly packaged organization, replete with division of labor, a structural hierarchy, and clearly defined roles (Cressey, 1969). The groundwork for Cressey's model can be found in the hearings chaired by Senator Estes Kefauver in the 1950s and those of Senator John L. McClellan in the early 1960s. Born of the testimony of Joe Valachi before the McClellan committee and Frank Costello (the "Prime Minister" of the underworld) before the Kefauver committee, terms such as Mafia, Our Thing, *Cosa Nostra, Capo, Consigliere,* made men, the Commission, and *omerta* came into common usage. Both sets of hearings were televised nationwide, and Americans had their first glimpse

into initiation rituals, and an organizational hierarchy with formal rules of behavior and an unwritten code or value set that earned violent physical retribution and even death for any who violated *omerta.*

In the early 1970s, researchers such as Joseph Albini (1971), Francis Ianni and Elizabeth Reuss-Ianni (1972), and Dwight Smith, Jr. (1975), began to question Cressey's typification. Could organized crime be a wholly Italian enterprise? What of the Irish, African Americans, Colombians, Chinese, and the vast and diverse collection of criminals who were being arrested for exactly the same criminal activities as the "Mob guys" but who were not of the Mafia. Weren't these criminals organized crime members too? And what of the Italians who were found operating outside the "family's" territory. What of the Brooklyn-based Gambino family member who was arrested for truck hijacking at Newark Airport, the domain of the Scarfo Mob. How did this fit into a model that said the boss tightly controls all activities of all members?

The debate is framed in this text by first presenting excerpts of Cressey's initial publication of his model (the concept is elaborated on in his classic book *Theft of the Nation,* 1969). Albini worked with Cressey; in fact, Cressey advised Albini when the latter was gathering material for his book on the Mafia. Ironically, *The American Mafia: Genesis of a Legend* (Albini, 1971) is a major voice arguing that organized crime is more than the Mafia and that however helpful *Theft of the Nation* is in understanding the phenomenon, it doesn't embrace the entire spectrum of organized crime activities and actors. Indeed, Albini argues that too much blame is put on Italians for all organized crime. Nevertheless, Cressey's book stands as the monumental work in the study of organized crime, and many criminologists believe that, given (a) the state of knowledge on the subject, circa 1965, and (b) resources limited mainly to government documents and Congressional testimony, without Cressey's seminal model, organized crime research would still be in the Dark Ages. Cressey moved organized crime from the pages of government documents into the milieu of academic theory and onto the front pages of the popular media. Albini writes of his close association with Cressey in Chapter 2, "Donald Cressey's Contributions to the Study of Organized Crime: An Evaluation." He says that Cressey "was not at the time [1967] very knowledgeable about organized crime" and, about Cressey's consultant paper (Chapter 1), "We see a researcher who is rightfully confused." These seem harsh words for a colleague, much more so because they are directed at the author of the most frequently referenced work in the literature on organized crime.

Charles Rogovin and Frederick Martens take issue with Albini in Chapter 3, "The Evil That Men Do." By implication, Albini is one of the evildoers. An example from the two chapters shows the close professional association these four authors (Cressey, Albini, Rogovin, and Martens) share. Albini asserts in his chapter that Cressey was apprehensive for his personal safety as a consequence of the information he had accessed during his research. Note that Albini's assertion was made in 1988, after Cressey's death. Rogovin and Martens say about the charge: "It strains credulity to believe

that Cressey ever seriously suggested that he was apprehensive. . . . Of the many people who knew and worked closely with Cressey, . . . none recall him ever expressing the apprehension." Continuing on a personal tone, these authors say that they cannot fathom "the exaggerations in which he [Albini] indulges in the development of his thesis" and "waiting until Cressey's death is to operate under a very fuzzy set of rules." Clearly, you can detect in Chapters 2 and 3 writers who know each other well and who have taken a position in defense or denigration of each other's methods and conclusions. The debate is not limited to such exchanges, but as Part 1 shows, the issue of who and what is organized crime is not yet settled, and the debate does indeed continue.

SUGGESTED READINGS

Abadinsky, H. (1983). *The criminal elite: Professional and organized crime*. Westport, CT: Greenwood.

Abadinsky, H. (1994). *Organized crime*. Chicago: Nelson-Hall.

Arlacchi, P. (1986). *Mafia business: The Mafia ethic and the spirit of capitalism*. London: Verso.

Blok, A. (1974). *The Mafia of a Sicilian village, 1860-1960: A study of violent peasant entrepreneurs*. New York: Harper & Row.

Doleschal, E., Newton, A., & Hickey, W. (1981). *A guide to the literature on organized crime: An annotated bibliography covering the years 1967-1981*. Hackensack, NJ: National Council on Crime and Delinquency.

Hess, H. (1973). *Mafia and Mafiosi: The structure of power*. Lexington, MA: D. C. Heath.

Kelly, R. J. (Ed.). (1986). *Organized crime: An international perspective*. Lanham, MD: Rowman & Littlefield.

Kelly, R. J., Chin, K-L., & Schatzberg, R. (Eds.). (1994). *A handbook of organized crime*. Westport, CT: Greenwood.

Moore, W. H. (1974). *The Kefauver committee and the politics of crime*. Columbia: University of Missouri Press.

Mori, C. (1933). *The last struggle with the Mafia*. London: Putnam.

Pantaleone, M. (1966). *The Mafia and politics*. New York: Coward & McCann.

Peterson, V. (1983). *The Mob: 200 years of organized crime in New York*. Ottawa, IL: Green Hill.

Ryan, P. J. (1995). *Organized crime: A reference handbook*. Denver, CO: ABC-CLIO.

1

THE FUNCTIONS AND STRUCTURE OF CRIMINAL SYNDICATES

DONALD R. CRESSEY

This chapter is extracted from, unquestionably, the major work in the study of organized crime. Originally published as Appendix A of *Task Force Report: Organized Crime* by the President's Commission on Law Enforcement and Administration of Justice in 1967, the report served as the basis for Cressey's *Theft of the Nation: The Structure and Operations of Organized Crime in America* (1969). The chapter's title, echoed in Cressey's book title, captures the quintessence of the debate about who and what is organized crime, how it is structured and operates, and how much of a threat to society it poses. Cressey's work is the catalyst that led to works of similar subject matter by Albini, Ianni and Reuss-Ianni, and Smith, Jr. Respectively, *The American Mafia, A Family Business,* and *The Mafia Mystique* built on or questioned the hierarchically structured, ethnocentric picture of the American Mafia drawn by Cressey. Herein is the bedrock for further study of organized crime. The excerpts—comparisons of American organized crime and its Sicilian cousin, the skeletal structure of organized crime, *omerta* and its workings, and "A Proposal for Study"—are the bare essentials for an informed examination of the rest of this text.

AMERICAN ORGANIZED CRIME AND THE SICILIAN MAFIA

In America, criminals have managed to organize a nationwide illicit cartel and confederation. This organization is dedicated to amassing millions of dollars from usury and the illicit sale of lottery tickets, chances on the outcome of horse races and athletic events, and the sale or manipulation of sexual intercourse, narcotics, and liquor. Its presence in our society is morally reprehensible because any citizen purchasing illicit goods and services from organized criminals contributes to an underground culture of fraud, corruption, violence, and murder. Nevertheless, criminal organizations dealing only in illicit goods and services are no great threat to the nation. The danger of organized crime arises

3

because the vast profits acquired from the sale of illicit goods and services are being invested in licit enterprises, in both the business sphere and the government sphere. It is when criminal syndicates start to undermine basic economic and political traditions and institutions that the real trouble begins. And the real trouble has begun in America.

It is one thing to make money in an illegal gambling enterprise, but it is another thing to achieve business monopoly by means of a simple weapon—a gun. It is one thing to amass a fortune in usury, but it is another thing to bribe a government official to get a construction contract. It is one thing to control gambling and most other illegal activities in a neighborhood, but it is another thing to demand, with a gun, a share of the butcher's profits, the baker's profits, the doctor's fees, and the banker's interest rates.

Although organized criminals do not yet have control of all of the legitimate economic and political activities in any metropolitan or other geographic area of America, they do have control of *some* of those activities in many areas. Members of crime syndicates have invested in a wide variety of businesses, and they are not operating those businesses legally, as the Kefauver committee showed over a decade ago. They continue to invest, and they continue to monopolize by force. Further, rulers of crime syndicates have strong interests in the government process, and they are "represented," in one form or another, in legislative, judicial, and executive bodies all over the country. They have gone beyond buying licenses to gamble from law enforcement officials and minor city officials and now are concerned with influencing legislation on matters as diverse as food services and garbage collection.

We recognize a danger. We cannot be sure of the degree of the danger any more than the observer of the beginnings of any other kind of monopoly can be sure of the degree of danger. If a large retail firm lowers its prices to a level such that its small independent competitors go bankrupt, that is free enterprise. If, after its competitors are forced out of business, the large

firm raises its prices above those existing when it had competitors, thus forcing consumers to pay a tribute, that is exploitive monopolistic practice. By analogy, rulers of crime syndicates are beginning to drive legitimate businesspeople, labor leaders, and other supporters of the ideology of free competition to the wall. They have established, by force, intimidation, and even more "legal" methods, monopolies in several relatively small fields such as the distribution of vending machines, the supplying of linen to night clubs, and the supplying of some forms of labor. . . .

During national prohibition in the 1930s, the various bootlegging gangs across the nation were largely composed of immigrants and the descendants of immigrants from many countries. An organization known as *Unione Siciliano* [*sic*] was involved. In 1930-1931, near the end of Prohibition, the basic framework of the current structure of American organized crime, to be described in the next section, was established as a result of a gangland war in which an alliance of Italians and Sicilians was victorious. During this war, the Italian-Sicilian alliance was referred to as "the Mafia," and the criminal operations of this establishment later were referred to as "the operations of the Mafia," just as crimes in Italian and Sicilian neighborhoods in the 1920s were attributed to the Mafia and the "Black Hand."

The Italian-Sicilian apparatus set up as a result of the 1930-1931 war continues to dominate organized crime in America, and it is still called "the Mafia" in many quarters. The question remains, however, whether this organization is the Mafia of Sicily and southern Italy transplanted to this country or whether it arose primarily as a response of hoodlums to their new cultural setting, some of the hoodlums being Italian or Sicilian immigrants knowledgeable about how to set up and control an illicit organization. For several reasons, this question is important.

First, it is a fact that the great majority, by far, of Italian and Sicilian immigrants and their descendants have been both fine and law-abiding citizens. They have somehow let criminals who are Italians or Sicilians, or Americans of Italian or Sicilian descent, be identified with them. Criminals of Italian or Sicilian descent are called "Italians" or "Sicilians," whereas bankers, lawyers, and professors of Italian or Sicilian descent are called "Americans." More Americans know the name *Luciano* than know the name *Fermi*. If the criminal cartel or confederation is an importation from Sicily and Italy, it should be disowned by all Italian Americans and Sicilian Americans because it does not represent the real cultural contribution of Italy and Sicily to America. If it is an American innovation, the men of Italian and Sicilian descent who have positions in it should be disowned by the respectable Italian American and Sicilian American community on the ground that they are participating in an extremely undesirable aspect of American culture.

Second, many of the Italian and Sicilian peasants who emigrated to America did so precisely to escape Mafia despotism. These persons certainly did not bring the Mafia with them. Were they once more dominated? Are any of them or their descendants now members of an illicit crime syndicate?

Third, in the late 1920s, Mussolini, Fascist Premier of Italy, had the Mafia of southern Italy and Sicily hounded to the point where some members found it necessary to migrate to escape from internal Mafia conflicts or from the official crackdown. The number entering America, legally or illegally, is unknown. Is it a mere coincidence that the Italian-Sicilian domination of American illicit crime syndicates and the confederation integrating them began shortly after Premier Mussolini's eradication campaign?

Fourth, if the American confederation is an import from Italy and Sicily and if it has retained its connections with the old country, then the strategy for eradicating it must be different from the strategy for eradicating a relatively new American organization. In other words, if it is but a branch of a foreign organization, then its "home office" abroad must be eliminated before control will be effective. Some American organized criminals themselves propagate the legend that their organization is a branch of the old Sicilian Mafia; this legend helps perpetuate the notion that the current conspiracy is ancient and therefore quite impregnable. If, however, the confederation is of recent American origin, then an all-out campaign by American law enforcement agencies working in America is called for.

Fifth, there is a tendency for members of any society or group to look outside themselves for the cause whenever it finds itself confronted with a serious problem or, especially, with an evil. In some cases, "looking outside" means attributing problems to the characteristics of individuals, rather than to the characteristics of the society or group itself. March and Simon (1958) have suggested, for example, that business managers tend to perceive conflict as if it were an individual matter, rather than an organizational matter, because perceiving it as an organizational problem would acknowledge a diversity of goals in the organization, thereby placing strain on the status and power. By the same token, the behavior of cold-blooded hired killers, and of the enforcers and rulers who order the killings, is likely to be accounted for solely in terms of the depravity or viciousness of the personnel involved, rather than in terms of organizational roles, including the roles of the victims. In other cases, looking outside the society or group for the cause of an evil means looking to another society or group. As Tyler has said, "When such a scapegoat can be found, the culture is not only relieved of sin but can indulge itself in an orgy of righteous indignation" (1962b, p. 334). If the Italian and Sicilian Mafia is, in fact, responsible for organized crime in America, then identifying it as the cause of our troubles is more science than scapegoatism. However, if the American confederation is a response to conditions of American life, then those conditions should be studied with a view to deciding whether they can be changed in such a way that the structure and subculture of organized crime will change.

The problem of assigning a name to the American confederation of criminals is, in part, a problem of answering the questions listed above. In a series of conferences at Oyster Bay, New York, some of the nation's leading experts on organized crime struggled to find a name for the organization, and as they did so, they indirectly responded to the above questions by saying that the American confederation should not be confused with the Sicilian Mafia. The conference group reviewed the names commonly used by the public and by some members of the confederation. All of them were rejected.

Mafia was rejected specifically because it is a Sicilian term referring to a Sicilian organization, and many participants in the American conspiracy are not Sicilian.

The term *Cosa Nostra* as describing everyone at all levels of organized crime also was rejected. The term incorrectly implies that all members of the conspiracy are Italian or Sicilian, and the term is unknown outside New York. The conference group did not say so in its reports, but the term is not even widely known in New York. Sergeant Ralph Salerno of the New York City Police has been processing cases of organized crime for 20 years. He has listened to hundreds of conversations between Italian-Sicilian criminals, and he has interviewed dozens of informants and informers. Other than the 1963 testimony before the McClellan committee, he has only twice (once before and once after the McClellan hearings) heard the term *Cosa Nostra* used to refer to the organization itself. If two members hear of an event relevant to their operations, one might say, "Questae una cosa nostra," but this is to say, "This is an affair of ours," not "I am a member of 'our thing' or 'our affair.' "

The conference group noted that, in Chicago, the members sometimes refer to themselves as *the Syndicate,* sometimes as *the Outfit,* but these terms were rejected because they are local. Thus, the Sicilian and Italian terms were rejected because they tend to stress the relationship to the "outside," whereas the Chicago terms were rejected because they do not stress this relationship.

The Organization is sometimes used by members and, although this term does not imply anything about a relationship between

the American organization and the Sicilian and Italian Mafia, it was rejected because it is "not very descriptive," meaning that it does not denote the relationship between the various branches in America.

The conference group accepted *confederation* as the best term. It should be noted that this term refers primarily to the organization of a *government.* The word *cartel* refers primarily to the organization of a *business.* The conference group concluded:

> All of these terms are generally applied to a single loosely knit conspiracy, which is Italian dominated, operates on a nationwide basis, and represents the most sophisticated and powerful group in organized crime. Practically all students of organized crime are agreed that this organization does not represent the total of organized crime, but there has been almost no attempt to name those organizations which constitute the remainder. (*A Theory of Organized Crime Control,* 1966, p. 10)

DETERMINANTS OF NATIONAL AND LOCAL STRUCTURES

The structure of the nationwide cartel and confederation, which today operates the principal illicit businesses in America and which is now striking at the foundations of legitimate business and government as well, came into being in 1931. Further, even the skeleton structure of the local units of the confederation, the "families" controlling illicit businesses in various metropolitan areas, came into being in 1931. These structures resemble the national and local structures of the Italian-Sicilian Mafia, but our organization is not merely the Old World Mafia transplanted. The social, economic, and political conditions of Sicily determined the shape of the Sicilian Mafia, and the social, economic, and political conditions of America determined the shape of the American confederation.

To use an analogy with legitimate business, in 1931 organized crime units across America formed into monopolistic corporations, and these corporations, in turn, linked themselves together in a monopolistic cartel. To use a political analogy, in 1931 the local units formed into feudal governments, and the rulers of these governments linked themselves together in a nationwide confederation that itself constitutes a government. Feudalism was the system of political organization prevailing in Europe from the 9th to the 15th centuries. Basically agricultural, the system meant that a vassal held land belonging to a lord on condition of homage and service under arms. The servant deferred to the lord and in other ways paid homage to him; the lord, in turn, protected the servant. The system was "hereditary" in the sense that the lord had custody of the heirs' property.

The structure of the Sicilian Mafia resembles that of ancient feudal kingdoms, and the Mafia probably is a lineal descendant of feudalism. The structure of the American confederation of crime resembles feudalism too, as it resembles the structure of the Sicilian Mafia. Like feudal lords and Sicilian Mafia chieftains, the rulers of American, geographically based families of criminals derive their authority from tradition in the form of homage and "respect." They allocate territory and a kind of license to do business in return for this homage. Nevertheless, the feudal local governments formed in 1931, and the confederation between them, are American innovations.

Certain American criminals, law enforcement officials, political figures, and plain citizens have known from the beginning that a nationwide confederation was established in 1931. Some of them have denied the existence of the apparatus because they are members of it. Others have for over 30 years been trying to convince the American public that the nationwide apparatus does, in fact, exist. We shall quote three such attempts to convince, occurring about a decade apart.

In a series of articles appearing in 1939, the former attorney for an illicit New York organization, a man who had occupied a position of "Corrupter" for the organization, but who later testified for the state, observed that a nationwide alliance between criminal businesses in America was in operation. This was not the first time such an allegation was made, but it dramatically foreshadowed statements that have been made in more recent years. We quote at some length because we later discuss the gangland war resulting in centralization of control:

When I speak of the underworld now, I mean something far bigger than the Schultz Mob. The Dutchman was one of the last independent barons to hold out against a general centralization of control which had been going on ever since Charlie Lucky became leader of the Unione Siciliani [sic] in 1931. . . The "greasers" in the Unione were killed off, and the organization was no longer a loose, fraternal order of Sicilian blackhanders and alcohol cookers, but rather the framework for a system of alliances which were to govern the underworld. In Chicago, for instance, the Unione no longer fought the Capone Mob, but pooled strength and worked with it. A man no longer had to be a Sicilian to be in the Unione. Into its highest councils came such men as Meyer Lansky and Bugs Siegel, leaders of a tremendously powerful Mob, who were personal partners in the alcohol business with Lucky and Joe Adonis of Brooklyn. Originally the Unione had been a secret but legitimate fraternal organization, with chapters in various cities where there were Sicilian colonies. Some of them were operated openly, like any lodge. But it fell into the control of the criminal element, the Mafia, and with the coming of prohibition, which turned thousands of law-abiding Sicilians into bootleggers, alcohol cookers and vassals of warring Mobs, it changed.

It still numbers among its members many old-time Sicilians who are not gangsters, but anybody who goes into it today is a mobster, and an important one. In New York City the organization is split up territorially into districts, each led by a minor boss, known as the 'compare,' or godfather. . . I know that throughout the underworld the Unione Siciliana is accepted as a mysterious, all-pervasive reality, and that Lucky used it as the vehicle by which the underworld was drawn into cooperation on a national scale. (Davis, 1939, pp. 35-36)

More than a decade after this statement appeared in a popular magazine of the time, many members of the public (and some law enforcement officers) still had no notion that an illicit cartel performed some types of crime across the nation. If they heard of "the Mafia," or "the Syndicate," or "the Outfit," or "the Mob," they did not believe what they heard or did not believe in its importance. They were shocked when in 1951 the Kefauver committee was able to draw the following four conclusions from the testimony of the many witnesses who had appeared before it.

1. There is a Nationwide crime syndicate known as the Mafia, whose tentacles are found in many large cities. It has international ramifications which appear most clearly in connection with the narcotics traffic.

2. Its leaders are usually found in control of the most lucrative rackets in their cities.

3. There are indications of a centralized direction and control of these rackets, but leadership appears to be in a group rather than in a single individual.

4. The Mafia is the cement that helps to bind the Costello-Adonis-Lansky syndicate of New York and the Accardo-Guzik-Fischetti syndicate of Chicago as well as smaller criminal gangs and individual criminals throughout the country. These groups have kept in touch with (Lucky) Luciano since his deportation from this country. (U.S. Congress, 1951, p. 150; see also Feder & Turkus, 1952, pp. 86-115)

The Structural Skeleton

Since the McClellan committee hearings, the tendency has been to label the nationwide cartel and confederation "Cosa Nostra" and then to identify what is known about its division of labor as the structure of "organized crime" in America. This tendency might be responsible for some of the misplaced skepticism about whether a dangerous organization exists. In the first place, calling the organization Cosa Nostra lets citizens believe that they are safe from organized criminals because their local bookie, lottery operator, or usurer is not of Italian or Sicilian descent. The term directs attention to membership, rather than to the power to control and to make alliances. In the second place, using

Cosa Nostra as a noun implies that the total economic and political structure involved is as readily identifiable as that of some other formal organization, such as the Elks Lodge, the Los Angeles Police Department, or the Standard Oil Company. This is obviously not the case. We know very little. Our knowledge of the structure that makes "organized crime" organized is somewhat comparable to the knowledge of Standard Oil that could be gleaned from interviews with gas station attendants. Detailed knowledge of the formal and informal structures of the confederation of Sicilian-Italian families in America would represent one of the greatest criminological advances ever made, even if it were universally recognized that this knowledge was not synonymous with knowledge about all organized crime in America. Because we know so little, it is easy to make the assumption that there is nothing to know anything about.

But we do know enough about the structure to conclude that it is indeed an organization. When there is a board of directors or governors, a president, a vice president, some works managers, foremen and lieutenants, and some workers and plain members, there is an organization.

As the former attorney general's testimony before the McClellan committee indicated, the highest ruling body in the confederation is the "Commission." This body serves as a combination board of business directors, legislature, supreme court, and arbitration board, but most of its functions are judicial, as we will show later. Members look to the Commission as the ultimate authority on organizational disputes. It is made up of the rulers of the most powerful families, which are located in large cities. At present, nine of the many such families are represented on the Commission. Three of the families represented are in New York City, one in Buffalo, one in Newark, one in Boston, and one each in Philadelphia, Detroit, and Chicago. The Commission is not a representative legislative assembly or an elected judicial body; families in cities such as Baltimore, Dallas, Kansas City, Los Angeles, Pittsburgh, San Francisco, and Tampa do not have members on the Commission. The members of the council do not regard each other as equals. There are informal understandings that give one member authority over another, but the exact pecking order, if there is one, has not been determined.

Beneath the Commission are 24 families, each with its Boss. The family is the most significant level of organization and the largest unit of criminal organization in which allegiance is owed to one man, the Boss. (Italian words often are used interchangeably with each of the English words designating a position in the division of labor. Rather than *Boss,* the words *Il Capo, Don,* and *Rappresentante* are used.) The Boss's primary function is to maintain order while at the same time maximizing profits. Subject to the possibility of being overruled by the Commission, his authority is absolute. He is the final arbiter in all matters relating to his branch of the confederation.

Beneath each Boss of at least the larger families, is an Underboss or *Sottocapo.* This position is, essentially, that of vice president and deputy director of the family unit. The man occupying the position often collects information for the Boss; he relays messages to him; and he passes his orders down to the men occupying positions below him in the hierarchy. He acts as Boss in the absence of the Boss.

On the same level as the Underboss is a position of Counselor (adviser), referred to as *Consigliere* or *Consulieri.* The person occupying this position is a staff officer, rather than a line officer. He is likely to be an elder member who is partially retired after a career in which he did not quite succeed in becoming a Boss. He gives advice to family members, including the Boss and Underboss, and he therefore enjoys considerable influence and power.

Also at about the same level as the Underboss is the Buffer. The top members of the family hierarchy, particularly the Boss, avoid direct communication with the lower-echelon personnel, the workers. They are insulated from the police. To obtain this insulation, all commands, information, money, and complaints generally flow back and forth through the Buffer, who is a trusted and clever go-between. However, the Buffer does not make decisions or assume any

of the authority of his Boss, as the Underboss does.

To reach the working level, a Boss usually goes through channels. For example, a Boss's decision on the settlement of a dispute involving the activities of runners (ticket sellers) in a particular lottery game, passes first to his Buffer, then to the next level of rank, which is Lieutenant or *Capodecina* or *Caporegima.* This position, considered from a business standpoint, is analogous to works manager or sales manager. The person occupying it is the chief of an operating unit. The term *Lieutenant* gives the position a military flavor. Although *Capodecina* is translated as "head of ten," there apparently is no settled number of men supervised by any given Lieutenant. The number of such leaders in an organization varies with the size of the organization and with the specialized activities in that organization. The Lieutenant usually has one or two associates who work closely with him, serving as messengers and Buffers. They carry orders, information, and money back and forth between the Lieutenant and the men belonging to his regime. They do not share the Lieutenant's administrative power.

Beneath the Lieutenants there might be one or more Section Chiefs. Messages and orders received from the Boss's Buffer by the Lieutenant or his Buffer are passed on to a Section Chief, who also may have a Buffer. A Section Chief may be Deputy Lieutenant. He is in charge of a section of the Lieutenant's operations. In smaller families, the position of Lieutenant and the position of Section Chief are combined. In general, the larger the regime, the stronger the power of the Section Chief. Because it is against the law to consort for criminal purposes, it is advantageous to cut down the number of individuals who are directly responsible to any given line supervisor.

About five Soldiers, Buttons, or just "members" report to each Section Chief or, if there is no Section Chief position, to a Lieutenant. The number of Soldiers in a family varies; some families have as many as 250 members, some as few as 20. A Soldier might operate an illicit enterprise for a Boss, on a commission basis, or he might "own" the enterprise and pay homage to the Boss for "protection," the right to operate. Partnerships between two or more Soldiers, and between Soldiers and men higher up in the hierarchy, including Bosses, are common. An "enterprise" could be a usury operation, a dice game, a lottery, a bookie operation, a smuggling operation, or a vending machine company. Some Soldiers and most upper-echelon family members have interests in more than one business.

Family membership ends at the Soldier level, and all members are of Italian or Sicilian descent. Between 2,000 and 4,000 men are members of families and, hence, of the confederation. But beneath the Soldiers in the hierarchy of operations are large numbers of employees and commission agents who are not necessarily of Italian-Sicilian descent, although some of them are Italian-Sicilian aspirants. These are the persons carrying on most of the work "on the street." They have no Buffers or other forms of insulation from the police. They are the relatively unskilled workmen who actually take bets, answer telephones, drive trucks, sell narcotics, and so forth. In Chicago, for example, the workers in a major lottery business who operated in an African American neighborhood were African Americans; the bankers for the lottery were Japanese Americans; but the game, including the banking operation, was licensed, for a fee, by a family member. The entire operation, including the bankers, was more or less a "customer" of the Chicago family, in the way any enterprise operating under a franchise is a "customer" of the parent corporation.

The positions outlined above constitute the "organizational chart" of the American confederation as it is described by members. Two things are missing. First, there is no description of the many positions necessary to the actual street-level operation of an illicit enterprise such as a bookmaking establishment or a lottery. Although we cannot outline the basic structure of all these enterprises, we must at least mention three principal operations—lotteries, bookmaking, and narcotics distribution. Arthur Sage, District Inspector of the Detroit Police Department and supervisor of police work in vice, liquor, and gambling in Detroit, presented to the McClellan committee a chart showing the hierarchy of the lottery enterprise supervised by one Detroit Section Chief (U.S. Congress, 1963). More than 100 positions are involved, but they are not unique, and further, some personnel occupy more than one position. Included on the chart or mentioned in the testimony are about 50 positions for "pick-up men," divided into five groups, each reporting to a substation supervisor. After the bet slips are collected at the substation, presumably by the substation supervisor, one or more of the trusted employees plays the role of messenger by taking them to the main office. The main office is depicted as having six workers, but their roles are not specifically identified. Someone at the main office tabulates the amounts bet, and someone determines which slips are winners, a role described as "bookkeeper." Another trusted person takes the proceeds to the Section Chief, who in turn passes a share up through the hierarchy.

The positions just described are in reference to what might be called "curbstone betting." In the operation of off-track bets on horse races and other contests, a similar set of positions is essential. In some such enterprises, a bookie, working on a commission basis, accepts bets verbally and telephones them to his supervisor. Other bookies accept bids from customers who telephone to place the bet. A bookie of this kind might employ 6 to 10 telephone operators, and a similar number of runners to collect bets and pay winners. The substation and messenger positions are similar to those in lottery enterprises.

Narcotics enterprises are organized like any importing-wholesaling-retailing business. At the top level are importers of multi-kilo lots. At the next level are "kilo-men," who handle nothing less than a kilogram of heroin at a time. A kilo-man makes his purchase from an importer-supplier and receives delivery from a courier. He dilutes the heroin by adding 3 kilograms of milk sugar for each kilogram of heroin. The product is then sold to "quarter-kilo men" and then to "ounce-men" and then to "deck-men," there being further adulteration at each stage in this process. Eventually, street peddlers dispense it in 5-grain packets called "bags" or "packs." The cost to the consumer is in excess of 300 times the cost of the original kilo.

Second, and more important, the structure described by members of the confederation is primarily the *formal* structure of the organization. The informants have not described, probably because they have not been asked to do so, the many *informal* positions any organization must contain. To put the matter in another way, there is no description of the many functional roles performed by the men occupying the formally established positions making up the organization. Businesspersons and managers know that identifying a position as that of, say, "vice president" is rather meaningless unless there is a description of what the person occupying the position does. And what he does is a response to an informal position he occupies at the same time he occupies the formal one; he may be "expediter" or "troubleshooter" or "psychotherapist," as well as vice president. In the confederation, one position of this kind is Buffer. This position has been identified by the New York police officers who watch family and confederation operations, not by the members themselves. The position is occupied by men who might also be occupying an "official," formal position such as Underboss, Lieutenant, or even some lower position. Later, we discuss other informal positions of this kind and the informal roles of the men who occupy them. Corrupter, Corruptee, Enforcer, Executioner, and Money Mover are some of these. Here we mention three informal or "unofficial" positions essential to the curbstone betting enterprise just described. The positions for lay-off man, for large lay-off man, and for come back man are essential to gambling enterprises, and the fact that they are included in the division of labor indicates why a gambling enterprise cannot be a "mom and pop" operation for long.

The division of labor essential to bookmaking does not stop at the street level. It is essential that the bookie insure himself against loss by making bets himself, in much the way a casualty insurance company re-insures a risk that is too great for it to assume alone. So that this is possible, the lay-off man position has been established. The bookie, sometimes called a "handbook operator," does not gamble. He pays the same odds as does the race track, but at the track these odds are calculated after deducting about 15% to 18% of the gross, this amount going to the track operators for taxes, expenses, and profits. The bookie pockets the entire 15% to 18%, less a percentage going to a family member for a license to operate, for corruption of police and political figures, and for "welfare" benefits such as bail and an attorney in time of need. However, because the bookie's customers do not necessarily bet on the same horses selected by betters at the track, the amount of money bet with him on losing horses sometimes is not enough to pay off those of his customers who have selected winners. He notes, before a race is run, that his books are out of balance. To get them in balance, he takes some of the money and makes a large bet with a lay-off man, who, like the bookie himself, operates on a percentage basis.

But when a number of bookies use the services of the same lay-off man, the latter's books may get out of balance too. Because he, like the bookie, is a commission agent rather than a gambler, he seeks a man occupying a position at the third level up the enterprise hierarchy, the large lay-off man. The men occupying this position reside in all parts of the country, but they keep in close touch with each other so that the overall amount of money handled by each of them will be bet on the various horses in the same proportions as is the total amount bet at the track. When this is the case, the bookie, the family members who license him, the lay-off man, the large lay-off man cannot lose; they simply split up the 15% to 18% of the gross. One large lay-off man takes in about $20 million a year, and his annual profit before expenses is about 4% of the gross, or $800,000.

If, just before a horse race, it looks as if there is some possibility that the persons occupying positions for large lay-off men might lose because their books are out of balance with the legitimate books at the track, they employ the services of a man occupying still another position in the division of labor, the come back man. Persons occupying this position function in such a way that the legitimate track betters themselves re-insure the bets taken by large lay-off men. The come back man is an "odds changer" who stands by at the race track. Just before each race, he opens a telephone line to a representative of the syndicated large lay-off men. When the latter's books are out of balance with those at the track, the person occupying the position of come back man is instructed to bet large amounts on specific horses, thus making the track odds approximately the same as the odds based on the proportions bet with the large lay-off men on each of the horses. "Lay-off action," together with the "come back money" system, is a principal device used by rulers of families and of the confederation to control all gambling of any consequence in America. Another device is coercion—extortion, muscle, and murder.

The skeleton structure we have outlined is by no means the structure of the organization operating America's illicit businesses. Even a skeleton has more bones than those we have described, as our discussion of informal positions and roles indicates. The structure outlined is sufficient to demonstrate, however, that a confederation of families exists. Investigating agencies have, since the time of the Appalachia meeting, documented the fact that the apparatus is tightly knit enough to have a corporate chain of command. Moreover, the names of the men occupying the major positions have been known for at least 5 years. The next important task for these agencies is that of depicting the numerous functional positions, formal and informal, making up the structure of the organization whose authority structure has been sketched out. Some aspects of the structure can be deduced from studies of function; details can be learned only by close observation of the interaction of members with each other. . . .

THE CODE AND ITS FUNCTIONS

The Code

We have been unable to locate even a summary statement of the code of conduct that is used in governing the lives of the members of American criminal families. There are several summaries of the Sicilian Mafia's code of *omerta,* or "manliness," and the popular assumption seems to be that such statements also summarize the code of American organized criminals. Although this assumption is not in itself improper, the implication is that the American code was simply borrowed from the Mafia. This is not correct, any more than it is correct to believe that the family structure and the confederation structure were simply borrowed from the Mafia.

The matter is complicated, of course, by the fact that the code of conduct for family members is unwritten. The snippets of information we have been able to obtain have convinced us that there is a striking similarity between both the code of conduct and the enforcement machinery used in the confederation of organized criminals and the code of conduct and enforcement machinery that govern the behavior of prisoners. This is no coincidence, for as indicated earlier, both the prisoner government and the confederation government are responses to strong official governments that are limited in their means for achieving their control objectives. To maintain their status as governors of illegal organizations, the leaders of the two types of organizations must promulgate and enforce similar behavioral codes.

We first discuss the code of prisoners and then summarize the code of American organized criminals. One summary of the many descriptions of life in a wide variety of prisons has suggested that the chief tenets of the inmate code can be classified roughly into five major groups (Sykes & Messinger, 1960, pp. 5-9). Sutherland and Cressey (1966, pp. 559-560) have shortened and rewritten this summary of the code as follows:

First, there are those maxims that caution: *Don't interfere with inmate interests.* These center on the idea that inmates should serve the least possible time while enjoying the greatest possible number of pleasures and privileges. Included are such directives as: *Never rat on a con; Don't be nosy; Don't have a loose lip; Keep off a man's back; Don't put a guy on the spot.* Put positively: *Be loyal to your class, the cons.*

Second, a set of behavioral rules asks inmates to refrain from quarrels or arguments with fellow prisoners: *Don't lose your head; Play it cool; Do your own time; Don't bring heat.*

Third, prisoners assert that inmates should not take advantage of one another by means of force, fraud, or chicanery: *Don't exploit inmates.* This injunction sums up several directives: *Don't break your word; Don't steal from cons; Don't sell favors; Don't be a racketeer; Don't welsh on debts; Be right.*

Fourth, some rules have as their central theme the maintenance of self: *Don't weaken; Don't whine; Don't cop out* (plead guilty). Stated positively: *Be tough; Be a man.*

Fifth, prisoners express a variety of maxims that forbid according prestige or respect to the guards or the world for which they stand: *Don't be a sucker; Skim it off the top; Never talk to a screw* (guard); *Have a connection; Be sharp.*

Prison inmates as a group do not give the warden and his staff their consent to be governed. By withholding this consent and developing their own unofficial government, they accomplish precisely what prison officials say they do not want them to accomplish—legally obtained status symbols, power, and an unequal share of goods and services in short supply. Organized criminals, like prisoners, live outside the law, and in response to this outlaw status they, like prisoners, develop a set of norms and procedures for controlling conduct within their organization. The five general directives making up the prisoners' code are, in fact, characteristic of the code of good thieves everywhere (see Irwin & Cressey, 1962). Specifically, the chief tenets of this thieves' code as it is found among organized criminals can be summarized and briefly illustrated as follows:

1. *Be loyal to members of the organization.* Do not interfere with each other's interests. Do not be an informer. This directive, with its correlated admonitions, is basic to the internal operations of the confederation. It is a call for unity, for peace, for maintenance of the status quo, and for silence. We have already discussed the decision for peace, based on this directive, which followed the 1930-1931 war. The need for secrecy is obvious.

2. *Be rational. Be a member of the team. Don't engage in battle if you can't win.* What is demanded here is the corporate rationality necessary to conducting illicit businesses in a quiet, safe, profitable manner. The directive extends to personal life. Like a prisoner, the man occupying even the lowest position in a family unit is to be cool and calm at all times. This means, as examples, that he is not to use narcotics, that he is not to be drunk on duty, that he is not to get into fights, and that he is not to commit any crimes without first checking with his superiors. A leader of an Italian-Sicilian family in a large city, accompanied by a low-status member of the family, passed a law enforcement officer on the street. The low-status man spat on the officer. The leader apologized profusely and, presumably, took punitive action against his worker. The low-status man was not, in the language of inmates, "playing it cool." The ruler of a different Italian-Sicilian family at one time temporarily stopped all lottery operations in his city because the business was drawing the attention of the police to the even more lucrative criminal activities of the family. As Tyler (1962a, p. 16) has observed:

In this era of the "organization man," the underworld—like most institutions that prosper within an established culture—has learned to conform. Its internal structure provides status for those who would plod along in workaday clothes. In its external relations, it affects all the niceties of a settled society, preferring public relations and investment to a punch in the nose or pickpocketing (see also Johnson, 1962, pp. 408-409).

3. *Be a man of honor. Respect womanhood and your elders. Don't rock the boat.* This emphasis on "honor" and "respect" helps determine who obeys whom, who attends what funerals and weddings, who opens the door for whom, who takes a tone of deference in a telephone conversation, and who rises when another walks into a room. Later we will show that emphasis on honor actually functions to enable despots to exploit their underlings.

4. *Be a stand-up guy. Keep your eyes and ears open and your mouth shut. Don't sell out.* A family member, like a prisoner, must be able to withstand frustrating and threatening situations without complaining or resorting to subservience. The "stand-up guy" shows courage and "heart." He does not whine or complain in the face of adversity, including punishment, because "If you can't pay, don't play." In his testimony before the McClellan committee, Mr. Valachi reported that juvenile delinquents appearing in police stations or jails are watched and assessed to determine whether they possess the "manliness" so essential to membership in the Italian-Sicilian confederation of criminals. This tenet of the code will later be discussed in more detail, in the section on recruitment.

5. *Have class. Be independent. Know your way around the world.* Two basic ideas are involved here, and both of them prohibit the according of prestige to law enforcement officials or other respectable citizens. One is expressed in the saying, "To be straight is to be a victim." A man who is committed to regular work and submission to duly-constituted authority is a sucker. When one family member intends to insult and cast aspersion on the competence of another, he is likely to say, "Why don't you go out and get a job?" The world seen by organized criminals is a world of graft, fraud, and corruption, and they are concerned with their own honesty and manliness as compared with the hypocrisy of corrupt policemen and corrupt political figures. A criminal who plays the role of Corrupter is superior to a criminal who plays the role of corruptee. . . .

A PROPOSAL FOR STUDY

One who tries to accumulate data on organized crime experiences somewhat the same frustrations as a policeman who seeks to eliminate it. Not the least of these is the frustration stemming from the fact that "organized crime" is not against the law. What is against the law is smuggling, selling narcotics and untaxed liquor, gambling, prostitution, usury, murder, conspiracy, and so forth. Careful studies of "homicide in America" can be undertaken because police and other government agencies routinely maintain files on homicide, inadequate as they may be for research purposes. . . .

In another publication, the conference group made the following seven statements about the characteristics of the type of organization they are working to combat: (a) Organized crime is a *business venture;* (b) the principal tool of organized crime is *muscle;* (c) organized crime seeks out every opportunity to *corrupt or have influence* on anyone in government who can or may in the future be able to do favors for organized crime; (d) *insulation* serves to separate the leaders of organized crime from illegal activities that they direct; (e) *discipline* is of a quasi-military character; (f) it has an interest in *public relations;* (g) members live *a way of life* in which they receive services that outsiders either do not receive or receive from legitimate sources (*A Theory of Organized Crime Control,* 1966, pp. 18-24).

Our view is that an "organized criminal" is one who has committed a crime while occupying an organizational position for committing that crime. This view has been taken in a roundabout way by one of the nation's leading legislative experts on organized crime, Senator John L. McClellan. His position is found in Senate Bill 2187, coauthored with Senator Frank J. Lausche and introduced in the 89th Congress on June 24, 1965—"A Bill to Outlaw the Mafia and Other Organized Crime Syndicates." Despite its title, the bill is designed to outlaw *membership* in specified types of organizations. Among the listed activities of these organizations, significantly, are the tendencies to corrupt and coerce. Although Attorney General Katzenbach raised questions about the constitutionality of the bill, its theoretical value should not be overlooked. The preamble to the bill—"Findings and Declaration of Fact"—attempts to describe in precise legal terms the characteristics of the organizations in which membership is outlawed. The attempt flounders because there is confusion of organizational structure, organizational goals, and values of members of the organization. Nevertheless, the second, fourth, and fifth points outlined below validate our argument that description of organizational structure, including description of positions of Corrupter, Corruptee, and Enforcer, are essential to understanding and controlling organized crime.

First, the preamble defines the objectives of the organizations in which membership shall be a felony: "There exist in the United States organizations, including societies and syndicates, one of which is known as the Mafia, that have as their primary objective the disrespect for constituted law and order."

Second, the preamble describes the types of crimes the members of the organizations perpetrate as they express their disrespect for constituted law and order. These are the types of offenses customarily called "organized crime": "The members of such organizations are recruited for the purpose of carrying on gambling, prostitution, traffic in narcotic drugs, labor racketeering, extortion, and commercial type crimes generally, all of which are in violation of the criminal laws of the United States and of the several States."

Third, the preamble acknowledges that members of such organizations share a code of conduct, one essential part of which is secrecy about membership and about organizational structure: "These organizations, such as the Mafia, are conducted under their own code of ethics which is without respect for moral principles, law, and order. . . . Secrecy as to membership and authority within such organizations is a cardinal principle." It is somewhat of a contradiction to specify that the value system of an organization is void of respect for moral principles, law, and order, for an organization is, by definition, an orderly arrangement of positions.

Further, as we have shown, members of criminal organizations place a great deal of stress on honor and honesty in their dealings with each other, a form of "moral principle." The framers of the bill obviously here had in mind specific *kinds* of moral principles, such as those proscribing *all* murders, not just certain of them.

Fourth, the preamble recognizes the essential alliance between such organizations and the public officials whose duty it is to prevent and repress crime: "The existence of these organizations is made easier through the use of bribery and corruption of certain public officials." In the terminology we have been using, the organizations include Corrupter and Corruptee positions for which men are recruited or trained.

Fifth, the authors of the bill explicitly recognize that a coercive system of justice is used in an attempt to maximize conformity to organizational authority and ethics: "Discipline and authority within such organizations are maintained by means of drastic retaliation, usually murder, and . . . similar methods are employed to coerce non-members." At least one position for an Enforcer of organizational order is a part of the division of labor.

Therefore, more than an opening of police files to researchers is essential, although this would be an important first step. New questions, different from those traditionally raised by police and prosecutors must be asked, and new evidence relating to the answers to those questions must be assembled. Moreover, researchers must learn more of the things police officers know but do not file in their reports, and must have access to the informants available to law enforcement agencies. Just as information on the economic, political, and social organization of a foreign nation can be obtained by means of interviews with defectors, so information on the economic, political, and social organization of the families operating in the United States can be obtained by conversations with informants. The American confederation of criminals will not be controlled until it is understood, and it will not be understood until its division of labor has been specified in detail so that it can be attacked as an organization.

2 DONALD CRESSEY'S CONTRIBUTIONS TO THE STUDY OF ORGANIZED CRIME

An Evaluation

JOSEPH L. ALBINI

The author presents an evaluation of the contributions of Donald Cressey to the study of organized crime. Beginning with the early era of research into this area of study—the 1960s—the author discusses the methodological and other problems faced by Cressey and other researchers. Then he describes Cressey's model of organized crime structure and function, with the goal of examining the internal consistency of the model itself and evaluating the major issues and problems inherent in its heuristic utility for researchers and its usefulness for law enforcement.

In the study of organized crime in the United States, two schools or models seek to describe and explain the structure and function of this form of criminal endeavor; one is commonly referred to as the governmental, law enforcement, President's Task Force, evolutional-centralization, or traditional view, whereas the other is generally conceptualized under such categories as a patron-client social system, informal structural-functional system, network system, or developmental association model.

It is a tribute to the late Donald Cressey that the *traditional or governmental conceptualization* has come to be known as "the Cressey model." This speaks both to Cressey's stature in the field of criminology and to the high regard with which he was held by members of the 1967 president's task force commission on organized

crime. Although, as listed in the *Task Force Report* (President's Commission on Law Enforcement and Administration of Justice, 1967, p. v), the commission had six consultants, Cressey towered over the others and came to be attributed the status of major spokesperson for the commission and its report. This stature had its origin in Cressey's consultant paper that was part of the report and was entitled "The Functions and Structure of Criminal Syndicates" (President's Commission, 1967, pp. 25-60).

His prominence as an authority on organized crime was not fully realized, however, until the publication of his book *Theft of the Nation* (1969), which gave a detailed description of the governmental conception of organized crime. This work was followed in 1972 by the publication of an extension of his Churchill College

Overseas Fellowship Lecture delivered at Cambridge University on May 3, 1971; this was entitled *Criminal Organization: Its Elementary Forms* (1972).

There is no question, then, that Donald Cressey had a powerful impact on the study of organized crime. The purpose of this chapter is to describe and evaluate both the strengths and weaknesses of his contributions to this area of study.

To begin such an evaluation properly, we must go back in time to the middle 1960s, which saw the beginnings of academic interest and research concerning the area of organized crime. It was an exciting time; it was a confusing time; it was an era of beginnings; it was an era plagued and yet scintillated by serious methodological problems and questions; it was an era without authorities on the subject; it was a time of fear and apprehension for researchers setting out to investigate a confused and confusing phenomenon—the answer to the description and explanation of the existence of organized crime in America. Ned Polsky (1967) had already noted that criminologists during this era believed it was impossible to conduct field studies in this area of research.

It is with nostalgia and fond memories that I go back to this era when I first met Don Cressey in Washington, D.C. The year was 1967. I was a recently graduated Ph.D. and had just begun to collect data for my study of organized crime, which was later to result in the publication of my book *The American Mafia* (1971).

At this time, both Cressey and I began with a belief in the existence of a secret society called, among many other names, "the Mafia." Along with Cressey, I spoke to Charles Rogovin and others associated with the president's task force on organized crime. My data at this time were very scarce, and as yet, I had not made contact with informants in the underworld and with police officials dealing with the organized crime phenomenon in various parts of the country.

Cressey was very gracious and tried to answer what I am certain must have appeared to him as the very broad, confusing, and complex questions of a naive and searching researcher in the field. What did emerge from these conversations was that Cressey, more so than the others with whom I spoke, was convinced of the existence of a secret criminal society. Along with "Mafia," it was now being called "Cosa Nostra."

At this point in time, I saw in Cressey's demeanor, his cautious and secretive manner of speech and other signs, that he was convinced of the ominous, terrorizing, and dangerous nature of the area of study we were now investigating. So convinced was I of his fear and beliefs that I seriously considered terminating my study. I confided this fear to Cressey, and he quietly assured me to continue my work in the area but, above all, he cautioned, "Be careful."

I mention this incident and conversation because I think this belief on Cressey's part helped formulate his unquestioning and, in many cases, uncritical acceptance of the government data. This is not meant as a criticism of Cressey; rather, it is an observation offered with a sympathetic understanding of where we researchers were, methodologically, during this era. We were searching for answers; yet, all we found was confusion. I honestly believe that if I had access only to the data that Cressey and the task force were given, I, too, may have come to accept the government's data as valid. In all fairness, Cressey, at this time, was not a specialist in the study of organized crime. He had no data other than that given him by sources drawn from the government, police, and one underworld informant—the celebrated Joseph Valachi.

It was obvious to me, however, that Cressey was not convinced that Valachi was a valid informant. Why do I say this? Because I had an opportunity to interview Valachi when he was imprisoned at Milan Prison in Michigan. I told Cressey of my intention to interview Valachi. He advised me not to bother doing so because Valachi was totally unreliable as a witness. Said Cressey of Valachi, "He will tell you only what he thinks you want to hear." I took Cressey's advice and never interviewed Valachi.

What is ironic, however, is that, in his writings, Cressey, though he takes issue with aspects of Valachi's testimony, nevertheless seems to give credence to much of Valachi's data. It would have been difficult, as a consultant to the 1967 task force, not to pay attention to Valachi in that, despite the fact that many witnesses gave testimony, it was Valachi's status as "the underworld informant" that seemed to capture the imagination of the *Task Force Report* writers and the general public.

I cannot help but believe that Cressey, though always attempting to keep a scholarly and objective view in his interpretations of the task force data, was captivated by the phenomenon that Dwight C. Smith, Jr. (1975) has so aptly termed *the Mafia mystique.*

Georg Simmel, many years ago, noted the power of the secret and the status that is gained by those who are privileged to know the secret (Wolff, 1964). I believe that Cressey was captivated by this secretive aspect of the government's conception of Mafia and Cosa Nostra. I, at the time, may have followed in his footsteps had it not been for the advantage of my having later made contact with numerous informants in the underworld and with police officials who presented data that completely contradicted those presented in the *Task Force Report.* These data set up an antithesis to my belief in the Mafia or governmental model, causing me to move to the opposite side of Cressey's position. Cressey's acceptance of a belief in the Mafia seems to have been followed by his development of the further belief that his life was in jeopardy because of his association and role with the president's commission. When I delivered a lecture at Cambridge University in 1973, 2 years after Cressey's lecture there, several faculty told me that Cressey gave them the distinct impression that he continued to believe he was engaged in a dangerous battle with organized crime and, specifically, with Cosa Nostra. This certainly would be a logical conclusion following from Cressey's belief in the existence of a secret society that sought revenge upon all those who trespassed into its territory.

I, too, as I have already indicated, had this fear until I realized that organized criminals, including my informants, couldn't care less

what type of data academics usually collect. These data, as my informants observed, were not being collected for the purpose of bringing legal action against them. My fears regarding this concern were ultimately put to rest in an interview with Ralph Salerno, a New York police official who was also a consultant to the task force. I asked Ralph whether I, as an academic researcher, had anything to fear from the organized criminals. He replied, "You are as safe as a baby in the arms of its mother." That certainly was safe enough for me. I would assume that Cressey talked with Salerno about this issue, as I am told that Cressey received much information from Salerno, who was one of the major police consultants to the task force. However, the fact that Cressey, unlike myself, was a member of an investigating body—the task force—may have caused him to view himself as a potential victim of organized criminal revenge. We, of course, know now, as my own work, both in the United States (1971) and in Great Britain (1975), and that of William Chambliss (1971), Tom Mieczkowski (1983), Francis A. J. Ianni and E. Reuss-Ianni (1972), and others have shown, that academics can research this area without their lives being placed in jeopardy. Needless to say, this ethnomethodological approach, as is typically true of all participant observation methodology, necessitates a keen awareness of role definition and the creation of innovative data collection techniques on the part of the researcher. It also is obvious now that consultants or investigators for government task forces have not been the victims of criminal retaliation. In any respect, having set the historical, social, and psychological stage of the era in which Cressey began his work on organized crime, let's turn to a description and evaluation of the model that he presented.

Cressey described the structure of organized crime as one consisting of a bureaucratic organization, with a hierarchy of ranks, a code of conduct for its members, and one, above all, that functioned as a secret society. This description has become so much a part of popular public thinking and knowledge that we need not describe it in detail.

Cressey believed that this organization consisted of 24 "families" located in various large cities across the United States. These groups or families were governed by a national group of Bosses known as "the Commission," which was the national overseer of the families.

Each family consisted of a hierarchy of ranks, with the most powerful being the Boss, second in command was the Underboss, followed by one or several Lieutenants, who in turn were in charge of the lowest ranks—the Soldiers or Button Men. Serving as an adviser or consultant to each group and having a rank equal to the Underboss is a *Consigliere* or Counselor (Cressey, 1969).

Cressey viewed the various categories of organized crime as being distinguishable and differentiated primarily on a continuum of hierarchy of development, the basis of which lay in one dimension—rationality. By rationality, Cressey (1972, p. 11) means the degree to which criminal organizations develop increasingly elaborate levels of complexity as they aim to achieve an "announced" criminal "objective." This development is reflected in the increasing number of participants or positions required to carry out the organization's objective and the degree of development of a division of labor. Thus, the more rationally organized the criminal group, the more complex and precise the role descriptions of its membership and the more sophisticated its division of labor. Cressey (1972, chaps. 2-4) describes six categories or levels of rationality as based on "key positions" that are present or absent in the organizational structure.

Thus, the most rational type, Cosa Nostra, has developed to the point that it has a Commission that oversees, plans, and coordinates the activities of a complex cartel or confederation of subgroups across the nation. Then, the remaining five categories that include organizational groups, such as professional thieves, have various levels of development. It is a scale conceptualization of levels of rationality in which basic or elementary key positions exist at the bottom of the scale, with the complexity and number of these positions increasing with each level so that the top level incorporates all the key positions.

Cressey (1972) himself seems to be aware that his typology is not a very thorough one in that he begins Chapter 2 of *Criminal Organization* with the following statement: "I cannot at this time present a detailed, accurate typology that incorporates the critical similarities and differences in the many kinds of criminal organizations" (p. 18).

Cressey was correct in this observation. Rationality, though an important element of organization, can hardly be adequately employed as the major distinguishing difference in constructing a workable typology of organized crime. Rationality represents only one dimension of structure and function. The works of John Mack (1973), Mary McIntosh (1975), and others have spoken to the complexity of the varying and confusing uses of criteria in the realm of establishing typologies for the study of organized crime.

The position with which Cressey has come to be associated, however, concerns his description of the sixth or most rationally organized form of organized crime—Cosa Nostra. Because this consists of Cressey's main thesis, the remainder of our discussion is an evaluation of the merits and difficulties that his thesis has presented for the study of organized crime.

One imagines that the stature that Cressey held as an internationally known criminologist at the time of his serving as a consultant to the president's task force placed him into a setting where he was asked to bring rationality to a set of data that, in itself, was totally confused and confusing. Cressey, as I said before, was not at the time very knowledgeable about organized crime. He was an academic and, like the rest of us in this area of research at the time, had virtually no research experience that could quickly and easily surmount the vast methodological problems that faced us.

Cressey obtained his data from those sources made available to the task force. Many of these sources, such as Joseph Valachi, had made their data public on the now famous nationally televised McClellan hearings before Congress (U.S. Congress, 1963).

As I indicated before, these data presented serious contradictions and many aspects of unclarity and confusion for researchers studying organized crime. We realize that Cressey was presented these data with all their deficiencies. We also realize that Cressey, like myself and most other Americans, scholars as well as the mass public, had already been given the unfounded belief or illusion of the existence in the United States of a national criminal secret society transported from Sicily and consisting of individuals of Italian descent. This society bore the name "Mafia." This information had been presented in 1950, also via nationally broadcast television during the now famous Kefauver hearings (U.S. Congress, 1951).

It is quite obvious that Senator Kefauver did not prove the existence of the Mafia in the United States; he simply made the public aware of the word itself. It would be a serious error in the sociology of knowledge, however, to underestimate the power of a word.

In his book *The Mafia Mystique* Dwight C. Smith, Jr. (1975), shows that the breeding grounds for belief in the Mafia were in existence in the media prior to Kefauver. Smith presents a powerful argument for the influence of television and the Kefauver hearings in creating what he calls "The Slippery Label"—*The Mafia* (pp. 142-144). Smith, in this term, captures the mystique and magic by which this slippery label, employed indiscriminately, has come to produce a simplistic, mythical, and romantic conception of American organized crime.

In keeping with Smith's observation, one can argue further that the current belief in the Mafia and the early days of television are closely correlated. Kefauver captured the imagination of the American public as the television camera for the first time gave America a "live coverage" of what the Mafia was like.

Books, primarily those of journalists, soon followed. These typically were historically nebulous and carried conceptually confusing explanations of the origins and structure and function of this newly discovered secret society—Mafia. Only one academic voice in the wilderness, Daniel Bell (1962), took the Kefau-

ver data to task and argued that Kefauver presented no real facts to prove the existence of the Mafia.

Later, historian William Howard Moore (1974) presented the argument that Kefauver, by creating a belief in this nationwide conspiracy of the Mafia, actually intended to promote himself politically and draw attention away from the Truman administration and the Democratic political machines across the nation.

What no one realized at the time of these hearings, however, was that Kefauver had planted the seed—the slippery label—Mafia—into the minds of the American public.

Slippery labels have one characteristic in common: They can be applied to different concepts, different organizations, different time periods, and a variety of other entities and be made to take on a semblance of truthfulness and authenticity.

When Cressey was faced with the data regarding Cosa Nostra and its existence, he was indeed faced with a confusion of terms, paradigms, definitions, and an underlying nebulous and "slippery" history of its origin.

This type of vast differentiation and confusion in data demanded careful, detailed research. This, of course, takes a great deal of time. It necessitates reading vast amounts of historical and other sources, many written in Italian. Cressey, it seems, was not given the time necessary for such detailed research in the preparation of his consultant's paper in 1967 (Cressey, 1967b). Smith (1975, p. 307) elaborates on this point:

In defense of Cressey's initial effort at Organized Crime theory, it should be pointed out that he worked under an exceedingly tight deadline. He was given less than fifty days, he explained at the fourth Oyster Bay Conference, to gain a basic understanding of a problem for which available information was scanty and confused.

Despite the fact that in 1967 Cressey had been pressed for time at this point in his research, one cannot argue that he was under a similar time pressure to publish his book *Theft of the Nation,* which appeared 2 years later.

His book, rather than offer more substantive and convincing data and arguments, instead was a more elaborate repetition of the ideas presented in his position paper in the *Task Force Report.* As Smith again notes, however, Cressey had now altered his ideas on two major points; first, whereas in his consultant's paper he argued for use of the neutral or non-ethnic term *Confederation* to describe organized crime, in his book, the term *Cosa Nostra* now becomes his choice; second, whereas in his position paper Cressey pleaded for government files to be opened to social scientists so that new questions could be asked, in *Theft of the Nation* there is no such plea (Smith, 1975, pp. 309-310).

Although a variety of reasons have been offered to explain this change in Cressey's outlook, the fact remains that he became dedicated to an exposition of a paradigm of organized crime as one that was in the hands of a secret, national, bureaucratic cartel consisting of very "rational" criminal entrepreneurs. We can see that Cressey made some quick, unexplained jumps in concepts. In reality, as Smith (1975, p. 309) notes, his decision to change his use of *Confederation* to *Cosa Nostra* occurred between April and November of 1967. He had made the switch in an article in *The Annals* (1967b), 2 years prior to *Theft of the Nation.*

When we evaluate Cressey's contributions to the study of organized crime, though we can appreciate the pressure associated with his role as a task force consultant faced with confusing data, we must, however, place this in proper evaluative perspective; that is, he was, above all, a social scientist, and specifically, a sociologist. This status and role carries with it the responsibility of applying scientific methodological procedures to the analysis of any given data so that the final conclusions are drawn from data whose nature and content have been scrupulously evaluated and objectively analyzed.

In Cressey's consultant's paper, we see a researcher who is rightfully confused; the data were confusing. In *Theft of the Nation,* we see a researcher who has found the answers and, in an effort to explain scientifically the structure and function of Cosa Nostra, strains and forces scholarship into his thesis.

The major flaws and assumptions with which Cressey began his analysis in *Theft of the Nation* and *Criminal Organization* become the flaws with which he cannot help but draw his confused conclusions. These major flaws are twofold: One, Cressey, as seen by his easy switching of terms, does not begin with an adequate, researchable definition of organized crime. At best, he begins with a description of a criminal organization that he first calls a "Confederation" and later "Cosa Nostra." If one examines for a definition of organized crime in either of his two books on the subject, one finds only descriptions of his various levels or degrees of rationality among organized crime groups. In both books, Cressey gives the impression that we should search for adequate definitions, but he never offers a clear definition. Instead, all that he offers is a description of various levels of rationality as these relate to the structure and function of various organized crime groups.

The second flaw in Cressey's two works surrounds his lack of critical evaluation of his data. Granted, he was using data that were given to him by law enforcement and an underworld informant, but irrespective of the source, data must be critically examined.

In my research, I was faced with many contradictions. I, like Cressey, also obtained information from law enforcement and underworld sources. It seems that Cressey, as well as the task force of 1967, did not take into account that each informant, whether from law enforcement or the underworld, has his or her own specific understanding, interpretation, and description of the phenomenon with which he or she is involved. That, unfortunately, is the nature of social reality. The contradictions in Valachi's and others' testimony presented to the McClellan committee were glaringly obvious. One would think that these, in themselves, would have caused Cressey to become doubtful about the description of the model of Cosa Nostra that he views as the culmination of the highest form of "rational" development. Valachi's usage of terms, including *Cosa Nostra,* was not precise. Why were these not questioned by Cressey, especially when he knew, as he told me in 1967, that Joe Valachi was an unreliable informant who simply told everyone what he or she wanted to hear?

Cressey commits another serious error when he accepts and presents his simplistic history of the origins of the Mafia in Sicily. He gives lip service to the fact that the Mafia in Sicily and in the United States may not be directly connected, but had he read the existing anthropological literature, such as the works of Boissevain (1966) and Blok (1966), he would have concluded that scholars did not then, as they do not now (Hess, 1973), believe that the Mafia in Sicily ever existed as a structured, formal secret society. As such, then, we wonder why in Chapter 7 of his *Theft of the Nation* he makes an issue of the value system that the Italians and Sicilians brought with them to the United States.

There is a serious historical weakness in Cressey's approach—that of isolating and limiting his historical analysis of organized crime to the period in American history when the Italian and Sicilian immigrants came to America. One has to ask, Was there no organized crime before this period? If there was, did it function any differently than it did with the arrival of the Italians and Sicilians? Cressey would not have been prone to ask this type of question because his definition, limited to that of a description of Cosa Nostra, forced him to begin his historical analysis with the so-called historical origins of that organization.

This is not to say that ethnicity and the value systems of ethnic groups are not important variables in the study of organized crime. Like "rationality" of organization structure, however, ethnicity must be viewed as a variable that becomes significant only when it is found in combination with a host of other variables that seek to explain the complex puzzle of organized criminal involvement. As such, Cressey missed a very insightful era of American history—the era before the arrival of the Italians and Sicilians—during which organized crime, operated by various ethnic groups with differing value systems, flourished and indeed operated within the same basic format as that carried on later by the Italians, Sicilians, and other ethnic groups.

This, in my opinion, is one of the most serious shortcomings of Cressey's and the *Task Force Report*'s conceptualization of organized crime: The conception is, for all practical research purposes, historyless in its approach.

Another problem with Cressey's analysis is his lack of awareness and concern regarding the sampling procedure employed in the collection of his data. It seems obvious to everyone that the McClellan Senate Subcommittee in 1963 called before it only those witnesses who would "fit" the stereotype of Cosa Nostra membership. It certainly appears obvious that this subcommittee, along with Attorney General Robert Kennedy, was seeking to develop and portray a more vivid stereotype of the slippery label created earlier by Senator Kefauver. Here again, however, we find Cressey limiting himself and caught up in the limitations of his definition.

His use of the Federal Bureau of Investigation (FBI) "airtels" to prove the existence of Cosa Nostra is also infested with a methodological weakness—mainly, circular reasoning that follows from an assumption of the hierarchy of Cosa Nostra ranks and positions and then interpreting or "fitting" the positions into place (Albini, 1971, pp. 250-254). Murray Kempton (1969) took Cressey to task on this and other issues through his critical analysis of "the De Cavalcante tapes." Annelise Graebner Anderson (1979, p. 33), who basically seems to accept Cressey's description of the structure of Cosa Nostra, nonetheless observes that "it is not clear from the De Cavalcante transcript exactly what the powers of the Commission are." Kip Schlegel (1987, p. 68) brings the most serious weakness of this use of wiretaps to a head when he writes: "Agents who record the information inject a bias in what they choose to record and how they describe the events in the memoranda they submit as evidence. Obviously these agents are trained to listen for key words and phrases relevant to pre-existing concepts of organized criminal activity."

Although Cressey, in *Theft of the Nation,* is thorough in the amount he writes on different aspects of Cosa Nostra history, structure, and function, he seems to write with the belief that volume of content equals verification and strength of argument. Hence, in Chapter 3, we find what Cressey describes as a "sketch" based on Valachi's testimony a very thorough discussion of the events leading up to "Purge Day" (September 11, 1931): the day, according to Cressey, when the Mafia came to an end and the contemporary structure of Cosa Nostra was formed. On that day and the 2 days following, Cressey tells us on page 44, "some forty Italian-Sicilian gang leaders across the country lost their lives."

One would think that because Cressey believed this story, he would have, as a researcher, at least questioned who these 40 people were, particularly because he believed that they held high positions equivalent to Boss, Underboss, and Lieutenant.

Even in the literature there was confusion as to the exact number of people killed; the number ranged from 40 to 90, depending on which source one examined (Albini, 1971, pp. 244-245). Alan Block (1978) reminds us that Valachi himself estimated the number of killings to be a mere 4 or 5. Yet, Cressey never questioned these data for their accuracy.

Since the time of Cressey's writing, Humbert Nelli (1976) and Alan Block (1978) have debunked this story by examining newspapers across the nation for stories of these killings during the Purge Day time period. They found no evidence for such a belief. Informants tell many stories. A researcher must take care to separate fact from fiction.

Cressey also simply overlooked other major contradictions that "glared out" in the data he was given. In his effort to support his major thesis—that of the high level of rationality existent in Cosa Nostra, he became oblivious to serious contradictions—among them (a) the belief in a rigid structure of authority, when instead we find underlings constantly disobeying and fighting their superiors; (b) the belief in an omnipotent Commission empowered to settle

disputes, when instead we find wars between Syndicate groups to be a continuous part of their interaction pattern; and (c) the belief in a position of Corrupter, when we know that corruption is a subtle and complex phenomenon that relies on the development and use of a complex web of social-legal networks.

Cressey did develop a model of organized crime that attempts to make rationality its major distinguishing feature. Yet, the data of many other researchers do not seem to agree with Cressey's conception. In my work both in America (1971) and in Great Britain (1986), I offer data and arguments that seem to indicate that syndicated crime has "rational" aspects but, in reality, can be better explained and understood as a loose-knit system of patron-client or network relationships, rather than as the manifestation of a rigidly organized, bureaucratic one.

We have come a long way since those days when both Cressey and I were the pioneers in this study. Much research has been conducted since 1967. Most of this research has not lent support to Cressey's model. And most of this research did not use Cressey's governmentally derived database. It seems that so long as we do not use that base, we cannot seem to find what Cressey found.

Among the critics, other than those already cited, who have questioned the Cressey or governmental model are John Mack (1975), Robert Kelly (1986), Gordon Hawkins (1969), Peter Reuter (1983), and Galliher and Cain (1974). But this does not mean that the issue regarding the structure and function of organized crime in the United States has been resolved.

Cressey has given researchers a model that details the government's position. The *FBI Law Enforcement Bulletin* (February 1987) featured an article by Sean McWeeney on the historical and current relationship between the Sicilian and the American Mafia that reaffirms law enforcement's support for Cressey's model.

Unfortunately, the basic ingredient of the argument regarding structure and function surrounds the differences that exist in the types of data and method of collection used by law enforcement or government sources and those employed by ethnomethodological researchers. The government contends, as did Cressey, that this material is secretive in nature and cannot be made public. It is difficult to evaluate these kinds of data. We would have hoped that Cressey would have upheld his original contention that the government files be open to social scientists; but, unfortunately, he did not. Nevertheless, at least the government subcommittees, task forces, and Cressey revealed their beliefs in writing so that we can evaluate the basis for their arguments. As we have noted, the lack of scientific rigor, the drawing of conclusions from weak and merely assumed historical and other sources, and the inherent, glaring contradictions in these writings have caused critics to become suspicious of this so-called secret data. As Jay Albanese (1983) notes, not only does the estimated number of members belonging to Cosa Nostra vary in these government sources—estimates range from 2,000 to 20,000 members—there is not even agreement as to how many families actually exist or in what cities they are located. Notice, the round figures of 2,000 and 20,000 certainly suggest guesses or estimates, rather than figures based on a factual or exact count.

Higher criticism in the 19th century used the Bible itself to argue that the biblical writings are riddled with historical and other inconsistencies. Those who have faith argue that these inconsistencies do not interfere with their faith. So, too, it seems, those who believe in the governmental model argue that the inconsistencies found in Cressey's model do not undermine their belief.

In scientific endeavors, though, drawing data from various sources allows researchers more extensive bases from which to draw conclusions. This was dramatically illustrated in my work in Great Britain, the entire account of which is reported in my chapter in Robert Kelly's (1986) *Organized Crime: A Global Perspective.* Suffice it here to say that data received from criminal informants in London led me to argue in a paper delivered at Cambridge University in 1973 that, in the operation of the pornog-

raphy enterprise in London, corruption involved officers at Scotland Yard. An official from Scotland Yard, present at the reading of that paper, took me to task, arguing that Scotland Yard had its own Internal Affairs Department and that members of that department or squad would certainly know whether such corruption existed. I stood my ground on the basis of my informant data. Several years later, this corruption was revealed and resulted in the arrest and conviction of several constables at Scotland Yard. How was it exposed? By bringing in a decoy constable from outside the London force; hence, the operation came to be given an appropriate title—Operation Countryman.

In conclusion, then, placing Donald Cressey's contributions to the study of organized crime into final perspective, Cressey has given researchers an explicit model of organized crime. Despite the fact that not all researchers agree with this model, it has offered us a model against which other models can and have been compared. Annelise Graebner Anderson (1979), for example, effectively employed the Cressey model in describing the similarities in and differences between Cressey's model and the organized criminal group that she studied.

As is often true in science, by analyzing and comparing the conceptualizations of one model against another, we can be in a better position to argue the strengths and weaknesses of each and the existence and merits of their logical consistencies or inconsistencies.

We have also learned from Cressey a lesson about taking on the role of consultant for government bodies. Observing the conditions under which Cressey was given data and asked to analyze it, we can appreciate the fact that these governmental investigating bodies ask scientists to lend credibility to their investigations but do not necessarily allow them the time or freedom of thought generally required for the execution of competent, accurate, and complete scientific inquiry. Further, we have come to realize that, all too often, government commissions have already drawn their conclusions before their investigations begin; hence, although we are not saying that this is true in Cressey's case, consultants are nonetheless often selected in terms of those who are more likely to lend agreement to the commission findings. One only need listen, as I did, to Edward Donnerstein (1987) tell the audience at a conference on sexuality of how his research findings were treated when he testified before the Meese Commission on Pornography: Evidently, his findings, irrespective of the fact that he is an expert in his field, were rejected because these findings did not fit with what the commission had been "mandated" to find. As related in Mieczkowski and Albini (1987), I had a similar experience with a government body investigating organized crime.

Along with these incidents, I heard at another conference a member of the President's Commission on Organized Crime voice his disenchantment with his own commission's findings. Justin Dintino, a member of the president's commission to study organized crime (created in July 1983 by an executive order from President Reagan) noted that the attention given to Cosa Nostra is fogging over the following realities: (a) 30% of all labor racketeering is not investigated because the participants are not defined or labeled as members of Cosa Nostra; (b) Cosa Nostra is made to appear the major organized crime menace to the country, whereas its involvement in organized crime represents only .001% of the total of all organized crime in America; (c) instead of Cosa Nostra, the number one problem in American organized crime consists of the Colombians and their involvement in cocaine distribution; and (d) despite the fact that the vote of the commissioners was 13 to 7, the press was told the vote was an even 9 to 9 (Dintino, 1986). Considering these experiences, it has reached the point where it almost causes a social scientist to feel a sense of apprehension when asked to be a consultant to one of these bodies because of the "unscientific" procedures that some of them employ.

Cressey, then, has given us a model and legacy of looking at the phenomenon of organized crime in America. It was a model that stemmed from his limited, descriptive definition of the phenomenon. It is unfortunate that his data were not open to the scrutiny of the scientific community; we would then be in a better position to evaluate it in its entirety. Despite these shortcomings, however, Donald Cressey left us with a model that has captured the imagination of the American public and has given social scientists a paradigm that they must examine as they continue their search for that mythical, mystical, but forever present reality of organized crime.

3 THE EVIL THAT MEN DO

CHARLES H. ROGOVIN
FREDERICK T. MARTENS

The authors respond to the viewpoints presented by Albini (in Chapter 2) regarding Donald Cressey's view of organized crime. They take issue with Albini's thesis that Cressey's model is inaccurate. They assert that this view of organized crime has stood the test of time.

The July 1988 issue of *Crime and Delinquency,* a well-respected criminology and criminal justice journal, was dedicated to the late Donald Cressey, a renowned sociologist/criminologist. Among the "tributes" to Cressey was a critique of his research on organized crime by Professor Joseph Albini of Wayne State University. This tribute, which purported to evaluate both the strengths and weaknesses of the so-called Cressey model of organized crime, dwelt upon contradictions in this model and attempted to explain where Cressey went wrong. In support of his thesis—that Cressey was essentially hoodwinked by the 1967 task force on organized crime and blindly accepted a preconceived model of organized crime—Albini uses his research (1971) and that of others to impugn

Cressey for a lack of scientific rigor. Although it is not our purpose to address Albini's study of organized crime, we do believe that his unfair critique of both Cressey's work and the *Task Force Report: Organized Crime* does not adequately or responsibly represent those products. It is thus our intent to clarify and expand the dialogue.

OUR PRECONCEIVED BIAS

Naturally, the first weakness that can and will be exploited by any critic is a real, apparent, or fantasized self-interest on the part of the subject researcher(s). Albini implies that Cressey was committed to a bureaucratic model of organized

AUTHORS' NOTE: We thank Peter Reuter for suggesting the title of this chapter.
EDITORS' NOTE: The authors use a first person, "I," style. Because there are two authors, they chose to differentiate who is saying what by prefixing certain passages with "I (Rogovin)" or "I (Martens)." You might find this distracting, but there was no other way to attribute statements to each author. Once alerted to the style, you should be comfortable with following the message.

crime as a result of being co-opted (by Joseph Valachi, a mobster, and various law enforcement officials, including Ralph Salerno, a veteran New York City detective). He may also contend that one of us (Rogovin) is committed to defending the 1967 *Task Force Report* because I was its director and personally worked with Cressey and others as part of a hastily conducted and meagerly funded research project. Moreover, Albini may imply that Martens works with Rogovin (as the executive director of the Pennsylvania Crime Commission, of which Rogovin is the vice chairman) and thus, both are committed, if not by ideology then by personal loyalty, to defend one another and the findings of the *Task Force Report*. In fact, nothing could be further from the truth.

In November 1979, I (Rogovin) and my former crime commission colleague G. Robert Blakley were part of an organized crime seminar at the University of Southern California. At this seminar, I suggested that perhaps the 1967 *Task Force Report* was not an all-encompassing analysis of organized crime in America. I said it may have been skewed toward Cosa Nostra as representative of the dominant model of organized crime, principally as a function of the data that had been available to analysts. Blakley, quite sharply, took issue with that suggestion and explicitly stated that he was convinced the research conducted by Cressey and others was accurate. In retrospect, I believe we were both right: Cressey's research was accurate but skewed in that it explored only one model— albeit, then and now, the most advanced form of organized crime, Cosa Nostra.

In contrast, Martens has taken to task the overwhelming reliance on the Mafia or Cosa Nostra model both in my writings (Dintino & Martens, 1983; Martens & Longfellow, 1982; Martens & Niederer, 1985), as well as in various public appearances throughout the United States, Canada, and Great Britain. In addition, Martens has had the opportunity to work with Reuter (cited in Albini's work as a critic of Cressey's research), as well as with Francis Ianni, Elizabeth Reuss-Ianni, Bob Kelly, Dwight Smith, and Justin Dintino. I have also critiqued Reuter's

research (Martens, 1983) and criticized Scarpitti and Block (1985) (cited by Albini as credible researchers) for "shoddy research" in their examination of the Mafia's role in the toxic waste industry (Martens, 1985a, 1985b, 1986). Although I certainly admit to and am proud of working for Rogovin, he has never sought to constrain my thinking (in fact, he unmercifully pushes me to expand it), nor has he held against me my writings questioning the overreliance by law enforcement on the Cressey model. Given these qualifications, we believe it is not only appropriate but also obligatory that we explore what Albini has chosen to ignore out of ignorance, convenience, or both.

THE *TASK FORCE REPORT: ORGANIZED CRIME*—HOW IT BEGAN

Organized crime was not one of the original areas of interest to the members of the President's Commission on Law Enforcement and Administration of Justice (1967; hereafter, the Crime Commission). However, through the thoughtfulness and tenacity of Henry Ruth, Jr., Deputy Director of the Crime Commission, $50,000 had been scraped together to fund a limited study of the topic. I (Rogovin) was recruited in March 1966, and we were to have a completed report no later than spring 1967. Henry Ruth, an incredibly intelligent, committed, persuasive, and determined man had persuaded Don Cressey, G. Robert Blakley, and John Gardiner to lend their talents to the task force effort. I persuaded Ralph Salerno to help, and with incredible luck, Tom Schelling agreed to look at the problems of organized crime. Clearly, the time frame to address this phenomenon was unrealistic, but the participants were eager to try.

Writing under the rubric of an "evaluation" of the contributions of the late Donald Cressey to the study of organized crime, Albini launches an attack that smacks of the polemical. Certainly, constructive criticism of the work of others is not only useful but also essential to the advance of knowledge across the range of academic disciplines. Nonetheless, a sense of fair play seems to suggest that Albini had more than 20 years during which he could have directly and publicly attacked Cressey for both methodological and conceptual errors in the development and articulation of Cressey's model of organized crime, and sought not to. Whatever the validity of Albini's criticisms may be—an issue to which we turn shortly—this is a situation where lawyers would say leeches have attached; that is, the passage of an inordinate period of time bars pressing a claim—whatever its possible validity. While acknowledging at several points in his article the grace and courtesy that Cressey—already a well-established scholar—extended to him, a newly minted Ph.D. in the early stage of his career, Albini has failed to reciprocate. Waiting until Cressey's death is to operate under a very fuzzy set of rules for engagement in academic battle.

Another preliminary objection seems appropriate in this context. For Albini to offer alleged, personal comments reportedly made to him by Cressey to buttress the position he asserts—at a time when Cressey is unavailable to respond—seems at least graceless and arguably involves the use of outrageous fabrication. It strains credulity to believe that Cressey ever seriously suggested that he was apprehensive about his personal safety as a consequence of the information to which he had gained access or that he would warn another researcher to "be careful" in such a context. Of the many people who knew and worked closely with Cressey at the Crime Commission during 1966 and others who spent time with him and appeared at countless programs with him thereafter, including Henry Ruth, Lloyd Ohlin, Ralph Salerno, and I (Rogovin), none recall him ever expressing the apprehension Albini attributes to him. Certainly, had Cressey ever seriously been concerned about the matters to which Albini adverts, he would have discussed the kinds of protective measures that one could take with the very people with whom he was involved. In fact, on all the occasions where he was involved with each of the foregoing people, Cressey was jocular about his work in the organized crime

field. On one occasion, I discussed with him why prosecutors who worked organized crime cases did not fear retribution—that is, because "Mob people" only killed witnesses who possessed evidence that could convict them. Cressey laughed on hearing that explanation and even more heartily when I told him prosecutors were essentially fungible, so that if one were to disappear or become otherwise unavailable, another could be easily found to try a particular case. In response, Cressey remarked that organized crime's lack of violent response toward prosecutions was an example of the rational employment or use of violence.

What Albini may very well have missed or ignored in his limited interaction with Cressey was the latter's sometimes whimsical sense of humor. On another occasion when the organized crime task force was at work, several of its participants, including Cressey, joined a recently appointed commissioner of corrections from one of the mid-Southern states for lunch. This official, who was aware of Cressey's interest in corrections, was proudly advising Cressey of the reforms he had initiated in his state's maximum security prison. As the litany ran on, Cressey looked at me (Rogovin) with a solemn face and said, "Take a note, a major prison riot within 1 year." Growing paler by the moment, the new commissioner remonstrated with Cressey and offered additional examples of his enlightened, reform administration. Still deadpan, Cressey listened and then addressed me (Rogovin) again: "Change that to a major prison riot within 6 months," he directed. As he later explained, this was his way of telling the commissioner that the new commissioner had seriously disturbed the existing social order within the prison and had adversely affected important vested interests for both guards as well as inmates and that a violent reaction was to be expected. That prison, in fact, exploded with a major riot well within Cressey's predicted schedule.

Put charitably, perhaps Albini's naïveté as a young academic led him to misunderstand something Cressey may have said to him. In any event, to many of those who knew him,

Cressey's sense of humor often helped leaven the difficult circumstances under which we worked at the Crime Commission. Among those things about him that some remember very well was the line we had not heard before, "No good deed goes unpunished!" If not original to him, he was at least the first to use it at the Crime Commission.

Without intending to diminish Donald Cressey's stature of contributions in any way whatsoever, it is inaccurate for Albini to suggest that Cressey "towered over" the other consultants who worked for the organized crime task force of the Crime Commission or that he was ever regarded as the "major spokesperson for the commission and its report" on organized crime. In fact, as Albini notes, although Cressey extended his initial work with the task force by the publication of *Theft of the Nation* (1969) and *Criminal Organization: Its Elementary Forms* (1972), he thereafter essentially withdrew from the field. After a brief spate of lecture appearances and some promotional work for his book, for reasons unknown to these writers Cressey did not pursue his earlier, successful venture into the morass that organized crime had presented. This was true, despite the fact that his work for the commission had created data access opportunities that no other academic had achieved.

In characterizing Cressey as "towering over" all the other consultants to the task force, Albini reflects either a parochialism unworthy of a senior representative of his discipline, sociology, or a penchant for creating a straw man whose destruction is used to reinforce a weak or indefensible position. Certainly, Thomas Schelling's work on the economics of organized crime, though too brief, stimulated other economists to enter the field (e.g., Reuter, 1983). John Gardiner's work (1967) on Wincanton was a very powerful and important contribution to the limited literature in the field. When measured in terms of determinable impact, the applied research of G. Robert Blakley on the evidence-gathering problems in organized crime was incredibly important. Blakley's consultant paper for the task force on organized crime provided the models for the revision of the law on electronic surveillance, immunity, and perjury (Blakley, 1967).

The fact that Joseph Albini has been regarded as a respectable and respected scholar makes inexplicable the exaggerations in which he indulges in the development of his thesis in his article. He compounds his statements as to Cressey's mental state with commentary that is either intentionally misleading or so recklessly inaccurate as to baffle those who have read Cressey's work in the past. He suggests that Cressey's acceptance of a belief in the Mafia seems to have been followed by his development of the further belief that his life was in jeopardy because of his association and role with the president's commission. Again, as far as we can ascertain, it would appear that only Joseph Albini ever became aware of this situation. Further, he describes Cressey as being a member of an "investigating body—the task force." This deliberately misleads the reader. The task force was no more an investigating body in the sense that that term has currency in the criminal justice field than was the Science and Technology Task Force of the Crime Commission. There were, in fact, no funds, personnel, or time to do original investigative work in the organized crime task force. At best, it could draw upon information in the hands of federal, state, and local agencies and seek to provide useful interpretations of that material. It is further astounding to find Albini discussing with apparent familiarity the nature and/or character of the data to which Cressey had access and upon which he grounded his conclusions. To the best of anyone's knowledge, and Albini makes no claim to the contrary, there is no evidence that Albini at any time ever had an opportunity to view any of the data on which Cressey was permitted to work or on which he may have relied. To suggest that contradictions, serious or otherwise, existed in these data, is the rankest of speculation and unworthy of a researcher of Albini's reputed stature. What was known to persons associated with the organized crime task force and the larger commission per se was that, for several years, the FBI had been conducting long-term, microphone surveillances (bugging) of Mafia or Cosa Nostra figures in various parts of the country. Institutionally, by 1966 the FBI was interested in some kind of dissemination of the product of that national campaign, especially because serious questions were being raised as to the utility of electronic surveillance in the organized crime field and, also, about the civil liberties implications of law enforcement activities in the organized crime field.

Perhaps the best rebuttals to a major thrust of Albini's "evaluation" of the validity of Cressey's thesis that a national criminal organization known as Cosa Nostra actually existed are found in the admissions of members of that very organization and in the conclusions of criminal trial juries.

Albini is critical of the Cressey-Salerno interaction at the task force. He implies that Salerno co-opted Cressey into a blind acceptance of a New York City-oriented Mafia model of organized crime. As articulate and persuasive as Ralph Salerno was and remains today, this fails to acknowledge Cressey's sophistication and appropriate scholarly skepticism. He was hardly a naive beginner; rather, he was a seasoned researcher—one whom it would have been very hard to bamboozle. Cressey and Salerno had never met before this undertaking, nor had the others. The aim of the task force work effort was to use the services of recognized authorities in their respective disciplines and to assemble four papers to describe the phenomenon commonly referred to as "organized crime." I (Rogovin) believe that not only was a credible job completed, especially when one examines what was produced by previous and subsequent commissions, but further, the *Task Force Report: Organized Crime* (President's Commission, 1967) towers over the others. This certainly is sustained in the debate, which still rages 20 years later. Moreover, I believe that Cressey's contributions to this report and the model he described have been validated in criminal prosecutions during the last 10 years. What is important, of course, about Cressey's contributions to the study of

organized crime is that this model spoke of a pattern of racketeering that occurred over time (it was not episodic) and was systemically related to the institutions of society. This view is the conceptual underpinning for Blakley's brilliantly designed, and at times maligned (Lynch, 1987b), Racketeer Influenced and Corrupt Organizations Act (RICO; Goldsmith, 1988). Ironically, RICO has been used not only against Cosa Nostra but also against Ferdinand Marcos, Lilco Power Company, and the Teamster's Union, and was being considered for use against Drexel Burnham (Eichenwald, 1988, p. D4). This, we believe, speaks to the vision and foresight that Cressey (and Blakley) brought to our understanding of organized crime and racketeering.

In looking back on the 1967 report, it seems appropriate to point out that although Cressey examined one dimension of organized crime, the one about which most data were available, Gardiner and Schelling did discuss other aspects of organized crime. Although Albini was asked to comment on Cressey's work and did, in fact, focus on the 1967 *Task Force Report,* he (Albini) could have at least recognized these contributions to the literature. The Wincanton study by Gardiner was certainly a classic description of organized crime, or a non-Cosa Nostra model, and the critical importance of corruption to its successes. Schelling's discussion on the business of organized crime (1971) is a seminal piece of economic research in the field. To ignore Blakley's work on the evidence-gathering problems in organized crime investigation and prosecution and to fail to credit its influence on Congress and various state legislatures is simply incredible, particularly because those statutory changes suggested have had major impacts against organized crime in a variety of modes. Persons must not be misled by Albini or others into believing that the task force focused only on Cosa Nostra; its focus and ultimate application were much broader.

Albini speaks of confusion, of a lack of refined methodology, of a time of fear and apprehension that characterized the era of research into organized crime in the 1960s. Although we are not as confident in Albini's description as he appears to be, we acknowledge that many highly recognized law enforcement officials claimed that Cosa Nostra did not exist. This belief, initially perpetuated by the FBI (Powers, 1987, pp. 332-334; Schlesinger, 1978, pp. 280-299) despite the massive amount of confirming electronic surveillance product that had been collected by the middle 1960s, was so strong that as late as 1965, the attorney general of New Jersey (and other states as well) claimed that organized crime (a synonym for Cosa Nostra) did not exist in New Jersey. Ramsey Clark (1970), the U.S. attorney general (1965-1967), minimized its importance when he stated:

> But we must not deceive ourselves—organized crime is a very small part of America's crime. What does it have to do with the juvenile offender who accounts for most of the increase in crime? True, it supplies some narcotics, and thereby contributes to drug-related crime. But the narcotics it supplies are a minor part of the total illegally consumed in America, and they will be found in one form or another, one way or another, while conditions causing the demand for them continue. What does organized crime have to do with street crime—murder, rape, assault, mugging, robbery? Practically nothing. Is it possible that one violent crime out of a thousand is committed by criminal syndicates, or results from their activities? Since America had more addicts of opiate derivatives in 1900 than in 1969, can addiction be fostered by organized crime? White-collar crime, protest, riot, school disturbances, the general violence of our environment are barely touched by organized crime. It only preys on them. We will no more make our streets safe or our society tranquil by eliminating organized crime than we would make the seas safe from sharks by eliminating the remora. The greatest harm we could suffer from organized crime would be to permit it to distract us from the major problems we face if we are to control crime in America. (pp. 83-94)

In the light of subsequent prosecutions in New Jersey and elsewhere in the United States, such a statement proved ludicrous (Hoffman, 1973; Lupsha, 1981). Cressey not only had available to him Salerno and Valachi, but he also had access to the reports of the Organized Crime

and Racketeering Section of the Justice Department. Those files contained summaries of the massive FBI electronic surveillance program directed against Cosa Nostra figures. It is remarkable that an astute, insightful, and sophisticated researcher such as Albini would succumb to the rather naive belief that Cressey, a skillful, skeptical, and cautious sociologist, was taken in by Valachi and/or misled by Salerno. Surely, Albini knows that, in the business of organized crime research, much is learned informally through interaction with police, prosecutors, and other criminal informants, many of whom cannot be identified. Furthermore, many of the data available to Cressey were subsequently reported by Sandy Smith (1967, 1968, 1969a, 1969b), an investigative reporter for *Life*. The history of this era is certainly not adequately characterized by Albini, who apparently failed to comprehend the political environment that preceded and followed the task force's inquiry.

Nonetheless, Albini raises one point that is certainly valid: the lack of historical perspective in Cressey's analysis of Cosa Nostra and organized crime. In his text *Theft of the Nation* (1969), Cressey attempts to address the history of Cosa Nostra, relying (because he was not a historian) on those more proficient in this discipline. He apparently made the same mistake as Ianni (Ianni & Reuss-Ianni, 1972) and others (Blakley & Billings, 1981; Bonanno, 1983), who have accepted the "Purge of the Mustache Petes" as a historical event. Although Albini contends that both Nelli (1976) and Block (1978) have disproved this event, we are not convinced that a survey of newspaper reports in 1931 represents a sound and acceptable research methodology. As Albini well knows, there is good reason to question both this methodology as well as the integrity of the research. Surely, Albini was aware of the lack of scientific rigor that his good friends Frank Scarpitti and Alan Block brought to their inquiry of the toxic waste industry (Scarpitti & Block, 1985), and yet he has remained noticeably silent. Given the shallowness of historical research on organized crime, to chastise Cressey for falling prey to what is still a historical enigma among organized crime researchers—"the Castellammarese War"—seems to us to be overreaching on Albini's part.

THE CRESSEY MODEL
HAS BEEN SUSTAINED

Perhaps the most egregious violation by Albini in his "tribute" to Cressey is: "Most research has not lent support to Cressey's model" (1971, p. 350). The volumes of evidence produced over the past 8 years, as well as the books that have been published by researchers, journalists, investigative reporters, private citizens, and members of Cosa Nostra, have corroborated Cressey over and over again. Why ignore Bonanno's (1983) autobiography of his life in Cosa Nostra? There is a great chapter on the "Commission" and its mode of operation. Read Fratianno's account of his life in Cosa Nostra (DeMaris, 1981). Seek out the wiretap product that was made public in the Commission trial in New York, a trial that resulted in the convictions of Tony Salerno, boss of the Genovese Cosa Nostra "family"; Tony Corallo, boss of the Luchese Cosa Nostra family; and others ("The Mob on Trial," 1986). Read the transcripts of the Scarfo trials in Philadelphia and critically evaluate the testimony of two Cosa Nostra members who became state's witnesses (Cooney, 1987a, 1987b; Mallowe, 1988). Obtain the transcript of the trial of Nick Civella in Kansas City (Turner, 1983, p. 30); the testimony of Cleveland Cosa Nostra Underboss Angelo Lonardo before the Permanent Subcommittee on Investigations (U.S. Congress, 1988); or the trial testimony in the Gennaro Angiulo case in Boston. Surely, the infamous "Pizza connection" trial (Alexander, 1988; Blumenthal, 1988); the reportings of Jimmy "the Weasel" Fratianno (DeMaris, 1981) or Joseph Bonanno (1983), Paul Meskil (1976), and Thomas Renner (Renner & Giancana, 1984; Renner & Teresa, 1973) are relevant pieces of research/literature ignored by Albini. Why are they given less credence than Albanese, Smith,

or Ianni? Why were Dintino's statistical data blindly accepted despite their lack of scientific rigor? Perhaps we should answer these questions because they were ignored by Albini.

Joseph Bonanno, the Boss of the Bonanno Cosa Nostra family, was exiled to Arizona in 1969. He subsequently wrote an autobiography (1983), self-serving in many respects, but informative in many others. And do you know what he says? Unexpectedly, he admits to being a member of the very Commission that Cressey described in the 1967 report. According to Bonanno, "The Commission was not part of my tradition. No such agency existed in Sicily. The Commission was an American adaptation" (1983, p. 159). Bonanno describes in some detail the inner workings of the Commission. As Bonanno puts it, the Commission was "an agent of harmony, [arbitrating] disputes brought before it" (p. 159).

Jimmy "the Weasel" Fratianno (DeMaris, 1981), the Underboss of the Roselli Cosa Nostra family, who became a well-paid but nonetheless credible government witness, was used at the Commission trial (in New York), as well as many others. Fratianno describes his initiation into Cosa Nostra and the structure of Cosa Nostra. According to Fratianno, "the Commission [is] made up of bosses from ten families; the five New York families, Buffalo, Philadelphia, Cleveland, Detroit, and Chicago" (pp. 3-19). Although there are certainly inconsistencies in his testimony (Albanese, 1985), is social reality or life ever totally consistent? Thomas DelGiorno and Nicholas Caramandi, both federally protected witnesses who were members of the Scarfo Cosa Nostra family (Philadelphia), have testified about the code of *omerta*. According to DelGiorno:

Q. Are you familiar with a code of silence?

A. Yes.

Q. What is the code of silence?

A. That you don't talk about the family.

Q. You don't disclose any of the information?

A. Right.

Q. What is your understanding as to the consequences for violating the code of silence?

A. You could be killed.

Q. Is it your understanding that by testifying in this courtroom you are violating the code of silence?

A. Yes.

The testimonies of DelGiorno and Caramandi resulted in the conviction of Nicodemo Scarfo in two separate trials, whereas in two other trials, they were apparently perceived as not credible. In the most recent trial that resulted in the conviction of Scarfo, the federal government proved beyond a reasonable doubt the existence of Cosa Nostra. Nonetheless, the standard of proof in a criminal prosecution is "beyond a reasonable doubt"—far greater than the civil trial standard, and most certainly greater than that employed for some scholarly research!

Vincent Teresa (a third-generation Mafiosi), who coauthored a text with Tom Renner (Renner & Teresa, 1973), disputes the generic name of Mafia and Cosa Nostra but does support the concepts of rationality and structure. According to Teresa, "There were made men, wiseguys, who were members of the Office. Some of the made guys . . . were called bosses. Patriarca was the top boss, the padrone" (p. 86).

Alexander (1988), in her treatise on the "Pizza connection" case, uses court testimony by Mafia informants, one of whom, Tomasso Buscetta, stated, "Cosa Nostra means Our Thing. If you use these words, it means: I belong to a Mafia family" (p. 43). Testimony regarding the structure of the Mafia was elicited from Buscetta, with titles and positions analogous to those described by Cressey. Blumenthal (1988), commenting on this same trial, wrote, "Buscetta's true value [referring to protected witness Tomasso Buscetta] . . . lay in his ability to describe the ritualistic and terrifying world of the Mafia" (p. 297).

Although we acknowledge the absence of advanced formal academic training for such persons, this alone does not diminish their truthfulness. Perhaps Albini is so fixated with academic credentials that these data are beneath him because they are often sensationalized and made the subject of media hyperbole (Albini, 1971; Martens & Niederer, 1985). It does, nonetheless, add to our knowledge and cannot be summarily dismissed. It seems odd that Albini's bibliography is also historyless, particularly since 1980 and later.

Let us concede, *arguendo*, the inadequacies in using such firsthand participant accounts as reliable source data. What do the "people of letters" say?

In a symposium proceeding, Kelly (1987b) stated that Ianni and Cressey were not saying anything different, just coming at the issue— Cosa Nostra structures—in alternative ways. According to Kelly, "Italian-American organized crime families may be something of a structural hybrid, superimposing the rational, efficient model of American corporations over a system patterned after the traditional extended family of southern Europe" (p. 23). Ianni (Ianni & Reuss-Ianni, 1972, p. 172) acknowledges the concept of rights and obligations that form alliances; the allocation of territory by these families or clans; a rigid code of familiar law; and "a common system of roles, norms, and values which not only *regulate* [emphasis added] the behavior within the family but also *structure* [emphasis added] relationships among the family." Does not Ianni's description depict a level of rationality and organization similar to, albeit not identical with, Cressey's model? Although Cressey and Ianni were of different disciplines (sociology and anthropology, respectively) and used different sources of data, nonetheless, their descriptions are quite similar.

Another formidable researcher cited by Albini, Nelli (1976), in addressing the 1967 report, stated:

Although the power of Italian organizations was exaggerated, the report—and other descriptions of syndicate crime published during the late 1960s and early 1970s—accurately pointed out that during the post-World War II decades Italians had made effective use of ethnic group cohesiveness and the family in order to reach a position of primacy in the American underworld. (p. 262)

Reuter (1983), an economist who has conducted the most insightful research of organized crime and Cosa Nostra in the last decade, never denies its existence (he questions its ascribed functions) and, in fact, stated, "The Mafia provides the most enduring and significant form of organized crime. It does indeed seem to span the underworld" (p. 175).

This leaves us with Dwight Smith (1971), a proficient and articulate theorist but one who has not conducted any substantial empirical research into Cosa Nostra or organized crime. Smith was certainly correct when he challenged researchers and practitioners to look beyond Cosa Nostra and examine illicit markets. He never dismissed Cosa Nostra in his 1971 article, however, but merely (and importantly) transformed the argument from one of criminal organizations to criminal markets. Smith raises many of the issues raised by Schelling (1967, 1971) and does give us the theory of illicit enterprise, a worthy contribution to the sparse literature.

In totality, it appears that the "criticism" of other researchers cited by Albini is inaccurate. Cressey may be criticized for the vigor and zeal he brought to describing Cosa Nostra, but his research need not be discredited or dismissed for exposing Cosa Nostra or describing what he interpreted the data as saying.

RELATIVE VERSUS ABSOLUTE STRUCTURE AND ORGANIZATION

Albini focuses his criticism on the bureaucratic, structured rationality of Cosa Nostra that Cressey depicted in both the 1967b and 1969 research. It is certainly true that Cressey did explain Cosa Nostra in terms of a corporate model. Does this mean that flexibility and informal systems of communications and control are necessarily absent? We believe that Cressey, an organizational sociologist, surely recognized the flexibility inherent in any social grouping

(Cressey, 1958, 1959, 1965, pp. 1023-1070; Cressey & Krassowski, 1957). In arguing that Cressey was wedded to this bureaucratic description, Albini fails to acknowledge these previous writings. Surely, within most organizations, whether it be Wayne State University, the FBI, or the Pennsylvania Crime Commission, there is a formal chain of command and an informal system of control and discipline. One Cosa Nostra family, such as Bruno's (the late Angelo Bruno of Philadelphia), may be less authoritarian than, say, the Scarfo Cosa Nostra family (its successor), yet both maintained a bureaucratic structure (despite Anderson's 1979 findings). Violations of the norms may be sanctioned differently from one Cosa Nostra family to the next. That does not imply that a structure is nonexistent; it suggests differences in management style, not organizational structure.

It appears to us that, in looking back on Cressey's research, the focus was on structure, with insufficient analysis of the management style and techniques used to maintain control in Cosa Nostra. This was not necessarily Cressey's fault; it may well have been a function of the types of data that had been collected and made available to him. We have been fortunate, in later years, to have Reuter, Ianni, Nelli, Albini, Haller, and others collect the types of data that provide us with insight into the informal systems of social control that function in these and other criminal organizations.

LACK OF DEFINITION OF ORGANIZED CRIME

When all else fails, attribute the deficiencies of research to lack of definitional quality. Albini and other critics are no strangers to this maxim (Maltz, 1976, pp. 338-346). They are so preoccupied with defining the phenomenon that they often lose sight of the purpose. They get lost in a definitional malaise and seem to dismiss the important characteristics of the phenomenon. This reminds us of Justice Potter Stewart's comment, "Maybe I can't define pornography, but I know what it is when I see it." Although we concede that it is certainly desirable to have precise quantitative definitions, it need not be obligatory, as Blumer (1969) so correctly noted. Cressey precisely described the discriminating characteristics of Cosa Nostra. Although they need not apply to all models of organized crime, they do represent organized crime in its more advanced and developed stage (Dintino & Martens, 1983; Stier & Richards, 1987).

THE CASUAL USE OF
STATISTICAL DATA BY ALBINI

Shockingly, we find that Albini (1988) closes his "tribute" to Cressey with quotes from Justin Dintino, a former New Jersey State Police official. In that way, Albini does exactly what he accuses Cressey of doing: He relies on the statements of Dintino (an ironic counterpoint to Albini's criticism of the Cressey-Salerno relationship), who was a member of the 1986 Commission on Organized Crime (Ralph Salerno). Here is where Albini is at his worst.

I (Rogovin) am a long-time friend of Dintino and was his colleague as a member of the Presidential Commission on Organized Crime. With him, I was one of those commissioners who objected vigorously to the substance of the commission's final report. Although reported by the press as a dissent to the final report, our views were, in fact, the statement of a majority of the commission. I (Martens) worked with Dintino while he was on the commission (and for 11 years prior to that as a member of the New Jersey State Police) and attended the seminar at which Dintino is alleged to have made those quoted statements. We believe this qualifies us to address the casual use of data that Albini ascribes to Dintino.

Our experience with Dintino certainly leads us to believe that he is a proponent of the thesis "There is more to organized crime than La Cosa Nostra" (Dintino & Martens, 1983). But contrary to the implication offered by Albini, Dintino does not deny Cosa Nostra, nor does he contradict Cressey's model. In fact, he is one of those who have testified and presented family charts of Cosa Nostra that adhere to the Cressey model (U.S. Congress, 1983, 1988).

The final vote of the 1986 commission, despite what Albini ascribes to Dintino or suggests that Dintino said, was, in fact, 10 to 9, the majority placing themselves against the "findings" of the commission. The dissent was, in fact, a majority report although not reported as such in the media. It is odd that Albini did not seek to verify the facts, but rather accepted uncritically press accounts, given his criticism of Cressey's lack of scientific rigor.

The remaining statistics ascribed to Dintino by Albini are even further flawed. We know of no acceptable research conducted by the 1986 commission (or any other government or nongovernment body) that indicated that 30 labor racketeering cases were not investigated because they lacked Cosa Nostra involvement, nor are we aware of any research that indicates that Cosa Nostra accounts for 0.001% of the organized crime problem in America. From what data these statistics are derived is anyone's guess. Why Albini would be trapped into repeating them says more about his desire to fit undocumented and unsupported data to his theory than it does about the nature of organized crime in the United States.

What is even more disturbing is Albini's belief (and perhaps Dintino's) that the Colombians represent the number one organized crime problem in America. It appears to us that their involvement in illicit markets is confined to cocaine (and perhaps some marijuana); they have not developed the systemic relationships with our institutions as other groups have (e.g., blacks, Asians, Italians, Jews, Irish); nor have they invested substantially in, or taken over, legitimate businesses or labor unions, as other groups have. In short, it is unfair, and certainly erroneous, to use the enormous amounts of money generated by the cocaine trade to define the seriousness of the problem. For Albini to adopt this statement, if it indeed was said, certainly demonstrates a lack of critical questioning. It also demonstrates perhaps how easy it is to be impressed with the credentials of a member of a presidential commission, even by one as intelligent, introspective, and cautious as Albini appears to have been.

THE FAILURE TO DISCUSS CRESSEY'S "APOLOGY" TO HIS COLLEAGUES

Albini has intrigued us with his failure to go into any detail in describing the skills and techniques that Cressey brought to the 1967 task force. In researching Cressey's work, we found an article that some may argue is an explanation of his research and analytic methodology, but it appears to be an apology to his colleagues. Cressey quite nicely and concisely describes how he came to his conclusions. It is a beautifully argued essay on organized crime research and the limitations imposed on the researcher(s).

What Cressey (1967b) essentially argues is that there is "no hard data on organized crime" and that, to solve this problem (and others), we must act like archaeologists—that is, seek "knowledge about inaccessible affairs from consideration of affairs accessible to study" (pp. 109-110). By using inferential reasoning, we can create and manufacture data "about both norms and interactions processes" (p. 110). He concludes:

> The social scientist who is an "organized crime expert" has an advantage over these other two types of scientists because he works with contemporary materials and therefore can comfortably make the assumption that "in the long run" the action scene which he has created by inference can be directly observed. This does not mean, of course, that eventually there will be no screens or filters on his perceptions. It means only that his perceptions will be strained through different screens and filters, those pertaining to empirical observation.

It is these different screens and filters that Cressey implores researchers to pursue, implic-

itly recognizing that his Cosa Nostra model was not, and perhaps would never be, the definitive statement on the issue.

WHERE DOES THIS LEAVE US?

Cressey's model of organized crime has stood the test of time. His research was visionary, though not necessarily all-inclusive. His legacy to the field of organized crime research, however, is well established. The facts remain: Cosa Nostra exists; it is structured and possesses a hierarchy; a Commission regulates interfamily conflicts; and Cosa Nostra families are located in the major cities of the nation. Criminal prosecutions have sustained this thesis.

Despite the vitality of the Cressey model, more needs to be done to explain the nature, scope, and dimensions of organized crime. The 1986 commission had the opportunity and resources but badly missed the mark in its work. Researchers using the techniques employed by Reuter, Ianni, Albini, Abadinsky, Cressey, Haller, and others need to explore organized crime in its totality. Black organized crime has escaped any meaningful inquiry. Asian criminal syndicates receive only superficial treatment. Hispanic organized crime appears to some to be only a Colombian and hence foreign phenomenon. And other non-ethnic forms of organized crime defy any substantive descriptions or explanations. The field remains essentially in a state of intellectual atrophy, with new research noticeably shallow. If history is any predictor of the future, we may be in dire need of an infusion of research funding from the federal government (as was the case in the post-1967 era) to encourage quality research. In the meantime, we will wallow about, engaging in rhetorical diatribes that do nothing more than spotlight the gross ignorance that pervades this field.

PART II

COMMENTARY

Your editors choose to stick to the theoretical for at least the next two chapters, and for good reason. Who and what is organized crime is not totally described in the "debate." All of Part 1 deals with the Italian version that literally burst on the scene in the mid-1960s. It is crucial to your understanding of organized crime generally that you understand how Cressey and his critics and supporters paved the way for further study. If not for these early pieces of research, we suspect that you would not be studying Russian or Chinese organized crime. But, however important the model supplied by Cressey, it does not describe all of organized crime.

This is an important concept. Cressey proposes a model. Others criticize it, provide different examples of criminal groups, describe different organizational structures, and even provide competing motives for why the group exists. An environmental or cultural *raison d'être* is supplanted by an entrepreneurial one; or race might be as powerful a force as ethnic succession (Ianni, 1974; Ianni & Reuss-Ianni, 1972). This is the nature of social science. We research a problem, one hopes, to do something about it. In an ideal world, the problem would be identified, the research done, and then some policy formulated to fix it. Usually, the

bandage is applied before we fully understand the problem—but that's another discussion. Suffice it to say that social science attempts an understanding of social and cultural phenomena to inform social policy. Hence, we present in Part 2 chapters that recognize Cressey's contribution and then respectfully suggest other avenues of study toward a more comprehensive understanding of the topic.

The title of Chapter 4 hints that we might be "trapped in the folds of discourse" should we continue to debate who and what is organized crime. Robert Kelly wonders whether we might be spending an inordinate amount of time "theorizing about the underworld." The inclusion of "Underworld" in the title may suggest that Kelly is also talking about those unseen beings of the netherworld, as does Joseph Albini in Part 3. He is not. Kelly's chapter bridges the gap between arguments about the value of Cressey's work and the later typologies that focus on the "business" of crime, the work of those researchers who argue that, above all other explanations, the Mafia exists to make money. This is a reasoned review of the debate about Cressey, done in an engaging style: On the one hand, Kelly highlights the commentary of Cressey supporters: "According to Rogovin

. . . Cressey's critics have situated their pulpits over a trapdoor" and then himself expresses some doubts about accepting Cressey's entire formulation because "Cressey tended to overestimate the extent of administrative centralization among Cosa Nostra groups." Before becoming too firmly entrenched on either side of the debate, closely read the section in which Kelly says, "Despite the differences in themes," we may perhaps accord (the Cressey/Albini models) them both "empirical equivalence" and prudently "oscillate between them for the sake of a more powerful and fertile perspective on organized crime." This is advice well taken.

A logical extension of Kelly's "theorizing" is Chapter 5, by Mark Haller, who argues, again, that Cressey's model may have relied too heavily on standard theoretical positions. For example, the bureaucracy described by Max Weber is a union headed by such as a CEO, with tasks divided and staff devoted to the common cause of making money. Labor is divided at the direction of the organization's leadership, and all work in tandem toward pecuniary ends. Regarding organized crime, Haller describes the opposite—mobsters working as individual entrepreneurs. He quotes one gangster: "The family don't run anything." Haller's warning that we best be careful about comparing apples and oranges when studying organized crime, that "It makes little sense . . . to compare an Italian American crime family to a Jamaican cocaine distribution group," is especially important in a text such as this, which examines international aspects of organized crime. Haller says, rather than compare "a Rotary Club and a department store" because both are organizations, the student of organized crime would be better served by getting to know the economics of disparate criminal operations and the ancillary associations that criminals have formed in aid and furtherance of the main criminal organization.

Above, we said that once you get by the theory, "it's all downhill." Start your slide. The material in Part 3 is dramatically different from what you've read thus far. Both of your editors are professors, so before we let you go, answer the following few questions: Does Cressey's model adequately depict what you know about organized crime? How would you compare a criminal family operating in Brooklyn, New York (or Philadelphia or Chicago), with a Columbian drug cartel—what methodology would you use? In view of Haller's argument that organized crime may be more individualistic and entrepreneurial than assumed, do you see any attraction to a life of crime in the "role model" theory—in other words, are wiseguys, wiseguys because they enjoy the life?

SUGGESTED READINGS

Anderson, A. G. (1979). *The business of organized crime: A Cosa Nostra family.* Stanford, CA: Hoover Institution Press.

Kane, J. (1992). *The crooked ladder: Gangster ethnicity and the American dream.* New Brunswick, NJ: Transaction.

Landesco, J. (1968). *Organized crime in Chicago.* Chicago: University of Chicago Press. (Original work published under the same title, Part III of the Illinois Crime Survey, 1929)

Nelli, H. S. (1976). *The business of organized crime.* New York: Oxford University Press.

Reuter, P. (1983). *Disorganized crime.* Cambridge: MIT Press.

Suttles, G. D. (1968). *The social order of the slum.* Chicago: University of Chicago Press.

4

TRAPPED IN THE FOLDS OF DISCOURSE

Theorizing About the Underworld

ROBERT J. KELLY

> There seems to be little doubt that many in the law enforcement community found Cressey's work for the President's Commission on Organized Crime (1967) and his later writings congenial. It seems uniquely relevant to their professional aspirations and agendas, but then there has been a certain amount of difficulty with the kind of organized crime represented in his work. Many scholars were never quite easy with his "model" and didn't finally believe in its actuality.

COSA NOSTRA: STRUCTURE, FUNCTION, MYSTIQUES

Most accounts of Cosa Nostra, official, scholarly, and popular, tend to emphasize the "business of crime." They say that criminals are oriented toward profits and pursue these unscrupulously in legal and illegal product and service markets. There appears to be wide consensus about the validity of this claim. Cressey himself is given to business and economic metaphors. In describing the origins of Cosa Nostra, he says when it all started and, as interesting, how we can make sense of its structure:

> In 1931 leaders of Sicilian-Italian organized crime units across the United States rationally decided to form monopolistic corporations, and to link these corporations together in a monopolistic cartel. To use a political analogy, in 1931 local Sicilian-Italian units formed into feudal governments, and the rulers of these governments linked themselves together in a nationwide confederation which itself constitutes a government. (Cressey, 1969, p. 35)

These momentous events occurred at the end of the "Castellammarese War," fought among factions of the Sicilian and Italian underworld, that culminated in the murder of Salvatore Maranzano. Joseph Valachi and others claimed Maranzano had formed the crime "families" from the amorphous groups of Sicilians and Italians loosely organized in adult gangs. The war, intrigues, and subsequent national reor-

AUTHOR'S NOTE: This work first appeared in the *Journal of Contemporary Criminal Justice, 8*(1), February 1992, and was revised for this edition.

ganization represent, for Cressey, a rationalizing process wherein the traditional Mafia evolved into a relatively complex organization that perpetuates selected features of the Old World cultural style of organization but that subordinates them to the requirements of bureaucracy. Cressey's sociological analysis is based on a shrewd grasp of power alignments; he argues that, by deposing the principal leaders of Old World Mafia clans, the new leaders formed smaller, feudal empires (families) with allocated territory and agreements to protect their local sovereignty. He further observes that his sketch of the outcomes of the 1929-1931 war is based mainly on the testimony and accounts of Joseph Valachi, and it appears to be a reliable chronology and narrative of events because it has been verified by police records—an independent source of confirmation. Cressey created a new paradigm of criminal structure and organization that functioned as an interpretive schema, a grid, that enables its users to shift through a pandemonium of information to arrive at the grist of events and processes.

COSA NOSTRA:
A SELF-FULFILLING PROPHECY?

Cressey acknowledged that most of his materials derived from access to law enforcement agency files (1967b). But where Cressey never expressed any reservations about the reliability of his data, other researchers have had similar experiences and have become skeptical of the research value in such files. This is a generic problem affecting all levels of law enforcement, from federal to local agencies. Information on organized crime is gathered by law enforcement agencies primarily for purposes of indictment and prosecution, and the agencies may be little concerned with other potential uses of their information. Further, law enforcement may be understandably reluctant to make available file data to researchers whose postures are those of professional disbelievers or who may, even inadvertently, betray confidences or portray law enforcement unflatteringly.

Confounding image problems and the sensitivities of information suppliers are issues concerning how intelligence gathering is shaped by beliefs. If law enforcement agencies believe that Cosa Nostra, for example, is the group worth the most attention and commit their resources accordingly, this tends to ensure that intelligence activities will focus on the doings of Cosa Nostra. More, consequently, is likely to be known about Cosa Nostra activities and members than about other groups. This knowledge, in turn, reinforces the belief about Cosa Nostra's prominence and dominance in organized crime. Conversely, ignoring other organized criminal groups may be construed as evidence of their lack of importance.

The president's commission has not entirely removed Cosa Nostra from center stage, although it acknowledges the existence and power of other criminal groups in the United States devoting time in hearings to Asian criminal gangs and their activities. The role of Cosa Nostra in labor racketeering and in the penetration of legitimate businesses where racketeers move diligently from benign investments to mask their illicit incomes to active control and domination of various industries suggests something about the dynamic nature of Cosa Nostra operations. It also suggests that the conventional view of Cosa Nostra as a highly centralized bureaucracy where power resides in the higher echelons of membership may be more apparent than real. Cressey's model has Soldiers sharing some of the profits with their Bosses and acting as their agents in the field. But the intrigues and liaisons in construction, waste, and kindred industries points toward arrangements that are more complicated and less neat than previously argued in the literature. Cosa Nostra members appear to be as distrustful and wary of each other as are law-abiding persons.

The evidence emerging from prosecutions and investigations in recent years implies that the role of the Commission of crime Bosses may not be as crucial in crime activities as the traditional model posits. It may be no more than Bonanno (1983) indicates: a forum with influence but no executive power that has respect and authority in interfamily disputes but only insofar as its individual members have respect.

The descriptive materials in official reports and studies (New York State Task Force on Organized Crime, 1988; Reuter, 1985) provide a glimpse of crime family members at work. Even newspaper accounts (e.g., *Newsday,* March 11, 1990) suggest that the crime families are loosely linked, engaged in temporary coalitions and alliances that come and go, and are very often as capricious as legitimate arrangements. Moore (1987) sees illegal firms and criminal entrepreneurs as closely resembling the erratic behavior of the real estate development industry. His basic point is that much illegal activity is neither routine nor systematic, but rather consists instead of many ad hoc deals in which frenzies of activity are followed by lulls.

Still other ramifications for the structure of Cosa Nostra have been embraced, unmodified since its inception, by the president's crime commission. Criminals active in the waste industry have developed a modus operandi that may be characteristic of other racketeering enterprises. In the waste industry, it seems that a structure of illegal activity (e.g., monopoly control of routes) has evolved around individuals who acquired a working knowledge of the industry and created networks with legitimate colleagues, regulatory officials, clients, and suppliers. The capacity to do business lay with individuals, not in a structure or with a criminal group per se. And over time, this business sector, infested with criminals knowledgeable about the business, led to numerous partnerships. The idea that crime families make deliberately concerted moves against targeted businesses and industries and commit resources to their domination may be mistaken.

The Scarpitti and Block study (1985) cites case after case in which those with organized crime ties were identified with several New York/New Jersey Cosa Nostra groups. They were part of a criminal milieu; many had reputations for particular skills and competencies in one area of commercial activity or another, and those who shared common experiences and backgrounds were likely to work with each other despite their loyalties and criminal affiliations with different crime families. A "structure" of organized criminality appears to have encrusted a business or industry because so many with criminal backgrounds and assets were present and active.

For all its flaws, the Scarpitti and Block study provides suggestive data that organized criminality is much more and more dangerous than ethnic gangs in vice activities who may branch out into legitimate businesses. Organized criminals are not exclusively members of Cosa Nostra but seem to be composed of greedy businesspeople as well as criminal types. Organized crime figures represented one element in the criminal collusions that affected the waste industry.

These studies and reports on the criminal trials of top Cosa Nostra leaders should arouse interests in reconsidering the Cressey model. In trials in New York City, prosecutors adopted the language of those under indictment or on trial as disclosed in electronic surveillance intercepts concerning the structure of their organizations. In the first trial involving John Gotti and associates, electronic surveillance intercepts reveal talk of "crews" (a term Valachi himself used to describe his group in the Genovese crime family). Crews appear to consist of members under a Capo who operate semiautonomously. The undercover FBI operative Joe Pistone similarly uses this term (Pistone & Woodley, 1987). Pistone's descriptions of everyday activities, as well as the semiautobiographical account of Henry Hill (Pileggi, 1985), provide source material about how contemporary criminal groups operate. It may suggest that the Cosa Nostra model fashioned by Cressey nearly 30 years ago is importantly different from the present. No doubt, many career criminals still operate in ways similar to those of their counterparts decades ago, but at the same time, the criminal opportunities available now suggest that new roles and lines of activity, and therefore organization, have taken a different tack and acquired a different look.

THE CRESSEY MODEL:
A THEORETICAL BLANKET
THAT SMOTHERS?

According to Rogovin and Martens (chap. 3, this volume), Cressey's critics have situated their pulpits over a trapdoor since subsequent research and evidence in the form of trial records, electronic surveillance, and numerous informers have, more or less, vindicated the claims of *Theft of the Nation* (Cressey, 1969). A close reading of Cressey's major work and other papers connected with its main themes, however, suggests that Cressey tended to overestimate the extent of administrative centralization among Cosa Nostra groups. Disclosures in trial testimony indicate that the crime families were often deeply divided not only by their personal ambitions but also by their networks of patronage (Salerno & Rincle, 1990). Even those committed to Cressey's versions of Cosa Nostra and the pivotal role it is alleged to play in American organized crime must be troubled by the shortcomings of a perspective that constricts and narrows the focus to a particular criminal entity within the underworld.

Still, what makes his work influential is the harmony between the topics of his research on organized criminality and the theoretical nature of his thinking. Cressey was only marginally interested in the problems raised by other, later analysts concerning ethnic succession; and he did not approach organized criminality as an expression of the social system with a view toward examining the continuities between the upperworld and the underworld. There are those considerations certainly, but his chief concern was with the factors that came together like an irresistible current to carry organized crime forward. In short, he wished to understand its internal dynamics, its mainsprings. Cressey no doubt believed that Cosa Nostra was the nucleus, the central phenomenon of modern organized crime—thus, the need to discover what made Cosa Nostra possible and what made it tick. In devising such a project, the analysis must go to the identifiable core: the internal structure of Cosa Nostra crime families.

This discussion leaves room for much speculation. Cressey was confronted by a major question: Why did Italian American criminal groups come to dominate organized crime in the United States? Whether this is a valid question, though many have disputed it, is beside the point; Cressey believed that Italian American groups had achieved hegemony in the underworld. If the question really is, as I believe it is, the crucial issue for him, then it shows why he centered his analysis on those characteristics thought to be unique to Cosa Nostra groups that paved the way for their ascension to power and enabled them to maintain it as long as they have.

The success of Cressey has much to do with the literary qualities of his work: His piercing yet apt imagery, his eye for revealing anecdotes, his infallible knack of sliding seamlessly between the petty and the major sinister detail informs yet also titillates. The "history" of organized crime sketched in Cressey's works reflect the fact that he was not a professional historian. But any history, whatever its conceptual apparatus, like all histories, involves intellectual presuppositions. Can there be such a thing as an "innocent" history? Historical interpretations are themselves located in history, indeed are history, the product of an inherently unstable relationship between the past and the present. His work, like any other, is a merging of a particular mind with the vast field of its topics, and it implies choices, preferences within the range of what might be studied.

The period of the Castellammarese War (1929-31) appears to be the key to what lies both upstream and downstream in organized crime for Cressey. For the same reason that the birth of Cosa Nostra is thought to have a beginning, it has no end; ethnic succession apparently has not fulfilled its predictions, at least in the short run, as the social lubricant of criminal mobility for minority criminals.[1] Seen negatively and lacking the chronological detail that historians appreciate, only the death of the pre-Prohibition underworld seems to be something of a certainty; the other, Cosa Nostra and large Prohibition gangs, contain a promise of such magnitude for growth and dominance that they become boundlessly elastic in terms of power and influence. Cressey sees the internal struggle among Italian gangs as the turning point in the form of organized crime in the United States.

The Castellammarese War transformed the Old World Mafia: The "Mustache Petes" gave way to the Young Turks who reshaped the Mafia and its ancillary non-Italian groups so that they were more smoothly aligned with social, economic, and political realities. "The basic structure of the nationwide cartel and confederation," writes Cressey, "which today operates the principal illicit businesses in America, and which is now striking at the foundations of legitimate businesses and government as well, came into being in 1931" (1969, p. 35). This reshuffling produced a Commission that replaced the Old World notion of a Boss of Bosses. The Commission is made up of the heads of the most powerful crime families. It functions as a judicial body making decisions in interfamily disputes. Not everyone agrees with Cressey's descriptions of the Commission, however. Bonanno (1983, chap. 13), for example, saw the Commission as a committee with decided influence on family matters but with no direct executive power.

These and other descriptions are presented with an absolutism that must make Cressey's sympathizers wince. A perspective that narrows all organized crime problems of any significance to the issue of whether we believe that Cosa Nostra pulls the strings on crime in the nation must be seen as deficient. Moreover, not all observers are persuaded that 1931 is the epochal event when the essential features of organized crime were fixed. Others have stressed Prohibition as the phenomenon that dramatically transformed organized crime in the United States (Fox, 1989).

If one is determined to preserve the idea of an objective break in the continuity of Italian American criminal organizations and to consider that fissure the alpha and omega points of Cosa Nostra history, one is bound to end up with some absurdities, whatever the interpretation advanced. And those anomalies—perhaps the term *absurdities* is too strong—become the more inevitable as the interpretation becomes more ambitious and encompasses more and more events within its orbit. One could say, for instance, that between 1929 and 1931, the entire structure of the Italian underworld was radically transformed because the Old World Mafia came to an end in America, as Cressey says. But the idea that between these same dates the social and economic fabric of the American underworld was reorganized from top to bottom as a consequence of a localized struggle among Italian gangs in New York City is daring but not very plausible.

The Castellammarese War, then, may not be a particularly useful explanatory concept—not more powerful than Prohibition, whose effects were felt nationally. Cressey apparently saw in the Castellammarese War the constitutive aspects of a major administrative upheaval in the underworld; and what is called Cosa Nostra (a phenomenon later inventoried, dated, and magnified as a new dawn) was but the acceleration of prior economic and organizational trends. By destroying the Old World Mafia, new leadership principles and policies came into play.

Especially troubling in all of this is Cressey's providential wandering in a field suffused with the narrative method as its principal source of information. His *Theft of the Nation* (1969) does not escape the tyranny of the historical actors' own conception of their experience, as he indirectly admits in his comments on sources. This may be why *Theft of the Nation* is more important for its methodology than for the thesis it advances. What separates Cressey from many modern writers on organized crime are method and the choice of empirical data. Cressey brings Cosa Nostra to life from the inside through colorful, sensational anecdotes interspersed with law enforcement information. Most social scientists today prefer not to install themselves within the phenomenon through immersion in its narratives. Rather, they look to discern the external social structural pressures that give rise to organized criminality. For those who conceptualize organized crime through market models, or as an element of the social system, or as a mechanism that emerged in response to contradictions between the legal system and the culture at large, the fixation on Cosa Nostra, or on any other specific crime groups, masks the real meanings and causes of criminal behavior.

The chronological narrative is less relevant to social science treatments today than in Cressey's era of research. Specific problems—drugs, vice, illicit market dynamics, racketeering—rather than periods are the focus of inquiries.[2] Nonetheless, the Cosa Nostra perspective is a powerfully explanatory device. Its simplicity provides the single-cause explanation of a major social problem. And Cressey has done much to synthesize the factors making up the Cosa Nostra mystique in a kind of logical balance sheet where history, structure, culture, and consequences are lined up in a systematic accounting of the past and the future.

Cressey (1969) argues that the Castellammarese War closed an era of Italian American crime and opened a new period that has shaped America's entire style of criminal activity since 1931. When those who brought down Maranzano attempted to restore the autonomy of individual groups—which they themselves were unable to respect as subsequent events are believed to have shown—they rediscovered the independence and inertia of the organized underworld and its recalcitrance even to powerful crime families—thus, the need for trade-offs and the compromises demanded by the interplay of means and ends among professional criminals (Kelly, 1987a). The Italian opponents of Masseria and then Maranzano, the "Americanized" factions of the Old World Mafia clans, did more than stop the autocratic power of the Boss of Bosses; they dismantled it as a system of power, replacing it with a structure more attuned to America's economic realities. Much like reformed drunks, the new Cosa Nostra leaders occasionally imposed their will harshly on other families but did so as an expedient, rather than on principle. The Castellammarese War represents a major benchmark in Cressey's interpretation of organized crime's evolution: It culminates in the overthrow of a system of power and not merely the substitution of one power for another, as in a coup d'état, but replacing one type of power for another. Perhaps Cressey also saw other implications such that the struggle between Italian gangsters went far beyond their internal squabbles as some have suggested (Stier & Richards, 1987).[3]

DIAGNOSIS AND THERAPY: INGREDIENTS IN THEORY CONSTRUCTION

In the wake of the bloodletting, the New World Mafia continued a vast process of social and economic integration with other ethnic gangs through never relinquishing its ethnic homogeneity or its dominance. This "reading" of Cressey is meant to emphasize the contexts in which his model is articulated. Fidelity to the main themes in Cressey's account is also meant to illustrate how he stitched together masses of data into a coherent account and why his perspective may be understood as a response to the problems and tensions current in the criminal justice and social science communities at that time; that is, it may be illuminating to situate Cressey's project, not as "caused by" certain irrepressible obvious features of organized crime in the United States, but to regard it as a distinctive picture reflecting conditions of law enforcement interests, strategies, and tactics, as well as criminological understandings of the phenomenon.

Cressey's work may be understood as posited in another assumption—namely, that social theorists always have some conception, not driven by the data alone, which may be either tacit or explicit, of the ills of their society and of possible remedies for them. A corollary of this view argues that all social theories embody the traces of social diagnosis and social therapy (Gouldner, 1976). Theories are never simply disinterested efforts to describe and explain social reality. One way in which social theories can be understood, then, is as analysis, clear or cryptic, of the causes and possible cures of social ills to which the theorist has been subjected. In Cressey's case, it is fairly clear what the milieu was like when he began his work. The

1967 task force was working in a period coming on the heels of major congressional investigations of Cosa Nostra, and the specific law enforcement conceptions of organized crime were prominently disseminated to the press, at hearings, and in legislative settings (Abadinsky, 1985, chap. 19). To discount these inputs and proceed as if they could be discounted in the interests of scientific objectivity is simplistic.

Theft of the Nation did not develop just through the cooperative efforts of friendly disciples and intellectual supporters who defend and extend a body of work in a cumulative and continuous manner. Indeed, theoretical continuity and cumulation derive as much from the mutual hostility of theorists as from their friendly collaboration. (It should not be forgotten that a corpus of work need have nothing to do with the sentiments through which workers in a field or discipline regard each other. Admirers and colleagues may contribute nothing at all to a theory, whereas critics arguing against a point of view may add much to its sophistication by their intellectual opposition calling forth a clarification and refinement not otherwise possible.)

Cressey's ideas seem to derive as much from polemical animus as from what they learn or borrow from friendly commerce with others. *Theft of the Nation,* and especially other works such as *Criminal Organization* (1972), may reflect the opinions of opponents as much as they do those of allies.

The chief aims of *Theft of the Nation* are not limited to "pure" description; they promise much more: There are numerous policy suggestions and recommendations for law enforcement agencies. No doubt, Cressey realized that it is harder to change the world than to simply comprehend it, and it is, therefore, easier to fail as an "applied" than as a "pure" social scientist—at least in terms of the different standards and aspirations that matter to each. Yet, he apparently thought the problems worth the risks. Consequently, he may have encouraged expectations that could not be easily realized and that might engender as much frustration as optimism.

MODELS AND METAPHORS: ORGANIZED CRIME AS A BUREAUCRATIC PHENOMENON

Discussions of Cosa Nostra are often referred to as the "Cosa Nostra model," yet seldom do critics or commentators pause to consider the presuppositions and implications of this characterization. Cressey, however, did. In several places, he is quite clear about his metaphorical analogues where Cosa Nostra is construed in terms of corporate bureaucracies and why these descriptions should be seen as "skeletal." There is also the recognition of the hazards of concentrating on Cosa Nostra to the exclusion of all else. And Cressey does this for at least two reasons, which were noted above. First, he believes that Cosa Nostra is the center of gravity of operational organized criminality; second, detailed knowledge of its formal and informal structures was lacking. What was known at the time suggested to Cressey and others that its organizational forms were not unlike those of legitimate formal organizations. If this were so, then such an organization possessed the added strength of being self-perpetuating and continuing beyond the life of its leaders and members. Because Cressey concentrated on the structure of authority and membership, leaving aside the informal relations and patterns of interactions, the work has been criticized because of its omissions and repeatedly attacked because of its inadequate database.

It seems to me that these criticisms ignore some facts about the circumstances of research in this area at the time and fail to acknowledge what Cressey attempted to do with the data available. First, the price of attempting to globalize an analysis means a loss of rigor and coherence. The omitted sides of criminal life can be accommodated by other studies that zero in on particular problems and aspects of Cosa Nostra that remain undeveloped. Second, given Cressey's interest in organization, he tried to establish some generalizations about the behavior of Cosa Nostra as an element in the criminal subculture of the United States. Although fragmentary and inconsistent in some respects, sufficient documentary evidence existed to permit some general correlations between the functions of the organization and the related social and economic factors. But he is able to do this only by averting his gaze from questions—sometimes very important and fascinating ones—about other features and characteristics of organized criminals; at least Cressey did not attempt to analyze the intricacies of gambling activities or drug trafficking, or the moral attitudes of suppliers and users, or their conduct in noncriminal roles as husbands or wives all at once. A theory or model attempting to embrace all these aspects of life would (as things are) lose in predictive power and in the precision of its results even if such a study would gain in comprehensiveness and richness. The more one wishes to cover, the more overweighted and, in due course, cluttered up and shapeless a model is bound to become if it is too ambitious, until it is scarcely a model at all because it no longer can cope with a sufficient number of actual cases. The utility of the model will steadily diminish as it attempts to grasp larger segments of information.

The Cosa Nostra model is a powerful descriptive device. The risk of fallacious inferences from inevitable irrelevancies and distortions is present in aggravated measure. Analogue models, in general, furnish plausible hypotheses, not proofs. Reliance on models may well seem a devious and artificial procedure, and it is reasonable to ask whether they are really necessary as an aid to understanding. Are the attendant risks of mystification and confusion unavoidable? Has Cressey succeeded in allaying such fears? Even the severest critics of the work will have to concede that Cressey's modeling has produced results, even if allowing that the allusions and comparisons to corporate, bureaucratic organizations may seem fanciful, carried to an extreme. This point of view, however, may reflect a myopic conception of doing science in the early stages of theory construction. Rigor at the formative stages of the classification of variables and the operationalization of testable items where Cressey was openly exploring the parameters of criminal organizational structures

seems out of place. In the incipient phases of the research effort, to impose demands on the scientific imagination that it produce well-ordered and carefully codified results may stifle research (Latour & Woolgar, 1986; Rogovin, 1990). What of the claim that a resort to the Cosa Nostra model is a mere crutch, a decorative embellishment designed to stimulate passions more than edify a problem? As Cressey himself says, compelling reasons for using the model had to do with the inadequacies of the data available so that a direct and exhaustive description of Cosa Nostra was not possible. Cressey (1969) is sensitive to the gaps in the database. He says:

> It will be some time before the investigating agencies will be able to depict the numerous functional positions making up the complete structure of the organization whose authority structure has been sketched out. Some aspects of the structure can be deduced from studies of function; details can be learned by close observation of the interactions between participants. (p. 140)

These remarks indicate that Cressey was conscious of the state of his work, that it was a beginning effort to elaborate on the formal dimensions of criminal groups. It was noted above that the Cosa Nostra model could operate to sabotage the very purposes for which it was invented. As a self-fulfilling prophecy, it could function as a mechanism whereby researchers and criminal justice practitioners selectively attend to information and discard that which does not fit into the Cosa Nostra matrix. In 1969, Cressey pinned his hopes on the existence of a Cosa Nostra structure that would have confirmed his model. The evidence collected by law enforcement agencies since then has shown signs of isomorphism between the model and the reality it is supposed to depict.

Two other considerations relating to the issue of the corporate structure of Cosa Nostra are worth examining. First, intertwined with the viability of models is the use of metaphorical language and imagery in describing criminal organizations. Sensing similarities between crime family structure and the organizational frameworks of legitimate business corporations, Cressey built his model of the former on the constructs of the latter. Given the paucity of criminal justice data, the strategy seems proper. But what is the point in applying corporate imagery and metaphors to describe Cosa Nostra organization? As pointed out above, model constructs and metaphor, which are inherent in modeling, may reveal new relationships by providing clues to heretofore ignored elements of the phenomenon. The similarities between legitimate corporate systems and criminal groups must have appealed to Cressey's instincts as an organizational specialist. Perhaps by using the corporate blueprint, Cosa Nostra structure could be carefully discriminated.

Another way of coming to grips with Cressey's approach is to see it as the application of a conceptual archetype developed in one sphere of research laid over another. Here, we have a systematic repertoire of ideas that do not literally apply to Cosa Nostra. Consequently, a detailed account of the archetype (the hierarchical model) used by extension analogically requires a list of key words and expressions with statements of their interconnections and their paradigmatic meanings in the field from which they were originally drawn to the field in which they are applied. This is supplemented by an analysis of the ways the original meanings become extended in their analogical uses. A cursory reading of *Theft of the Nation* shows that, in the main, these analytic requirements were met.

In this procedure of employing the model, I see nothing to be deplored on the ground of general principles of sound method. Of course, there is the ever-present threat that the analogue model will be used metaphysically so that its evaluation empirically will be permanently insulated from disproof. The more persuasive the model, the greater the danger of its becoming a self-certifying myth. These issues aside for the moment, a good model can meet the demands of experience.

Because of its durability and flexibility, an analysis of the Cosa Nostra model's structural components would be justifiable if only to reveal its weaknesses and vulnerabilities. The model illustrates the following elements:

1. *The criminal activities undertaken by Cosa Nostra are rational.* One may regard the bureaucratic structure of command and authority as a technology that shields and protects the family's vital inner core—its leadership echelon.

2. *The viability of Cosa Nostra families depends on their skill in adjusting to changes in their operational environments.* The organizational suppleness of Cosa Nostra groups had not been sufficiently emphasized until Cressey pointed this out and observed their skill in exploiting illicit opportunities. Further, crime families deploy their resources very effectively in response to pressures not only from law enforcement but also from clients and criminal competitors. The "ameliorated situation" of mutually hospitable accommodations involving systemic corruption that neutralizes law enforcement, sufficient retaliatory capacity that stymies criminal rivals, and opportunities to seek out new sources of income seem to be the principal critical tasks of these organizations.

3. *A hierarchical system of authority and command, which appears more or less intact over the 50 years in which data have been collected, does not obviate against a variety of organizational formats for generating illegal profits and infiltrating legitimate businesses.* As Ianni (1974) noted and as testimony before the president's commission suggest, associational networks of individuals are marked by an emphasis on mutual trust, bound together by close interpersonal relations founded by ties of ethnicity, by neighborhood propinquity, or through the criminal subcultures that operate as organized criminal groups. In addition, criminal activities may be described through entrepreneurial models in which a network of individuals from within the same crime family, or across family lines, or those involving nonfamily members is formed in order to earn a mutual profit. These networks tend to

exhibit bureaucratic trappings, depending on the type of illicit activity engaged in.

4. *Since Cressey's work, the research tends to show that how organized crime is defined may very well depend on the perspective, the model, that affords a vantage point for the observer.* Along these lines, Cressey's point of view is very much from the top down; Ianni, in contrast, sees things from the inside and emphasizes the informal side of relationships.

The growing body of research literature illustrates the complexity of organized criminal activity. This suggests that the struggle over the definitions of organized crime may be misconceived. Maltz (1990) has labored mightily to tease out the distinctive elements that make up organized crime. As he confesses, that task seems insurmountable beyond descriptions of certain regular attributes. Cressey took pains to tell us why it has proved so elusive. Organized crimes do not possess common characteristics: Some criminal conspiracies that are of interest involve behavior that falls under the social category of organized crime, but not all; some, but not all gambling; some, but not all cases of assault and murder; some, but not all cases of prostitution; and so on. From this it is a short step to Cressey's view that what distinguishes organized crime from any other form of crime is that it is committed by a person occupying a position in an established division of labor (no matter how flexible) designed for the commission of crime. This says that any organized criminal's activities are coordinated with the activities of other criminals by means of rules that are precise or vague but that nonetheless specify duties, obligations, expectations, and rights in much the same way that an accountant relates to a clerk, a chief executive officer, or a factory worker in a firm. Therefore, positions in criminal organizations need to be known, as well as how the positions are connected to each other and how they, as a system, differ from legitimate systems if efforts against them are to succeed. The RICO statutes are an expression of Cressey's perspective (Ryan & Kelly, 1989).

Albanese (1989) has offered helpful clarifications on the definition problem. As with Cressey, Albanese argues that organized crime does not exist as a distinctive type of criminal behavior but is best understood as characteristic of a larger category of behavior—"organizational crime"—and that most organizational crimes occur as a deviation from, or variation on, legitimate business activities, whether they involve products or services. "On the other hand," Albanese explains, "organized crime . . . takes place through continuing criminal enterprises that exist to profit primarily from crime." And, "organized crime does not exist as an ideal type, but rather as a 'degree' of criminal activity or as a point on the 'spectrum of legitimacy'!" (pp. 5-6).

Has Cressey's perspective generated useful results? Has it enabled law enforcement to devise effective anticrime campaigns and strategies? The answers to these questions are not clear. Had Cressey's model been taken seriously, then it would be apparent that the elimination of a Boss, much like the removal of a chief executive officer, would not, should not, seriously impair the operations of an organization. Removing an individual from a "position" may not produce a crisis. If crime families are built around the personal charisma and power of individuals whose presence is indispensable to the conduct of business, then the attrition rate among crime family leaders through criminal conviction would have destroyed them some time ago. Top Bosses and leaders in organized criminal groups have been prosecuted, convicted, and deported for more than a half century, yet no significant decline in activity or profitability of criminal enterprises seems to have occurred, according to estimates presented in the report of the President's Commission on Organized Crime (1986).

Cressey himself may have believed that strategies designed to eliminate the heads of crime families would effectively erode their power, but his model of Cosa Nostra structure suggests just the opposite. *Organization* means a system of consciously coordinated activities articulated through rules that imply "positions."

The most important thing that law enforcement can learn from Cressey is how that coordination is accomplished and sustained.

With *Theft of the Nation,* Cressey succeeded in writing himself into criminological history yet again. But as he doubtlessly knew, this is not a task one can ever accomplish alone; every text is at the mercy of its readers. Seldom has a social scientist, brought in at the last minute with little prior knowledge or experience, achieved such a comparable apotheosis.

APPENDIX:
CRESSEY AND ALBINI:
IS THERE THEORETICAL BIVALENCE?

Conceptual models fix the mesh of the nets that analysts drag through information in order to describe and explain structure and action of a phenomenon. To extend the metaphor a bit further: Models direct analysts to cast their nets across select ponds, at particular depths, to catch their prey. These tools are more than simple angles of vision or approaches to a phenomenon. Each framework consists of a cluster of assumptions and categories that influence what the analyst finds puzzling, how questions should be formulated, where evidence might be, and what counts as a satisfactory answer to questions posed.

Although Cressey's and Albini's work produces somewhat different descriptions and explanations of the same phenomenon, and at another level their models may eventuate in different explanations of quite different occurrences, it seems worthwhile to consider the degree to which they share similarities such that their work may be theoretically interchangeable. Another way of putting this is to ask whether Cressey and Albini complement each other. Both fix on the broad national context, the larger national patterns of organized crime and the shared public images of it, and both seek to illuminate the organizational structures of organized crime.

This situation can be illustrated by examining some key concepts in two works (Albini, 1971; Cressey, 1969) that appeared at approximately the same time and addressed the same phenomenon but from different perspectives. Albini's book has been positioned in the literature as a critique of Cressey's work and as an alternative to it (Duggan, 1989). Generally, the formulations of organized criminal activities in both works are empirically equivalent: Cressey and Albini rarely disagree factually; rather, they part company in the interpretations of the data available at the time. Cressey refers to Italian American "crime families" known as Cosa Nostra, and Albini talks about "syndicated crime."[4]

It may be stretching matters, but it seems that most, if not all, of the implicative connections between the observation categoricals and the statements containing the terms *Cosa Nostra crime families* or *syndicated criminal groups* in the one theory formulation are matched by the same implicative connections in the other theory with the two terms rewritten. The observation categoricals (the empirical databases) remain identical—if the terms *Cosa Nostra crime families* and *syndicated crime groups* do not appear in the observed sentences. If we imagine a situation in which (a) *Cosa Nostra crime families* and *syndicated crime groups* are switched and (b) neither term appears, we arrive at a point where there is empirical equivalence but logical incompatibility because, for the one (Cressey), properties are attributed to *Cosa Nostra crime families* that the other formulation (Albini's) denies to *Cosa Nostra crime families* but attributes to *syndicated crime groups.*

The natural response is that the two formulations are really minor variations on the same phenomenon pitched in different words and that the one may be translated into the other by transposing or switching terms. A more general intuitive reaction to theories that seem to run parallel is that whenever terms extraneous to the observation categoricals themselves occur where they can be reinterpreted or construed so as to reconcile them with either theory without disturbing the empirical content, the conflict between the two theories may be superficial.

Albini offers an interesting—and, unfortunately, somewhat neglected—characterization of the main lines of thinking about organized criminality. In a chapter devoted to the genesis and development of what he refers to as *syndicated crime* (because the more familiar *Mafia* has clandestine connotations that distort analysis), he constructs a conceptual model with two major dimensions: the evolutional-centralization and developmental-associational approaches. Briefly, the *evolutional-centralization model,* which has been widely disseminated by the media and government investigative bodies, assumes that organized crime in the United States derives from the Mafia—an alien conspiracy of Sicilian origins. Subsequent events have transformed its character, but the organizational core remains intact. The other perspective, the *developmental-associational model,* which Albini adopts and endorses as a more realistic account of organized criminality, sees it as emerging out of social and economic conditions prevailing within American society at specific periods in history. The developmental-associational approach does not deny that the Mafia or Cosa Nostra exists as such; it assumes, on the contrary, that it is one type of criminal organization among numerous others. The burden for Albini is the extent to which the evidence supports either conceptualization.

Cressey's project involves issues that also drive Albini's analyses, but the former allots considerably more space and energy to discussions on the internal structure of crime families. Both writers raise the fundamental issue of organization. They ask in different ways, Just how organized is organized crime? And, What are the main structural ingredients in that organization? For Cressey, Cosa Nostra crime families draw some of their ethos and élan from the subcultures of the Mafia and *Camorra,* but they are scarcely clones of southern Italian *cosche* and criminal bands. Nevertheless, even though the traditional Mafia may have evolved into a relatively complex organization that perpetuates, at best, selected features of the older peasant organizational form, subordinating them to the requirements of bureaucratic norms in some of the criminal enterprises, the term *Mafia* has held on, and organized crime has come to be synonymous with Mafia for many. Albini and Cressey readily acknowledge this fact.[5]

Perhaps it is possible to persuade ourselves somehow of the empirical equivalence of the Cressey/Albini formulations despite the differences in themes governing their respective projects. Then we should recognize the two as equally well warranted. We might even, as I think it may be prudent to do, oscillate between them for the sake of a more powerful and fertile perspective on organized crime.

If a scientific theory is under tension from the twin forces of evidence and system, then Cressey/Albini qualify as the seedbeds for more refined theoretical elaboration. Albini's orientations imply that theoretical terms should be subject to observation, the more the better, and the more directly the better, other things being equal. Cressey's temperament lends itself to systematization, the simpler the better, other things being equal. If either of these intellectual impulses were left unchecked by the other, both would issue in something ungainly: in the one case, a mere record of discrete observations, and in the other, the perpetuation of a myth without a substantial foundation.

We settle for a trade-off. Within reason, simplicity of theory is achieved by recourse to terms that may relate only indirectly, intermittently, or tenuously to observation (Chambliss, 1975; Cressey, 1967a; Kelly, 1990). It may be that heuristic values traded off—evidential and systematic—are themselves incommensurable and that this creates tensions between researchers of different tastes and tolerances as to how much evidential dilution they are prepared to accept for a given systematic benefit, and vice versa. On the one hand, those who prize the evidential side are the readier to gerrymander their language so as to excise one or another segment of information dependent on sources that appear self-serving and therefore less than reliable. On the other hand, those favoring the systematic side are the readier to round out findings and gain smoothness by accepting some incremental adipose tissue clinging to their databases.

Whether one's inclinations lean toward simplicity of theory or its solid factual grounding, it is pertinent to acknowledge the costs that fidelity to either imposes.

NOTES

1. Before World War II, Prohibition gangsters and Italian groups assiduously cultivated political allies and supporters. Since then, among blacks, Hispanics, and Asians, the systematic corruption of political machines appears to be less intensive and successful, or perhaps machines themselves have shielded themselves to resist criminal penetrations (Kelly & Schatzberg, 1987; Schatzberg, 1990).

2. Not all commentators find many recent approaches to organized crime particularly fruitful. Fox (1989) chides writers who describe organized crime as another type of private enterprise gone astray:

> During these five decades the analogy of organized crime as just another form of private enterprise could be tested at different times and places. In the end the analogy made little sense. Gangsters most depended on muscle, not on market forces. American capitalists, for all their failings, did not habitually extort bribes, beat up people, and kill their business rivals. Organized crime was not productive but parasitic in function. It generally did not produce goods or services or develop new products and markets. It merely leeched on those who did. (p. 220)

3. Stier and Richards (1987) offer an interesting evolutionary model of criminal development that begins with predatory street gangs, matures into parasitic types, and then into more sophisticated symbiotic groups where gangs become integrated into the legitimate economic system. The Stier and Richards analysis seems rooted in Cosa Nostra history and is predicated on Cressey's model where symbiosis is a natural development step for organized crime groups.

4. Albini (1971) offers a definition early on in his book. He writes:

> In a very broad sense, then, we can define organized crime as any criminal activity involving two or more individuals, specialized or nonspecialized, encompassing some form of social structure, with some form of leadership, utilizing certain modes of operation, in which the ultimate purpose of the organization is found in the enterprises of the particular group. (p. 37)

5. One might ask peripherally whether it is the differences between scholarly writing on organized crime, as compared with popular accounts, that explain public confusion. It is indeed worrisome that government commissions selectively attend to some groups and types of crime and ignore others. Whether it is publicity pressures or the convenience of informational sources is hard to say. Whatever the reasons, the results are harmful because a distorted picture is fed to the public, which in turn demands law enforcement responses and control policies that bear little relation to reality (see Abadinsky, 1985, chap. 17, Part 3).

5 BUREAUCRACY AND THE MAFIA

An Alternative View

MARK H. HALLER

Cressey's bureaucratic interpretation of organized crime families has been the dominant view of the subject. The author of this chapter reviews the problems associated with the bureaucratic definition and suggests some alternative viewpoints.

The dominant interpretation of the organization and functions of Italian American crime "families" derives from Donald Cressey's remarkably influential book *Theft of the Nation* (1969). Among the features of the book is the author's description of the now-familiar formal structure of the families. That structure consisted of some 24 families (including 5 in New York City), each with a Boss, an Underboss, *Consigliere, Capos,* and Soldiers. Above these families, a Commission, consisting of about nine of the most influential Bosses and dominated by New York, directed and coordinated "organized crime" in America.

Some have argued that, if this or a similar structure can be confirmed, then Cressey was essentially correct in his analysis of organized crime in America. Actually, of course, this structure had been described by Joseph Valachi in highly publicized testimony before a U.S. Senate subcommittee and had been widely trumpeted in the press and popular magazines (Maas, 1968). Although Cressey depicted the structure in greater detail than others, this was not his chief contribution. Because the goal of social science is to integrate theory and facts, what made Cressey an influential criminologist was his impressive ability to bring theoretical clarity to various areas of criminological research. The problem is that, in his analysis of Italian American crime families, he often applied a theory that had limited relevance. The authoritative

AUTHOR'S NOTE: This chapter is a revised version of a paper given at the Academy of Criminal Justice Sciences in Denver, March 15, 1990. I am grateful to the Pennsylvania Crime Commission for providing unlimited access to its files to study the structure of the Philadelphia family in the 1970s and 1980s. I am especially grateful to the staff of the commission for their friendly help and advice. In addition, I thank Frederick T. Martens and Richard Kedzior for their critical comments on this chapter. They would nevertheless wish me to add that the views expressed in the chapter are my own.

way he did so has tended to make more difficult any subsequent attempts to reach a consensus concerning the role of Italian American crime families within the underworld.

In a book rich in anecdotes and complex in its analysis, the predominant theory that Cressey applied to Italian American crime families was the idea of bureaucracy—a theory rooted in Max Weber's seminal essay (Gerth & Mills, 1946, pp. 196-244) and elaborated by several sociologists in subsequent years. This theory described complex, ongoing organizations that were hierarchically structured to achieve rational goals, were characterized by formal rules, and consisted of individuals having specialized functions and skills within the hierarchy. The President's Commission on Law Enforcement and Administration of Justice, which gave Cressey access to FBI interceptions and other intelligence data not available to social scientists generally, provided him with a remarkable opportunity to apply the concept of bureaucracy to a wide range of information. Despite some vigorous and sometimes misdirected early criticisms (Albini, 1971; Hawkins, 1969; Smith, 1975), Cressey's view largely prevailed and remains a standard interpretation.

In this chapter, after suggesting two significant problems with the bureaucratic theory of organized crime, I offer an alternative formulation.

THE FAMILY AS A PROFIT-MAKING BUSINESS

One aspect of Cressey's analysis was to present a crime family as a hierarchical and rationally structured bureaucracy that was both an underworld government and a business enterprise. The chief problem lies in Cressey's description of the family as a business enterprise. In describing the family as a business, Cressey generally argued that a Boss presided over an organization characterized by staff and line positions devoted to a rational search for profit. The Boss, then, was roughly like the CEO of a business corporation.[1]

The evidence, though, points to another view. Rather than the family being a business enterprise, members (and their associates) are involved in independent legal and illegal activities that are their own and from which they derive income. (As one long-time Philadelphia family member once stated emphatically, "The family don't run anything."[2]) A *family,* then, is a group that is separate from a member's economic ventures and to which members belong roughly in the same way that legal businesspeople might join a Rotary Club. (Although the Rotary Club may have businesspeople as members,[3] it is not itself a business.) For the members, a family can serve at least three functions.

First, the families are somewhat like blue-collar fraternal organizations in providing male bonding and social prestige for members. The belief that a person is a member brings respect on the street corners and in the bars and nightclubs where they hang out, brag, gossip, and arrange their deals. Many take seriously the social bonds that are forged among members and displayed at marriages, funerals, and other occasions where they exchange gifts and acknowledge their loyalties to each other. Within the organization itself, of course, elevation to *Capo* or Boss brings with it special marks of respect that are often reflected in a ritualized demeanor that recognizes a person's position within the family.

Second and more important, perhaps, crime families act like businessmen's associations in providing members with contacts and mutual assistance that can be useful in pursuing their own careers. Those who are beginners hope that more experienced Mob members will direct business their way and perhaps offer attractive partnership opportunities. More successful businessmen will wish to wheel and deal among their equals, make selective investments in the enterprises of younger men, and participate in a network of underworld gossip and exchange of information. For most members, a significant advantage of membership is that criminal entrepreneurs outside the family often wish to have a family member as a partner in an enterprise. Membership can, in short, expand a member's money-making opportunities by placing him within a network of similar entrepreneurs who wheel and deal for their mutual benefit.

Third, successful involvement in varied money-making ventures requires certain minimal rules and expectations so that others can be expected to honor their obligations and, therefore, the outcome of economic ventures can be somewhat predictable (Best & Luckenbill, 1982, chap. 10). For legitimate businesspeople, predictability is provided by government laws and regulations, as well as by rules sponsored by private associations such as the Better Business Bureau or the American Bar Association. Such rules and the means to enforce them are lacking in the underworld. Italian American crime families, then, constitute a kind of informal government that has perhaps been unique within the American underworld.

The need for predictability is made clear by an incident in the Philadelphia area in the late 1970s. Two family associates involved in a surety bond fraud decided that they might need to offer a $100,000 bribe to the state insurance regulators. Although the junior partner in the fraud agreed to contribute $25,000, he was understandably worried that, if the bribe scheme failed, he might not get his money back. He therefore took his problem to an acquaintance who was a family member; and the member, in turn, went to Angelo Bruno, the family Boss. Bruno guaranteed that the money would be returned. (After the bribe attempt fell through, the money was, in fact, returned.) Bruno's guarantee created a predictable structure that facilitated the scheme.[4]

Generally, though, predictability results not from personal guarantees, but rather from the development of mutually understood rules of ethical behavior. In Philadelphia, as in other cities, it was a settled tradition that, at the initiation ceremony, new members took a solemn oath of loyalty to the group and were warned of criminal activities that were forbidden to members.[5] These were prostitution, kidnapping, counterfeiting, and dealing in illegal drugs. Presumably, the activities were proscribed because

they were seen to be dishonorable, disruptive, or likely to bring severe criminal sanctions. More important, members were expected to act in an honorable and "ethical" manner in dealings with other members and associates (see Bonanno, 1983). They were not to attempt to steal business from each other. A numbers banker, for example, was not to try to recruit someone else's numbers sellers. Members were expected to repay their debts, not to cheat or embezzle from joint businesses, and to carry out obligations to which they had agreed. More generally, they were to provide mutual favors that would aid other members in their business activities. A member who owned a restaurant and wished to install a cigarette machine, for instance, would offer the business to a member in the cigarette vending business. The families, then, have been the source of rules and expectations so that members and associates could lend and borrow money, enter into partnerships, and carry on their various business and hustling ventures (Anderson, 1979, pp. 44-49; Haller, 1991; Salerno & Tompkins, 1969, pp. 105-148).

The system goes beyond the informal establishment of rules of ethical behavior. Although families vary in the degree to which family leaders exercise oversight in monitoring the illegal activities of members, leaders in all families probably mediate disputes among members and associates, either by offering informal advice or by holding formal hearings where the dispute is presented for resolution (Abadinsky, 1983, chap. 11; Reuter, 1983, chap. 7). There are sanctions to enforce the decisions, including the periodic use of the death penalty. The legitimation of violence by the families to enforce rules, of course, sharply differentiates them from most legal fraternal organizations or businesspeople's associations.

Although the families are not themselves businesses, then, they nevertheless have exercised a variety of important and overlapping functions in the social and economic lives of members.[6] First, they have been blue-collar fraternal organizations in which members gain comradeship and male bonding through selection to join a more-or-less secret society with a long history and mysterious rituals. Furthermore, the families serve some functions of a businessmen's association. Members make useful business contacts, learn about business opportunities, and perform mutual favors for fellow members and their associates. Finally, the families can be seen as informal shadow governments. Among members and associates, a common law of behavior sometimes provides a structure of predictability and a system of dispute resolution that includes penalties for noncompliance.

ILLEGAL ENTERPRISE

If we look not at the structure and functions of the families, but instead at the money-making activities of the members, we find a markedly nonbureaucratic world, compared with the legitimate economy. Members own and operate their hustles and their businesses independent of the family. Whether they join in a partnership to back a numbers bank, put money on the street in a loan-sharking operation, or assume an interest in a bar or vending machine company, they are largely independent entrepreneurs. Indeed, to the extent that the business is illegal, they not only are small-time independent entrepreneurs but also operate outside the red tape of city, state, and federal laws and regulations. Unlike legal businesspeople, illegal entrepreneurs seldom withhold taxes or Social Security and obviously feel no obligation to maintain written files for government inspection.

The spirit that comes through in most transcripts of their conversations is their sense of being outside the bureaucratic society around them—outside the 9-to-5 routine, outside the rules and red tape. They describe themselves as being "on the street." More than most Americans, they have control over their time and enjoy negotiating deals, taking risks, and plotting legal or illegal schemes to make money. A successful entrepreneur, far from being a specialist within a hierarchy, can lead a varied day.

He may negotiate a loan to a small businessman in the morning, take calls from numbers runners in the afternoon, meet for gossip in a restaurant for dinner, and oversee a high-stakes crap game until early morning.

Many of the members' activities are not even ongoing firms, but instead are short-term, opportunistic ventures. These may consist of a partnership to smuggle a truckload of cigarettes from the Carolinas to New York or Philadelphia, a chance to shake down a local dealer in illegal drugs, or the planning of a bankruptcy fraud arising from the failure of a legal businessman to meet payments to a loan shark. Often, their economic activities, then, are short-term hustles that arise in that shadow world that links legitimate and illegal businesses (e.g., Pileggi, 1985).

Even when members of Italian crime families operate ongoing illegal enterprises, they are often small scale and informally organized. As Reuter (1983, chap. 5) has argued convincingly, illegal enterprises have lower capitalization, fewer personnel, and less formal management than comparable legal businesses. Many of those involved are only part-time, operate with loose supervision, at best, and the enterprises tend to be decentralized.

A numbers bank, for instance, sells numbers through numerous sellers in regular contact with customers. Many sellers have legitimate jobs that bring them into contact with the public: bartenders, barbers, family grocers, operators of newspaper kiosks. They peddle numbers as a sideline to their regular work, keeping a fixed percentage of the money bet with them and turning the rest over to the bank. They are part-time commission agents running a relatively independent operation, not bureaucrats whose work is directed by a hierarchy. The headquarters of a numbers bank will often be a telephone or two in a small office where the banker—or one or two part-time clerks—records the bets over the telephone. Between the banker and the seller are often pick-up men who also work on a commission and settle with the bank weekly (Anderson, 1979, chap. 3; Carlson,

1940; Haller, 1990; Reuter, 1983, chap. 2). Other illegal businesses, such as loan-sharking or sports bookmaking, likewise exhibit largely informal, nonbureaucratic structures (Anderson, 1979, chap. 4; Haller, 1991; Reuter, 1983, chap. 4; Seidl, 1968).

Members of crime families, in short, are generally independent entrepreneurs who have carved out a world of opportunistic ventures and informal illegal enterprises within the interstices of a larger and more bureaucratic society. The structure of the underworld gives free rein to personalities who take pleasure in deals, hustling, and risk taking. To see them as cogs in a bureaucracy misses a central characteristic of their economic endeavors.

CONCLUSION

The analysis here provides a perspective to reconcile the two major theories currently put forward to explain what is often referred to as "organized crime" in the United States. One theory—a bureaucratic model that derives from the work of Cressey and others—stresses hierarchy and the dominating influence of Italian American crime families. Yet, precisely because Cressey often claimed that the families were profit-making bureaucracies, he set the stage for a rival theory that emphasized the illegal or illicit enterprises that constituted the money-making activities of underworld entrepreneurs. After all, most underworld entrepreneurs have not been associated with Italian American crime families, yet have earned money from numbers gambling, sports bookmaking, loan-sharking, and other activities engaged in by those associated with crime families. A theory that appears to limit organized crime to those who are associated with crime families either denies a place for many criminals engaged in the same types of enterprises or must be broadened to include all those engaged in criminal enterprises. This set the stage, then, for theories of organized crime that emphasized the criminal enterprises (Haller, 1990; Reuter, 1983; Smith, 1975).

The apparent tension between the two theories can be avoided by recognizing that they refer to different structures. Those who emphasize criminal enterprise are describing the businesses and other money-making ventures of criminal entrepreneurs. They are concerned with understanding the economic structure of the organized underworld, whether engaged in by Italian Americans or by other criminal entrepreneurs. Those who stress the bureaucratic model generally analyze the social organizations (e.g., Italian American crime families) that provide a shadow government and various services within the underworld. Perhaps for clarity of thought, only these latter groups should be designated "organized crime."[7]

When an emphasis is placed on the economics of criminal enterprise, the differences between those associated with Italian American crime families and the wider underworld blur. Numbers banks, whether operated by African Americans, Latinos, or Italian Americans, are similar in their structure because they must respond to the same internal economic needs and external environment (just as department stores managed by businesspeople who are members of a Rotary Club are similar to department stores managed by businesspeople who are not Rotary Club members). When the underworld is examined through the lens of criminal enterprise, we find that it is held together—or divided—by economic ties, more than by coordination through ties forged by Italian American crime families. Illegal entrepreneurs negotiate partnerships and extend credit to each other, bookmakers lay off bets with each other, drug dealers buy from and sell to each other, and in numerous ways hustlers negotiate, cooperate, squabble, and compete. Bureaucracy and hierarchy become less important as explanatory tools, and various informal systems of cooperation and competition emerge as crucial factors that structure criminal enterprise (Haller, 1990).

Paradoxically, although the perspective outlined here stresses the ways, in their money making, the members of Italian American crime families have resembled the larger underworld of criminal enterprise, the perspective also identifies ways the Italian American underworld may have been unique. Italian American crime families have provided a structure of contacts, mutual favors, and quasi-governmental functions that have assisted the members in their money-making activities. Other criminal entrepreneurs have generally operated without such a separate structure. This difference, then, sets the stage for a comparison of the Italian American underworld and the larger world of criminal enterprise of which they have been a part.

First, though, it is important to be clear about the appropriate comparison in order to avoid comparing apples and oranges. It makes little sense, for instance, to compare an Italian American crime family to a Jamaican cocaine distribution group. One is largely a social group that serves its members' business interests; the other is a business group distributing illegal drugs. It is like comparing a Rotary Club and a department store. Instead, the appropriate study is to compare a Rotary Club and a Chamber of Commerce or to compare a department store to other department stores.

A central goal in the study of the organized underworld, then, should be an understanding of the economics of loan-sharking, numbers gambling, drug dealing, labor racketeering, and the numerous other illegal ventures often classified as part of the organized underworld. They are, after all, the heart of what criminal entrepreneurs do in pursuing a criminal career. Such studies will involve the economic factors that shape the enterprises, the geographic factors that underlie the locations of criminal dealing, and the law enforcement policies that provide an environment within which entrepreneurs operate.

But there is another, perhaps less important, study: a comparison of those associations that criminals have sometimes formed to assist in their illegal activities. In the early 1900s, for instance, pimps in New York City founded the Independent Benevolent Association as a sort of mutual aid society (Woolston, 1969, p. 86). In 1928, the independent black numbers and policy bankers in Detroit formed the Associated

Numbers Bankers. This association, formed to maintain black control of the banks in the Detroit region, continued through the 1930s. It regulated the pay-off odds to limit competition, retained an attorney to provide advice and legal representation, and probably coordinated corruption activities for the banks (Carlson, 1940, pp. 54-55). In recent years, it has been suggested that various motorcycle gangs, whose members deal in drugs and carry on other criminal activities, may serve many of the same functions as the Italian American crime families (e.g., President's Commission on Organized Crime, 1986, pp. 58-73). Probably most relevant, though, have been the Chinese tongs that sometimes structured illegal activities in the early days of America's Chinatowns or the tongs and triad groups that have more recently become a factor in criminal activities among new Asian immigrants to this country (Chin, 1990b). In both longevity and the diversity of the criminal activities of members, Italian American families may prove to be unique. Nevertheless, much may be learned by exploring systematically the range of organizations that criminal entrepreneurs have, from time to time, put together to assist them in their criminal ventures.

NOTES

1. Although Cressey (1969) generally treated crime families as rationally organized businesses (e.g., see the chart on pp. 146-147 in his book and its explanation), he also sometimes analyzed his evidence in a manner consistent with the view in this chapter (e.g., p. 118 of his book). He seemed at times to recognize the lack of fit between his bureaucratic model and the evidence available to him.

2. Confidential interview, July 27, 1989.

3. The distinction made here between the Italian American crime families and the independent businesses of members is the same as the distinction that Anderson (1979, p. 2) makes between the "firm" and the "organized crime group."

4. Pennsylvania Crime Commission, File No. 111-1-51/157 (May 9, 1978).

5. The many members of the Philadelphia family who became government witnesses provided markedly similar descriptions of the initiation ceremony; see the testimony

of Thomas DelGiorno in the trial *U.S. v. Nicodemo Scarfo et al.* in U.S. District Court for the Eastern District of Pennsylvania, Dec. 5 and 7, 1987.

6. For a discussion of ethics by family members, see, for instance, the conversation of Angelo Bruno and Sam DeCalvacante, February 11, 1962, published in *The FBI Transcripts* (New York: Lemma Publishing, 1970), and the conversation of Harry Riccobene and Louis Marchetti in FBI transcripts at the Tyrone DeNittis Agency, Oct. 2, 1977.

7. Reuter (1983, p. 175) seems to suggest defining organized crime so that it would refer to such structures only.

PART III

COMMENTARY

If you jumped to this part, looking for the Devil, enjoy Albini's Chapter 6—it's an entertaining piece. However well informed about the Devil you might want to be, it is important to us that you study in a stepwise fashion; otherwise, we would not have worked so hard to put these chapters into their current layout. You don't have to return immediately to the Introduction and Part 1, but you should go back there after dispensing with Part 3. We hope the devilish connection and the memoirs whet your appetite to study the whole book.

Chapter 6 gives reasons to pause and think about what (or how or why) we know the Mafia is real. FBI Director J. Edgar Hoover staunchly refused to publicly acknowledge the existence of organized crime until such time (circa 1965) that the Kefauver and McClellan committees had paraded gangsters before the public to tell, firsthand, of their criminal activities. The meeting of crime Bosses at the home of Joseph Barbara in Apalachin, New York, in 1957 and the ensuing media coverage did much to alter Hoover's stance. The congressional hearings are noteworthy for the repeated references to "facts" that were otherwise not supported by the evidence. Broad television coverage brought the likes of Joe Valachi and Frank Costello into

U.S. homes. Avid viewers were regaled with stories of burning icons in the hand, bloodletting, oath taking, and generally a heretofore unheard of organization of men who go around the countryside robbing, looting, hijacking, maiming, and largely wreaking havoc on all who oppose them. Especially prurient were the accounts of what happens to those who violate *omerta,* the code of silence. Half a horse being left on Steve Allen's doorstep (a fact) got translated in the *Godfather* movie as a horse's head being put on the traitor's silk sheets. Tales of genital mutilation, eye poking, stabbing, and other gruesome practices spread without regard to their factual basis. One killing became 100; 1 business taken over, 1,000. And, what Dwight Smith (1975) calls "the Mafia mystique" grew to proportions well beyond its real effect. As long as it didn't affect them directly, it seems Americans were ready and eager to believe whatever was said about this mysterious but somehow intriguing group of mobsters.

Observers such as Jay Albanese have remarked: "Like the existence of God, the nature of organized crime in North America has been based largely on unprovable assumptions" (1985, p. 46). Albini points out (chap. 6, this volume) that Joe Valachi said at the 1963 hearings he had never used the word *Mafia*. "That did not matter," says Albini, "because the conclusion had already been reached that *Mafia* and Valachi's new term *Cosa Nostra* were the same thing." Throughout these hearings runs a theme of reaching a conclusion without regard to what the evidence actually showed. If, for example, a gangster said he *was not* a member or denied knowledge of a national syndicate that controlled organized crime, the very denial was taken as proof positive of the syndicate's existence. It was the code of silence at work, said the senators (and others, most notably the news media). It was quite plausible, as far as the public was concerned, that fear of violent retaliation forced Mafia members to deny their membership. After all, what else can we expect? Conversely, when Frank Costello and Joe Valachi said they *were* members of organized crime, that "fact" proved the existence of the Mafia. Had they gainsaid membership, the "fact" would have been interpreted to produce exactly the same conclusion. Wouldn't it be preposterous to expect a Mafioso to confess at a congressional hearing that he really was a criminal—more so, that he was a member of organized crime? *Omerta* forbade such confessions. In any event, the hearings were designed to uncover organized crime on a large scale, and they did.

The media were in full flower with their coverage of both the Kefauver and McClellan hearings. Regrettably, the coverage fed, and at the same time fed on, the same mythology, circular reasoning, and mutual support as did the congressional investigators. Mieczkowski and Albini (1987) parsed the government and media reports published at the time and found that each cited the other for support of their findings. Of course, the accounts of what and who was organized crime matched. They had to match because they relied on each other for "the facts."

Soon after the 1967 President's Commission on Law Enforcement and Administration of Justice published its findings, Albini (1971), Ianni (1976), Moore (1974), Hawkins (1969), Smith, Jr. (1975), and other voices largely crying in the desert started to challenge the depiction of organized crime that was fast becoming cemented into the public cognizance. Never denying the existence of the Mafia or the need to combat it, these scholars did research independently, without reliance on the preconceived notions supplied in the popular press and government publications. A different picture emerged, but it never got to the same audience as the former accounts. Accordingly, we continue to see Al Pacino and Marlon Brando playing the role first mentioned by Donald Cressey. In fairness to Cressey, he never described what the poetic license of Mario Puzo created or how the role is interpreted by Pacino, Brando, and others. Nevertheless, the media product is what has caught and firmly entrenched itself in the idea that Americans have of organized crime. That idea may not be wholly accurate.

Gordon Hawkins wrote in 1969 of "God and the Mafia," and 9 years later Albini and Bajon (1978) entitled an article "Witches, Mafia, Mental Illness, and Social Reality: A Study of the Power of Mythical Belief." That last mouthful encapsulates the chapter presented here about what the Mafia and the Devil have in common. It should alert you against accepting at face value everything written about organized crime. Some sage said: Believe half of what you see and even less of what you hear or read. The topic of this text should be treated no differently. Scholars have spent an awful lot of time investigating the widely distributed picture of organized crime, finding it wanting, and providing us with alternative notions of the structure and organization of this kind of criminality. Organized crime can be found in many forms, but be clear on one point: The Mafia does exist. It just doesn't exist the way most of us think it does.

Thomas Firestone, in Chapter 7, does not argue for or against the existence of the Mafia directly. He accepts that the Mafia is alive and doing business, some $50 billion each year. Rather, he calls attention to our inability to get to know this "highly secretive organization that executes those who break its code of silence." Using a unique research technique that relies on first-person accounts (almost half of the works cited are written by or about gangsters), Firestone argues that personal self-interests are now dominant over *omerta* and that the growing number of people in the Witness Protection Program from the ranks of organized crime portend the death of the Mafia as it is currently structured. Firestone helps us understand (a) why people become mobsters, (b) how the Mafia is structured, and (c) why so many mobsters are breaking the code of silence and "turning state's evidence."

Without stealing too much from the chapter, it seems that cultural deviance theory, or differential association, offers the best explanation for initial entry into organized crime. Sutherland's differential association theory says—if one of the most often cited pieces of criminological research can be condensed into a single phrase—that we learn at the parent's knee. Our role models are, more often than not, other than our parents, but the theory still applies. The biographies of the mobsters reveal that "their neighborhoods exalted the local gangsters," who in turn "encouraged" the local children to "follow in their footsteps." Firestone goes on to extract from the memoirs evidence that the Mafia is, at the same time, a highly structured corporation and a group of individual entrepreneurs loosely connected to a "feudal lord" by the need for protection from other mobsters. It is more what Ianni (1976) and Albini (1976) first called a "primitive government" than a modern corporation. In any event, Firestone makes a cogent argument that the Mafia is alive and well but, if the memoirs can be believed, might be just on its way out.

To his last question about Mafioso-turned-protected-witnesses, Firestone replies that it is more an aging process than the effect of new prosecutorial weapons that has resulted in so many more Mafia defections of late. As Mob ranks are infused with new members, traditional cultural beliefs wane. Joe Bonanno, an old-time Boss of one of New York's crime families be-

moans: "My tradition has died in America." Bonanno was once kidnapped by rival mobsters who held a gun to his head while some other gang Bosses decided Joe's fate. Bonanno had inadvertently incurred their displeasure—probably because he couldn't keep his own workers under control. A gang war was under way, and Bonanno was seen by the others as having lost control of his family. The word on the street during the kidnapping was that Joe "Bananas" had been marked for death. He survived to retire in sunny Arizona, from which retirement he writes of his sorrow over the loss of the old ways. "Friendships, connections, family ties, trust, loyalty, obedience" lie by the wayside in favor of the more modern ways that disdain cultural prerogatives in favor of economic relationships.

Will the Mafia erode to nothingness, as Firestone suggests? Indeed, is the Mafia less than what it is said to be in Part 1? Does Albini's chapter raise any doubts about the existence of the Mafia as you know it? Can we believe what exposed criminals say in their memoirs or while in the witnesses protection program from whence they bargain for preferential treatment? You'll find the answers—and many more questions—in the pages that follow.

SUGGESTED READINGS

Block, A. A. (1983). *East side-west side: Organizing crime in New York, 1930-1950*. New Brunswick, NJ: Transaction.

Block, A. A. (1991). *Perspectives on organized crime: Essays in opposition*. Norwell, MA: Kluwer Academic.

Chandler, D. L. (1975). *Brothers in blood: The rise of the criminal brotherhoods*. New York: E. P. Dutton.

Fox, S. (1989). *Blood and power: Organized crime in 20th-century America*. New York: Morrow.

Pitkin, T. M., & Cordesco, F. (1977). *Black Hand: A chapter in ethnic crime*. Lanham, MD: Littlefield, Adams.

Sterling, C. (1990). *Octopus: The long reach of the Sicilian Mafia*. New York: Norton.

6

THE MAFIA AND THE DEVIL

What They Have in Common

JOSEPH L. ALBINI

The Mafia and the Devil are both found to be the creation and product of a belief in a mythological system. Often, the attendant mythologies are creations of journalists, government investigation committees, and law enforcement officials, not based on fact, and serve as scapegoats whose true incidence of criminality belies the attention they receive from those who create the myth and a public who would rather stigmatize others than themselves.

The Mafia and the Devil, if they are studied and understood from an empirical perspective, are both found to be the creation and product of a belief in a mythological system. Typically, we assume that mythologies are created for, and are believed only by, children. We fail to acknowledge the fact that mythologies are also created by and for adults. We fail to recognize the fact that mythologies fulfill personal and social needs within the society of which they are a part. We fail, above all, to acknowledge that people will kill or otherwise try to subdue anyone who is unwilling to agree with or accept their mythological belief. Mythology is power, and its belief brings into existence all manner of functionaries that gain and hold social positions entrusted with the responsibility of making certain that the mythology is kept alive and, above all, that the majority of the populace continues to believe in it.

THE MYTH IN HISTORY

It is indeed odd but critical to the understanding of mythology that, historically, those stories that college students currently read in courses on ancient Greek and Roman mythology are not stories at all if we recognize the fact that, to the ancient Greeks and Romans, these were real beliefs. The practice of ethnocentrism allows us today to pass judgment on the ancient Greeks and Romans by reducing their religious beliefs to that of mythology. We fail to understand that Hercules and Atlas were "real" people in the religious belief system of their time. Today, we laugh at that thought and say, "How could anyone believe in the superhuman feats that these two mythological heroes performed?"

Yet, the "higher criticism" movement of the mid-19th century in Germany caused people to ask the same questions about Moses and Jesus. These critics asked: "How can we believe that the Red Sea really parted or that the dead were raised from their graves?" The difference lies in the fact that current religious belief has the same components as yesterday's mythologies, with the difference that current religious belief is accepted by many as truth. It is difficult for those who today believe in the biblical doctrines of Judaism and Christianity to accept the possibility that, someday in the distant future, college students in other cultures or perhaps our own will be reading the biblical stories as the mythological beliefs of a bygone era. Yet, as true as that may be, during the era when mythology is viewed as true, it is a powerful force.

THE CREATION OF MYTHS

The Mafia

Let's turn now to an examination of two current mythological beliefs—the Mafia and Devil cults—in an effort to demonstrate how these mythologies were created and what functions they serve in contemporary society. If one examines carefully the conditions and forces that gave birth to the contemporary beliefs in the existence of the Mafia and Devil cults, one readily discovers that these were the creations of one or more of the following institutions, agencies, professions, or businesses: government investigating committees, law enforcement agencies, journalists, and freelance writers.

The Mafia had its birth in the United States as the invention of the now famous Kefauver committee in 1950. Armed with absolutely no understanding of the word, let alone any aspect of its existence in Sicily, Senator Kefauver succeeded in making *Mafia* a terrifying household word. Backed by Harry Anslinger and agents from the Federal Bureau of Narcotics, the Kefauver hearings produced not one shred of evidence as to the existence of this so-called secret society; but that was not the purpose of the Kefauver hearings. These hearings were meant to be exactly what they were—a great television

show. As William Howard Moore (1974) argues, this show was devised to draw attention away from the shortcomings and fiascoes of the Truman administration. The show did that; but it did much more. It implanted a symbol in the minds of the American public—the symbol that slowly evolved into a gestalt system of symbols described by Dwight Smith, Jr. (1975), as "the Mafia mystique."

Soon, journalists armed with Senator Kefauver's production of absolutely no evidence found a reader's market in which it paid to create more lack of evidence. Reid gave us his best-seller *Mafia* (1954), which included several paragraphs describing how the Mafia began in Sicily. Thousands of papers have been written by scholars still trying to understand all the forces that created the Mafia in Sicily, not as a secret society, but as part of Sicily's social system; yet, Reid managed to condense that history into a few paragraphs.

But here is the first point we must understand about mythological belief: The average person is bored by scholarly writings, so just a few paragraphs will do. When it comes to building mythological beliefs, it is the conclusion that matters; the facts on which the conclusion is based are irrelevant.

Along with Reid, *Time, Newsweek,* and other magazines were soon featuring stories on the Mafia, with covers that laid the symbols of what the Mafia consists of firmly in the American subconscious mind—hatchets, ropes, chains, knives, machine guns, and above all, a mental and physical profile of what a "Mafioso" looked like. It turns out that he looked very much like an Italian.

But it would not be too long before U.S. television audiences would be shown a real-life Mafioso, Joseph Valachi; he appeared during the McClellan hearings in 1963. There was only one problem: Valachi said he had never used the word *Mafia.* That did not matter because the conclusion had already been reached that *Mafia* and Valachi's new term *La Cosa Nostra* were the same thing. Valachi did not concede that; the president's task force did. After all, what did Valachi really know? Evidently, not very much, or at least not very much that made any sense to serious students of organized crime. But we must understand that Valachi was not presented to the American public for his knowledge. He was presented to further solidify in the minds of the American public a mental picture of the ominous, evil, secret society that had taken over America.

If the McClellan investigators had really wanted to conduct a valid investigation, they certainly would have questioned the many inconsistencies in Valachi's testimony. Valachi scarcely made one statement without contradicting himself with the next. He told of how powerful the Cosa Nostra Bosses were and then told about how no one obeyed them. His term *La Cosa Nostra* makes no sense in its Italian usage as a term signifying an organization. The words cannot grammatically be used in that manner. But that does not matter. It sounded good. Valachi described a structure of Boss, Underboss, Lieutenant, and Soldier that was so particularly simple and elusive that it could apply to any organization. Yet, the McClellan committee was excited about discovering the secret about absolutely nothing. But that is the other powerful ingredient of mythological belief: creating excitement over nothing.

Next, and suddenly, Donald Cressey said that there was something to this nothing. He wrote *Theft of the Nation* (1969), a book that pretended to elevate this simple structure of nothing to a theoretical system worthy of being taken very seriously and, above all, worthy of serious sociological study. Soon, Italian terms such as *Don* and *Godfather* that were part of legitimate Italian culture were reduced to words that applied only to the Mafia.

If Cressey had read the works written by anthropologists long before the McClellan hearings, he would have known that the Mafia in Sicily is not and never was a secret society, but rather was and is part of Sicily's historical and social system. As such, it could not be transported to the United States as the McClellan committee and Cressey sought to argue. We wonder why Cressey and the McClellan investigators saw the Mafia as the greatest threat to

the United States when, as Block and Chambliss (1981) point out, the government's own records at the time of the hearings showed that only 16% of those organized criminals convicted between 1953 and 1959 had Italian surnames.

But when one is building mythology, one must follow a simple rule: When the facts do not fit, simply force them to fit or completely disregard them. And that is exactly what freelance writers, journalists, and the McClellan investigators did. In a futile effort to try to argue that Cosa Nostra was a new version of the Mafia, they came up with "purges" in which the "Old Mafia" members all across the United States were killed. No bodies were found. Serious researchers have looked frantically through newspaper obituaries, but not one shred of evidence has turned up. We should have known it was only a story when even the originators of the purge story could not give us any names; in fact, they could not even agree on the number that had been killed. What is worse, as Jay Albanese (1983) notes, the government and the newspapers and magazines still cannot agree on how many Mafiosi exist today. But they do agree that we should be terrified over the fact that Cosa Nostra is so powerful that it has even corrupted our government. Ironically, while America was watching movies about this menace, our government, through the CIA, was evidently allowing various operators such as Manuel Noriega in Panama and Khun Sa in the Golden Triangle to deal drugs in return for intelligence information. Neither of these traffickers had Italian surnames. And so, the Mafia has come to serve as a mythological belief that excites the imagination, entertains the public, and draws attention away from real social issues.

Interestingly, the government commission reports and the media reinforce each other in creating and sustaining this belief. Thus (as Mieczkowski and I [1987] have found), when presenting the sources of evidence to support each other's findings, the government reports cite the news magazines as their source and the news magazines cite the government reports. Is there any wonder that they are in total agreement? Is there also any wonder why the large body of serious scholarly researchers who have collected their own data have not been able to find evidence to support a belief in the Mafia? Government investigators argue that these researchers would find the Mafia if they used the government's data, and of course we would, but then we would not be researchers.

And so, while America was being titillated with Cosa Nostra stories, its streets and neighborhoods have become havens for crack houses; daily, citizens, many of them children, are being killed by syndicates battling one another openly in the street. Virtually every ethnic group has become involved. The Colombians, government sources tell us, are responsible for 80% of all cocaine imported into the United States. But who do we still fear the most—the Mafia. Why? Because the image of the portrait implanted by mythological belief is far more powerful than reality. That is, unfortunately, the power of mythological belief: It takes on the form of reality.

The Devil Cults

And so, joining in the Mafia in this world of mythological distortion of reality, we now have the current hysteria of Devil cults. Belief in the Devil is a mythological one that developed out of Judaism and Christianity. One can safely argue, however, that Christianity gave the Devil the high-ranking status he holds today. Historically, and currently, the Devil has been used to take away the shame and responsibility from humans who have committed hideous or brutal acts. Note that, when such acts are committed, we refer to them as "inhuman." We thus try to make it appear that humans are not capable of committing such acts. Thus, in the past, when horrible, hideous crimes were committed, werewolves or vampires—that is, humans possessed by the Devil—were blamed. Humankind evidently cannot face itself for what it is, humans capable of committing horrible deeds. And so we take comfort in believing that the Devil makes people evil.

Unfortunately, horrible crimes are also committed by people who say that God told them to do it. In such cases, we are quick to argue that such people are deranged. Why, then, do we not argue the same when the people say the Devil made them do it? The answer is simple: The Devil is bad and God is good; so, God cannot make us do bad deeds. We must remember that both the belief in God and the belief in the Devil are mythical beliefs. Neither can be absolutely proved except from within the belief system of the individual person. Yet, for many individuals and groups, both God and the Devil are very real entities.

Historically, we know that witches (those people who, as the belief goes, sold their souls to the Devil to receive power) were discovered and put to death. The Salem Witch Trials and the Inquisition are the best examples. But we should not be surprised that government tribunals entrusted to find witches always do. Why? Because they are the ones that decide what characteristics witches possess. Once accused, if a witch denies being a witch when interrogated, that in itself is absolute proof that he or she is a witch. We now see the power of those investigating bodies entrusted with the ability to label. In this respect, we recall Senator Kefauver's reactions to those Italians called before his committee and asked the question, "Are you a member of the Mafia?" If they replied no, Kefauver and the committee said this was definite proof that they were of the Mafia. And so, neither those branded as witches nor those labeled as Mafiosi had a chance. To be accused, in itself, is to be convicted.

As we look at the current hysteria concerning Devil cults, we find that, like the Mafia, it is the creation of journalists who want to excite the public but do so with unfounded facts and the creation of certain types of law enforcement agents, now called "cult cops," who, like the witch hunters of old, often see themselves as winning a battle for Jesus. Not so ironically, we find that these officers, like the Mafia investigators, get their facts from the newspapers, and in turn we find that the newspapers obtain their facts from these officers. So, too, as Robert Hicks (1990a) notes, these officers typically come from fundamentalist religious backgrounds, where the Devil is viewed as real and terrifying. Some of these officers are born-again Christians with a born-again zeal to strike a blow for the Lord. It should be emphasized that these officers themselves believe in and are frightened by the power of the Devil; hence, they are projecting their own fears into their work. They are largely responsible for creating the rumors about the existence of Devil cults (Hicks, 1990b). In all fairness to law enforcement, we should note that many officers out there are trying to halt the hysteria by evaluating the real facts and trying to bring some reasonable explanation to the so-called Devil cult crimes.

We must appreciate the fact that the Devil is very real, not only to cult-orientated police officers but to many Americans as well. The Devil and his staff have even been sued in court for having caused the plaintiff his downfall by placing deliberate obstacles in his path (*United States ex rel. Gerald Mayo v. Satan and His Staff,* 1971). The court did not take issue with the question of the existence of the Devil; instead, it argued that the plaintiff had not supplied the court with a mailing address for the Devil and therefore the court could not serve the Devil the proper papers.

The real issue concerning Devil cults is that of determining whether or not their members really commit the so-called hideous crimes they are suspected of committing and of trying to determine exactly how the Devil is involved in the commission of these crimes. Among the crimes the cult cops are reporting are serious mutilations of animals in satanic rites; the brutal killing of newborn babies to obtain sacred blood to enhance personal power; the desecration of cemeteries to obtain bones and other body parts; the sexual abuse of children to pay homage to the Devil; the forcing of women to dance nude and have sex with members of the group; and a host of other bizarre behaviors.

Are these crimes, in fact, happening? According to the cult cops and the believing public, they are. According to law enforcement statistics as reflected in indictments, they are not.

Here, again, as in the case of creating the Mafia, we see the journalists at work. The best-selling book *Cults That Kill,* by Larry Kahaner (1988), is a perfect example. The book consists of report after report by cult cops, professed Satanists, and various authorities on cults. The blurb on the cover reads: "This book is a shocker." In my opinion, the only thing shocking is that, after all the presentation of gory details, there is no indication that any of these crimes ever occurred or resulted in an indictment. All that such books contain is so-called facts presented in such a way as to give the reader the creeps. Just as journalists in the 1960s were trying to convince Americans that the Mafia had control of America, journalists today are trying to tell us that we should not venture outdoors because the Devil's disciples are waiting to grab us and turn us into something to eat for their evening meal. This is a total absurdity—but it sells books.

It also raises the status of the police detectives who go looking for these Satanists. As Hartsfield (1985) observes, in America, historically and socially, the role and status of the detective have been mutually tied to those of the professional criminal. As a detective, one gets more points for chasing clever criminals, as compared with ordinary ones. Thus, in the 1960s, those detectives who were "Mafia hunters" won status for dealing with the supposedly clever criminal mind of a Mafioso. Today's "cult cops" get points for doing battle with the "evil mind" of the Satanist. Yet, neither the Mafia hunters nor the cult cops realize they are fighting a creature of their own mental creation and their overworked imagination. As was true of the Mafia, those journalists writing about satanic cults manufacture interest and fear, not by the facts they present, but rather by how they present an absence of facts.

Some years ago, the "mystery" of the Bermuda Triangle held the nation spellbound with journalists reporting the many ships that disappeared in the triangle. The disappearances sounded awesome. But did these journalists go searching for evidence as to what really happened to these ships? Of course not. If the ships were found, that would not sell books, and what would happen to the mystery? Kusche (1983), by simply using original sources, was able to solve the so-called mystery. The ships had been shipwrecked or simply abandoned in other parts of the world, some as far away as Ireland and Africa, long after they had safely gone through the Bermuda Triangle. So much for that absurdity.

The case of the satanic cults is the same. The craze began in the late 1980s. No doubt, like the Beatles and rock music, it came from England. As Valiente (1989) notes, in the 1940s and 1950s, England had an outbreak and rebirth of witchcraft hysteria. As is true today in America, the newspapers in England were stunning the public with horror stories of satanic disciples who were killing newborn babies as sacrifices, molesting children, and dancing in the nude. Three individuals—Aleister Crowley, Gerald Gardner, and Alex Sanders—loomed as basic figures in the witchcraft movement. Crowley called himself "The Beast" and indeed evidently himself engaged in various forms of sadomasochism. This, however, would not be the first time an Englishman openly engaged in sadomasochism. The practice is so common in England that it has come to be called "the English vice." We can hardly argue that Crowley got his ideas concerning sadomasochism from the Devil. Here is the point: Crowley was a self-made Devil. He never advocated killing babies or adults as sacrifices to Satan. The only proof that he was The Beast came from him; and this is true of all those who claim they are Satanists. All they have to do is say they are, and in their minds and the minds of those who believe them, they are of Satan. But whose reality are we dealing with here? Just because people proclaim that they are Napoleon, are they? This is the ridiculous aspect that lies with the fear that cult cops and society have of the Satanist.

In any respect, England went through its phase of satanic care with not one indictment. The difference between the craze in the United States and that in England was that the police in England saw the newspaper stories for what they were, just stories. No cult cops emerged in England.

In the United States, the satanic scare has created a bizarre reaction on the part of police, with cult cops daily warning the public about the menace and presenting seminars to police officers across the country to teach police the techniques of detection and investigation of cases involving satanism. In 1988, 50 such seminars were presented in Virginia alone.

Along with the influence of Aleister Crowley, the American cult cops have added that of an American Satanist, Anton LaVey, the creator of the Church of Satan and author of *The Satanic Bible*. Certainly, Anton LaVey does not recommend killing babies; in fact, it has always been known that he would not allow recruits admission into his church if they even expected to dance in the nude or to have sex. His church, it appears, is just a harmless outlet for people looking to increase their self-esteem. It is true that members are taught how to put hexes on people. They do. Then they wait. Eventually, something bad happens to everyone. When it happens to the person on whom the hex was placed, however, the member who placed the hex on the victim says with joy, "I got him," and everyone in the cult rejoices. If one believes in hexes, then, this power is something to reckon with. The rational mind, however, knows that successful hexes are nothing more than chance occurrences.

Nonetheless, cult cops get all excited if they stop a teenager for a traffic violation and find a copy of LaVey's book in the vehicle. Here, they conclude, is definitely a Satanist. One cult cop was shocked when he learned that LaVey's book is openly available at most bookstores. He was keeping his copy hidden because he thought he had a rare, devilish work. These officers would do well to remember that, every year, numerous people kill, assault, brutally beat, or molest children and commit a host of other violent horrible crimes because, they maintain, God told them to commit the act or they got their ideas from reading the Bible. On the basis of these occurrences, should officers not be suspicious of teenagers who have a copy of the New or Old Testament sitting by their side when stopped for a traffic violation? We make this point merely to stress the illogicalness of behavior that can be brought about by obsessive thinking.

It is difficult to decide who is more naive—those who profess to be Satanists or the cult cops who go chasing them. Neither can claim any real knowledge about satanism because there really is no one book or source that has the satanic secrets. As Valiente (1989), herself a practicing witch, notes: Folklore based on oral tradition is the only pathway by which witchcraft lore has been passed down to modern witches. No authentic book describes what a Satanist should or should not do. However, certain signs such as the "horned hand," the "swastika," the "moon-crescent and a star," the "pentagram," black candles, and other symbols have come to be used by those who play at satanism.

Aside from the use of these symbols, where is the evidence for all the fuss? In an attempt to bring sense to nonsense, Robert Hicks, himself a law enforcement specialist, is one of the severest critics of cult cops. He argues that these officers have no facts; instead, they get their facts from newspapers, and their knowledge of satanic and cult involvement with crime is "rife with error and ignorance" (1990a, p. 276). Like those trying to create the Mafia, cult cops are prone toward simply distorting facts and denying those facts that do not fit their theory.

One horrifying series of stories that shocked the nation was one telling of the many cattle mutilations that were the result of Devil cult rites. Again, law enforcement itself, through the investigation of FBI agent Kenneth Rommel, Jr. (Hicks, 1990a, p. 281), showed that these so-called mutilations turned out to be nothing more than the result of the natural actions of animal scavengers and predators. So, too, Kenneth Lanning, another FBI agent who has investigated satanic crime, concluded that "there are no cases in the United States in which devil-worship itself was the sole motivation for any murder" (p. 281). Or as Carlson and Larue (1990, p. 27) clarify Lanning's meaning further: "There are no instances of a stranger being

kidnapped and ritually sacrificed solely for the purpose of glorifying the devil." So much for the Devil and his sordid influence.

As with the Mafia, symbols are used by journalists and cult cops to strike the mind's emotional, rather than rational, center. In murder trials, satanism takes the platform where prosecutors try to argue that Satan caused the person to commit the act. Thus, the best-selling book *Across the Border* (Provost, 1989) tells the story of the now famous Matamoros drug killings in northern Mexico. The subtitle of this book is *The True Story of the Satanic Cult Killings*. As Hicks (1990b) notes, however, the so-called satanism here turned out to be nothing more than a drug dealer who, like Charles Manson before him, used whatever symbolism and ritual he could to scare the Devil into or out of his rivals and his own followers.

As Victor (1991) observes, the current satanic scare is a process of the creation of rumor-panics that often happen in places or locations where there is a great deal of social and economic stress. Like most forms of hysteria, people often feel safer if they can focus on some cause of their woes. In this case, it is the satanic cults. Similarly, rather than blame themselves for their desire to use drugs in the 1960s, Americans found it easier and more exciting to blame those foreigners from Sicily who brought the Mafia to America and addicted a drug-virgin country.

In the case of Satanists, the current belief is that they are committing all the brutal crimes in this country. As Stevens (1990) so astutely observes, police and other reporters are saying that as many as 60,000 children are killed by satanic cults each year. FBI statistics, however, indicate that a total of 23,000 murders occur in the entire United States each year. So how did the police come up with the remaining thousands of killings? They simply used their own fear and imagination.

This speaks to the basic issue of the function of the satanic scare. It draws attention away from reality. Americans cannot face the fact that they really do not need the Devil to create evil. They do quite well on their own.

As for the popular craze of teenagers being interested in the Devil and manifesting this by listening to heavy metal music, remember that when jazz first appeared on the American scene more than 100 years ago, the racist belief emerged that because jazz had its roots in African ritualistic music, it was "the Devil's music." Lyons (1988) observes in his very sensible book on satanism that many teenagers profess to believe in the Devil and listen to his supposed messages in rock music because belief in the Devil is the one psychological weapon left in the modern teenage subculture through which adolescents can shock their parents and other adults. Somehow, teenagers believe that if they profess this belief, it will give them status. They do get status, but only from those who have themselves bought into their belief system.

For all the hype about Satanists, crime statistics in the United States show that when it comes to homicide, the average American is probably safer with a Satanist than with members of his or her own family or friends. And, according to FBI statistics on date rape, women are probably safer going home with a Satanist they just met at the bar than they are with their friends or acquaintances with whom they have a date.

CONCLUSION

And so the Mafia and satanic cults turn out to be mythologies. But they are harmful ones. I personally know of too many stories of honest, law-abiding Italians who, in the 1960s, could not obtain jobs or lost their jobs because their employers thought they belonged to the Mafia.

I know of a mother who watched in horror as her house burned down, knowing that her newborn baby was inside it and could not be rescued. That was traumatic in itself. More traumatic, however, was her arrest when police found, among the ruins, a book on magic. They suspected she had killed her child as part of a satanic ritual. Fortunately, her lawyer was able to talk sense into the police and she was released.

So, in conclusion, the Mafia and the Devil cults are the creations of journalists with overactive imaginations, government investigation committees that are basically self-serving, and law enforcement officers with a religious fervor and a fear of their own making. They originate from facts that either do not exist or are based on profound exaggeration and serve as scapegoats for an American public that cannot face itself for what it is. These are what the Mafia and the Devil cults have in common.

7 MAFIA MEMOIRS

What They Tell Us About Organized Crime

THOMAS A. FIRESTONE

Researching the Mafia has become easier with the number of ex-mobsters who have published *memoirs* detailing their careers in organized crime. This body of literature helps explain (a) why people become mobsters, (b) how the Mafia is structured, and (c) why so many Mafiosi are breaking the Mob's code of silence. Traditional criminological theories mirror and are supported by descriptions in the various memoirs of answers to these three questions. On the basis of this literature review, the paradox of the prisoner's dilemma, in which each conspirator manages to destroy the entire conspiracy to protect his own interests, suggests that the erosion of trust and loyalty among Mafiosi portends a similar fate for the organization to which they belong(ed).

According to Wharton Econometrics Forecasting Associates (1986), the Mafia earns approximately $50 billion each year at an annual cost to the U.S. economy of $18.2 billion in economic output, 414,000 jobs, and $77.20 in per-capita disposable income. Despite its impact on the U.S. economy, the Mafia has only rarely been the subject of serious academic analysis. As Peter Reuter writes, "The scholarly literature on organized crime and illegal markets in the United States is quite modest. . . . No major studies have substantially increased our understanding of either phenomenon. The empirical studies are very few" (1983, p. 5). Reuter attributes the absence of Mafia scholarship to "scholarly disdain for popular passions" (p. 5). It is

much more likely, however, a result of the lack of primary source material. The Mafia is, after all, a highly secretive organization that executes those who break its code of silence.

Fortunately, researching the Mafia has become easier as some ex-mobsters, most of whom became government witnesses, have published memoirs detailing their careers in organized crime.[1] Although some of these memoirs have reached best-seller lists, they have never been the subject of academic analysis, which is surprising, given the general lack of information on the Mafia. Therefore, in an attempt to make use of this new resource and to enhance the understanding of organized crime, in this chapter I critically review and analyze the evidence contained in the memoirs. Specifically, I use the memoirs to explain (a) why people become mobsters, (b) how the Mafia is structured, and (c) why so many mobsters are breaking the Mob's code of silence by testifying against their former crime "families." The choice of these questions follows the structure of the memoirs, which generally begin with a description of the author's youth and early involvement with the Mafia, then proceed to an extended discussion of the author's day-to-day life in the Mob, and culminate with an explanation of the author's decision to "turn" and cooperate with the government. Before addressing each issue, I review the relevant secondary literature to place the evidence from the memoirs in context.

WHY PEOPLE BECOME MOBSTERS

To understand the origins and persistence of the Mafia, it is necessary to understand why people become Mafiosi. Three sociological theories address this question. The first of these is *strain theory,* which argues that crime is a substitute path to success for those who have been denied the opportunity to succeed by legitimate means. As Robert Merton (1968), the father of strain theory, wrote:

> Crime and vice constitute a "normal" response to a situation where the cultural emphasis upon pecuniary success has been absorbed, but where there is little access to conventional and legitimate means for becoming successful. . . . [O]f those located in the lower reaches of the social structure, the culture makes incompatible demands. On the one hand, they are asked to orient their conduct toward the prospect of large wealth . . . and on the other, they are largely denied effective opportunities to do so institutionally. . . . In this setting, a cardinal American virtue, "ambition," becomes a cardinal American vice, "deviant behavior." (p. 198)

Thus, strain theory would hypothesize that people become mobsters to acquire the wealth, power, and status that society prevents them from obtaining through legitimate means (Bell, 1960, pp. 127, 143; arguing that organized

crime serves as "a route of social ascent and place in American life" and that gangsters of the Prohibition era were merely "seeking to become quasi-respectable and establish a place for themselves in American life").

A second sociological theory of crime, generally known as *differential association* or *cultural deviance theory,* explains crime in terms of socialization and environment. Specifically, it argues that people become criminals because they "learn" criminal behavior from role models, usually friends or family members. The influence of these role models, the theory posits, rubs off on the subject and, if not offset by countervailing examples of law-abiding behavior, results in the subject's becoming a criminal. As E. H. Sutherland, the developer of differential association theory, wrote: "A person becomes delinquent because of an excess of definitions favorable to violation of law over definitions unfavorable to violation. . . . When persons become criminal, they do so because of contacts with criminal patterns and also because of isolation from anticriminal patterns" (Sutherland & Cressey, 1974, p. 88).

Proponents of differential association theory argue that the criminal socialization process can take place across entire communities, which then develop "criminal subcultures." People who are born into these communities are likely to grow up with friends and role models who are criminals and are thus likely to become criminals themselves. Thus, according to this theory, delinquency can often be explained by the fact that the delinquent grew up in a neighborhood dominated by a culture of crime. [For this reason, differential association theory is often referred to as *cultural deviance theory.* An example: "Differential association is a principle of normative conflict which proposes that high crime rates occur in societies and groups characterized by conditions that lead to the development of extensive criminal subcultures" (Sutherland & Cressey, 1974, p. 89); also, Shaw and McKay (1942, p. 73), explaining youth gangs in terms of "the presence of a large number of adult criminals in certain areas (which) means that children there are in contact with crime as a career and with the criminal way of life."] Thus, differential association theory would argue that people become mobsters because they grew up in communities dominated by the Mafia, with mobsters as their role models.

In contrast with differential association theory, which sees crime as the result of an individual's absorption of community norms, a third school of thought, usually labeled *control theory,* argues that crime is caused by alienation from the surrounding social institutions. According to control theory, the more an individual is involved with society, the more likely he or she is to develop law-abiding behavior. Conversely, the more an individual is separated from society, the more likely he or she is to become a criminal. Thus, according to Hirschi (1971), a leading exponent of control theory, "Delinquent acts result when an individual's bond to society is weak or broken" (p. 16). Specifically, Hirschi identifies four elements of the bond between the individual and society—(a) *attachment* (defined as involvement with others, (b) *commitment* (defined as investment of personal resources in a legitimate goal), (c) *involvement* (defined as involvement in conventional activities), and (d) *belief* (defined as acceptance of national social values)—and argues that the likelihood of delinquency in any particular case is inversely proportional to the strength of these four elements. As applied to the Mafia, control theory would argue that people become mobsters because, as children, they were cut off from the most important socializing institutions (e.g., family, church, school, community) and, as a result, failed to develop the discipline and habits characteristic of law-abiding behavior (Lombardo, 1991, p. 12; relying on control theory to make the case that organized crime is the product of weak communities).

In short, strain theory sees crime as the result of the tension between socially induced aspirations and an individual's inability to realize those aspirations through legitimate means. Control theory sees crime as the product of a deficit of law-abiding attitudes resulting from insufficient connection to community institutions. And cultural theory sees crime as the result of socialization into the values of a criminal community or subculture.

Evidence From the Memoirs

Evidence from the memoirs suggests that cultural deviance theory offers the best explanation of the social roots of organized crime. Specifically, it reveals that most of the authors became mobsters because they grew up in neighborhoods dominated by the Mafia, with gangsters as their role models.

Repeatedly, the authors describe how their neighborhoods exalted the local gangsters and encouraged neighborhood children to follow in their footsteps. For instance, Henry Hill, a former associate of the Lucchese family in New York and his coauthor, Nicholas Pileggi, describe Hill's neighborhood of Brownsville-East New York as "the kind of neighborhood that cheered successful mobsters the way West Point cheered victorious generals" (Pileggi, 1985, p. 33). As Pileggi writes,

> In Brownsville-East New York wiseguys were more than accepted—they were protected. Even the legitimate members of the community . . . seemed to keep an eye out to protect their local hoods. (p. 38)

Like most children in the neighborhood, Hill grew up idolizing the local gangsters and aspired to be a "wiseguy." As he explains,

> I used to watch them from my window and I dreamed of being like them. At the age of twelve my ambition was to be a gangster. To be a wiseguy. To me being a wiseguy was better than being President of the United States. . . . To be a wiseguy was to own the world. (Pileggi, 1985, p. 13)

In the same vein, Tony Frankos, formerly a freelance enforcer for several New York families, points to the fact that he grew up in Hell's Kitchen, a neighborhood dominated by the Irish Mob, as the cause of his delinquency. As Frankos explains:

Many in Hell's Kitchen viewed [the local] Irish gangsters as Robin Hoods . . . [they] drove Buicks, Lincolns, and Cadillacs . . . seemed quite glamorous, and were apparently able to acquire anything they wanted. On a subconscious level . . . I wanted to be like them. (Hoffman & Headley, 1992, p. 21)

Nick Caramandi, a former Captain in Philadelphia's Scarfo family, also points to neighborhood culture as a crucial factor in his criminal development. Caramandi explains that he grew up in South Philadelphia, a neighborhood in which the Mafia is one of the "dominant institutions" and that, according to Caramandi and coauthor Anastasia, "has stocked the mob for three generations, supplying a core group of thieves, loan sharks, extortionists and murderers" (Anastasia, 1991, p. 31). Thus, Caramandi explains that when he was growing up in South Philadelphia, he and his friends worshipped "the guys from the neighborhood with connections and juice—the bookmakers, gamblers, and loan sharks" who worked for the local Mafia family (Anastasia, 1991, p. 139). Caramandi remembers feeling "intoxicated" by their power and "want[ing] to be one of them." Whenever he had money in his pocket, Caramandi recalls, he dressed up "like a South Philadelphia wiseguy in a tailored suit and silk tie . . . playing the role of a mobster long before he became one" (Anastasia, 1991, p. 34).

Vinnie Teresa, formerly an associate in New England's Patriarca family, also points to neighborhood as a prime cause of his delinquency. Teresa explains that he grew up in Revere, a town he describes as "owned" by the Mob, and remembers being impressed by the "polished limousines" and "flashily dressed hoodlums" he saw at gatherings of the local crime Bosses (Renner & Teresa, 1973, p. 36). As a child, Teresa recalls, he considered these congregations of gangsters "more significant than the summit conferences of world leaders" (Renner & Teresa, 1973, p. 36). Similarly, Jimmy Fratianno, who eventually rose to become Boss of the Los Angeles Mafia family, describes his

background as "classical American Mafioso" (DeMaris, 1981, p. 3). As Fratianno explains, he grew up in Cleveland's Little Italy, always aware of the fact that "the Italians on the hill had something special going for them" and wanting to be part of that "something special" (DeMaris, 1981, p. 20). Fratianno especially remembers being impressed by the power of gangsters when, at the age of 6, he saw three men gunned down in front of a local speakeasy (DeMaris, 1981, p. 3).

Although he has not written one of the memoirs under examination, it is worth noting that Sammy "the Bull" Gravano, former Underboss of the Gambino family and lead witness against John Gotti, also pointed to neighborhood culture as the key factor that drove him to the Mob. When asked on cross-examination at Gotti's trial why he became a gangster, Gravano explained: "When you grow in a neighborhood like I grew in [Gravano grew up in Bensonhurst, a heavily Italian neighborhood in Brooklyn] and you grew with the people I grew with, it was an environment. . . . It was an environment. It was not something—I just grew with it. It didn't seem wrong. The whole life style didn't seem wrong" (Blumenthal & Miller, 1992, p. 293).

The memoirs also illustrate, as differential association theory would predict, that these values are usually concretized for the aspiring mobsters in the form of particular role models. For instance, Joe Cantalupo, formerly an associate of the Colombo family in New York, explains that he became involved with the Colombos because he was impressed by the family's Boss, Joe Colombo. Cantalupo recalls that Colombo seemed to "have it all," including "the expensive things in life that I wanted" (Cantalupo & Renner, 1990, p. 51). He appeared to be "a man of respect, a man of immense power who . . . could have anyone he chose eliminated" (Cantalupo & Renner, 1990, p. 50). Thus, Cantalupo writes, "I admired Colombo . . . [he] alter[ed] my life irrevocably" and "became a teacher for me, a sort of professor of the college of street smarts" (Cantalupo & Renner, 1990, pp. 11, 51). Similarly, Vinnie Teresa remembers being particularly influenced by the example of his mobster uncle, Sandy, who "bought suits like they were candy" and would think nothing of handing the young Teresa three expensive suits out of his closet for no reason at all (Renner & Teresa, 1973, p. 36). Teresa recalls, "To me, this looked like this was the answer. I'd think: 'I don't know what this guy's doing. but whatever it is, I want to do it' " (Renner & Teresa, 1973, p. 36).

Along the same lines, the memoirs also indicate, again following differential association theory, that many mobsters are drawn into the Mafia by their families. For instance, Michael Franzese, former Captain in the Colombo family and son of Sonny Franzese, a notorious Mob enforcer of the 1950s and 1960s, explains that he became a mobster because he "admired" his father and viewed him as "a role model I thought I could emulate" (Franzese & Matera, 1992, p. 34). "I was my father's son," Franzese writes, "and . . . if he wanted me to become a member of La Cosa Nostra, I wasn't going to question it" (Franzese & Matera, 1992, p. 88).

Similarly, Bill Bonanno, formerly *Consigliere* of the Bonanno family and son of the family's Boss, Joe Bonanno, also attributes his decision to the influence of his father.[2] As Gay Talese, who authored Bonanno's story, writes: "The main reason [Bonanno joined the Mob] was that he loved his father, was part of him, and could not, would not, disassociate himself from him" (1971, p. 67). According to Talese, Bonanno claimed that he felt "too close, too involved . . . [and too] . . . influenced by certain values of the old country" to break away from the lifestyle he was born into (1971, p. 52).

At the same time that they lend support to differential association theory, the memoirs contain evidence disconfirming the strain and control theories of organized crime. With the exception of "Joey," the pseudonymous author of *Killer*, who claims that he started in crime at the age of 11 because his poverty left him with no choice (Fisher, 1973, p. 26), none of the mobsters claim to have chosen crime because

they were denied the opportunity to pursue a legitimate career. In fact, quite to the contrary, most of the authors indicate they could have had legitimate careers but simply preferred to be criminals. For instance, Hill, whose view on this point seems typical, explains that he and his colleagues considered legitimate careers depressing and viewed those who pursued them as "suckers." According to Pileggi, in the view of Hill and his friends,

> Anyone who stood waiting his turn on the American pay line was beneath contempt. Those who did—who followed the rules were stuck in low-paying jobs, worried about their bills, put tiny amounts away for rainy days, kept their place, and crossed off workdays on their kitchen calendars like prisoners awaiting their release—could only be considered fools. . . . To wiseguys, "working guys" were already dead. (1985, p. 37)

Hill goes on to explain that he was repulsed by the conventional "working stiff" life his father led and swore, "My old man's life wasn't going to be my life" (Pileggi, 1985, p. 16).

Similarly, Franzese explains that he could have become a doctor but gave up his premedical studies because the Mob promised faster and easier money. As he explains: "I faced a decade of intense study before I could become a doctor. There was a quicker route to success. . . . the money that could be made [with the Mob] . . . excited me" (Franzese & Matera, 1992, p. 60). Bill Bonanno also had other opportunities. As Talese points out, Bonanno grew up with wealth, acquired a "superior education in boarding school," studied agricultural engineering at the University of Arizona, and operated several legitimate businesses, including wholesale food markets and real estate trading firms, before turning to crime (Talese, 1971, pp. 37, 41, 50).

By the same token, there is little evidence of the social alienation that control theory identifies as the cause of crime. In fact, most of the authors had decent upbringings and, as youths, were involved with their families and surrounding social institutions in a healthy way. For instance, Franzese's description of his child-hood seems a model of wholesomeness:

> My father schooled me in athletics [and] taught me how to hit and catch a baseball. . . . When Dad wasn't grooming me to be a shortstop, the Catholic schools were molding me into a responsible citizen. I started at St. Ann's Grammar School in New Hyde Park, then graduated to Holy Cross High School in Flushing. I spent two years as an altar boy at St. Ann's Catholic Church in Garden City, frequently rising at five a.m. so I could get dressed and ride my bike to church for six o'clock Mass. (Franzese & Matera, 1992, p. 32)

Similarly, Bonanno went to boarding school, where he "learned to ride horses and brand cattle, dated blond girls whose fathers owned ranches; and later, as a student at the University of Arizona, led a platoon of ROTC cadets across the football field before each game to help raise the American flag before the national anthem was played" (Talese, 1971, p. 9). In college, Bonanno "attended classes punctually, joined student groups, supported the football team and . . . was popular with his classmates" (Talese, 1971, p. 37). In the same vein, Joe Cantalupo explains that he had a good relationship with his family, held summer jobs, graduated from West Islip High School, and joined the army, where he distinguished himself as a paratrooper (Cantalupo & Renner, 1990, p. 12).

Conclusion

It is widely accepted that crime is rooted in poverty, despair, and a breakdown of social institutions. The memoirs, however, suggest that the causes of Italian American organized crime are more cultural than socioeconomic. As the mobsters themselves explain, most of them became criminals, not because they lacked other opportunities or had deprived upbringings, but because they were raised in communities in which becoming a gangster was seen as a legitimate and even desirable career path.

This finding raises the question of why such communities, with such seemingly inverted value structures, exist. Unfortunately, an-swering that question requires an inquiry into Italian history and culture, which is simply beyond the scope of this chapter, whose contribution must therefore be limited to simply posing the question.

STRUCTURE AND OPERATIONS OF ORGANIZED CRIME

If law enforcement is to combat the Mafia, it must understand the Mafia's structure and be able to locate the power center within each family. Absent such knowledge, resources will be spent on prosecutions that, even if successful, will have little effect on the Mob's operations. Analysts have developed two models that purport to describe the Mafia's structure. One, which I call the *corporate model,* depicts the Mafia as a highly structured organization in which power is concentrated at the top of a formal hierarchy and the criminal activities of members are planned and coordinated by the Bosses. The other, which I call the *feudal model,* portrays the Mafia as a relatively unstructured collection of criminals held together only by informal patron-client ties. To determine which of these two models is more accurate, and thereby contribute to the development of more effective law enforcement strategies, in this section of the chapter I examine the assumptions on which each of these theories is based and then test these assumptions against the evidence in the memoirs.

Corporate Model

The model of the Mafia as a highly structured organization comparable with a modern corporation has long been popular among academic criminologists, journalists, and the law enforcement establishment. For instance, the President's Commission on Law Enforcement and Administration of Justice (1967; long the standard work on the American Mafia) concluded that the "structures" of organized crime are "as complex as those of any large corporation" and are "subject to laws more rigidly enforced than those of legitimate governments" (President's Commission, 1967, in Conklin, 1973, p. 27). Similarly, Ralph Salerno, a former police officer who wrote a scholarly study of organized crime in 1969, portrayed the Mafia as a "highly organized" criminal "confederation" whose structure "parallels" that of a major corporation (Salerno & Tompkins, 1969, p. 85). At the same time, Donald Cressey wrote a similar book that also depicted the Mafia as a highly integrated organization structured in the same way as many "large legitimate corporations" (Cressey, 1969, p. 110).

Moreover, the corporate model has retained its popularity over time. For instance, a 1986 presidential task force described Cosa Nostra as a "highly structured" criminal group that, "like any other bureaucracy carries out its purpose over a period of time" (President's Commission on Organized Crime, 1986, pp. 26-27). Similarly, *Fortune* magazine, in a cover story on the Mafia, also espoused this view, reporting that "the organization chart of a crime family or syndicate mirrors the management structure of a corporation" (Rowan, 1986, p. 24).

The corporate model is based on several distinct assumptions about the Mafia's structure. First, it assumes that the Mafia is like a corporation in that all its activities are planned and coordinated from a single power center (cf. Clark, 1986, p. 21; "The single most important fact" about the structure of modern corporations is that "managerial power is legally centralized"). For instance, Cressey (1969) writes, "Decision-making [in the Mafia] is concentrated at the top of the hierarchy. . . . a low-status member is expected to surrender his own will to the authority of his superiors" and "place [himself] almost completely at the disposal of the rulers to be used as the latter see fit" (p. 225). Furthermore, Cressey claims, every mobster's activities are coordinated with those of other mobsters "by means of rules, in the way the activities of a cashier in a retail firm are coordinated with the activities of a stockroom clerk, a sales person, and an accountant" (p. 313).

Second, proponents of the corporate model argue that the Mafia, like a modern corporate bureaucracy, is characterized by a high degree of functional specialization and division of labor (cf. Parsons, 1947, p. 330; modern bureau-

cracies defined by "specified spheres of competence . . marked off as part of a systematic division of labor"). For instance, Salerno contends that responsibilities in a Mafia family are delegated in a very sophisticated manner, with members occupying specialized positions equivalent to those of president, executive vice president, chairperson of the board, divisional vice president, general manager, personnel director, public relations manager, general counsel, and security officer (Salerno & Tompkins, 1969, p. 85). Similarly, Cressey (1969) writes that the Mafia, "like the corporations which it resembles," has "specialized positions for . . . presidents, vice presidents, staff specialists, works managers, foremen, and workers" (p. 110). Cressey's chart illustrating his conception of the Mafia's structure is a standard staff and line, boxed, depiction. Also espousing this view, the 1967 Presidential Commission on Law Enforcement and Administration of Justice identified specialized positions in each family for "enforcers," "corrupters," and others (Conklin, 1973, p. 27).

Finally, proponents of the corporate model argue that promotions in the Mafia, as in a corporate bureaucracy, are made on the basis of demonstrated expertise, rather than of personal connections or "politics" (cf. [Weber] In modern bureaucracies, "candidates are selected on the basis of technical qualifications"; Parsons, 1947, p. 333). Thus, Cressey (1969) writes that "the history of organized crime since 1931 shows a tendency to shift from a system in which rank authority was dominant to a system in which authority based on expertise is becoming equally important" and concludes that "the rulers of organized crime have . . . found it necessary to recognize and reward the special kinds of technical competence possessed by men occupying the various positions making up the organization" (p. 224).

Feudal Model

A second approach, developed primarily by academic sociologists and anthropologists, rejects these assumptions and depicts the Mafia as little more than a loose agglomeration of criminals organized, if at all, along kinship lines. For instance, anthropologist Francis Ianni (1976) argues,

> There is *no* [italics added] formal organization or confederation of Italo-Americans in organized crime called *Mafia, Cosa Nostra,* [italics added] or anything else. There are numbers of Italo-Americans who are involved in organized crime. . . . But they are not held together by a national membership organization with a ruling council or even some shared conspiracy in crime. (p. 55)

Although Ianni concedes that Italian American gangsters may be organized in families, he points out that "membership in a 'family' is not like membership in a gang or an organization. A member does not receive a salary. He is usually engaged in his own activities. Members of families may even be competitive with each other" (1976, p. 55). According to Ianni, whatever structure there is to the Mafia is defined by "the looser form of obligations and protections of the south Italian system of family and kinship," not by some formal organizational structure. Thus, Ianni concludes, "the closest model is a feudal one wherein a member swears fealty, receives protection and provides his services to protect others when asked" (p. 55).

Sociologist Joseph Albini (1976) takes a similar view: "Rather than consisting of a rigid, formally structured organization with specific rules and regulations," Albini writes, "syndicated crime is best described . . . as a system of loosely structured patron-client relationships in which the roles, expectations and benefits of participants are based upon agreement or obligation and whose size and function is basically determined by the activity in which it is involved" (p. 24). Thus, in Albini's view, the Mafia is an umbrella organization consisting of disparate criminals who organize themselves as gangs on an ad hoc basis for specific jobs and only look to the organization for backup support in these endeavors (also, Reuter, 1983, argues that illicit markets in the United States operate autonomously, devoid of organization or control by a single, or even several, power centers).

Evidence From the Memoirs

The memoirs contain evidence supporting both of these views, thus suggesting that the truth lies somewhere between them. First, the memoirs reveal that the Mafia is, in many ways, highly structured. For instance, several of the authors confirm that the Mafia is organized nationally with 24 families operating in 20 cities (New York has 5 families; the other 19 cities each have 1) and with a ruling Commission consisting of the most powerful Bosses settling disputes among the various families (e.g., Maas, 1968, p. 75, describing creation of the Commission and national organizational structure and territorial division in the wake of the Castellammarese War in 1931; Bonanno, 1983, pp. 59, 205, describing the creation of the Commission in 1931 and subsequent political infighting on the Commission over the next 30 years; and DeMaris, 1981, p. 21, explaining that the purpose of the Commission is to settle disputes among different families).

Second, the memoirs reveal that all 24 families share the same sophisticated organizational structure. As several of the authors detail, at the top of each family are the Boss and his two main advisers, the Underboss and the *Consigliere.* Beneath them are several *Capos,* or Captains, each of whom supervises a crew of Soldiers, the lowest level of "made" members. Each Soldier, in turn, supervises a crew of associates, who are affiliated with the family but have yet to be formally inducted into it (Maas, 1968, p. 75, describing adoption in 1931 of an organizational blueprint for all families; and Pistone & Woodley, 1987, p. 116). Associates are usually up-and-coming mobsters who aspire to membership or more experienced criminals who cannot be "made" because they are not Italian (Maas, 1968, p. 14; Valachi explains that "the members of the Cosa Nostra are united by one great common bond: they must be Italian"; Pileggi, 1985, Henry Hill could not be made because he was part Irish).

The maintenance of such a sophisticated and uniform structure with a national Commission probably makes the Mafia the most structured criminal organization in the world. Not even groups as sophisticated as the Japanese Yakuza, the Colombian drug cartels, or the Chinese triads have a single ruling body equivalent to the Mafia's Commission. Although this evidence lends support to the corporate model, the memoirs also highlight several features of the Mafia's structure that undermine the corporate analogy.

First, the memoirs contain substantial evidence indicating that the Mafia's criminal activities are not centrally coordinated, with particular tasks assigned to those most suited to carry them out. Rather, it seems, as Albini and Ianni suggest, that mobsters (both made men and associates) enjoy a great deal of autonomy and engage in a wide variety of criminal activities with very little coordination from above. For instance, Michael Franzese, a former made member in the Colombo family, explains: "We weren't given a salary or put on somebody's payroll. It was up to each man to make his way" (Franzese & Matera, 1992, p. 96). Franzese also recalls: "[As a new inductee] I was invited to go on various stickups and burglaries . . . but always declined. That was okay. The Mob doesn't choose a job for its members" (Franzese & Matera, 1992, p. 93). Similarly, Joe Cantalupo, formerly an associate with the Colombo family, also explains that he was free to do whatever he wanted so long as he brought money into the family. Thus, Cantalupo recalls that "the rules of the game were simple. Make money any way you can" (Cantalupo & Renner, 1990, p. 28).

Second, the memoirs reveal that all of the authors engaged in a wide variety of criminal activities without specializing in any particular area. For instance, "Joey" writes, "I . . . smuggle narcotics and cigarettes; hijack trucks; bootleg perfumes, records and eight track tapes; run card games; work the numbers; do a little muscle work; book some bets; make pornographic movies; put people in contact with shylocks; fence some stolen goods; and now and then scalp some tickets" (Fisher, 1973, p. 24). Similarly, Caramandi claims to have participated in crimes as diverse as extortion of drug dealers, blackmail, sophisticated bank fraud, and labor racketeering schemes (Anastasia, 1991). Likewise, Cantalupo describes his involvement in activities as widely disparate as money laundering, hijacking, real estate fraud, and jewelry heists (Cantalupo & Renner, 1990). Similarly, Teresa claims to have participated in bank robberies, fencing stolen goods, fixing horse races, and stealing securities (Renner & Teresa, 1973).

Third, contrary to Cressey's assumptions, these activities were not planned or coordinated by the ruling circles of the authors' respective families. Rather, as the Albini/Ianni model suggests, the role of the Bosses and Captains seems to have been limited to that of "patrons" rendering passive support to the criminal activities of their "clients." Thus, the memoirs portray the Bosses as resolving disputes, establishing and maintaining territorial boundaries, and protecting members' operations from encroachment by other gangsters or law enforcement officials, but not planning or coordinating crimes to be carried out by their Soldiers. In return for these services, the memoirs explain, the Bosses, like feudal lords, took a cut of the profits made by those under their protection.

For instance, Henry Hill explains: "The guys who reported to . . . Paulie [Lucchese family Captain Paul Vario] . . . thought up the schemes. . . . [They] had to make their own dollar. All they got from Paulie was protection from other guys looking to rip them off . . . what Paulie and the organization offer is protection for the kinds of guys who can't go to the cops" (Pileggi, 1985, pp. 56-57). Similarly, Joe Valachi, formerly a Soldier in the Genovese family, made the same point when he told the McClellan committee that all he ever got from Cosa Nostra was "protection" and explained that, as a Soldier in a Mafia family, "You get nothing, only what you earn yourself" (cited in Albini, 1976, p. 33).

That the Mob Boss functions more like a feudal lord than a modern CEO is also confirmed in *Boss of Bosses,* an account of the daily life of former Gambino Boss Paul Castellano written by two former FBI agents O'Brien and Kurins (1991). They base their account on Castellano's private conversations that they monitored through a listening device planted under Castellano's kitchen table. As the wiretapped conversations reveal, Castellano almost never left his house and spent most of his time at his kitchen table, entertaining offers to support criminal ventures initiated by others, providing advice and guidance to Captains, resolving disputes among subordinates, and collecting a cut of the profits from the crimes committed within his jurisdiction (O'Brien & Kurins, 1991).

Thus, the evidence from the memoirs suggests, as Ianni and Albini hypothesize, that the Mafia functions more like a primitive government than a modern corporation.[3] In this connection, it is worth noting that Ronald Goldstock, director of the New York State Organized Crime Task Force, made the same point in an interview, explaining:

> The Mob's always been looked at as a corporation—"bigger than GM." But it's not. It's more like a government. In a corporation, people at the bottom carry out the policies and perform the tasks assigned to them by executives at the top. In the Mob, the people at the bottom are the entrepreneurs. They pass a percentage of their income upward as taxes in return for government-type services: Resolution of disputes, allocation of territories, enforcement and corruption services. (Stone, 1992, p. 29)

At a more abstract level, the memoirs also suggest that the corporate analogy is inapposite because rank and status in the Mafia are understood in ways more typical of a feudal or aristocratic society than a modern bureaucracy. Specifically, the memoirs reveal that made members of the Mafia take on a status similar to that possessed by a ruling elite in aristocratic systems and entirely uncharacteristic of functionaries in a modern bureaucracy. For instance, according to Pistone,

> A made guy has protection and respect. . . . [As a made man] *You are elevated to a status above the outside world of "citizens." You are like royalty* [italics added]. In ethnic neighborhoods . . . nobody has more respect than a made guy. A made guy may not be liked, may even be hated, but he is always respected. (Pistone & Woodley, 1987, p. 77)

At another point, Pistone explains that his Mob mentor, Lefty "Guns" Ruggiero, demanded recognition of his status as a made guy in all sorts of little ways, including making Pistone book flights and carry his luggage when the two traveled together (1987, p. 161). Similarly, Nick Caramandi explains that, as a made man, "You become like a god. Your whole life changes. You have powers that are unlimited" (Anastasia, 1991, p. 223). In a television interview, Caramandi expanded on this point, explaining, "If it's raining, 50 umbrellas come out. If you sneeze, 50 handkerchiefs come out. People can't do enough for you" (ABC News, 1992). Franzese also recalls that, on being made, "I was treated with awe and respect. The mantle was there. I couldn't see it or feel it, but everyone around me felt its weight" (Franzese & Matera, 1992, p. 97).

The memoirs also indicate that a strong status hierarchy is maintained among made members, although the distinctions among them are not as dramatic as those between members and nonmembers. For instance, Pistone reports that when he asked Lefty Ruggiero, a made member of the Bonanno family, whether they could go into a restaurant where the family's Boss Carmine "Lilo" Galante was eating, Ruggiero responded:

> Donnie, you don't understand nothing sometimes. In the first place, Lilo don't sit down with anybody except captains or above-bosses. He don't sit down with soldiers or below, like me and you. . . . You can't even talk to this guy. You got to go through somebody higher, somebody that can talk to him. (Pistone & Woodley, 1987, p. 150)

Status is also considered important in interfamily relations. For instance, Martin Light, a "Mob lawyer" who testified before the President's Commission on Organized Crime (1986), explained the procedures a Boss must follow before executing a made member of another family:

> He would have to sit down, or get a message with someone of similar rank; in other words, he

wouldn't do it himself, he would tell his under boss or *consigliere* that . . . so the under boss would then call for a meeting with the under boss, say, of the Gambino family. In other words, you have to be of equal rank. (President's Commission on Organized Crime, 1986, p. 319)

The maintenance of such status distinctions suggests a strong disanalogy between the Mafia and a modern bureaucracy. As political sociologist Ken Jowitt (1983) has argued, premodern, status-based systems are characterized by invidious distinctions between members of the ruling corporate group and outsiders. In such systems, according to Jowitt, those higher in rank, like the mobsters described above, will often demand tribute payments and dramatic displays of deference in recognition of their superior status.

Needless to say, such practices are incompatible with modern bureaucratic systems. For instance, according to Weber, in modern bureaucracies individuals are accorded only the power and status inherent in the office they occupy. Because they occupy these offices only temporarily, they are never seen as anything more than "human" (e.g., Weber, in Parsons, 1947, p. 328; "In the case of legal authority, obedience is owed to the legally established impersonal order. It extends to the persons exercising authority under it only by virtue of the formal legality of their commands and only within the scope of authority of the office"). Therefore, the invidious distinctions between made men and associates and the humbling displays of deference required of associates to made men (and made men to their superiors) suggest that analogies between the Mafia and a modern bureaucracy misunderstand status relations in both.

Conclusion

As the evidence in the memoirs reveals, the Mafia is highly structured, perhaps more so than any other criminal organization. At the same time, however, the memoirs reveal that characterizing the Mafia as a modern corporation or bureaucracy is inappropriate for two reasons.

First, the Mafia lacks the centralization of power, coordinated planning, and functional differentiation characteristic of modern corporations. Second, relations among Mafiosi are characterized by premodern status distinctions, in which superiors are not seen as simply more experienced or more qualified, as in a modern bureaucracy, but rather, like royalty, are accorded an almost superhuman status that is reaffirmed through dramatic displays of deference.

THE DECISION TO INFORM

Prior to 1980, only two made members of the Mafia, Joe Valachi and Jimmy Fratianno, had ever publicly broken *omerta,* the Mafia's ancient code of silence. Since 1980, however, 16 made members and dozens of associates have testified against their former crime families. These turncoats have included figures as powerful as Sammy "the Bull" Gravano, former Underboss of the Gambino crime family; Alphonse D'Arco, former Underboss of the Lucchese family; Peter Chiodo, formerly a Captain in the Lucchese family; and "Crazy Phil" Leonetti, former Underboss of the Scarfo family.

Analysts have offered two theories to explain the sudden breakdown of *omerta.* The first, which I call the *law enforcement theory,* claims that new prosecutorial weapons created by the 1970 Organized Crime Control Act (OCCA) significantly strengthened the government's hand and enabled prosecutors to turn mobsters who would otherwise have stayed silent.[4] According to this theory, three provisions of OCCA have been particularly important. First, the liberal rules of joinder provided by RICO enable prosecutors to join previously severable offenses and defendants, thus making it easier to obtain convictions in organized crime cases.[5] Second, the draconian penalties provided by RICO mean that a conviction will likely result in a very long prison term and seizure of the defendant's assets.[6] Third, the Witness Protection Program, by providing effective protection for witnesses (no member of the program has ever been killed), means that one can talk without risking one's life. Thus, according to the law enforcement theory, these three provisions working together have changed the decision calculus of mobsters faced with the choice of testifying or standing trial. Prior to implementation of OCCA, mobsters faced relatively mild sentences and knew that the risk of being killed for cooperating was fairly high. Now, as a result of RICO and the Witness Protection Program, conviction is much more likely, sentences are harsh, and the chance of being killed for cooperating is remote. As a result, cooperating is a much more attractive option today than it was 25 years ago.[7]

Thus, as Goldstock (n.d.) writes, by "creat[ing] new leverage against potential witnesses," OCCA has "revolutionized" law enforcement's approach to organized crime and has enabled the government to break the Mob's code of silence (p. 4). Similarly, Ostrow (1991) argues that "the key [to cracking *omerta*] has been skillful use of . . . RICO . . . and development of an effective Witness Protection Program" (p. A1; also McFadden, 1987, p. A1, explaining the rash of Mafia informers in terms of the "the lure of a witness-protection program and the threat of heavy prison sentences").

The second theory of the breakdown of *omerta,* which I call the *generational change theory,* argues that the current generation of Mafiosi, born during the baby boom, lacks the moral cohesion of preceding generations and consists of men willing to "rat out" their friends to save themselves. Specifically, proponents of the generational change theory argue that mobsters of earlier generations, being relatively new to the United States, were more closely tied to the Italian American immigrant community and thus more imbued with traditional Sicilian notions of duty, family, loyalty, and honor. Members of the current generation, in contrast, are more likely to have grown up in ethnically mixed neighborhoods, or even WASP suburbs, and are therefore more imbued with American notions of individualism. Thus, journalist Michael Stone (1992) writes,

The old-timers . . . were closer to their Southern Italian roots and the codes of honor and silence on which the Mafia had originally been founded. In America, they were tested in the street gangs of insulated Little Italys and, by the time they joined an organization, were tougher and more seasoned than today's inductees. (p. 24)

Similarly, Goldstock (n.d.) claims,

The years . . . following [Valachi's] testimony saw the beginning of important changes. New soldiers were initiated into *Cosa Nostra* who were second and third generation Americans. These new members had grown up with a different system of values: those of their contemporaries. They joined the Mob not because it was the honored society, but because it was a means by which they could profit financially. The ties that bound them together were not those of kinship and respect, but, in many cases, of dollars and cents. (p. 2)

Similarly, from other authors: "This new breed of Mafia would save its own skin. The yuppie wiseguy does not have the old loyalties. . . . This new breed breeds informers" (Nadelson, 1992, p. 729); McFadden (1987) argues that the Mafia's problems with informants are rooted in the contrast between "younger, reckless, flamboyant mobsters . . . and elders who . . . would rather die than break the code of silence" (p. A1).

Thus, according to the generational change theory, the collapse of *omerta* is the result of the accession of a new generation of mobsters devoid of the old loyalties and values and unwilling to subordinate their personal interests to those of their Mob families. This argument stands in strong contrast to the law enforcement theory, which argues that members of the current generation are more likely to talk, not because they are weaker, but only because they are subject to new and more intense forms of prosecutorial pressure.

Evidence From the Memoirs

Evidence from the memoirs suggests that although new prosecutorial weapons have played a role in spurring mobsters to talk, the collapse of *omerta* is primarily a result of the erosion of traditional Mafia values attendant upon the most recent generational turnover. First, the memoirs reveal that the mobsters *themselves* subscribe to the generational change theory. For instance, Caramandi complains that "the Mafiosi today, they're not like the old-timers of yesterday. Like in the thirties, forties, and fifties. . . . Today it's betrayal, deceit, envy, jealousy, viciousness. It's not like it was" (Anastasia, 1991, p. 349). Similarly, Teresa claims that "the New York mobs are in trouble now" because "a lot of the respect, the discipline is gone." According to Teresa, the "punks" in the American Mafia lack the "respect" and "honor" still instilled in young Sicilian Mafiosi (Renner & Teresa, 1973, p. 350). In the same vein, Fratianno complains that, in contrast with the old days, "greed and jealousy" are now "destroying [the Mafia] from within" (DeMaris, 1981, p. 515). Similarly, Bonanno, the former Boss of the Bonanno family, who prides himself on being a Sicilian "man of honor," also sees a serious erosion in the Mob's values over time. Thus, Bonanno (1983) laments,

My tradition has died in America. The way of life that I and my Sicilian ancestors pursued is dead. What Americans refer to as "the Mafia" is a degenerate outgrowth of that life-style. . . . Friendships, connections, family ties, trust, loyalty, obedience—this was the glue that held us together. In America, however, and increasingly throughout the industrialized world, the glue that holds people together is their economic relationship. Trade and work are the basis of the new culture. The sons and grandsons of the Sicilian immigrants absorbed the new values. (p. 404)

The memoirs also provide some concrete examples of the contrast between the current generation and its predecessor in this regard. For instance, Cantalupo and Franzese, both sons of mobsters, state that their fathers disapproved of their decisions to talk and would not have talked under similar circumstances. Cantalupo reports that his father tried to persuade him to break his agreement with the government and go into hiding rather than testify against the Colombo family (Cantalupo & Renner, 1990, p. 6). Similarly, Franzese explained in a recent interview that his father "wouldn't even think" of talking and "would never agree with what I've done" (ABC News, 1992). Franzese points out that his father has spent more than 20 years in prison, with 30 years remaining on his sentence, and has never talked despite repeated offers from prosecutors. Franzese considers his father "the ultimate Mob Soldier" and implies that such behavior is characteristic of his father's generation (Franzese & Matera, 1992, p. 268).

Franzese also relates an illustrative anecdote on this point. He recalls that when he and his father were summoned to an official Colombo family "sit-down" at which they thought they would be killed, his father insisted that they go, despite his son's protestations, because he believed that following Mob rules was more important than anything else, including one's life or family: "We have been given an order," Franzese recalls his father saying, "We must obey. . . . We are sworn to obey. . . . The oath and the life is more important than any two individuals. I'm going to go. And you must follow" (Franzese & Matera, 1992, p. 202). Franzese's response to this grandiloquent invocation of Mob values was simply, "Don't give me that shit!" (p. 202).[8]

In the same vein, Talese explains that Bonanno, another memoirist born into a Mob family, also differed with his father on traditional Mob values. According to Talese (1971), "The younger Bonanno . . . seemed impatient with the system, unimpressed with the roundabout ways and Old World finesse that are part of Mafia tradition" (p. 5). Bonanno considered it "absurd" that he was still stuck in the "insular ways" of his father's world and considered himself a "modern man, lost in times, grinding old axes" (Talese, 1971, p. 9).

The mobsters' explanations of their decisions to talk also suggest an erosion of traditional Mob values. For instance, in explaining their decisions to cooperate, several of the mobsters confess to a Machiavellian venality incompatible with traditional Mob notions of self-sacrifice and loyalty to other family members. Cantalupo explains that he cooperated with the FBI because he thought he could do well for himself by trading the FBI information on his friends for money and protection (Cantalupo & Renner, 1990, p. 141; "Maybe I could be an underworld spy, a big wheeler-dealer with federal protection; maybe I could use all my connections with all the mob people to my advantage and make money for myself . . . and nobody would ever be the wiser"). Fratianno admits that he cooperated to make money and feed the FBI information on other mobsters whom he wanted to do in. According to Fratianno's coauthor, Jimmy "resolved to give the FBI only information that would serve his purpose in his effort to gain control of the San Francisco family. If he played his hand carefully, they could be very helpful. He liked that idea. The FBI, not only helping him, but paying him for doing in his enemies" (DeMaris, 1981, p. 332). Similarly, Franzese's explanation for cooperating, that he became a born-again Christian under his wife's persuasion, though much loftier than Cantalupo's or Fratianno's, also suggests a willingness on the part of the current generation to place other values over the Mafia (Franzese & Matera, 1992, p. 282). Cooperating out of devotion to God is as much a violation of Mob traditions as cooperating to avoid prosecution and is thus also symptomatic of the disappearance of traditional Mob loyalties.

The concrete effect of this erosion of values on *omerta* is illustrated by the authors' explanations of their decisions to talk. Specifically, these discussions reveal that the decline in values has created an atmosphere of mutual distrust that makes talking more likely. Several of the authors claim that they talked because they feared that their colleagues would suspect them of talking and would thus try to kill them. Thus, Henry Hill explains that he decided to cooperate after being arrested for dealing drugs, not to avoid a RICO indictment, but because he feared that his partners would kill him rather than take the chance that he would become an informant. Hill writes,

I knew that arrest on the drug charge made me vulnerable. Maybe too vulnerable to live. There wouldn't have been any hard feelings. I was just facing too much time. . . . The fact that I had never made a deal before, the fact that I had always been standup, counted for nothing. . . . From where my friends stood, I was a liability. I was no longer safe. (Pileggi, 1985, p. 268)

Caramandi also decided to talk after being arrested, not because he wanted to reduce his sentence, but because his Boss, Nicky Scarfo, fearing that Caramandi might cooperate, put a contract out on him (Anastasia, 1991, p. 325). Cecil Kirby, formerly an associate with the Toronto family, also decided to cooperate because he suspected that his Bosses no longer trusted him and were planning to kill him. Kirby explains: "I knew a helluva lot about their operations and the crimes they were involved in. Because of that I figured that I would either disappear or I'd be killed at some meeting, like my predecessor" (Renner & Kirby, 1987, p. 6). Along the same lines, Fratianno claims that "senseless killings" have created an atmosphere of insecurity in which people become informants "because it [is] the only way they [can] save themselves or strike back" (DeMaris, 1981, p. 515).

Thus, as the memoirs reveal, rather than trust their arrested subordinates not to talk, the current generation of Mafia leaders prefers to kill them, thereby, ironically, ensuring that they will talk. The connection between this practice and generational turnover is elucidated by Caramandi, who claims that he and five other members of the Philadelphia family would not have turned had Angelo Bruno, the traditional Mob Boss who had ruled Philadelphia for 30 years, still been in power, rather than his flamboyant and paranoid successor Nicky Scarfo. Anastasia (1991) paraphrases Caramandi's views:

Bruno would have let Caramandi take his shot in court, confident that the mobster would do the right thing. In turn, Bruno would have made sure that Caramandi's family was provided for. If Caramandi had been convicted, he would have spent his time in prison under the mob's protection and would have returned to the Bruno family once he had finished serving his sentence. . . . The process, the system, the organization would have remained intact. That was the old, time-honored way the mob took care of its own and ensured its continuity. (p. 343)

In contrast with Bruno, Scarfo reacted to the arrest of any of his Soldiers by trying to have them killed. As a result, six made members of his family flipped and became government witnesses.

According to Caramandi, the difference between Bruno and Scarfo is symptomatic of the difference between the current generation of mobsters and their predecessors. Moreover, Caramandi claims that the shift from the Bruno style to the Scarfo style destroyed the Philadelphia family and, he implies, is destroying the Mafia as a whole. Thus, Anastasia (1991) writes: "Angelo Bruno had ruled the Philadelphia Mob for more than twenty years. He used an iron fist covered with a velvet glove. Nicodemo Scarfo saw no need for the glove. In the end, that made all the difference" (p. 343).

Conclusion

As the old adage about honor among thieves suggests, criminal conspiracies have always been plagued by the paradox of the prisoner's dilemma, in which each conspirator, in seeking to protect his or her own interests, manages to destroy the entire conspiracy. What made the Mafia so successful for so long was its ability to create and maintain a level of trust that allowed its members to avoid the prisoner's dilemma. Mobsters who were arrested didn't talk because they trusted their Bosses to take care of them and their families. Bosses didn't try to kill arrested subordinates because they trusted them not to talk. As the memoirs indicate, this trust and loyalty seem to be eroding, and with their disappearance, one must wonder whether the Mafia is not far behind.

NOTES

1. The most important of these memoirs are the following. Their authors/subjects are listed in parentheses:

Quitting the Mob: How the "Yueeie Don" Left the Mafia and Lived to Tell His Story (Michael Franzese) (1992)

Contract Killer: The Explosive Story of the Mafia's Most Notorious Hit Man (Tony Frankos) (1992)

Blood and Honor: Inside the Scarfo Mob—The Mafia's Most Violent Family (Nick Caramandi) (1990)

Body Mike: An Unsearing Exposé by the Mafia Insider Who Turned on the Mob (Joe Cantalupo) (1990)

Mafia Enforcer: A True Story of Life and Death in the Mob (Cecil Kirby) (1987)

Donnie Brasco: My Undercover Life in the Mafia (Joe Pistone) (1987)

Wiseguy: Life in a Mafia Family (Henry Hill) (1985)

A Man of Honor (Joe Bonanno) (1983)

The Last Mafioso (Jimmy Fratianno) (1981)

Honor Thy Father (Bill Bonanno) (1971)

The Valachi Papers (Joe Valachi) (1968)

My Life in the Mafia (Vincent Teresa) (1973)

Killer: Autobiography of a Hit Man for the Mafia ("Joey") (1973)

It should be noted that the author of one of the books I have listed, Joe Pistone, the subject of Donnie Brasco, was actually an undercover FBI agent who lived as an associate of the Bonanno family for 6 years. Although he was not actually a mobster, Pistone's account is based on extensive firsthand experience with day-to-day life in the Mafia, and I have therefore used his book as a source for the second part of the chapter.

2. Bonanno's father also wrote a memoir, *A Man of Honor,* which is discussed later. Neither of the Bonannos, however, ever cooperated with the government in any way.

3. Although the family leadership generally take a "hands off" approach, the memoirs also reveal that the Bosses do sometimes restrict the activities of their family members. For instance, almost all the authors, including Franzese, Caramandi, Fratianno, Hill, Cantalupo, and Valachi, report that their families maintained strict prohibitions against drug dealing. Fratianno, for example, reports that on being made, he was told that the three rules he would always have to obey were (a) never betray the secrets of Cosa Nostra, (b) never violate the wife or children of another member, and (c) never become

involved with drugs (DeMaris, 1981, p. 2). Caramandi repeats a similar story (Anastasia, 1991, p. 216).

There is also evidence of similar prohibitions on exploitation of women. For instance, Fratianno claims that pimping is considered a "disgrace" because "only creeps live off women" (DeMaris, 1981, p. 516). Similarly, O'Brien and Kurins (1991) report that, during the Castellano surveillance, they recorded a Mob pornographer, Robert DiBernardo, complaining that Castellano disapproved of his activities and considered it inappropriate for the Mafia to be involved in such a dirty business.

At the same time, though, the memoirs also reveal that these rules do not significantly restrict mobsters' activities. For instance, several of the authors claim that the ban on dealing drugs was (and is) routinely violated. Thus, Maas (1968) paraphrases Valachi as reporting, "[Despite] the command to get out of narcotics . . . the temptation for quick profits was too much, and individual members, particularly those short on cash, persisted in handling heroin secretly" (p. 197; also, Cantalupo & Renner, 1990, p. 155—Colombo family rule against drug dealing routinely violated and enforced sporadically; Pileggi, 1985, p. 192—Hill and other associates of Lucchese family were heavily involved in cocaine trafficking; and DeMaris, 1981, p. 477—Fratianno turned to drug dealing when he needed money).

Furthermore, the memoirs reveal that even if mobsters obey the ban on drugs, they can still collect a percentage of the profits from the drug trade by extorting money from independent drug dealers. For instance, Caramandi explains, "You couldn't deal drugs, but you could . . . do anything you wanted with [drug dealers]. Steal from them, rob them, make them pay a street tax." And, indeed, Caramandi reports that extortion from drug dealers was one of his biggest money-making activities (Anastasia, 1991, p. 198). Similarly, according to Maas (1968), Valachi claimed that Vito Genovese formally adhered to the ban on drug dealing but always took "a cut of the take" from those who did in exchange for his promise to "look the other way" (p. 197).

Evidence also suggests that the Mob makes money from pornography in the same way. For instance, Fratianno refers to a friend's description of the family's policy on drugs as being the same as the policy on pornography: Extortion from dealers is acceptable, but selling drugs or pornography oneself is not. Fratianno quotes his friend as saying, "The families here deal with [drugs] like they do

porno. They shake down dealers, but don't touch none of that shit" (DeMaris, 1981, p. 485). Similarly, in the same conversation in which he complained about Castellano's disdain for the pornography business, DiBernardo made clear that Castellano was still willing to take a cut of the pornographer's profits for himself. DiBernardo was recorded as saying, "He [Castellano] uses me. 'Look at D. B. [DiBernardo]—he makes his money in pornography! Like he's some kinda high-and-mighty! Mr. Fucking Clean. Does it stop him taking his cut?' Sorry, Paul, you don't wanna touch those dollars—there's pussy on 'em. Ha! He'll take 'em anyway. He wants it both ways. Get paid. Act clean" (O'Brien & Kurins, 1991, p. 232).

4. The OCCA provided for, among other things, testimonial immunity, increased jurisdiction for the federal government in gambling enforcement, enhanced sentencing in organized crime cases, grand jury reports, the Witness Protection Program, and the Racketeer Influenced and Corrupt Organizations Act (RICO) (Goldstock, n.d., p. 4).

5. As Robert Mueller, former assistant attorney general in charge of the Justice Department's Criminal Division, said: "RICO gives you the ability to pull together the various criminal acts committed by various persons in an organization [and present them] in one courtroom. . . . Both the jury and the judge understand the scope of criminal activity" (Ostrow, 1991, p. A1).

6. For instance, Anthony Salerno, Tony "Ducks" Corallo, and Carmine Persico, all convicted under RICO in the Commission Case, each received 100-year sentences. Similarly, John Gotti, convicted on 13 RICO counts, received a life sentence.

7. Since the passage of the federal sentencing guidelines in 1984, which significantly increase sentences for almost every federal offense and eliminate the possibility of parole, law enforcement's bargaining hand has been strengthened even further, and some analysts point to the sentencing guidelines as an important factor in the breakdown of *omerta*. For instance, criminal lawyer Alan Chaset notes that because of the sentencing guidelines, "there are people who have never thought of being a snitch, a dimedropper . . . coming in as soon as they can, and telling everything they know about everyone they know in hopes of getting a reduction" (Tyre, 1991, p. 10).

8. As it turned out, Franzese and his father did go to the meeting but were able to talk their way out of their problems and thus avoid execution (Franzese & Matera, 1992, p. 203).

PART IV

COMMENTARY

In Chicago, the criminal enterprise made up of Italian American Mafiosi is called "the Outfit." Its membership, organizational structure, and criminal activities mirror those of any other of the Mafia families. Justifiably, you might think of the Outfit as a legacy from the Prohibition era and Al Capone. The current group finds it roots in street gangs with names like the Ragen's Colts and the Valley Gang or in gangs whose members were identified by association with its leader: Mike "King Mike" McDonald, John "Bathhouse" Coughlin, Michael "Hinky Dink" Kenna, and William "Big Bill" Thompson each lent his name to the gang he led (Abadinsky, 1992, p. 159). The Volstead Act was a godsend that filled the coffers of these gangs. Characteristically of organized crime, when goods or services are prohibited, it will supply the demand—at a price.

Fred Martens, coauthor of Chapter 3 in this text, once replied to the question of how one defines organized crime by saying (here paraphrased): The true test of an enterprise's organizational integrity is its ability to exist after its major source of income has been removed. In other words, is the enterprise so well put together, so diversified, so strongly structured that it will continue to find products and markets for

them when its prime income source is no longer available? American organized crime, and particularly the Outfit, passes Martens's test. Although Capone and company made money in bootlegging liquor, by 1933 and the repeal of the Eighteenth Amendment his organization was all of the above and well able to withstand the loss of its major commodity. Gambling, extortion, bust-out schemes, hijacking, loan-sharking, labor racketeering, and a host of other criminal activities filled the bill. It takes a good measure of administrative acumen and practice to handle the logistical problems associated with delivering sufficient booze and beer to keep a thirsty nation sated for about 15 years. The planning, staffing, directing, coordinating, and recruitment of staff to run such an operation is imbued with a life of its own; once in place, it is difficult to extinguish it.

Robert Lombardo, author of Chapter 8, argues that the staying power of the Outfit may have had some support from a quarter that should not surprise you—the public. Like the existence of the Devil, we all "intuitively" know that without the demand for illegal goods and services, the supply would dry up. We just don't think about it, preferring instead to attack the supply side. The numbers player who bets a few dollars, hoping to hit a 600 to 1 payoff, seldom thinks about where the gambler's profits go. Out of sight, out of mind, gets translated in real life to out of sight, into the Mob's treasury to finance loan sharks, drugs, the takeover of businesses, and whatever else Mob Bosses do with their profits. Lombardo reports the results of his interviews of street-smart folks who know the Outfit. Like any good academic, he provides us with some theoretical underpinnings for his research, suggesting that all organizations are fluid, adapting to their environments as needs demand. This is "contingency theory" and, as do Kelly and Haller (this text, Chapters 4 and 5, respectively), Lombardo believes that a more fruitful approach to understanding criminal organizations would include both the bureaucratic and decentralized models, or at least the best approach would pick and choose elements from them both.

Lombardo defines the environment in which the Outfit operates to include clearly delimited positions for Bosses, members, and associates (bureaucratic model) and an organized public made up of gamblers, thieves, and wanna-bes. The latter are people who want to be part of the Outfit but, for reasons of ethnic ancestry, ineptitude in criminal dealings, or other shortcoming, are not allowed membership. The key to this chapter is Lombardo's argument that a large part of "the public" is organized to provide a ready source of participants for organized crime activities and that although not formally made members, they are an integral part of the Outfit. Regards the individual, Lombardo says the symbiotic dependencies between the Outfit and the public cause everyone involved to order their lives according to their beliefs about organized crime, and, in fact, they consider organized crime an accepted part of their society. Ergo, whether connected, a client, or peripherally associated, each individual plays a role in organizing crime.

The chapter is an especially insightful look at the "social organization" of organized crime because it relies on interview data supplied by police officers, federal prosecutors, and investigators, authors, associates of organized crime figures, gamblers, bookies, and actual organized crime members. You should find the verbatim accounts of the interviews enjoyable reading, but be alert against being lulled into a mind-set that ignores the real worth of the information they contain.

Chapter 9 relies on personal interviews and direct observation, as well, but adds information from official reports and government documents to round out the database. The locale remains the same; the cast of characters changes. In this relatively short piece, Robert Davidson examines organized crime groups of Asian ethnicity. He attempts to discover comparative differences and similarities between these groups and the better-known American gangs.

This is a descriptive piece. Davidson is less concerned with theoretical niceties than he is with trying to pin down the kinds of criminal activities that Asian criminals are involved in. Heroin importation and distribution comes first to mind about Chinese gangs, but Davidson "assures" us that the laundry list of traditional organized crime activities—larceny, gambling, loan-sharking, prostitution, protection rackets, extortion, smuggling, and so on—are all in the tool bag. Certain ethnicities tend to specialize— for example, the Vietnamese, in home intrusion robbery; the Fukienese Chinese, in illegal alien smuggling—but all Asian gangs are into drug trafficking and the crimes listed above.

The research presented here mirrors that done by Kelly, Chin, and Fagan (1993) in New York City. They, like Davidson, point to the use of street gangs, a more fluid, less structured criminal entity than the groups identified as tongs and triads, as the muscle for the latter. The Asian criminal groups that better fit the definition of organized crime in terms of sophistication, organization, and ability at political and law enforcement co-optation use the Asian street gangs as strong-arm enforcers or debt collectors, gofers, hit men, and doers of the generally more risky tasks that need to be done to keep an organized crime group in business. Although Davidson does not directly say so, his depiction of the associations between street gangs and organized crime groups echoes what Lombardo says of the Italians: For many, organized crime is an accepted part of the social system.

This text is about organized crime globally. We believe that "international aspects" should include examples from the United States. Accordingly, the first half of Part 4 provides a glimpse at one small part of the American version. It might serve as a benchmark or comparative basis when studying the remaining chapters. This is not to say that Lombardo and Davidson describe all of American organized crime. They tell but one part of the entire story. Nevertheless, what is happening in Chicago is sufficiently reminiscent of organized crime generally that these two examples provide a good sounding board for fine-tuning your study of international organized crime.

Lest you think that organized crime operates only in big cities, as described by Lombardo and Davidson, Chapter 10 moves your study to the international scene, to no less prestigious a place than the Vatican, where bankers turned bandits to sate the ubiquitous profit motive. Maurice Punch examines the precursor event to the Bank of Credit and Commerce International (BCCI) scandal that so rocked the international money markets—the case of the Banco Ambrosiano in Italy. Punch presents another idea that is widely known but seldom articulated: Organized criminals need banks to perform covert and illicit services for them. The gravamen of his analysis is the observation that international regulation of banks is sporadic and ineffective, a ready field on which to play games of financial chicanery. Every large organization uses banks, and the Vatican is no exception. Archbishop Marcinkus, the head of what is commonly known at the Vatican Bank, said, "You can't run the Church on Hail Marys." It is a very different context, however, when the bankers resort to criminal means to carry out their deals. Marcinkus is seen as part of a complex web of financial wizards who exploited lax banking regulations to engineer a system of fraud and falsification of international proportions. Punch identifies the major participants in the scheme and an "incredible supporting cast"

of politicians, military men, journalists, businessmen, secret agents, and even two Popes— John Paul I and John Paul II. Again, we see the mix of criminals and facilitators that so deeply embeds organized criminality into the social fabric as to make it indecipherable.

While you read this account, pay close attention to the personal connections that grease the skids of financial manipulations. The diplomatic status of the Vatican serves to cloak the crimes, as well as the cabal of complicit enablers, a tracing of whom leads to the highest levels of Italian society. Underlying Punch's tale of an aftermath of suicides, questionable deaths, and long prison terms is the disquieting notion that the main characters are not organized criminals. The account begs the question whether the activity is organized crime when the actors do not fit the role of gangster. It also echoes our comments in the Introduction that it seems wherever people are, organized crime is. We hope you will be equally concerned with definition. A helpful reading in this regard is a two-part article in the *Columbia Law Review* in which the author suggests "organized crime is, what organized crime does" (Lynch, 1987a, p. 687).

Chapter 11 keeps us on the continent. David Carter continues the focus on fiduciary matters, with an analysis of trends in entrepreneurial crime in Eastern Europe. With the breakup of the Soviet republics, news accounts abound about organized crime elements plying their trade in commodities as diverse as Pepsi and plutonium. Carter's report calls attention to the traditional denial of threat (ala J. Edgar Hoover and the Mafia) until well past the reason for the threat has surfaced.

This qualitative piece relies on the author's interviews with ranking law enforcement officials around the world. Of special note is Carter's retelling of initial reactions to his suggestion that Americans are threatened by the emerging organized gangs in the former Soviet Bloc nations. The counterarguments were something akin to "it's not likely because they are too far away," "they aren't sophisticated enough," "it would be too difficult," "there is nothing for them to exploit from the United States," "they don't speak the language," and so on. Carter's research contradicts each of these arguments. Indeed, he concludes that North America, particularly the United States, is "dearly" a target of the East European criminal enterprises. As do most of the authors of the chapters in this text, Carter describes the structure and nature of the organization(s) under study. In this case, the nature is entrepreneurial, increasingly global, and rapidly growing in scope and influence. Given the lessons thus far learned, we best take heed of the warning from Carter to intervene now, not play catchup as we have done in the past.

Lombardo and Davidson did not consult each other before doing their research, yet somewhat eerily, their respective descriptions of people associated with organized crime but not actually a part of it use words that mean the same. Lombardo (Chapter 8) speaks of Italians, Davidson (Chapter 9) of Asians, and both say, in effect, that the organized crime group is surrounded by a contingency of wanna-bes and hangers-on that do the bidding of the gang leaders. The supporting contingency is part and parcel of the social fabric, and they make it easy for organized criminals to blend into that fabric. Punch (Chapter 10) sheds some light on the problem of separating "legitimate" actors from criminals. Today, more than ever, organized crime confounds efforts to identify those involved because they clock themselves in legitimate businesses when "in fact a criminal enterprise has been subsumed in the folds of that cloak" (Ryan, 1990, p. 4).

Are the individuals involved in the BCCI and Banco Ambrosiano scandals really organized criminals or just legitimate business folk gone astray of the law? What of Lombardo's description of the hard core members of the Outfit—the crew, the made guys, the Outfit guys, the connected guys? Is it a usable characterization? What have you learned from it? Because it is the more extensive, use Lombardo's description of the "organized public," with particular attention to it being the demand side of illegal markets, to extrapolate to Davidson's discussion of Asian organized crime groups being the major suppliers of hard drugs to America. Are the two analogous? And finally, what side of the argument are you on regarding the threat from East European gangs as described by Carter? Is he an alarmist or someone worth heeding?

SELECTED READINGS

Abadinsky, H. (1983). *The criminal elite: Professional and organized crime.* Westport, CT: Greenwood.

Booth, W. (1991). *Triads: The growing global threat from the Chinese criminal societies.* New York: St. Martin's.

Chin, K-L. (1990). *Chinese subculture and criminality: Nontraditional crime groups in America.* Westport, CT: Greenwood.

Kaplan, D., & Dubro, A. (1988). *Yakuza: The explosive account of Japan's criminal underworld.* Reading, MA: Addison-Wesley.

Landesco, J. (1968). *Organized crime in Chicago.* Chicago: University of Chicago Press. (Original work published under the same title, Part III of the Illinois Crime Survey, 1929)

Lasswell, H. D., & McKenna, J. B. (1977). *The impact of organized crime on an inner-city community.* New York: Policy Sciences Center.

Posner, G. C. (1988). *Warlords of crime: Chinese secret societies—The new Mafia.* New York: McGraw-Hill.

8 THE SOCIAL ORGANIZATION OF ORGANIZED CRIME IN CHICAGO

ROBERT M. LOMBARDO

Based on an analysis of interview data, this research argues that neither the bureaucratic model nor the patrimonial model of complex organizations adequately explains traditional organized crime as found in Chicago today. The author suggests that the open systems perspective, and in particular the contingency model, better explains the true nature of organized crime. In addition, the author describes the organizational structure of the Outfit, the traditional organized crime group in Chicago, and argues that positions exist within the Outfit for made guys, Outfit guys, and connected members. In addition, the author argues that the Outfit has an organized public made up of gamblers, thieves, and wanna-bes who provide support for the activities of the organization and recruits for the Outfit itself.

Since the 1950s, sociologists have debated the structure of traditional organized crime in the United States. As a result, two basic positions have emerged. The first position portrays a nationwide association of Italian American criminals bound together by a rigid code of conduct within a rational, bureaucratic structure with an elaborate division of labor and detailed general rules of conduct. The second position presents a system of Italian American criminal units tied together by a patrimonial network of social relationships within a structure that is not rational, but traditional.

This debate would put traditional organized crime somewhere on a continuum between a rationally defined formal organization and a naturally organized criminal group. As a rational organization, "Cosa Nostra," as it is often referred to, would be organized in the pursuit of relatively specific goals and exhibit a formal social structure. In contrast, the natural systems perspective maintains that members of Cosa Nostra are not necessarily guided by their organization's goals but do share a common interest in the survival of the system and engage in collective activities informally structured to secure this end. They are, fundamentally, social groups attempting to adapt and survive in their particular circumstances. As such, these organizations can be seen as ends in themselves.

The view that traditional organized crime follows a bureaucratic structure can be traced to the work of the 1967 President's Commission on Law Enforcement and the Administration of Justice. It referred to Cosa Nostra as a group of 24 crime "families" whose membership was exclusively men of Italian descent working within structures as complex as those of any large corporation (p. 1). The task force detailed the internal structure of each family, and the bureaucratic analogy was subsequently given wide circulation by Donald Cressey (1969) and Ralph Salerno (Salerno & Tompkins, 1969), two task force consultants who authored popular books in the field.

Cressey and Salerno both suggest that Cosa Nostra closely resembles a formal organization. They argue that it is a complex system, like a business or government bureaucracy, with a specialized division of labor rationally designed to achieve specific goals. They present a picture of a hierarchical organization, with orders coming from the top and passing through various levels to the workers, who operate under official rules of conduct based on the code of the Sicilian Mafia. Such a code would lend itself to the belief that Cosa Nostra is a rationally organized group. These rules are vaguely stated and not permanently recorded, however, and as such are actually more characteristic of patrimonial systems than formal organizations.

In contrast with the findings of the task force is a view that conceives of Cosa Nostra as a band of ethnic criminal gangs whose structure can best be understood in terms of culture and kinship (Ianni & Reuss-Ianni, 1972) and patron-client relationships (Abadinsky, 1983; Albini, 1971). Ianni (Ianni & Reuss-Ianni, 1972, p. 108) writes that Italian American crime families are not formal organizations like governments or business corporations, rationally structured to maximize profits and carry out tasks efficiently. Rather, they are traditional social systems organized by action and by cultural values that have nothing to do with modern bureaucratic virtues. Ianni argues that Italian American organized crime can be better explained by examining kinship networks. Membership is based simply on blood, marriage, godparenthood, and fictive relationships.

The bureaucratic view of organized crime has also been criticized by Albini (1971, p. 229), who writes that Cosa Nostra consists of criminal syndicates in a loose system of power relationships, in contrast with a rigidly organized secret society. Albini (1971, p. 155) characterizes the *bureaucratic model* as the "evolutional" approach, which assumes that Italian American organized crime represents the evolution of the Sicilian Mafia. He offers the "developmental" approach, which sees organized crime as emerging from social conditions and factors within American society itself.

Abadinsky (1983, p. 165) also takes exception to the bureaucratic model of organized crime. Although he found that rules and other signs of formal organization do exist, he contends that patron-client networks are better able to describe the structure of organized crime than bureaucratic analogies. For example, Abadinsky states that the Soldiers of an organized crime family act as patrons to nonmember clients, both legitimate and criminal (p. 108). The Soldier, in turn, is a client of a higher-ranking member, a Lieutenant. Lieutenants are the clients of the Boss, who together with other Bosses form a loose network based on kinship, friendship, mutual interest, and tradition.

Attempts have been made to integrate rational and natural systems theory into what has been described as the *open systems perspective* (Scott, 1981). One such attempt, the *contingency model* (Lawrence & Lorsch, 1967), might help in explaining the true organizational nature of Cosa Nostra. Contingency theory stresses that the form an organization takes is determined by its environment: The more homogeneous and stable the environment, the more appropriate will be a formalized and hierarchical form; the more diverse and changing, the more appropriate a less formalized organic form. Simply put, the contingency argument suggests there is no one best way to organize. All organizations have fluid structures that adapt to changes in their environments.

The contingency argument is supported by the work of Annelise Anderson (1979, p. 34), whose research revealed that organized crime does have a hierarchical structure similar to that described by Cressey, though not as complex. She found that traditional organized crime groups did have positions of Boss, Underboss, Lieutenant, and so on but that they also included various "Associates" who were not true members themselves. These Associates carried out many activities necessary for the success of the group and entered into patron-client type arrangements with its members. They ran both illegitimate gambling activities and legitimate business fronts for the criminal organization.

Anderson's research was an important contribution to the study of organized crime in that it bridged the gap between the bureaucratic and patron-client models of organizational structure. Yet, it seems that her findings have gone unnoticed. For example, the 1986 President's Commission on Organized Crime rejected the bureaucratic notion of its 1967 predecessor and accepted the more decentralized version offered by Albini (1971), Ianni (Ianni & Reuss-Ianni, 1972), and Abadinsky (1983) without mentioning the fact that the structure of each organized crime group may contain elements of both the bureaucratic and patron-client models.

My research attempts to resolve the ongoing debate surrounding the structure of traditional organized crime through an examination of "the Outfit," the established organized crime group operating in the Chicago area. The Chicago Outfit is a particularly interesting subject for research because no empirical examination of this group has been done since the original 1929 publication of John Landesco's classic book *Organized Crime in Chicago*. In conducting this analysis, 25 in-depth interviews were conducted with people who have firsthand knowledge of the activities of traditional organized crime in Chicago. These people include police officers, federal prosecutors and investigators, authors, associates of organized crime figures, gamblers, bookies, and actual organized crime members themselves.

The data used in this study were collected without any preconceived deductive scheme, and the findings reported here were developed during the process of this research. All interview data were analyzed by using the constant comparative method advocated by Glaser and Strauss (1967, pp. 105-112). In addition, the gathered data were also cross-checked with other empirical sources. No data are reported in this study unless two or more persons gave the same information or other sources were available against which to check the accuracy of the data.

Past research revealed that it was often necessary to conceal the identity of informative sources when dealing with traditional organized crime. Further, it was learned that anonymity was the first step in obtaining cooperation from knowledgeable persons. As a result, confidentiality and anonymity have been strictly adhered to, and the identity of many of the interview sources used in this analysis will remain undocumented.

The formal structure of the Chicago Outfit is well defined. Newspaper and popular accounts of the activities of the Outfit suggest that positions exist for Bosses, members, and associates who are said to be "connected." This research uncovered evidence that the Chicago Outfit has an organized public, composed of gamblers, thieves, and wanna-bes (people who "want to be" associated with the Outfit), that provides a ready source of participants for organized criminal activities, as well as recruits for the Outfit itself.

This report is divided into two sections. In the first section, I describe the formal structure of the Chicago Outfit and its criminal activities. In addition, I argue that people who are connected to organized crime are, in fact, part of the formal organizational structure. In the second section, I describe the people with whom the Outfit is regularly in contact and suggest that they, too, are an integral part of the Chicago Outfit.

THE CRIMINAL ORGANIZATION

The Chicago Outfit is divided into six "street crews": Taylor Street, Grand Avenue, 26th Street, the North Side, Rush Street, and the suburb of Chicago Heights. The 26th Street Crew is also referred to as the "Chinatown" Crew because of its proximity to Chicago's Chinese community. The derivation of the term *Outfit* was described by a former member:

> Well you were trying not to say that I belong to the syndicate or organized crime. It was supposed to be a secret, the "Outfit." Nobody was supposed to know what that meant except the guys involved and then it got out of hand.

Schoenberg (1992, p. 77) traces the beginning of the use of the term *Outfit* to the days of Johnny Torrio. He reports that it was not a name of consequence, like the lurid usage of the term *Syndicate* as used by crime reporters and novelists. The Outfit was a casual name gang members used when they were talking among themselves and about their group. For example, they would say, "I joined the Outfit 2 years ago."

Except for the Bosses, most members of the various crews do not know the members of the other crews. Each crew works independently of the others, but, as explained by John Hinchy, former deputy chief of detectives of the Chicago Police Department, when somebody "picked up the phone," they were all aligned. Each crew did its own thing, but when it came down to business, they were all allies.

The Outfit has a membership of 191 persons, including 4 senior statesmen, 6 Street Crew Bosses, and 181 members who are usually referred to as "Outfit guys." It should be noted, however, that the composition of the Outfit and the number of members varies according to which agency you contact and when you ask. The designation of the six crews used in this analysis comes from a 1987 organizational chart prepared by the Chicago Police Department. The Chicago Crime Commission (1990, pp. 4, 12) also reports six crews, which it characterizes as 26th Street, the West Side, Elm-

wood Park, the North Side, Grand Avenue, and Lake County. The commission estimates approximately 66 members of the Outfit but "more than 300 individuals who derive significant portions of their income from mob operations."

The Chicago Police Department, except for the case of the Rush Street Crew, uses the "original historic designations" to identify the various street crews—that is, the names of the neighborhood areas in which each of the street crews evolved. The Chicago Crime Commission (1990, p. 4) points out that the use of the original territorial name to designate each street crew is often done for the sake of convenience and that every crew still has some presence in each of these community areas although crew members now venture wherever criminal opportunities arise.

Members of the West Side, Elmwood Park, and Lake County Crews as indicated by the crime commission, by and large, correspond to the members of the Taylor Street Crew as indicated by the Chicago Police Department. The need for this further diversification of the Taylor Street Crew can be explained by two factors: (a) the resettlement of many Taylor Street residents in the Chicago suburb of Elmwood Park and (b) the Taylor Street Crew's eventual takeover of gambling in the Lake County, Illinois, area.

A review of the history of the Chicago Outfit indicates that the organization has also been characterized in other ways over the years. For example, in 1970 the *Chicago Today* newspaper ("Nobody Today," 1970) divided the Outfit into four segments: Cicero, Melrose Park, the North Side, and the South Side. The creation of the Cicero Crew in the 1970s can be explained by the then crime syndicate Boss Joey "Doves" Auippa maintaining an office in Cicero, Illinois. On February 17, 1985, the Outfit was similarly divided by the *Chicago Sun-Times* into three segments: the West Side Group, the South Side Group, and the North Side Group. An examination of the membership of the South Side Group, as indicated by the *Chicago Sun-Times,* revealed that it was composed of members of both the 26th Street and Chicago Heights Crews.

Variation in street crew designation can largely be attributed to population migration. For example, in the 1960s, many people from the Taylor Street area moved to the Chicago suburb of Melrose Park, just as they later moved to Elmwood Park. According to Special Agent Thomas Moriarty of the Internal Revenue Service in Chicago, these towns received an infusion of people associated with organized crime when members began to move off Taylor Street. Many crime syndicate figures, such as Joey Auippa and Rocco Infelice, moved there, and other members followed.

A more recent variation in street crew designation centers around the division of the North Side Crew. The Rush Street and North Side Crews had traditionally been one but are now divided into two separate crews. The North Side Crew, made up of mobsters from other sections of Chicago, was imported into the area to handle organized crime activities north of the North Side community area and into Chicago's northern suburbs. The Rush Street Crew is made up of the remnants of the original North Side Crew, who continue to control what little organized crime activities remain in the Rush Street area. One explanation for the division of the North Side Crew is the unavailability of new recruits in the North Side neighborhood. This community has been completely changed as a result of social and economic development and is no longer viewed as an organized crime area. The old Sicilian neighborhood in which "North Side" organized crime activity was previously centered no longer exists.

Evidence also suggests criminal specialization among the various street crews, although it appears that gambling is the major activity of each crew today. According to Howard Shapiro, former head of the Justice Department's Organized Crime Strike Force in Chicago, virtually every member of the Outfit is now involved in some type of gambling operation.

The Grand Avenue specialty is burglary. According to Chicago Police Department and Chicago Crime Commission records, 65% (20) of the 31 members of the Grand Avenue Crew have been arrested on more than one occasion for burglary or have been suspects in a major burglary. The 26th Street Crew is noted for truck hijacking, or cartage theft as it is called in Chicago. The North Side/Rush Street Crew is noted for its vice operations: prostitution, pornography, and liquor law violations.

Many of these criminal specializations can be related to the ecological aspects of each area. For example, the North Side contains Rush Street, Chicago's adult nightclub entertainment district. The 26th Street area contains many railroad yards and associated shipping and trucking terminals, thereby providing the opportunity for cargo theft. Chicago Heights, located on the southern edge of the Chicago metropolitan area, has a reputation for automobile theft and chop-shop operations. According to Paul Sieler, an experienced Chicago Police Department intelligence officer, for some reason the south suburbs had better auto thieves and as a result there were chop shops all over the local area and in Indiana that were controlled by the Outfit.

The 1990 Racketeer Influenced and Corrupt Organizations Act (RICO) prosecution (*U.S. v. Rocco Infelice et al.* 90-CR00087-1, F.2d 1990) of a group of Chicago crime syndicate figures gives an inside look at street crew activities today. In all, 20 members of the Chicago Outfit were indicted and charged with 42 counts of racketeering. According to the indictment, there existed in Chicago a criminal organization sometimes referred to as the Joseph Ferriola Street Crew. This street crew was part of a larger criminal organization commonly referred to as the Chicago Outfit or the Chicago Mob. "Ferriola Street Crew" is another name for "Taylor Street Crew." Joseph Ferriola was the Boss of the Taylor Street Crew during much of the time of this investigation.

The indictment states that the Ferriola Street Crew existed primarily for the purpose of providing income to its members in several ways, including:

> ... the operation of various illegal gambling businesses such as sports bookmaking, parlay cards, and casino games; the collecting of interest,

known as "juice" on usurious loans made by the enterprise; the collecting of protection money known as "street tax" from various illegitimate as well as questionably legitimate businesses; and the use of the proceeds from these activities in the enterprises and in other business ventures.

To accomplish the purposes of their criminal conspiracy, members of the Ferriola Street Crew were charged in the indictment with the murder of several people who either posed a threat to the street crew or who failed to pay street tax for operating various illegal enterprises. Members of the crew were also charged with engaging in an illegal gambling business and extortionate credit practices stemming from that business. In addition, various members of the crew were charged with extortion and the failure to file federal income taxes.

The indictment also states that the purpose of the Ferriola Street Crew was to recruit and retain members and to maintain loyalty, discipline, and control over the members of the illegal enterprise. To carry out these activities, the street crew maintained the following structure: a leader or Boss, assistants to the Boss, supervisors of the various income-producing activities, and agents and employees who were compensated out of the earnings of the enterprise.

The role of the Boss of each street crew is further defined in the 1992 RICO indictment (*U.S. v. Sam Carlisi et al.* 92-CR1064, F.2d 1992) of 11 other members of the Outfit in Chicago. This indictment states:

The "boss" of the crew was ultimately responsible to the head of the Outfit and was required to ensure that the leadership of the Outfit received a share of the proceeds from the crew's activities.

According to the data gathered here, the head of the Outfit in Chicago is more of an arbiter than a director of a large corporation. Each street crew, for the most part, acts totally independent of the other crews, and each Boss is solely responsible for the activities of his crew. The head of the Outfit settles disputes between the crews and may handle relations with those outside the organization, such as corrupt public officials and organized crime groups in other cities. Agent Moriarty believes that the street crews defer to his authority in order to avoid violence and the news media attention that is associated with it.

The Chicago Crime Commission (1990, p. 4) states that each street crew of the Chicago Outfit is headed by a *Capo,* or Captain, who is in charge of the crew. Each crew is composed of *made members,* who are sometimes referred to as Soldiers, and associates, who are said to be "connected." In charge of all the crews is a Boss and a second in command, the Underboss. Also, Advisers are usually older successful members who serve as elder statesmen.

It should be noted that there is some disagreement about the various terms used to describe positions within the Outfit. Sieler reports that members of the Chicago Outfit never use the terms *Soldier, Capo,* or *Cosa Nostra* when speaking about themselves. These terms originated in New York and with Joe Valachi. Valachi, a self-admitted member of the New York Genovese crime family, testified before the Senate Permanent Subcommittee on Investigations (McClellan committee) in 1963 regarding the existence and structure of organized crime in America.

Made Guys

Within the Chicago Outfit, there is a definite distinction between being a Boss and being a worker. According to Jack Hinchy, to be a made guy, one has to be a Boss, not just a member. The head of the Outfit and his advisers are said to be Bosses. The heads of the street crews and their Lieutenants, persons with a definite area of responsibility, are said to be Bosses. As reported by Richard Weber, a longtime Chicago Police Department gambling investigator, being a made guy grants certain rights and privileges that other members do not have. Made guys can order other people to do things, and they are the ones who receive most of the money earned by the Outfit's illicit enterprises.

Becoming the Boss of a crew is a good indication that the member has been made. Associating with made guys and assuming responsibility within the organization are also indications of who is likely to be a made guy. Chuck Giancana (Giancana & Giancana, 1992, p. 242), brother of one-time Outfit chieftain Sam Giancana, writes that you knew how high up the ladder a guy was by the men he hung around with, by how many people he required to conduct business, and by the job he held.

To be a made guy, one also has to be Italian, and not just any kind of Italian, but Southern Italian, Neapolitan, or Sicilian. Some non-Italians could carry great stature within the Outfit because of their advanced age or accomplishments within the organization, but they were not made guys. Take Jewish gangster Lenny Patrick, for example. As explained by Jerry Gladen of the Chicago Crime Commission, Lenny Patrick grew up on the West Side of Chicago and went to the penitentiary for armed robbery. After he came out, he became associated with the Outfit and eventually controlled gambling in the Jewish community. Although he was a Boss and killer in his own right, he could never be a made guy because he was not Italian.

It is commonly believed that another requirement for becoming a made guy is that you must have killed someone in furtherance of crime syndicate business. Giancana (Giancana & Giancana, 1992, p. 242), however, states that a guy didn't necessarily have to kill someone to be made if he had powerful friends to protect him from such dirty work. This position is supported by the data collected in this analysis. According to a gambler and associate of organized crime figures in Chicago, to be "made," one just has to be sharp, know his business, and be able to make money.

Evidence suggests that one can get credit for killing someone else by assisting in a murder, as opposed to carrying out the actual killing itself. For example, William Jahoda, a government informant, used Chicago gangster Solly D'Laurentise as an example. Agent Moriarty reports that Jahoda told federal investigators that he did not know whether Solly D'Lauren-tise had killed anyone himself but that the Outfit may have given him credit for being present and helping to "set up" bookmaker Hal Smith. Just being there and knowing about it may have counted.

Becoming made may also involve a ceremony. Jahoda also told federal law enforcement officials that the Infelice Street Crew made people the old way:

> D'Laurentise said in '86, or '87 that Infelice told him that he had been expecting that he was getting (Infelice used the term) "made." And Infelice didn't go into great detail but he said that "we do it the way they used to do it." Jahoda said do you mean with the paper and the fire, and Infelice said yes.

Outfit Guys

Reporting to the made guys are the Soldiers, or members of the various street crews. In Chicago, they are commonly referred to as "Outfit guys." There is a distinction between being a made guy and being a Soldier. There is also some disagreement regarding whether Soldiers are, in fact, made guys. The Chicago Crime Commission, for example, states that each crew consists of Soldiers who are made guys (1990, p. 4). This is not consistent with the data gathered here. For example, in a statement given to the FBI (1988, p. 3), crime syndicate figure Gerald Scarpelli stated that he was not a member of organized crime although he readily admitted being part of one of the street crews, collecting juice money and participating in some murders. Scarpelli obviously attributed membership to being a made guy.

Gerald Scarpelli is a good example of an Outfit guy today. Scarpelli was originally from the Taylor Street neighborhood (FBI, 1988, p. 3). Scarpelli told the FBI (p. 4) that he was a member of the street crew currently run by Ernest Rocco Infelice (Taylor Street Crew). He stated that his principal duties involved the collection of street taxes (payments made to organized crime for the right to conduct some type of unlawful activity, such as gambling). Scarpelli also told the FBI that he was not currently collecting juice payments on behalf of the Chicago Outfit. He did admit, however, that he had collected such money in the past. With regard to street tax, Scarpelli stated that he was personally responsible for 15 individual accounts, mostly bookmakers, and a few "whore houses" run by organized crime figure Vito Caliendo.

Scarpelli's duties also involved the identification of new illegal activities to tax. J. Kenneth Lawrie of the Organized Crime Strike Force in Chicago explained how this works:

> They develop their own leads and then go back and say I got this guy who is doing something and I checked everywhere and he is not paying anyone else. The Boss checks and then gives him the OK. He checks to see if this guy belongs to anyone else. If no one knows this guy, then they go out and tell him he knows the rules and he has to pay. He either pays tax or enters into a 50% partnership with the Outfit. Tax is usually $1,500 to $2,000 a month. The guy usually doesn't complain because he is making enough money and doesn't want trouble. Whatever money that is collected is usually given to the Outfit Boss, who then gives a portion of it back. They get a portion of their own criminal activities, not the full benefit of it.

Scarpelli stated that he received a salary of $2,000 per month for collecting street tax for the Chicago Outfit (FBI, 1988, p. 5). In addition, Scarpelli committed various acts of violence as part of his duties, admitting to participation in three murders and two beatings. He was never paid money for his participation in these crimes because they were just part of his responsibilities as a member of the Outfit (FBI, 1988, pp. 6, 23, 24). To supplement his income, Scarpelli also committed burglaries and admitted to having taken part in three Brinks armored car robberies. According to Lawrie:

> If Scarpelli pulled a stick-up and he was going to be straight with his Boss, he would have to go back to his guy and give him a portion. . . . You would have to get permission in advance. Then do the deal. Then your profit would be cut back.

According to Scarpelli, he was only receiving $24,000 a year in salary from the Chicago Outfit at the time of his arrest in 1988. This is not very much money! He was even told at one point by his Boss that he should not participate in any "scores" (thefts). One may ask why Scarpelli would continue to involve himself in organized crime activities. According to Lawrie, being an Outfit guy made one "important." Being an Outfit guy provided a certain status that people found rewarding and were attracted to.

The fact that Scarpelli did not make a lot of money from his organized crime activities highlights that the status provided by membership is often more important than the financial benefits it provides. The status of membership seems to take on even greater importance at the lower end of the organized crime hierarchy. These data indicate that much of the money made by the Outfit moves up the organizational structure, leaving relatively small amounts to be paid to those at the lowest levels—small payments, when compared to the risks they take. It seems, therefore, that people are not in organized crime solely for the money. They are also in it for the prestige associated with membership.

Despite the prestige that accompanies membership, not everyone involved in the Chicago Outfit wants to become a made guy—or an Outfit guy, for that matter. According to one Chicago bookie, many people associated with the Outfit are happy just being bookmakers. Although being a bookmaker is not an important position, it is one that makes a lot of money. Even some Outfit guys themselves are reluctant to become made guys and take positions of authority because the federal government will target them for prosecution.

Connected Guys

Besides made guys and Outfit guys, the criminal organization of the Chicago Outfit also consists of associates who are said to be "connected." There is a definite distinction between membership and being connected. Made guys and Outfit guys are members; connected guys are not. Just because someone has access to the

Outfit does not mean that he or she is connected. Giancana (Giancana & Giancana, 1992, p. 242) states that being connected meant you did business with the Outfit. Giancana himself was a connected guy. As the brother of crime syndicate leader Sam Giancana, Chuck Giancana was employed by the Outfit as a bookie and the manager of a hotel owned by the Chicago crime syndicate.

The fact that connected people are part of the criminal organization, but not seen as members of the Outfit, is highlighted by a Christmas party hosted by the Chicago Heights Crew at the Alcazar Club in Chicago Heights. Agent Moriarty reports that Albert Tocco, the head of the crew, separated wire room clerks (connected employees) into a different party room from the made guys and Outfit guys.

People doing business with the Outfit are generally only connected to the person they are working for. According to a former member of the Outfit,

> Guys that are associates like guys that are bookies, bookmakers. They will say that they are connected, but they are only connected to the guy that they are answering to, and he is answering to somebody else.

Family members and professional people who work for the Outfit are also said to be connected. As explained by Lieutenant Thomas Spanos of the Chicago Police Department, Jack Cerone made his son a lawyer in charge of a union. Is he in the Outfit, or is he not? He is a legitimate lawyer, but he is taking care of all Outfit business, so he is still connected. Only people who are beneficial to the Outfit become connected. An associate of some organized crime figures elaborated:

> If you are a bookmaker, yeah, you're beneficial to them. It's an ongoing activity. Other than that, if you are a truck hijacker, you bring the load and now the load is gone and you are out of money 2 weeks later, you can't go to them and ask for money for your kids. They don't want to know nothing. The deal is over with. There is no pen-

sion, there is no hospitalization. Nothing like that. You are what you are. That's it.

Being connected has its benefits. According to Paul Sieler, being connected grants one the ability to pick up the telephone and get a favor done if you had a problem they could resolve. But Giancana (Giancana & Giancana, 1992, p. 243) reports:

> If a man got a favor from an Outfit member, he was involved more than he imagined. He might get lucky and never have his marker called in or he might be called on to hit his best friend or take a fall on a murder rap for a total stranger. The possibilities were limitless.

Being connected also enables one to go to the Outfit with business propositions, both legal and illegal. It doesn't make you a member, but as explained by a Chicago gambler, being connected meant,

> You were recognized. You could sit down and have a cup of coffee. Come to them with a score or a venture that is profitable, and you might get some assistance or help. If you are connected, you are worthy of being listened to.

Being connected to the Outfit gives a person status. A person who is connected is said to carry some "weight." As explained by a former juice victim,

> [Connected people] get a certain gratification because of the people that they come into contact with. . . . It's power knowing that someone is connected. If he gets into trouble, he feels that he can go to people to get help in straightening things out.

During the 1960s, the Chicago Police Department listed approximately 3,015 people as being associates of organized crime in Chicago. As of the latter part of 1992, approximately 1,500 people were listed as having some form of connection to the Outfit. As described by a person having firsthand experience with organized crime in Chicago,

There are a ton of guys that will never see the chart. These guys go down and work in City Hall. They work in the Bureau of Sanitation. There are so many guys that are real Outfit guys that we don't know about. Did you read Hoheimer's book? He was never known for years, an Outfit burglar. Nobody knew anything about him except the Outfit. There are still guys like that, but not many.

THE ORGANIZED PUBLIC

Most organizations operate in an environment in which they are not related to the public they routinely contact. For some organizations, however, the public in contact is actually part of the organization. This situation routinely occurs in prisons and mental institutions (Blau & Scott, 1962, p. 79). Neither institution would exist without inmates. It also occurs in organizations that provide a service, such as schools because of the presence of students.

What makes organized crime in Chicago unique among criminal endeavors is that the public the Outfit is in contact with is also part of the organization. This public may be as diverse as an individual gambler or thief and a person who simply wants to be associated with organized crime. Although gamblers, juice loan victims, and thieves all use services provided by the Outfit, they are also part of organized crime. Although they are not made guys, Outfit guys, or connected people, they are critical to the survival of the organization. Someone who was once connected explained:

> They're protected. It is like you go to the bank and get a loan for your house. You can then go and get a checking account. They will accept you before they take anybody else. They will help you out with a car loan. So if you are on a juice loan with a guy, you can always go to him for whatever.

Gambling and professional theft are particularly important for the continuation of organized crime in Chicago because they provide social structures that support this deviant group. Gambling and professional theft provide distinct sets of activities that not only produce income but also identify the public the Outfit is in contact with. Support for organized crime is also provided by a segment of the public that defers to organized crime activity and seeks to be associated with members of the Outfit. These wanna-bes also provide willing participants for the organized public contacts of the Outfit.

Gamblers

The Chicago Outfit makes most of its money through illegal gambling. There is some casino gambling and a few card games, but these events are becoming a thing of the past. Today, most illegal gambling is on sporting events. Virtually all illegal gambling in the Chicago area is strictly controlled by the Outfit. The control of illegal gambling takes two forms: Outfit gambling and street-taxed gambling. *Outfit gambling* is operated directly by street crew members who have people working for them in wire rooms (places where bets on horse races and sporting events are called in over the telephone) or at dice and card games. Also, some independent gambling operators, usually bookies, pay *street tax* to the Outfit. As related by a Chicago bookie:

> In order to book, you have to get the OK. It is accepted that you have to pay in order to book. I have to split 50/50. For that, I get the right to book. It is a tax. If you make money legitimate, you pay taxes. If you make money illegally, you pay the "Outfit."

The importance of gambling for the Chicago Outfit goes beyond the revenue it produces. Gambling also provides a setting in which some important organized crime activities are carried out. Gambling provides access to juice loans; provides a means of identifying gambling operations that are not paying street tax; creates opportunities for violence; and provides a mechanism for identifying potential burglary victims. Gambling also provides a mechanism for introducing people to organized crime and a setting for organized crime recruitment.

In reference to loan-sharking, a former juice loan victim explained:

> Let's assume you gamble. You lose your money and go to a loan shark. Now you are obligated. The shark has permission from the Outfit to give out money at the game and has paid the street tax to whoever gave permission for the game.

Gambling provides a means for the Outfit to identify potential street tax victims. As explained by a Chicago gambler:

> Most gamblers know many other guys. I might ask you, where are you going tonight? "I am going up to Deerfield to gamble with a bunch of guys. Some Jews, a couple of Greek restaurant owners, some Italian guys." And you hear that. You may go to another poker game and talk to a guy who is obligated to the Outfit for money. So the guy goes to his juice man and tells him the information for a break on his juice. They may knock something off what he owes if the information checks out. They send someone to the game and tell them they need the OK. If they don't cooperate, they may even call the police.

A person who doesn't cooperate could also be taken care of in other ways. He might be "found in a trunk at O'Hare Field" (Chicago gambler). Violence is also perpetrated against those who fail to pay their gambling and juice loan debts. A Chicago bookie explained:

> If a gambler gets behind, they will talk to him and try to get him to straighten out. They don't like to kill people for a small amount of money because it draws too much heat from the police. But if a guy gets too far behind, and everyone knows, they will kill him as a lesson to others.

Only "deadbeats" fail to pay their "just" debts. These debts, though illegal, are seen as just because no one is made to gamble or borrow money from the Outfit. According to J. Kenneth Lawrie, crime syndicate enforcer Frank Schweis

stated in secretly recorded government recordings that people deserve to get killed if they do not "follow the rules."

Gambling also provides a mechanism for identifying potential burglary and theft victims. As Robert Cody of the Chicago Crime Commission notes:

> Take a good bookie like Bobby Lewis. If he goes to a house to collect a bet and sees a good score, you can bet he is going to tell somebody about it and get cut in for a piece.

Dice and card games provide a setting for the exchange of information about organized crime activities. A Chicago gambler provided the following example:

> There is a card game northwest. Wiseguys gravitate there. Everyone talks: Who is playing? Who is dealing. . . . In that gravitation, you can come into contact with those involved in the gambling end. That takes into consideration the loan-sharking that is involved because you know who to go to if you want to get money and whatever you pick up "on the earee" so to speak: Who is a burglar? Who is hijacking trucks, and so on. You are not part of it, but you actually see explanations of it.

Gambling provides a setting for organized crime recruitment. This is accomplished in two ways. First, bookies and game operators can become members of a street crew if they are productive. Agent Moriarty explains:

> Gambling is the most labor intensive part of the Outfit. They have to have phone clerks. They have to have collectors, and you don't have to be a genius to be any of these things. Answer a telephone, write down a bet, clear a line. And it is a great recruitment tool to see how someone is.

Second, card and dice games provide a setting where information is exchanged on potential members. As described by a Chicago gambler:

I am into stolen cars. You are into chop shops. We come into contact with one another (at a card game). That's number one, we come into contact. He may have a kid. I may go to him and say I need your kid. Let's say he had gone to the can and served 3 years. He came out and is looking for something to do. Well, all right, he may option. Here is what will be asked of you. They have that kind of information.

Thieves

Professional theft is another activity that supports organized crime in Chicago. It provides both a source of revenue and potential recruits for the Outfit. Revenue is derived from street tax, as well as from the proceeds of criminal activity. Some Outfit guys are thieves themselves, as was demonstrated by the life of Gerald Scarpelli. Other thieves are also connected with the Outfit.

Street tax is paid by burglars and thieves for the right to steal in the Chicago area. Not all thieves pay street tax. Only those associated with the Outfit pay street tax. As explained by Richard Weber:

If you are a connected guy and you are a burglar, you are like a half-made guy or a wiseguy, then you are working for somebody. You don't freelance. You can freelance, but you better pay the guy that you're working for.

Street tax is also paid by thieves who are residents of street crew neighborhoods. Weber says,

If I am a guy from 26th and Princeton and I am hanging around and conspire with a couple of other guys to go out and break into the Jewel and they find out that I did it, they would probably want their piece. You had better come to them and say I did it, here is your end.

Street tax is not paid by blacks, Latinos, or inner-city street gang members who engage in professional theft. It is only paid by thieves who understand about the Outfit because they are controllable. A gambler and one-time connected guy explained:

They have to grab somebody they can control. Somebody that knows about you. The PR [Puerto Rican] don't know about you. The PRs got their own thing. You have to speak the language, in other words.

Professional theft also provides a ready source of recruits for organized crime. Jerry Gladden says the following about thieves who aspire to membership in the Outfit:

[They] go to these social clubs they have in the neighborhoods, card rooms [places where people play cards]. They sit there 8 to 10 hours a day. There are two or three wheel men. A safe guy. A guy like Joe Vento, who was good with keys. He would train the young burglars from Grand Avenue. Ronnie Jarrett used to train the young juice collectors on how to make silencers. Everybody trains everyone else. They would sit there and wait for someone to come in and tell them they have a job. They would then drive away in a cool car. The next day, you would hear about them in maybe Ohio following a jewelry salesman.

The life of Frank Cullotta provides an excellent example of the relationship between professional theft and organized crime. In a series of articles excerpted from federal court documents, Levin (1983a, 1983b, 1983c) reported that Cullotta was born in the Grand Avenue neighborhood of Chicago and eventually moved to the northwest side of the city, where he met Tony Spilotro, who was also originally from Grand Avenue. They quickly became friends and began stealing together.

By the time Cullotta was 15, he was committing armed robberies of taverns and gas stations. By 18, he had graduated to robbing bank messengers, which netted him a new car and a substantial amount of money. Frank was also committing home invasion robberies and burglaries. In 1960, he went to jail for 1 year for the burglary of an appliance store. After he came out of jail in 1961, Cullotta returned to stealing.

During the time Cullotta had been in jail, Tony Spilotro had become involved in the loan-sharking business and the Chicago Outfit. According to Goodman (1983a), Spilotro was working for Chicago mobster Sam DeStefano. DeStefano was a notoriously violent individual who had killed his own brother for using drugs. Dubbed the "Marquis de Sade" of the Chicago Outfit, DeStefano himself was soon found murdered. The prime suspect was Tony Spilotro. At age 27, Spilotro had become the youngest loan shark and hit man in the Chicago Outfit.

Eventually, Cullotta was offered positions on two different street crews. Lawrie states that Tony Spilotro told Cullotta,

> Soon you are going to be with us. You are going to go in to see this guy Joe Lombo. They are going to ask you to go with him or Dominick. If you go with Dominick, you will be my guy and work with me.

Cullotta chose to go with Spilotro and moved to Las Vegas, where Tony had set up shop as the chief emissary of the Chicago Outfit. It was Spilotro's job to ensure that Chicago mobsters received their share of income from the Las Vegas casinos in which they had acquired a hidden interest. In Las Vegas, Cullotta worked for Spilotro, leading a contingent of burglars known as the "Hole in the Wall Gang," so-named because they would cut holes in walls of buildings in order to enter without setting off the burglar alarms (Goodman, 1983b).

Cullotta was arrested twice in 1981. While in jail, Cullotta realized that Tony Spilotro had failed to care for his family while he was in prison. This was a signal to Cullotta that something was wrong. When he eventually learned that Spilotro had decided to have him killed, Cullotta decided to cooperate with the federal government and testify against Spilotro and others in exchange for protection for himself and his family.

Although the life of Frank Cullotta provides a colorful example of the relationship between professional theft and organized crime, the importance of professional theft for the Outfit in Chicago seems to be diminishing. Today, the Outfit is much less involved in burglary and truck hijacking than it was just a few years ago. Gambling is now the main activity of the Chicago Outfit. According to the majority of the people interviewed in this analysis, today virtually every member of the Chicago Outfit is involved in some form of illegal gambling.

Wanna-Bes

Wanna-bes are persons who "want to be" associated with the Outfit. They will do anything to ingratiate themselves with Outfit associates. Tony Carduf, a retired Chicago Police Department intelligence officer, states that a wanna-be could be a "working stiff" or a man in business who just wants to be around Outfit people. Wanna-bes are distinct from gamblers and thieves, although gamblers and thieves can themselves want to be part of the Outfit. What distinguishes wanna-bes is that they generally have some other jobs.

Wanna-bes are people who like to be where the action is. They gamble, buy stolen property, and can be heard discussing news reports of the latest arrests of crime syndicate figures. Wanna-bes like the excitement. As described by a Chicago gambler,

> [Wanna-bes] like the atmosphere. It is like a need. It's like doing heroin. Once you see a gangster, you want to be like a gangster.

Jack Hinchy believes that wanna-bes are attracted by the aura of secrecy and the romanticized version of organized crime that is glorified in such movies as *The Godfather.* They are into the organized crime lifestyle. They romanticize about it. They think this is a great way to live. Wanna-bes also think they are important because they associate with Outfit guys. A Chicago gambler provided the following vignette:

> It is like the guy who owed the gangsters $50 and would give them $5 a week juice and never pay

the $50 back because he wanted to see the gangster every week. He wanted the contact.

A Chicago bookie pointed out that "it is clout to be known by wiseguys." However they get to know them, whether it be from the neighborhood or by some other means, legitimate people, businessmen, judges, lawyers, and doctors all befriend these people because it gives them stature. They can say when they see organized crime figures on television that they know them.

Despite the stature provided by knowing Outfit people, it is interesting to note that the term *wanna-be* is a derogatory designation. According to an associate of some Chicago organized crime figures, no one can use the term *wanna-be* around these people:

> If I would say that you are a wanna-be, to me and my friends you are a guy that is lacking. A guy that comes to mind now is a very wealthy man. I don't know his business, but he is always with them. He is a wanna-be. He don't need them. He's got everything. He's got a big car. What's he doing with these guys?

Some wanna-bes are content with just hanging around with Outfit guys. Other wanna-bes do become Outfit guys. If someone likes you and you do a good job, then you might be given the chance to move up. You would begin by being a gofer, a person regulated to menial tasks. For example, Richard Weber suggests that you may be told:

> "Run over there and tell so and so to do this." "Do this or that." Whereas a Soldier would be more trusted with important things. "We need to have this done." Or, "You are going to work this place, work a wire room, or steal a truck."

The Victims of Organized Crime

The concept of an organized public as it pertains to the Chicago Outfit is supported by the fact that innocent people are rarely the victims of organized crime activity. Innocent people do become the victims of robberies and burglaries perpetrated by the Outfit, but as explained by Jerry Gladden, they are rarely the victims of extortion or violence perpetrated by the organization. Why? One Chicago gambler explained that "innocent people call the police."

A Chicago bookie argues that "there must be some type of obligation in order to be a victim." This obligation is created through voluntary participation in gambling, loan-sharking, participation in connected burglary crews, and other involvement with organized crime. As an example, John Hinchy offers the following:

> Say a guy owns a factory and he likes to gamble and he gets into them [the Outfit]. Now he is into the bookmakers and he goes sour on paying them back. They move in a guy as his partner, and the next thing you know they own a company.

One's obligation to the Outfit can also be created by asking them for help:

> Someone breaks your windows and you go to the Outfit and say: "These kids are really bothering me, can you help me out?" say for a figure or a favor. After you ask him for the help, he visits you for a free meal every week. Now you are on the hook. But you bought into it. You joined.

Success as a result of past involvement in organized crime activities can also create an obligation. For example, four members of the Outfit's North Side Crew were found guilty of extorting money from various Chicago area businesses, some of which had past ties to organized crime (*U.S. v. Mario Rainone et al.* 91-CR 727, F.2d 1991, U.S. District Court for the Northern District of Illinois). Two of the victims, Myron and Philip Freedman, are the owners of Myron and Phil's Restaurant in Lincolnwood, Illinois, a popular hangout for gamblers and organized crime figures. Both had reportedly been bookies before opening their restaurant and thus obligated and prone to victimization.

If an organized crime figure extorts money from a legitimate person, it is said that he will "lose his edge." As described by a Chicago gambler and onetime connected person:

> If you fuck with guys doing stuff illegally, then he is not supposed to go anywhere [to the police]. It is hard for him to go anywhere. With a legit guy, you are going out of your territory. You are into illegitimate persons. You have to stay in your realm.

The same notion applies to the juice loan business. Paul Sieler explains:

> Nobody is going to give you a juice loan because you need money. If you and your wife are having a hard time making ends meet, nobody is going to give you a juice loan. You are not going to get one. You only get a juice loan when you are doing things that the Outfit allows. The gamblers, the druggies.

SUMMARY AND CONCLUSION

This research has sought to determine the true organizational nature of traditional organized crime in American society, if Chicago serves as a model for organized crime generally. The data gathered indicate that the Outfit, the traditional organized crime group operating in the Chicago area, exhibits elements of both the bureaucratic and patrimonial models. The division of labor within the Chicago Outfit—made guys and Outfit guys—suggests that the organization has a hierarchical structure. At the same time, connected guys, gamblers, thieves, and to some extent, wanna-bes appear to be in patron-client relationships with individual members of the Outfit. As such, it would seem that the contingency argument best describes the organization of the Chicago Outfit. It is an open system that adapts to the external circumstances it confronts.

The establishment of the Lake County faction of the Taylor Street Crew and the fact that the various crews have had different criminal specialties also support the contingency argument. The organizational structure of the Chicago Outfit has changed as people have moved from city to suburban areas as is evidenced by the Cicero and Elmwood Park Crews. And the criminal specialties of the various crews are often dependent on the ecological characteristics of the area in which they are based.

Contingency theory also provides a suitable explanation for the emergence of traditional organized crime. The conditions that gave rise to organized crime are rooted in the environment, and not in the rational decisions of the groups' members. Organized crime as we know it today came about because Prohibition fostered an alliance between vice entrepreneurs, machine politicians, and the criminal underworld. In short, organized crime could not have been invented until the structure of society was ready to accommodate it. If organized crime is a rationally organized phenomenon, any group setting about to "do" organized crime would be able to similarly organize. We know that this is not the case. Traditional organized crime has never been duplicated in this country.

Although support for the contingency argument is an important finding, probably the most important fact found by this research is that some people order their lives according to their beliefs about organized crime. The members of this criminal organization and its organized public defer to the Outfit and look on organized crime as part of the accepted structure of their society. Whether a made guy, Outfit guy, or connected guy, whether a gambler, thief, or wanna-be, they are all part of organized crime.

LAW ENFORCEMENT INFORMANTS

Investigator Robert Cody—Chicago Crime Commission, May 1992

Detective Anthony Carduf—Chicago Police Department (retired), August 1992

Deputy Chief John Hinchy—Chicago Police Department (retired), June 1992

Investigator Gerald Gladden—Chicago Crime Commission, July 1990

J. Kenneth Lawrie—U.S. Attorney, Northern District of Illinois, October 1989

Special Agent Thomas Moriarty—Internal Revenue Service, Chicago, Illinois, November 1992

Detective Richard Weber—Chicago Police Department, July 1992

Howard Shapiro—U.S. Attorney, Northern District of Illinois, November 1988

Detective Paul Sieler—Chicago Police Department, August 1992

Lt. Thomas Spanos—Chicago Police Department, October 1988

9

ASIAN GANGS AND ASIAN ORGANIZED CRIME IN CHICAGO

ROBERT L. DAVIDSON

The primary purpose of this chapter is to present findings of a preliminary examination into the existence and extent of activity of Asian street gangs and Asian organized crime in Chicago. Information was acquired through field study, personal interviews, direct observation, official reports, and government documents. The author defines and distinguishes between criminal gangs and organized crime groups. Links between Asian street gangs and Asian organized criminal groups in Chicago are examined. In addition, relationships between Asian criminal groups in Chicago and other U.S. cities and international crime groups are highlighted. Suggestions directed toward more effective investigation procedures and policy decisions are recommended.

It should be stated clearly at the outset of this chapter that the majority of Asian Americans and Asian immigrants are hardworking, productive, law-abiding citizens and people. Unfortunately, however, as is the case with all races and ethnicities, inevitably a small but problematic percentage will be involved in criminal activity. This chapter is directed toward the criminal activities of this small criminal minority.

Until the last few years, Asian gangs and Asian organized crime have been regarded as less than priorities when compared with other ethnic gangs and criminal organizations. This began to change in 1984 as a direct result of information presented by representatives of national and international law enforcement agencies via public hearings conducted concerning Asian organized crime by the President's Commission on Organized Crime (1986). Some law enforcement officials predicted that Asian organized crime would become the most serious organized crime problem of the 1990s (e.g., Butterfield, 1985).

Therefore, during the last 18 years or so, public and official attention has been more closely focused on the increasing levels of criminal activities by Asians. Certain areas in the United States have higher concentrations of Asian populations than others. The most obvi-

ous examples are New York City, San Francisco, Southern California, and Houston. Consequently, these areas reflect more serious levels
and frequency of Asian criminality. Increased
numbers of both legal and illegal Asian immigrants have resulted in the significant and rapid
growth of the Asian population in the United
States.

The rather limited literature and scientific
examination of Asian criminality in the United
States, as might be expected, tends to focus on
the large, urban Asian populations. Many me-
dium-sized and smaller communities, however,
are beginning to experience considerable Asian
population growth and criminal activity. As a
result, I have chosen to explore the above-
mentioned phenomena in a Midwestern city of
prominence, Chicago.

DEMOGRAPHICS

According to 1990 census figures, Chicago has
a population of 2,783,726. Of that total popula-
tion, 104,141 are listed as Asians and Pacific
Islanders. Only 1,046 of this figure are Pacific
Islanders, leaving a total Asian population in
Chicago of 103,095. For a breakdown of the
Chicago Asian population by nationality, see
Table 9.1.

METHOD

Because of the nature of the topic, this chapter
presents many obstacles that must be overcome.
The primary problem involves the fact that the
people involved usually prefer to protect their
criminal operations and organizations by intimidation, violence, and silence and by shroud-
ing themselves in secrecy. Additional problems
involve the fact that much of the crime occurring in Asian communities goes unreported and
that many Asian victims are reluctant to even
discuss criminal groups that operate in their
neighborhoods (Chin, 1990b). Also, reliable
available scientific data are limited. Much of the
available data must be considered incomplete,

TABLE 9.1 The Asian Population of Chicago

Nationality	Population
Chinese	23,233
Filipino	29,309
Japanese	6,865
Asian Indian	14,649
Korean	13,857
Vietnamese	4,200
Cambodian	1,572
Hmong	115
Laotian	567
Thai	1,952
Other Asian	6,776

SOURCE: U.S. Bureau of the Census (1990).

at best, because of a reluctance of law enforcement agencies to collect and classify crimes
according to ethnic background of the offenders, as well as the confusion over defining and
labeling crimes as "gang related" (Knox, 1994).

Therefore, much of the time, any attempt to
examine these topics must be approached
through indirect sources and methods. Information for this chapter was acquired through direct
observation, field notes, official reports and
documents, academic literature, and professional conferences and by personal interviews with reliable, knowledgeable, and confidential sources.

RESEARCH ISSUES

An initial issue that arises is defining and differ-
entiating organized crime from criminal gangs,
adult and/or juvenile. *Organized crime* is defined by the Omnibus Crime Control Act of
1970 as "the unlawful activities of the members
of a highly organized, disciplined association
engaged in supplying illegal goods and services, including, but not limited to gambling,
prostitution, loan-sharking, narcotics, labor racketeering, and other unlawful activities of members of such organizations."

At the risk of offering a basic and rather
oversimplified definition for *criminal gangs,* I

refer to *Merriam-Webster's 10th Collegiate Dictionary* (1993, p. 479) with "a group of persons working to unlawful or antisocial ends." Knox (1994) suggests that a *gang* is established when a group "exists for, or benefits substantially from, the continuing criminal activity of its members." He further states that it need not be income-producing criminal activities.

How does one differentiate between these two criminal groups? Part of the answer is dependent on the level of development of a criminal group. A criminal gang may include several elements that are shared in common with an organized crime group. Both are in the business of sustaining themselves and generating profits through criminal activity.

The major differences lie in the level of sophistication, organization, and capability. Aside from the more obvious involvement in crime, organized crime groups vary most significantly from gangs in their ability to engage in corruption and to penetrate legitimate businesses. Knox (1994) illustrates these points clearly via a "group/organization crime continuum." Indeed, Knox demonstrates the possible evolution of a "group" not initially identifiable as a gang and suggests intermediate formative stages through which some groups become criminal gangs and may eventually evolve into true organized criminal groups.

In this chapter, the above definitions are applied to the examination of issues involving Asian criminal activity in Chicago. The information in this chapter may or may not reflect similar situations and issues relative to Asian gang and Asian organized criminal activity in other areas and cities of the United States.

THEORY

I propose to establish that Asian organized criminal groups and Asian street gangs are operating in Chicago. I further suggest that Asian crime in Chicago is operant at two different, though related, levels via a synergistic relationship between Asian organized criminal groups and local Asian street gangs and that there are national and international links with criminal tongs and/or triads.

ASIAN ORGANIZED CRIME

In addition to other criminal activities, "most Asian Organized Crime groups traffic in drugs" (U.S. Congress, 1990). Chinese organized crime groups operate on both the East and West Coasts of the United States and are major figures in drug trafficking. They are the largest importers of heroin from Southeast Asia (Martin & Romano, 1992).

Asian organized crime appears to function on at least five levels. Level 1 involves international Asian organized crime groups. Chinese triads are known to be major bulk heroin traffickers operating out of Southeast Asia. Level 2 involves domestic organized crime groups. This level is represented by criminally influenced Chinese tongs that engage in "venture based" bulk heroin deals with Chinese triads. Level 3 involves criminal tong distribution of heroin to Asian street gangs. Level 4 involves criminal tong heroin distribution to other, non-Asian criminal groups. Level 5 involves local distribution.

Asian criminals active at the more sophisticated levels of organized crime tend to be more mature, more experienced, and more discreet in their criminal activities. Street gang criminals are younger, less experienced, and more overt in their activities and violence. A synergistic relationship exists between the two criminal groups and is illustrated in the following way: The domestic Asian organized criminal groups, support the street gangs with money, weapons, and the privilege of operating in various geographic areas, as well as a certain amount of security and protection. These services are offered in exchange for the street gang's loyalty, enforcement, security, and protection functions relative to the organized group's activities, including extortion, gambling, prostitution, and drug trafficking. Evidence also suggests that some Chinese triads, in particular the Wo Hop To of Hong Kong, have acquired direct influence over some San Francisco Asian street gangs (Bergman, 1990).

Triads are secret Chinese criminal organizations that originated in China as political organizations and, in turn, have evolved into criminal organizations, most of which are based in Hong Kong. Triads and other Asian criminals have connections to sources of Southeast Asian heroin from the Golden Triangle. Law enforcement agencies have established that triad networks of criminals provide conduits for a large percentage of the heroin coming into the United States. It is not difficult to grasp how the criminal connections lead right down to the Asian street gangs for distribution. Evidence also suggests that Chinese organized criminal groups act as middlemen or brokers for bulk quantities of heroin sold to other non-Asian criminal groups and street gangs for distribution.

Tongs are Chinese business associations. The two most well known tongs in Chicago are the Hongmen and the Hip Song. It should be emphasized that some tongs are legitimate business organizations. Some of the legitimate tongs, however, may have criminals among their members. Also, some tongs are dedicated criminal organizations involved in organized crime activities. Usually, only the leader of an Asian street gang has direct contact with a tong (Chin, 1990a).

GENERAL INFORMATION RELATIVE TO ASIAN STREET GANGS IN CHICAGO

According to my sources, Chinese gang activity does not appear to be as much of an "overt" crime problem as it was 5 to 8 years ago. Chinese community leaders have been working hard to promote Chicago's Chinatown as a safe area, free of gang influence and violence. It is portrayed as a place where anyone is welcome to visit, eat, tour, and do business. Chinatown appears to be a well-organized community, and its population is more homogeneous in that it is heavily Cantonese Chinese. This does not mean that Chinatown is crime-free, however.

Because of the "underground nature" of crime, it is suspected that activities still involve gambling, prostitution, protection rackets, extortion, and drugs in Chinatown. If this is the case, the Chinese criminals are very discreet and thereby avoid public and police attention. Some of the more established Chinese criminals are involved in organized crime and may be associated with tongs or triads. They may have worked their way up through street gangs over time to their current positions.

It appears that the Chicago Chinese are rather successful as far as keeping their children off the streets, out of gangs, and in school. For the most part, if a Chinese criminal entrepreneur has need of personnel for criminal activity or support (e.g., enforcers to protect gambling operations or collect debts), he or she tends to employ Vietnamese gang members.

The "Little Village," on the north side of Chicago, is a much more heterogeneous area with a population of Chinese, Vietnamese, Thai, Cambodians, Laotians, and blacks. This community appears to be considerably less organized and more dysfunctional.

Street Gang Membership

Gang membership can be very fluid, with individuals floating easily from one gang to another. In the past, criminal street gangs tended to be ethnically homogeneous. Currently, however, the movement appears to be toward ethnically mixed gang membership, as evidenced by the Chinese/Vietnamese and Cambodian/Laotian groups.

It appears that Asian gang affiliation among high school students generally fits the social formula involved in affiliation factors of other ethnic gangs (Wang, 1996). The organization, structure, values, and behavior, however, may be significantly different from those of other ethnic gangs.

It has been suggested that some Asian gangs should not be called gangs at all because they differ in so many ways from the behaviors that are used to define "gangs" in the United States. Examples include the lack of initiation practices like "jumping in" or the fluid nature of changing from one gang to another.

Despite this argument, it appears that at least some younger Asian criminal street groups are starting to identify with or copy traits of more traditional U.S. street gangs. One Chicago source suggested that some younger Asians are starting to Americanize in a negative way by emulating "gang bangers" in dress and attitude and are even selling rock cocaine on street corners. Perhaps this information ties in with the appearance of "new generation" Chinese criminal street gangs that have no ties or history with tongs or triad subculture and that are emerging in newly established Chinese communities (Chin, 1990a).

In terms of gender, members of Chicago Asian criminal gangs are primarily male. Some teenage girls are involved, but they are mostly gang members' girlfriends and fringe or hangers-on types.

Asian gang members in Chicago do not usually openly admit gang membership and therefore do not usually display colors, tattoos, and graffiti and thus identify "turf" or other practices, which is typical of the black or Hispanic/Latino gangs. This low-profile "gang affiliation" behavior is especially typical of Vietnamese gangs in other parts of the United States as well.

Structural and Dynamic Components

The highest concentrations of Asians tend to be in U.S. coastal regions such as California and New York, which also provide the initial arrival destinations for many Asian immigrants. Recruitment of street gang members is most successful among recent adolescent immigrants who have difficulty with the English language, fail in school, lack contemporary job skills, and experience difficulty with socialization (Chin, 1990a).

I suggest that Chicago's Asian community is smaller numerically and that Asian street gangs do not access the large adolescent immigrant recruitment pools. This results in smaller gangs

and comparatively less Asian criminal activity than found in the larger Asian population areas. The Asian criminal gangs in Chicago reportedly have 30 to 40 members, maximum. These represent the "hard core" members. There is also usually a contingency of inactive members and peripherals or hangers-on.

As mentioned, many Asian street gangs are so loosely structured that some experts hesitate to identify them as gangs. This is especially true of Vietnamese gangs. Chicago Asian street gang members tend to change their personal names and, in some cases, the names of the gangs frequently. Some gangs are short term or "venture based" and never take on a name. They do not usually have formal recruitment or initiation rites or turf to identify and defend, as is typical of the black and Hispanic/Latino street gangs. They usually do not have a problem with people who become inactive or who want to change groups.

Each gang may have one or several gang leaders. Even the title "leader" may be a misnomer if taken in the context of a disciplinarian giving, and followers executing, orders. One source explained that rather than have a formal leader, some gangs are more likely to follow a "person of strong personality." Also, it was stated that the "strong personalities" tend to emerge and recede within the gang over periods of time. Some leaders often tend to look out for and recruit their members by providing them with money, "crash pads," weapons, and so on. A group may form temporarily for one or more criminal activities as casually as they might team up for a neighborhood "pick-up" basketball game. Two or three individuals may conspire to target a victim, calculate that they need more people to do the job, and recruit these on the street or at the local pool hall. Often, they tend to know one another casually or by reputation, and that may be all the reference needed.

Types of Offenses

Most Asian street gangs tend to engage in a full range of criminal offenses, including murder, aggravated assault, simple assault, armed and unarmed robbery, various levels of larceny, gambling, loan-sharking, prostitution, protection rackets, extortion, robbery, smuggling, and drug trafficking. Some offenses are gang-generated at the street level, and some result directly from working for Asian organized crime groups. The types of offenses preferred may vary slightly from one ethnic group to another. These tendencies or preferences are illustrated by the fact that Vietnamese gangs tend to be involved in most of the home invasion robberies. The Fukienese Chinese are heavily into the smuggling and kidnapping of illegal immigrants. The Fukienese in Chicago have even been involved in a failed attempt to kidnap.

The Nature of Targeting Victims

Typically, Asian gangs and criminals tend to target their own communities and people as victims. Some evidence suggests, however, that their criminal activities are beginning to spill over into non-Asian neighborhoods and involve non-Asian victims (Chin, 1990b).

Asian gang members sometimes focus on business proprietors or Asians displaying wealth (e.g., by way of expensive cars, adornment with expensive jewelry) and engage in home invasion robberies. Many Asians do not trust banks and tend to keep large amounts of cash at home, thereby providing easy targets for criminals. Typically, the gangs "raid" the home, bursting in wearing ski masks and brandishing automatic weapons. The victims are threatened, intimidated, and sometimes tortured into telling where the money and valuables are hidden. Occasionally, these robberies may result in rape or murder of victims or both.

Asian gang members also tend to rob and extort Asian businesspeople. Some researchers suggest a connection or pattern to the behavior. Gang members often will offer protection to a business owner for a fee. If the owner refuses, then the same group later will harass or even rob the owner. Later, the owner is told that if he or she had paid the protection money, the gang could have "protected" the business from the robbery. The following study is a case in point.

A Case Study: Extortion

In 1990, a female Korean nightclub owner in Chicago was victimized by a Chinese gang led by Andrew Lee. Lee was known by the street name of "Kojak" because of his shaved pate. His gang members used a typical scam: They went into the business, started fights, and otherwise created disturbances that scared off customers. They would also sometimes eat, drink, physically tear up the place, and leave without paying. Then, Lee approached the owner and offered her, for a fee of $200 a week, protection from the "troublemakers." Eventually, she gave in and paid.

When Lee later tried to extort additional protection money from the club owner, she refused to be victimized any further and went to the police. A surveillance was set up by the gang task force outside and within the victim's club. Eventually, Lee returned to the club and the owner led him and a few of his cohorts into her office. After some small talk, she excused herself for a few minutes to allow the surveillance team to record any conversation by the suspects while she was not present. After she returned to the office, Lee was taped trying to extort more money from her. Charges were filed against Lee, but he died of natural causes before he could be brought to justice.

Many variables impede successful police investigation of these crimes, not the least of which is a reluctance or failure to report. Details of these issues are beyond the scope of this chapter, however, and remain subject to future investigation.

ASIAN GANGS ACTIVE IN CHICAGO

A few members of the Flying Dragons, a Chinese gang, are active in Chicago's Chinatown. These are primarily Fukienese connected with the New York branch of the Flying Dragons. Currently, there is no known activity in Chicago by the Chinese gang called Ghost Shadows, from New York City, whose origins date back to the 1970s (Chin, 1990b). Known Vietnamese gangs are the Flying Dragons, Local Boys, Wolf Boys, and the GAP "family."

The Cambodian/Laotian gang is called the Local Boy Bloods. They began to appear on the Chicago scene in approximately April of 1996. They are unique among Chicago Asian gangs in that they tend to resemble the black and Hispanic/Latino gangs as far as displaying gang affiliation by wearing bandannas, tattoos, and so forth.

The City Kings and the Akhroes are Filipino gangs. The Akhroes reportedly began as a school fraternity. However, they eventually became involved in the beating death of a Cambodian youth and other criminal activities. The Filipino gangs are reportedly hated by everyone, including the Southeast Asians, whom they refer to as "Gooks." For a listing of Asian street gangs by nationality that are currently active in Chicago, see Table 9.2.

GANG CONNECTIONS TO OTHER CITIES IN THE UNITED STATES AND ASIA

Investigating agencies have confirmed connections between Chicago Asian criminals and Asian criminals in other U.S. cities and Asia. One illustration is the connection between the Chicago Fukienese and the New York City Fukienese (Chinese Flying Dragons). Evidence also suggests that Chicago is a transit point for Asian heroin enroute from Seattle, Vancouver, and Calgary to New York City, Boston, Philadelphia, and Washington, D.C. The distribution route then goes to Houston, San Francisco, and Los Angeles (U.S. Congress, 1990).

DISCUSSION AND CONCLUSION

This chapter provides a preliminary examination of Asian crime in Chicago. I suggest that, although direct evidence may be minimal, the heroin trafficking patterns identified by federal, state, and local investigators would support the premise that Asian organized criminal activity

occurs in Chicago. Organized criminals are present, if for no other purpose than to support and facilitate the international transit of Southeast Asian heroin from the western United States and Canada to the eastern seaboard. In addition, Chicago police investigations substantiate incidents of extortion, gambling, prostitution, loan-sharking, and other crimes that typically represent organized criminal activities.

I have established that criminal Asian street gangs are active in Chicago and that they have connections with domestic and international Asian organized crime. I further suggest that Asian criminal activity in Chicago is currently less intense and more discreet than in the larger coastal cities with higher population concentrations of Asians. The characteristics of Asian crime in Chicago appear to involve more mature criminal organizations that hire Asian street gangs as Soldiers for security and other services. I also suggest that the more experienced criminal organizations prefer to keep a low profile to facilitate the smooth, uncomplicated transit of Southeast Asian heroin. This low profile is, in part, accomplished and maintained by using Asian street gangs for the more overt and violent aspects of criminal business.

Although Asian street gangs are fewer in number and generate lower numbers in criminal statistics when compared with Chicago's black and Hispanic/Latino gangs, they cannot be ignored or underestimated. Asian criminals—in particular, the Chinese criminals—are connected and instrumental in the transit of Southeast Asian heroin. In addition to being a transit city, Chicago is also a heroin distribution center for the Midwest (Grant, 1992).

This study has generated many additional issues and questions requiring further exploration and study. Further and more in-depth field studies are recommended. Policy decisions and adjustments, to be appropriate and effective, must be based on solid data. Government, social, and law enforcement agencies can assist with the collection and accumulation of data by amending their reporting processes to include pertinent information relative to all offenses involving Asians. Data must be collected

TABLE 9.2 Asian Street Gangs Currently Active in Chicago

Chinese	Vietnamese	Filipino	Multiethnic
Flying Dragons	Flying Dragons	City Kings	Local Boy Bloods (Cambodian/Laotian)
Fuk Ching	Local Boys Wolf Boys GAP Family	Akhroes	

NOTE: Data to compile this table were gathered from interviews with confidential sources.

concerning not only race but also culture and ethnicity (e.g., language, family, business/social contacts locally, nationally, and internationally).

Law enforcement agencies must continue to improve the classification and sharing of information and resources at all levels, domestically and internationally. The most prominent group of this nature in Chicago is the Asian Organized Crime Task Force, which involves the combined efforts of the FBI, the Chicago Police Department, and the Illinois State Police. Other cities with Asian or Chinese gang task forces are San Francisco, Los Angeles, Monterey Park (CA), New York, Vancouver, and Toronto.

Efforts should also be made to recruit Asian officers with skills in various languages and dialects. This recommendation is made, not so much for the purpose of increasing Asian victim reporting (which is desirable but involves complexities beyond the scope of this chapter), but for the purpose of infiltrating Asian criminal gangs and organizations to gather intelligence. American-born Asian and non-Asian law enforcement officers also need training in foreign cultures to overcome "culturally induced obstacles that can frustrate investigations and prosecutions" (Kelly et al., 1993).

Finally, as Asian criminal groups and activities increase internationally and in the larger U.S. coastal cities, the governments of smaller cities, including those in the Midwest, would be remiss not to expect and prepare for increased levels of Asian criminal activities in their areas.

10 BANDIT BANKS

Financial Services and Organized Crime

MAURICE PUNCH

The BCCI scandal revealed that international control of banks is lax and that governments, as well as organized crime, need the services of financial institutions. This author focuses on a precursor to BCCI by analyzing the case of Banco Ambrosiano in Italy. Roberto Calvi took Banco Ambrosiano to expansion and success; but in the process, he let organized crime infiltrate the bank for its own purposes. This act proved fatal, and he was murdered. The ensuing scandal exposed the involvement of the Vatican and implicated politicians, businesspeople, and secret services in a range of dubious and even criminal practices. The affair tended to be seen as an Italian scandal, but it should have been a forewarning that the "system" of international regulation needs reforming. In essence, banks are vulnerable to penetration by organized crime; a maze of offshore havens conceal control of companies and the trail of currency; and business, governments, and security services have an interest in not fundamentally altering the situation that led to the collapse of Banco Ambrosiano and, a decade later, the spectacular bankruptcy of BCCI.

The aura of respectability and reliability with which banks like to surround themselves will never be quite the same since the Bank of Credit and Commerce International (BCCI) was founded in 1972 and grew to be the seventh largest private bank in the world; when it collapsed in 1991, it was the biggest bank closure in financial history. In its 19 years of existence, it attracted and was used by terrorists, security services, drug barons, dictators, arms dealers, and devious businesspeople and politicians (Adams & Franz, 1992; Kochan & Whittington, 1991). The BCCI scandal exposed two important features of contemporary financial services. First, effective international regulation of banks operating cross-nationally is sporadic and ineffective. Second, governments and organized criminals *need* banks to perform covert and illicit services for them. These two elements were mercilessly revealed in the trials and publications surrounding BCCI. The affair attracted enormous publicity because it was played out

115

largely in the United States and the United Kingdom. It threw up an incredible cast of "folkdevils"—Marcos, Duvalier, Somosa, Saddam Hussein, the Medellin and Cali drug cartels of Colombia, and Manuel Noriega—that ensured widespread press coverage in the Anglo American media. This publicity tended to overshadow the fact that there had virtually been a dress rehearsal for BCCI some 10 years earlier. But the lessons had not been learned, and the signals had been largely forgotten.

I am referring to the case of Banco Ambrosiano and Roberto Calvi. This Italian banking scandal of the early 1980s demonstrated that organized crime had infiltrated the bank and that it pursued criminal ends by exploiting the loopholes in international financial regulation. In retrospect, it is not so surprising that this affair was treated as something of an extreme and untypical case and that every effort was made to restore confidence in the financial system. First, the legitimate interests of Italian commerce and industry were immense and needed to be protected from any loss of confidence in financial institutions. Second, and more important, we now know that Italian society was characterized by intimate and intricate links among business, politics, and organized crime. What was long suspected has emerged with stark clarity in the virtual political revolution that is changing the face of Italian society. The Mafia's attempt to intimidate the judicial authorities, with the brutal murders of two investigating magistrates, provoked a popular outcry that demanded a cleanup of public life. Many of the sinister and subterranean interconnections that have now been unearthed—of massive bribery, corruption in business and politics, and the omnipresent role of organized crime (in the north of Italy, and not just in its southern strongholds; and within legitimate firms, and not just in traditional criminal enterprises)—were evident in the Ambrosiano case. The judicial operation "Clean Hands" made an enormous impact as criminals, businesspeople, and politicians were arrested. But it took a substantial political earthquake to dislodge the deviant edifices of Italian society.

Two major explanations have been proposed for why the process of exposure was so prolonged. On the one hand, the weaknesses in international regulation of financial services are exploited to the full by legitimate companies seeking any financial or fiscal advantage that such opportunities provide. This makes it relatively easy for illicit enterprises to push those possibilities for criminal purposes. On the other hand, governments and security services need banks both for covert purposes and for tracking criminals and terrorists. Both of these elements tend to keep the weaknesses in the system from being effectively tackled. This perhaps helps in explaining why the Calvi case was conveniently seen as a typically "Italian" affair and swiftly forgotten. It took the truly spectacular exposure of the BCCI empire to push home the message that international regulations had proved powerless to prevent this massive fraud and that "reasons of state" may have prolonged the bank's life considerably (thereby duping thousands of depositors who might have saved their money if they had been informed in time).

In essence, the collapse of Banco Ambrosiano should have warned us that those staid cathedrals of capitalism, the banks, had become essential to organized crime and that it had proved all too easy to penetrate their sober and respectable walls. And, as a reminder of missed signals and as an example of a failure to learn, I present here the case study of Calvi and Banco Ambrosiano. It is rooted in Italian society, but it is also highly informative about the growing sophistication of organized crime and its manipulation of international financial services.

THE CASE:
MONEYLENDERS IN THE TEMPLE:
CALVI, BANCO AMBROSIANO,
AND THE VATICAN

"You can't run the Church on Hail Marys."

"I may be a lousy banker, but at least I'm not in jail."

(Statements attributed to Archbishop Marcinkus)

The Actors in
an Italian Scandal

The transformation of a leading Italian bank into a fraudulent financial empire, and its subsequent spectacular collapse, would undoubtedly have attracted considerable external attention in any event; but the case of the collapse of Banco Ambrosiano was truly exceptional. Its downfall brought to light a staggering cast of characters enmeshed in intrigue, secrecy, politics, and the underworld. It was called "one of the biggest things in Italian history, because everyone's involved" (Gurwin, 1984, p. xvii). Most startling of the revelations that emerged was a connection with the Vatican that induced worldwide interest.

Who were the major players? Archbishop Marcinkus headed the IOR (Instituto per le Operere di Religione; commonly known as the Vatican Bank), which was strongly linked with Banco Ambrosiano, and at one stage even faced a warrant for his arrest. Sindona was a highly successful banker, nominated by the American Club for the Man of the Year Award in 1974, who built up a web of fraud and falsification in international banking that earned him a 25-year prison sentence in the United States. He introduced Roberto Calvi, director of Banco Ambrosiano, to the Vatican Bank. Licio Gelli was an archmanipulator with strong right-wing sympathies who was associated with the Fascists, Klaus Barbie, Juan Perón, and Italian terrorists and who recruited an impressive cross section of the Italian elite into his P2 Masonic Lodge (among them, the banker Calvi). Flavio Carboni was a minor businessman, yet with strong connections to the underworld and extreme right-wing terrorism, and he accompanied Calvi on his last, fateful trip abroad. In the background was an incredible supporting cast that included politicians, military men, journalists, businesspeople, secret agents, and two popes—John Paul I and John Paul II (the former dying suddenly in circumstances that excited rumors of poison and coverup). Indeed, some key figures associated with the case were eliminated, whereas the more fortunate ones merely

had to nurse permanently stiff joints as a memento of the Banco Ambrosiano affair.

The main figure, however, was undoubtedly Roberto Calvi, who worked himself up from clerk to become head of Italy's largest private bank. At various stages, he became involved with Sindona, Gelli, Carboni, and the Vatican and began to construct a complex fraudulent network of companies abroad. After the bank came under increasingly intense scrutiny in 1982, Calvi fled to London and was eventually found hanging from some scaffolding under Blackfriars Bridge. An inquest jury brought in a verdict of suicide, but this was altered to an "open" verdict at a second inquest that indicated the death could have been caused by murder (an opinion widely held in Italy). Calvi bequeathed a bankrupt bank, the collapse of which represented the worst financial scandal in postwar Italian history and led to the exposure of a trail of devious and dubious connections within the highest echelons of society and, by implication, the Vatican. Shock waves reverberated throughout the international banking community.

The setting for this intricate and tantalizing drama was an Italian society that had recovered in near miraculous fashion from the rubble of war. The newly buoyant economy, however, was still faced with numerous prewar regulatory restrictions, but standards of auditing and accounting did not keep pace with developments. In addition, the small Milan stock market was easily manipulated by a few major players. Generally, commentators note that modern Italian society has been continually dogged by the lack of strong central government, by the favoritism of party politics ("clientelism"), by the failure of many regulatory and government agencies to implement effective legislation, and by behavior posited on "secrecy, back door, personal connection, special allegiances, private codes of honour and justice" (Johnson, 1983, p. 12), out of which grew the Mafia and its Neapolitan counterpart, the Camorra. Furthermore, it is maintained that the "amassing of personal fortunes by individuals, and the exploitation of public life for this end, is part of the fabric of Italian society"

(Johnson, 1983, p. 12). Italy is, then, a modern industrial democracy, yet a deep ambivalence runs right through institutional life in terms of a powerful hidden economy. The perception is that, to get things done, one needs access to submerged power, and that in some respects the structural weaknesses politically, economically, and socially are compensated for or manipulated by hidden societies and by the pious facade of religion.

The rich ingredients of the Calvi case, with interconnections among politics, terrorism, and the banking world, are not unique to Italy, as the BCCI scandal informs us. Ambition, connections, favoritism, and deviousness are also not monopolies of Italians. And yet the story of Banco Ambrosiano does strongly reflect certain elements of Italian society, and these have to be taken into account in placing the case in its proper cultural context. One essential factor, for instance, in explaining the prolonged success of the bank's dubious transactions lies precisely in the relationship between the Vatican as a sovereign state and Italian society. The Vatican's special diplomatic status and its otherworldly religious allure are a central component in explaining how a major financial institution could be taken over for criminal purposes, how it could be protected from effective intervention for such a long time, and how it could continue to outfox the international banking world.

The Bank and Calvi

Banco Ambrosiano was founded by a priest in 1896 as a Catholic bank aimed at counteracting the "lay," or non-Catholic, banks that in late 19th-century Italy were often associated with Freemasonry. It became known as the "priests' bank," and its stronghold was Milan, in the industrial north of Italy, far from Rome (the seat of political power) and even farther from the south and Sicily, where other norms applied and that was treated by northerners as virtually a separate country (with sayings such as "That's where Africa begins"). The bank was small, conservative, and solid. People had confidence in it.

Roberto Calvi joined Banco Ambrosiano in 1947 and made rapid progress up the hierarchy because of his capacity for hard work and because the industrious young man was fortunate enough to find a powerful patron in the chairman. His rise also coincided with the strong expansion of the Italian economy in the 1950s that provided new opportunities and that Calvi seemed able to anticipate with fresh, innovative plans. In 1963, for instance, a holding company was opened in Luxembourg that later became known as Banco Ambrosiano Holding (BAH) and that was to play a central role later in Calvi's schemes. The bank grew both domestically and internationally. In 1975, Calvi reached the top when he was elected chairman. Because of the religious origins of the bank and its connection with the Vatican, Calvi was colloquially referred to as "God's Banker."

By all accounts, Calvi was a highly gifted banker. At the same time, he is described as somewhat one dimensional in that he was aloof and secretive, lacking the silky skills of the traditional patrician bankers. He came from a modest background and retained a strong insecurity that was cloaked by reserve, coldness, suspicion, and secrecy. He never felt at home with his fellow Milanese bankers, not to mention the wheeling and dealing politicians of Rome, and he found solace within his close family circle. Some people even thought he was basically naive (Gurwin, 1984, p. 36). Ambitious he certainly was, and he set about transforming this sleepy, provincial bank into an international merchant-bank. In so doing, he attracted the attention, admiration, and fear of others; at the height of his power, he was described as the "most feared, hated and courted private banker in Italy" (Gurwin, 1984, p. xvi). Employees were proud of the bank's success, the press dubbed him dynamic and innovative (the only "real" banker in Italy), and he received an award for his contribution to the economy from the hands of the Italian president. On the surface, Calvi was a supremely successful banker representing the new generation of fresh-thinking entrepreneurs cast up by the country's economic revival. He could have enjoyed an outstanding career. Behind the scenes, however, in the heavily guarded and secretive enclave of his fourth-floor office at the headquarters building in Milan, Calvi had three concerns that ultimately led to his downfall and that of the bank he built up so assiduously.

First, the law was an obstacle to his plans. Restrictions were in force on the export of currency, and it was illegal for banks in Italy to own industrial companies. To realize his ambitions, Calvi had to bend the law. Second, he wanted personal control of the bank, and to ensure that no shareholders could challenge him, he devised a secret plan by which the bank would virtually own itself with shares that Calvi had "parked" in companies abroad. Third, and crucial, he felt vulnerable to interference from the world of government, with which he was not familiar and which he believed was dominated by shadowy cliques of powerful men. He became convinced that the real power in Italy was hidden—*potere occulto*—and that he had to insure himself against it.

To a certain extent, all Italians are aware of the existence and importance of hidden power, the *sotto-governo* (undergovernment). But to Roberto Calvi, a particularly insecure and personally isolated man, it became something of an obsession. He was convinced, says one banker, that "in the world, only a few obscure persons command and decide, and that it's important to have connections and friendships with these circles." Carlo Calvi (his son) said that his father "was fascinated by secret societies" (Gurwin, 1984, p. 36). Calvi came to dominate Banco Ambrosiano completely. Its board comprised deferential and compliant ciphers who followed his bidding and who rejoiced uncritically in its success. His ambition, however, brought him to bending the law to achieve his ends, whereas his isolation, insecurity, and ostensible naïveté led him to seek allies to negotiate and manipulate for him in those areas where he felt himself a clumsy stranger. The first "fixer" to spot Calvi's combination of flair and vulnerability was the banker Sindona.

Sindona

Sindona was a Sicilian (and, like Calvi, of modest origins) who was brought up with an empathy for those two vital and even interrelated institutions in southern Italy—the Church and the Mafia. He developed a powerful ambition for wealth, power, and connections. Sicilians traditionally like to think of themselves as "sly, nimble, quick-witted . . . to be naive is ultimately to be *fesso* . . . the opposite of *fesso* is *fuerto* or *scaltro*—the sly knowingness which is able to fox authority, to get things done, to bend rules" (Steinberg, 1989, p. 13).

Sindona set out to evade the country's banking, tax, and foreign-exchange controls in order to construct a financial empire based on companies in fiscal paradises, such as Luxembourg and Liechtenstein, through which he could operate on the Italian stock exchange. Basically, the idea was simple, and it was to be copied by Calvi later. Money circulated through a "shell" company abroad, to an offshore investment company, and then back into Italy. This enabled him to evade Italian laws and to smuggle millions of lire out of Italy. Sindona was like Calvi in possessing a "memory of steel, a swift imagination, and a capacity to keep a secret," but in contrast with Calvi, he was a good communicator with "charm, sparkle, humour" (Cornwell, 1984, p. 39). At home and abroad, Sindona was regaled as a great banker, a dynamic entrepreneur, and "the only financier in our country who has a modern and dynamic mentality: a modern vision of business" (Gurwin, 1984, p. 18). Giulio Andreotti (a former prime minister) even extolled him as the "savior of the lira."

In the rise of Sindona, ingredients and characters recur in the case of Calvi. Sindona cultivated the Vatican, turned to Licio Gelli to lobby for him, had underworld connections, and sought a mentorlike relationship with Calvi. In essence, Sindona built a fortune based on illegality. When one particularly ambitious Italian venture came to nought, however, he turned his attention to the United States and bought control of the Franklin National Bank. Basically, he was engaging in "enormous and reckless foreign exchange speculation and falsifying records to cover up the resulting losses" (Gurwin, 1984, p. 23). When his empire collapsed—the demise of the Franklin National Bank was the biggest failure in U.S. banking history—severe reverberations on the Milan Stock Exchange took several years to remedy, and the collapse contributed to the international financial crisis (that had followed the first oil crisis of 1973).

Sindona had offered Calvi his tutelage, his contacts, and his connection with the Vatican. But from being a widely feted banker, he had become bankrupt, facing criminal charges in Italy and in the United States. In 1974, warrants for his arrest on grounds of fraud and falsification were issued in Italy, but he fled to Taiwan. In his absence, he was sentenced to 3½ years in jail. Later, he received a 25-year prison sentence in the United States and was extradited to Italy, where he died in prison when poison was placed in his coffee.

The Vatican had its financial fingers severely burned by the collapse—there were reports of amounts varying from $30 million to $300 million—and the escapade, potentially so damaging to the Holy See's reputation, should have served as a severe warning. Yet, somehow the dubious connections among Sindona, the Vatican, Calvi, and Gelli did not prevent a similar scandal occurring a decade later. This is especially remarkable because Sindona himself actually helped open the can of worms about Banco Ambrosiano. In their relationship, Sindona clearly thought that they had strongly favored Calvi, and for a Sicilian, a favor implies an obligation; but when Sindona was in deep trouble, Calvi—and the Vatican—dropped him like a hot brick. Sindona then engineered a highly embarrassing rumor campaign in pamphlets and posters that displayed remarkably accurate information about Calvi's dubious share transactions and secret Swiss bank accounts. Apparently, Calvi paid off Sindona and the campaign ceased, but an even more potent barb had proved irreversibly damaging in that Sindona had sent a most compromising letter

for Calvi to the Italian Central Bank. In the aftermath of the Sindona scandal, it was likely that the regulatory authorities, to bolster international confidence in Italy's tarnished financial market, would mount a sharpened control campaign. And now the authorities had been alerted to the shadow side beneath the glitter of Banco Ambrosiano and Roberto Calvi.

The Vatican

The Vatican is a tiny state within a state, its 109 acres being considered sovereign territory. Although it enjoys a religious aura of piety and respectability as the focal center of the world's Catholics, it also has mundane preoccupations such as salaries for its staff and expenses for its upkeep. In the 1970s, it was in need of money for several reasons and sought alliances with bankers. A key figure in this development was Archbishop Marcinkus, a tall, sociable, sporty American who became a highly visible organizer of papal tours abroad and who took over the running of the IOR, the Vatican Bank. Much earlier, in the 1940s, the Vatican had enabled wealthy Italians to export capital, and the Vatican's status as a virtual domestic "offshore" haven soon made it attractive to businesspeople:

"IOR is the best off-shore bank you can think of," notes Umberto Venturini of the business weekly *Il Mondo*. "Instead of having the unsavoury reputation of a bank in the Caribbean, they have the moral backing of the Church. They are not answerable to any central bank governor, there's total secrecy—and no pope has ever been elected for his financial acumen." (Gurwin, 1984, p. 11)

In effect, people like Sindona and Calvi used the IOR as a conduit for moving currency out of the country in a way that evaded effective control. In turn, the Vatican took an increasing part in the network of foreign companies, with Marcinkus, as archbishop, actually sitting on the board of Banco Ambrosiano Overseas. The obsessive secrecy of the Vatican, allied with its privileged status outside Italian law, means that accurate information on the actual workings of the IOR is meager; but it later emerged that the Vatican owned a string of ghost companies that were at the center of the Ambrosiano scandal. At one stage, when Calvi's world was tottering in 1981, he approached Marcinkus for support and received "letters of comfort," which have no legal status but which were used to reassure some anxious bankers abroad. In a sense, this prolonged the impending collapse that outraged some creditors who might have got off more lightly if the debts had been exposed earlier. Marcinkus issued them in return for a letter from Calvi, absolving the Vatican of financial responsibility for any subsequent claims. When the scandal broke, the Vatican denied knowledge of the ghost companies. Later, it emerged that the Vatican owned Manic SA of Luxembourg and at least 16 ghost companies. (Calvi's son accused the Vatican of a "blatant lie" and even maintained that the Vatican was the real owner of Banco Ambrosiano; Gurwin, 1984, p. 172.) This news was potentially enormously damaging to the Vatican. The embarrassment was heightened by the arrest warrant issued against Marcinkus in 1987 for "fraudulent bankruptcy" (*Time,* 1987, p. 27). The Vatican refused to accept the warrant, and for a period, the archbishop remained confined within the Vatican's precincts. Later, the warrant was declared invalid by the highest judicial organ in Italy, against which no further appeal is possible (De Volkskrant, 1987). Although the exact figures have never been published, it appears that the Vatican paid some $250 million as part of a settlement that enabled the Italian government to sign a new concordat with the Vatican state in 1984. Marcinkus's career was irretrievably damaged. He was not made a cardinal, no longer accompanied the pope on his travels, and eventually resigned from the IOR in 1989.

The Vatican had been involved in two major financial scandals involving Sindona and Calvi. It had been revealed as the owner of a string of tiny companies that had run up massive debts. Suggestions were made that some of the secret financial deals involved Solidarity, the Polish trade union, and had potential implications for East-West relations. The Vatican's response was one of pained innocence: It had been taken for a "colossal ride," and its "sins were those of naivety and inexperience" (Cornwell, 1984, p. 229). In effect, it had been duped by Calvi. But there can be no doubt that the Vatican had allowed itself to be used for criminal purposes in two successive scandals and had left an unhealthy impression of secrecy, deviousness, and even duplicity. For some, the Vatican had simply been a knowing accomplice to fraud (Cornwell, 1984, p. 247) and had opened itself to charges of aiding and abetting criminals.

Gelli and the P2

Licio Gelli was one of these slippery power brokers who emerged to lubricate the Byzantine world of Italian politics. He was a past master at *sotto potere* (hidden power) based on information and contacts; and he was associated with intelligence agencies, Latin American dictators and death squads, arms dealing, and right-wing terrorism. His dubious reputation as an archmanipulator earned him the nickname "Puppet Master" (Gurwin, 1984, p. 53; Willan, 1991). He was associated first with Sindona, and then he embraced Calvi. While investigating Gelli's relationship with Sindona, the authorities unearthed a membership list of the P2 Freemasons Lodge, of which Gelli was Grand Master. He had proved able to draw in 962 prominent people whose names, when made public, staggered even the Italian public, who are reared on a juicy diet of scandals.

Over a period of about ten years Gelli was able to recruit to his most secret of secret lodges in Italy, three Cabinet ministers, 40 MPs, the head of every branch of the Armed Services, the head of the Intelligence Services, and senior officers in banks and corporations, who between them gave access to and, information being a form of power, some control over an enormous array of deals, contracts, preferments, and appointments. (Moorehead, 1984, p. 19)

Roberto Calvi was on the list. He seems to have been initiated into the lodge by Gelli in 1975, and at some stage he started paying him. Gelli had powerful friends in almost every area of public and economic life and could valuably lobby to protect Calvi's interests. But at a price. For there was an element of blackmail, and even of a massive protection racket, in his dealing with people, and the "protector" of Calvi soon became his manipulator. Gradually, Calvi was drawn into a web that ensnared him in increasingly dubious transactions that saw Banco Ambrosiano money flow to Latin America and be slushed to Italian political parties (allegedly to the tune of 88 million lire) and to the Swiss bank accounts of Gelli. The Puppet Master had found another victim.

Gelli fled Italy in 1981 when his secret files were uncovered. Later, disguised and with a false passport, he personally attempted to transfer $100 million from one of his Swiss bank accounts and was arrested and imprisoned to await extradition. He escaped from the allegedly "escape-proof" prison of Cham Dollan near Geneva by bribing a guard and with the help of a helicopter hired by the arms dealer Adnan Kashoggi (De Volkskrant, 1990). It was hinted that some members of the Italian secret services were involved in the rescue and that later, in France, Gelli was protected from arrest at the hands of pursuing Italian officials by elements of the French secret services. The Italian authorities now formally acknowledged a link between the P2 and Banco Ambrosiano and that Gelli was in possession of $100 million of Ambrosiano money (Gurwin, 1984, p. 165). After several years in Latin America, Gelli gave himself up to the Swiss authorities in 1987. In Italy, he has been sentenced to 18 years in prison for offenses that included involvement in the "blood bath" of Bologna, in which 85 people were killed by an explosion at the railway station in 1980. Because of "heart trouble," he was released provisionally from prison. Some sources maintain that this is the result of his continuing influence. Many of those mentioned in the P2 list still hold high office. Indeed, it is even insinuated that he has set up a new P2 and protests in his autobiography—The Truth

[*sic*]—that P2 was legal and respectable (De Volkskrant, 1990).

Gelli represents the dark and sinister side of Italian society, and his influence on Calvi was malign. The isolated and insecure banker, ambitiously determined to protect his empire, was vulnerable to an unscrupulous manipulator who drew Calvi deeper and deeper into intrigue and illegality.

Front for Crime

Until the early 1970s, Calvi had advanced his own career and built up Banco Ambrosiano in ostensibly impeccable fashion. There was no evidence of criminal practices. But in his desire to seek external protection and to realize his continuing ambition, Calvi sought the company of people like Sindona and Gelli—and later Carboni—who had strong connections with illicit business deals and even with the underworld. In effect, Calvi allowed Banco Ambrosiano to be appropriated for criminal ends. It began with the Sindona-Vatican connection and led to an intricate international network of deception. Like Sindona, Calvi set up holding companies in Luxembourg and Liechtenstein, where supervision was weak and the Italian Central Bank had no authority. There was a chain of holdings, subsidiaries, and ghost companies in Zurich, New York, and Nassau, and Nicaragua, Panama, and other Latin American countries. The holdings sprouted a profusion of shell companies with strange-sounding names— they were "little more than an entry in a lawyer's books" (Cornwell, 1984, p. 70)—that were managed by Calvi but owned by the IOR, which put the companies beyond Italian scrutiny. On paper, they were worth millions of dollars, but they could be started with a token capital of $10,000. For instance, "Andino," in Peru, contained "assets" of $890 million in 1980, but its board meetings were held in Switzerland or Luxembourg, whereas decisions were effectively made in Milan. Several ghost companies' directors were Ambrosiano employees, among them the telephone operator at a Bahamas bank

(Cornwell, 1984, p. 34). The basic tactic was simple:

> Calvi would purchase Italian shares and then re-sell the shares to a foreign company secretly controlled by him. He would then buy the shares back at an artificially high price. The result: several million dollars have been smuggled overseas in violation of Italy's foreign exchange control laws. (Gurwin, 1984, p. 20)

The essence was to conceal, to control, and to evade regulations. This enabled Calvi to buy into Italian companies against the law, to manipulate the stock exchange, to illegally strengthen his own company, and to create opaque channels for illicit transactions probably related to arms, drugs, terrorism, and bribes. In this high-risk game, two issues were crucial. One was that the authorities should not be able to uncover who had real control; the other was that there had to be a measure of sound financial decision making behind the deceptive facade to ensure that economic reality would not eventually intrude to thwart the banker's intricate constructions.

Three factors contributed to Calvi's downfall and the bank's demise. First, Calvi used illegal transactions to gain control of two banks and a large insurance company in Italy (a deal in which Sindona and the Vatican were involved). Second, and again using the Vatican as cover, he spirited some 15% of the shares of Banco Ambrosiano through his overseas maze out of the country at a cost of $60 million, giving him control of the bank. Third, Calvi was induced to buy into the Rizzoli media group, which published the influential daily newspaper *Corriere della Sera*. This deal originated with Gelli and the search for influence and political clout even though this involvement in a newspaper was illegal. Indeed, Calvi stated, "All my problems began when I bought Rizzoli," and Gurwin (1984, p. 54) maintains "in making the loan to the ailing Rizzoli company Calvi had violated every principle of prudent banking." All three could have got Calvi into trouble, perhaps not of such a catastrophic kind, but in a sense the

perfidious influence of exploitive figures in his career led Calvi to increasingly take decisions that should have been directly opposed to his banking acumen.

Somewhere along the line, Calvi had started paying money to those devious people in his life. There were "commissions," loans, bribes, and questionable transactions that no one at the bank really dared to question. Millions were funneled away to obscure destinations (and, after the collapse, some $400 million remained unaccounted for). Was Calvi fully conscious of what he was doing, or had he lost control and was he in the grip of people who were squeezing him? As each shady figure passed on—first Sindona and then Gelli—another one seemed to be ready to take his place. Thus did Flavio Carboni appear, and he inveigled himself into Calvi's confidence. Carboni had some very tough companions, and Rosone (second man of the Banco Ambrosiano) said, "These people make you afraid just by looking at them." Rosone received gunshot wounds in the legs that reinforced his point (his attacker turned out to be an underworld figure who was then shot by bodyguards and who had been sent by Carboni to act as a "frightener"; Gurwin, 1984, p. 86). Later, it turned out that Calvi had paid Carboni around $14 million, but precisely for what remained obscure. Calvi not only was keeping bad and dangerous company, but some of his illicit schemes were also on the point of unraveling.

The Regulatory Response

To a large extent, the machinations of Sindona and Calvi were made possible by the weaknesses of the regulatory mechanisms in Italy: The small Milan Stock Exchange was easily manipulated, the banking and currency regulations were not difficult to sidestep, and the Italian Central Bank was powerless to investigate the Vatican's IOR and shell companies abroad—and, of course, by the structural opportunities offered by the nearly uncontrollable network of offshore financial institutions. For instance, although the Luxembourg holding was called a "bank," it was not one, and consequently the Luxembourg banking authorities were not empowered to control it. The increasing linkage of formal financial markets, however, meant that Italian scandals could have rapid and severe international consequences while the Italian economy needed a measure of stability and confidence to attract capital. In the mid-1970s, the lira was in difficulties, the country faced mounting deficits and high inflation, and the Communist Party grew in strength, which brought a stronger left-wing influence in the political spectrum. One measure that was passed, designed to stem the flow of illegal currency exports, was Law 159, which criminalized the offense and, crucially, made its enforcement *retrospective*. The aftermath of the Sindona affair, moreover, was bound to bring parliamentary and press attention and a revived regulatory alertness.

Increasingly, indications were that Banco Ambrosiano warranted investigation. Sindona's venomous letter to the Central Bank had sowed the seed of distrust. The Bank of Italy, responsible for the supervision of about 1,000 banks, is a professional and highly respected institution. In 1978, it sent 12 inspectors to Banco Ambrosiano. The bank's subsequent 500-page report was scathingly critical. In brief, it displayed concern about lack of information, weaknesses that could affect other banks, suspicions on the chain of control, the weakness of the organizational structure, the level of undercapitalization, breaches of the banking laws, and "supine and acquiescent auditors"; and it concluded with the necessity for restructuring the bank (Cornwell, 1984, p. 91f). Two breaches of the currency regulations were attributed to Calvi personally, and this information was passed on to the judiciary. At this stage, the regulators were closing in on Calvi and the bank.

Then a most disturbing episode occurred. The military-style police, the *Carabinieri,* entered the Central Bank and arrested the principal inspector for the Banco Ambrosiano case on the grounds that he had concealed evidence in another inquiry. Only the advanced age of the

governor saved him from a similar humiliation. Given that banks in Italy are all connected to political allies, and tough inspection will elicit enemies, it can only be assumed that this was a "counter-attack to teach the bank a lesson" and the "inspector had been muzzled" (Cornwell, 1984, pp. 99, 101). Inevitably, this gross interference in the investigatory wing of a central bank in a major European country brought powerful protests from home and abroad. The various charges were dropped, and the officials concerned were later rehabilitated.

This crude warning to the Bank of Italy only meant a stay of execution for Banco Ambrosiano. For within a short time, the authorities had regained their confidence and were prepared to launch an assault on the financial world when 38 bankers were arrested in 1980 in relation to a savings bank scandal. The financial police, the *Guardia di Finanza,* also turned up at Banco Ambrosiano, demanded the surrender of Calvi's passport, and warned him that criminal charges were imminent on the grounds that he had failed to report share dealings as demanded in Law 159. This restriction on his movements must have been a severe psychological blow to Calvi, who was used to attending the key meetings of the international banking world. In addition to stricter regulations and controls related to the declaration of interests held by Italian banks abroad, a new regulatory regime was ensconced at the Milan Stock Exchange, where the supervisory committee (CONSOB) was pushing under new leadership for consolidated balance sheets, the disclosure of true share holdings in quoted companies, and other trading rules as found elsewhere in Europe (Cornwell, 1984, p. 130). All these were signals that the regulatory net was tightening around Calvi. The pressure increased on him in 1981 when it was revealed that he was a member of a secret society (the P2 Lodge) and when it emerged that he was improperly involved in a newspaper and had also broken currency regulations. Calvi was arrested and spent 2 months in jail, which proved shattering for this very private man. He even attempted suicide, although this was interpreted by some as merely a tactic to generate sympathy for his plight. But he was exposed as vulnerable to pressure, and under interrogation he had declared himself ready to reveal names with regard to politics, the IOR, and the P2 ("I'm just the last wheel on the cart," said Calvi, "try to understand, *Banco Ambrosiano* is not mine. I'm simply in the service of someone else . . ." Gurwin, 1984, p. 74).

Although he retracted much of his statements, this episode may nevertheless have alerted his "good friends" to his weakness and to the threat he posed if he should talk. He was sentenced to 4 years in prison and was fined 16 billion lire but was released on appeal. The board at the bank then reconfirmed his position unanimously; and thus, a man with a criminal conviction hanging over his head went on running the largest private bank in Italy!

The Roof Caves In

From his conviction onward, Calvi was a man trying to stave off the inevitable. The Vatican Bank helped out with the "letters of comfort" but would assume no financial liabilities. There was a short-lived involvement of Carlo de Benedetti, the dynamic entrepreneur who had revitalized Olivetti, but he left after 65 days, complaining of a "wall of rubber" and airing his grievances to the Bank of Italy. When the first full disclosure on the Milan Stock Exchange came, the stocks of Banco Ambrosiano declined precipitately. Rosone, the deputy chairman of the bank, was shot at in the street. And, very significantly, Calvi was, for the first time, defeated at a boardroom vote. Soon afterward, he was smuggled out of the country. News of his disappearance set off a landslide, and Rosone said later, "Banks deal in confidence, and we just ran out" (Cornwell, 1984, p. 186).

It soon became clear that Banco Ambrosiano was bankrupt, and appeals for a rescue to the IOR fell on deaf ears. In his absence, Calvi was stripped of his powers, the Central Bank was notified, and Banco Ambrosiano was placed in the hands of commissioners. Calvi's secretary jumped to her death from a window in the bank building. Inevitably, some skeptical Italians

asked whether she was perhaps helped on her way.

London

Calvi left Italy in the company of some rather unsavory companions, and via a circuitous route he arrived in London. He had once more talked of revealing all, of naming names, and of implicating the Vatican. He warned his family to get out of Europe and to go into safe hiding; he told them, "Something really important is happening, and today and tomorrow all hell is going to break loose" (Cornwell, 1984, p. 196). With him was always a black briefcase containing his most secret documents. On June 18, 1982, his body was discovered hanging from scaffolding under Blackfriars Bridge. His body was partly immersed in the Thames, and his pockets were filled with money and stones. There were possible elements of Masonic symbolism in the manner of his going. Much later came indications of Mafia involvement, suggesting that Calvi was considered dangerous in that he was threatening to reveal too many secrets, and accordingly, he was expertly strangled and left hanging on the scaffolding ("Breakthrough," 1991). Once more, the Italian pattern of potential witnesses being prevented from disclosing unpleasant truths had been repeated; and Calvi's black bag had disappeared (a bishop was indicted in Italy on charges of receiving stolen property in relation to buying back from criminals potentially incriminatory documents for the Vatican; "Breakthrough," 1991). During this period, Calvi was accompanied by Carboni and some of his cronies. Carboni was later arrested and charged with several crimes, including involvement in the shooting of Rosone (presumably because he was getting too inquisitive). Calvi spent his last days as a fugitive, in the company of criminals. On the eve of his death, he informed his daughter that

he was on the verge of completing it (a deal)—and that it could solve all his problems. "Things are going ahead slowly," he said, "but they are moving. . . . A crazy marvelous thing is about to explode which could even help me in my appeal. It could solve everything." But the conversation also contained an ominous note: "I don't trust the people I'm with any more." (Gurwin, 1984, p. 117)

The next day, the man who was once hailed as Italy's leading banker was ignominiously dangling from scaffolding with a rope around his neck, not far from one of the world's major financial centers, the city of London. The career of "God's Banker" had come to a sad and violent end.

The Mess

The dimension of the collapse that emerged after these dramatic events was on a scale that threatened to severely damage international confidence in Italy's financial institutions. The Luxembourg holding company was revealed to have a loss of $1 billion and total debts in the order of $1.2 billion. It was now clear that Banco Ambrosiano was facing a terminal crisis of both solvency and liquidity. A spate of lawsuits among the various parties involved in the crash followed. The Bank of Italy, for instance, refused to honor all the debts because much of the activity of Banco Ambrosiano took place in areas where the Bank of Italy had no control. A rescue attempt by a consortium of Italian banks failed. The Vatican sanctimoniously denied any responsibility for the debacle, but it did take the unprecedented step of appointing three "wise men" to investigate the Vatican's financial operations. Later, the Vatican was forced to admit that it owned a string of tiny companies that owed Banco Ambrosiano some $1.1 billion. A joint commission of Italian and Vatican experts also began an inquiry, and the Italian team became convinced that the Vatican had been a knowing accomplice to fraud (Cornwell, 1984, p. 247). The Italian government sought a political agreement with the Vatican on long-standing issues and the IOR scandal, but the Vatican's still vehement denial of responsibility stood in the way of a settlement. In 1984, a concordat was signed between the Italian government and

the Vatican after years of delicate negotiations, and it was preceded by a settlement among the Vatican, the Italian authorities, and 120 foreign creditor banks. The $250 million contribution from the Vatican toward claims amounted to a virtual admission of responsibility.

COMMENT

In this country, everything depends on the "good friends"; my "good friend" is sure that you will get the job you want, so you can go ahead and apply for it. This is our way of doing things. This is our mentality. In other words the Sindona, P2 and Calvi scandals are products of a mentality and a system. As a government official puts it: "Unless we change the rules of the game, another Calvi can be born." (Gurwin, 1984, p. 199)

The complexities and multiple layers of the Calvi affair almost beggar analysis; but it tells us something about international banking, Italian society, personal ambition, and the shadowy, interlocking world of politics, finance, religion, terrorism, drugs, organized crime, arms smuggling, right-wing regimes, and secret services. And it reveals that certain segments of banking are indispensable conduits for the dubious and hidden transactions of the underworld, and the "upperworld," to the extent that even a respectable and thriving bank can become a criminal institution.

Financial Structures

The key to the schemes of Sindona and Calvi lies in the convoluted network of "offshore" tax havens that evade external control, impose minimal internal inspection and external auditing, and espouse secrecy as fervently as Switzerland. In Europe (Luxembourg and Liechtenstein), the Caribbean, and Latin America, there are possibilities for legitimate business—but also for crooks and government agencies engaged in crooked business—to seek maximum fiscal advantage with a minimum of supervision. The consciously created loopholes and inviting weaknesses in the international banking system are central to this case, which illustrates the "ease with which a natural deceiver could exploit the opportunities offered" by that "system" (Cornwell, 1984, p. 248).

Italian Society

The context for this drama was a postwar Italian society that experienced a fluctuating economic recovery from the war, a long period of political instability (left- and right-wing terrorism; the murder of Aldo Moro, a former prime minister), and several scandals that brought down governments (e.g., the Lockheed affair of the early 1970s, the oil scandal of the late 1970s). Everything in the country—favors, jobs, contracts, and protection from interference—depends on the shifting bases of power among the contending political parties. Their absorption in negotiation and manipulation and in reaping the fruits of their favors almost precludes a strong, serious, and responsible central government (so Italy is sometimes referred to as a "blocked democracy" and the stranglehold of the parties on public life as "partyocratie"; *NRC Handelsblad,* 1991).

Also at work is a very powerful duality running through Italian society between the surface "front" presented to the outside world and a submerged world where the "real" business is conducted, in the underground economy (*economica sommersa*), in the hidden power structure (*sotto potere*), in secret groups (*potere occulto*), and in the underworld (*malavita*). Notorious examples of the latter are the criminal organizations of the Mafia and Camorra, which reflect and propagate widely held notions of honor, secrecy, silence (*omerta*), and revenge. This means that, in Italian society, nothing is quite what it appears to be and that public figures have to engage in constantly shifting and intricately subtle role playing.

Personal Motives

The Calvi case is almost a Faustian morality play related to power, ambition, and greed. Sindona, Calvi, and Marcinkus were all highly ambitious. The first two decided at some stage that illegality was necessary for them to achieve their ends; the archbishop, either naively or cunningly (depending on one's interpretation of his motives and behavior), acquiesced in rule bending. Probably, the trio could have had successful and unblemished careers by following legitimate paths, but they clearly wanted more than those paths offered. In terms of criminal careers and of identifying potential criminal behavior in business, it is important here to note that Sindona and Calvi were internationally respected bankers with whom many major banks were only too willing to do business and who were regaled as geniuses (even as saviors of the economy) and as daring innovators. Their strategy was to employ a solid, respectable facade behind which they constructed a fraudulent empire, and they were able to conceal that criminal core until a very late stage in their careers. Until exposed, they were identical to successful, straight bankers and indistinguishable from them. To take the concept of "career" a little further, the case has an element of adoption and tutelage in that Sindona took Calvi under his wing and taught him the financial wizard's bag of tricks; when Calvi was looking for "good friends" to protect him in places of power and influence, he soon found Gelli, and later Carboni, courting him to provide their services. Calvi's ambition led him to illegality and to keeping bad company because he became a captive of the people and processes that came to dominate the hidden part of his existence. In those circles, "friendship" tends to be conditional, manipulative, and exploitive; Sindona went from mentor to bitter enemy, Gelli from protector to blackmailer, and Marcinkus from ally to a Pilate, washing his hands of responsibility. At the end, Calvi—"a stiff, formal man with a highly developed sense of conspiracy, fascinated by secret societies and the occult"— had become a victim of his own ambitions, his own suspicions, and his own compatriots. He lived in a "continuous passage from one bunker to another," from armored car to fortified building, surrounded always by bodyguards (Moorehead, 1984, p. 19). He was the captive of forces he could not control.

Global Multinationals of Crime

Calvi claimed at times to be only a small cog and that others controlled him. In his story, one often gets the feeling that beyond the visible antics of the well-known players is a much deeper, sinister web of connections that somehow interlinks the worlds of finance, politics, religion and ideologies, the media, terrorism, arms smuggling, drug trafficking, secret services, right-wing regimes, and organized crime. It is an area that is obviously difficult and dangerous to investigate, and it is open to the wildest of fantasies and conspiracy theories. Here, one can only touch on the subject and hint of characters and connections in this case that raise disturbing but nearly impenetrable questions. These are related to the death of Pope John Paul I (was it because he was investigating the IOR?); the Catholic Church's aims in Eastern Europe and Latin America; the support of dictatorial regimes and the direction of their death squads; the sale of Exocet rockets to Argentina via the illicit arms market at the time of the Falklands/Malvinas crisis; the activities of extremists in Western espionage agencies (with or without covert political support); and the activities of left- and right-wing terrorists and the support they derive from governments and/or politicians in the East and West. And then there are the new "multinationals" of crime—the old, agrarian criminal societies such as the Mafia, which have grown into sophisticated corporations with extensive global tentacles—who profit from this finance-politics-international crime nexus because they are of value to both sides of the ideological divide and will operate as dealer, trafficker, launderer, pimp, bag man, intimidator, burglar, or executioner.

Religion

Bishops are not supposed to frequent brothels, and it is strange here to find prelates, archbishops, cardinals, and even popes becoming entangled in financial intrigues. But the Vatican is a sovereign state, with instrumental ends and mercenary needs. The heightened activities of the Catholic Church in the 1970s created a demand for funds, and the Vatican does own a bank. So religion is an essential thread running through this case. Banco Ambrosiano had been born as the "priests' bank" in terms of promoting Catholic against lay banks; its statutes required shareholders to produce evidence of their baptism and a recommendation from a priest; and it became intimately interlocked with the Vatican. And it was precisely that connection, between high and sometimes dirty finance and the money needs of the Holy See, that added such a powerful element to the scandal. In effect, the Catholic Church had been involved in crime, and its protection had enabled Calvi, and before him Sindona, to build criminal empires. There is no doubt that the reputation of the Vatican was severely tainted by all this, and its obtuseness, secrecy, denials, deviousness, calculative delays, and slippery evasion of responsibility clashed starkly with its otherworldly moral ethos. The machinations of Sindona, Calvi, and Marcinkus could not have taken place if the IOR had been run as a proper bank. Behind the walls and holy aura of the Vatican, the IOR operated as an offshore bank, beyond Italian supervision and auditing, which employed the shield of religion, the preeminence of the pope, and the immunity of its sovereign state to provide opportunities for criminals, to protect them from control, and to deny any responsibility for the consequences.

Control

I wish to touch here on three aspects of control. First, the regulatory context of the case is embedded in postwar Italian society where the expansion of the economy was not matched by equivalent developments in legislation. Some control measures dated from before the war and were designed to deal with different circumstances. Later, they were hindrances to businesspeople who operated under more restrictive measures than elsewhere in Europe. In a sense, the failure to match legislation and control with the developments in the economy and with mechanisms in use elsewhere meant that Italian businesspeople were encouraged to bend the law to get things done while, at the same time, they could easily avoid supervision. Second, it is clear that Calvi was preeminent at Banco Ambrosiano and that there was no real internal curb on his activities. The board was servile, meetings were a ritual, and no one questioned his authority or his decisions. There was no effective control by board, shareholders, or accountants that might have checked his absolute power, particularly when his decisions began to stray from sound banking logic. Third, external control was revealed to be amenable to political persuasion and interference. The most notorious example was the punitive raid on the Bank of Italy to "muzzle" it. The magistrature, particularly in Rome, was also shown to be prone to bend under external pressure. In addition, CONSOB, the supervisory organ of the Milan Stock Exchange, failed conspicuously to curb the manipulation of the market. In brief, the regulatory environment could be said to have stimulated rule bending and to have proved incapable of exerting effective control of financial markets. This was exacerbated by Calvi's total dominance at Banco Ambrosiano, which simply subverted internal control, and by an external control structure that was vulnerable to political interference.

Victims

The crimes of Calvi created undoubted victims. There were the 40,000 creditors of Banco Ambrosiano who had been encouraged to invest in the bank; the employees (a much reduced in size, new Banco Ambrosiano was resurrected from the old one); and the many foreign creditors who had been "burned" and who found the Bank of Italy and the Vatican reluctant to help them. Then there were the opponents, critics, journalists, magistrates, and regulators who faced humiliation, intimidation, injury, and even death if they were too inquisitive or too energetic. Threats, blackmail, and violence run

darkly through the case and are significant aspects of trying to unearth deviance in Italian society. Finally, there was Calvi himself, who paid with his life for his involvement with Sindona, Marcinkus, Gelli, Carboni, and with some shadowy figures from the underworld. His initially brilliant career ended with him as a fugitive, scuttling across Europe, and with a faked suicide that spelled out a warning to all those who threatened to lift the veil on certain powerful, underground forces: It can cost you your life.

The Media

The subterranean activities of politicians, officials, and businesspeople may be partly checked by revelations in tough, independent, and investigative media that are not open to external influence and manipulation. Calvi was able to own, illegally, the most influential newspaper in the country, and Gelli had journalists tied up in his P2 network. After the scandal journalist Mino Pecorelli published incriminating stories on Gelli's past, he was murdered within hours (Gurwin, 1984, p. 64). One element of control, an independent and fearless media, was difficult to operationalize in Italy.

Trust and Confidence

A major "victim" of substantial financial crises is confidence in the international system linking banks and in the banks themselves. The international system and its outlet in stock exchanges and markets is a highly sensitive and delicate instrument that is sometimes all too responsive to various political and industrial tremors. The so-called secondary banking crisis following the first oil crisis of 1973 was definitely exacerbated by the Sindona scandal. The collapse of the Franklin Bank in 1974 was the biggest default in U.S. banking history, and the Federal Deposit Insurance Corporation (FDIC) was forced to fork out $2 billion in compensation. Calvi and the Banco Ambrosiano affair severely dented the reputation of the Milan Stock Exchange, undermined confidence in

Italian financial institutions, and even had international repercussions. The Milan Stock Exchange lost 4 trillion lire, then around $3 billion, in what was called the "Calvi effect"; the Bank of Italy had suffered severe loss of face; and in the early 1980s the world banking community once more faced a spate of bleak news related particularly to the growing foreign debt issue. Then the exchange was hit by the Banco Ambrosiano crisis, which was one of the largest bank failures since the war (Gurwin, 1984, p. 78); and as Rosone stated, "A bank sells confidence, only confidence."

Finally, the case reveals the convoluted, multilayered aspects of a complex, major scandal. Of course, it is a story of greedy men and overweening ambition, but it is also a lesson about finance, politics, and regulation in the rich cultural context of postwar Italian society. The roles were played out, and the script enacted, according to specific conditions at specific times. What unfolded was related to shifting coalitions of power, control, and submerged forces that constantly changed the parameters of the "system" even though the players were aware of the culturally bound rules of the game that enable people to negotiate the shifts and ambivalences between "front" and "back" in Italian public and corporate life. Several dualisms run through Italian society—between north and south, between clarity and intrigue (representing two conflictory mentalities according to the journalist Piero Ottone; Gurwin, 1984, p. 87), between piety and cruelty, and between surface government and hidden groups with ostensibly the "real" power. In a sense, Calvi fell prey to those dualisms: He was a cold northerner, not at home in Rome and a world away from Sicily; he was the brilliant banker with an obsession for secrecy and for hidden power; he was a dominating figure in his own circles but became apparently *fesso* (naive) to

be preyed upon by those who were *scaltra* (quick-witted). Personally and professionally, he even began to lead a double life. A lawyer for Calvi at his trial in 1981 maintained,

Calvi's fatal flaw was that he had a dual character or, as Mazzola put it, "two brains". . . "Brain number one is good. It's the brain that has built *Banco Ambrosiano* into a big, solid, prosperous, well-run bank. Brain number two thinks that the world is run by conspiracies." Calvi's dual nature was reflected in the financial empire he created. "It was two banks," says an American banker in Milan. "One was a normal Milanese bank, heavy in deposits. And then there was this other institution (the foreign network) that nobody understood." Initially a gifted and feared magnate, he set in motion a chain of events that took control of him and led remorselessly and tragically to his own downfall and death. As such the events have to placed in the context of that "system" to which he was responding; *Ambrosiano* was the ultimate example of what could go wrong with the system at large. (Gurwin, 1984, p. 199)

"It was a mutant child of an imperfect financial structure, of the political parties' unquenchable thirst for money, of the secret ramifications and connivances of a distorted state, of the unresolved relations between Italy and the tiny sovereign state of the Vatican, planted in the heart of its capital" (Cornwell, 1984, p. 25). But systems are no more than the people who comprise them. The deep emotional involvement of people in their work, and their powerful ties with the organization to which they devote much of their lives, was expressed by Rosone. With a somewhat melodramatic Italian touch, he said, "I did what I could to save the bank. I loved it the way one can love a woman"; more prosaically, Calvi summed it all up when he commented bluntly, "For that amount of money, people will kill" (Gurwin, 1984, pp. 203, 204).

11 INTERNATIONAL ORGANIZED CRIME

Emerging Trends in Entrepreneurial Crime

DAVID L. CARTER

The author explores changing trends in international organized crime, with particular attention to changes in Eastern Europe. Discussions and findings are based on research both in the United States and abroad at various police organizations, law enforcement intelligence agencies, related government organizations, and international organized crime entities. Among the findings are the growth in comparatively short-term criminal alliances, diversity among the commodities of crime cartels, and growth in transnational criminal alliances. It was also found that East European organized groups are diverse, violent, and will engage in changing "structures" to maximize profits in any given enterprise or in the criminal trafficking of commodities.

When I first proposed the idea that East European organized crime would have a significant influence on the United States, initial reactions were something akin to "It's not likely," "They are too far away," "It would be too difficult for them to substantially enter the American crime market," "They are not sophisticated enough," "They don't have anything to exploit in the United States," and "They don't speak the language." And the arguments continued.

Think, however, a decade and a half ago: Had we been forewarned that small groups of criminals from the rural areas of Colombia would form together in criminal enterprises that would have a dramatic influence on U.S. social problems, not to mention amassing vast amounts of

money to corrupt people and influence portions of our economy, our reactions may have been similar. Yet, the impact of the Medellin and Cali drug cartels is all too real. Our acceptance may have also been reluctant if forewarned about an organized crime group from a small Caribbean island that would be extensively involved in drug trafficking in the United States, with a particular penchant toward violence. Yet, the influence of Jamaican posses throughout North America became pervasive. Although the role of the Mafia is now legend, many government officials, particularly J. Edgar Hoover, refused to acknowledge that organized crime existed until its presence could no longer be ignored after the fateful Appalachia, New York, discovery of the "Commission" meeting. In essence, denial has played a historical role in America's response to organized crime—a role that has not served us well.

In specifically addressing the international nature of organized crime, the United Nations Economic and Social Council observed:

> International experience shows that organized crime has long ago crossed national borders and is today transnational. . . . It should be noted that aspects of the evolutionary process undergone by society may make powerful criminal organizations even more impenetrable and facilitate the expansion of their illegal activities. (1992b, p. 32)

It is suggested that organized crime from Eastern Europe[1] is one of the next substantial organized crime threats to North America. Furthermore, East European organized crime has the ability to surpass the Colombian drug cartels' influence for several reasons. Not the least of these reasons is the diversity of commodities and the opportunities for power and wealth afforded by the significant political, social, and economic changes occurring throughout Europe and the close bond the United States has with the European Community (EC) on a range of fronts.

Acceptance of change in known patterns of behavior and practices is always difficult. The tendency is to deny that change may occur; instead, we cling to the status quo. Yet, this dogmatism does not bode well for our ability to prepare for potential change. This is the circumstance in which we find the problem of East European organized crime. With the limited information we have now, it is all too clear that such groups exist and are growing. It is similarly clear that they have targeted the United States as a result of the potential wealth that such groups may reap here. My research expands our knowledge of these groups, explores the threats they pose to the United States, and describes the emerging vision of organized crime as entrepreneurial crime.

PURPOSE AND PROBLEM

Although crime has always had international dimensions, in recent years it has appeared to grow, taking on new characteristics, particularly as related to organized criminal activities. Several factors on a global level have contributed to this: (a) changing sociopolitical environments in Eastern Europe, the Middle East, and the Pacific Rim; (b) government instability in Africa and Eastern Europe; (c) growing common markets of trade in Europe, the Pacific Rim, Africa, and North America; and (d) growth in the ease and speed of travel, telecommunications, and data transmissions. The change in international organized crime includes the emergence of new groups—crime cartels—as well as the diversification of organized crime "targets" and a "restructuring" of criminal enterprises toward models that are somewhat different from our traditional experiences. These are important for both understanding the trends that are occurring and for developing countermeasures to the organized crime threat.

My initial attempts to quantify both the trends and the effects of emerging organized crime proved to be unreliable for several reasons. First, crime-related data were extremely difficult to obtain because either they were not collected or the validity of the information was highly suspect. Second, given the transnational nature of the criminal enterprises, it was virtually impossible to segregate the data effects despite what was estimated by the authorities of each country. Third, the data that do exist vary so widely in structure and definition that comparisons are highly speculative. Finally, the growth of many crime groups has been so fast that the effects of their influence simply cannot be determined because law enforcement and intelligence agencies are still attempting to determine who the "players" are.

As a result, the intent of this study was to qualitatively explore current trends in the growth of organized crime groups, including their characteristics and commodities or enterprises. In this process, specific attention was given to East European organized crime because it appears to be expanding most rapidly, yet little is known about these groups, even among law enforcement agencies. In this regard, I learned early in the project that one initial assumption was erroneous. It was assumed that some type of organized crime "families"—such as the five Mafia groups in Italy and Sicily[2]—could be identified and documented in Eastern Europe via a case study approach to learn more about the nature of these enterprises. What I learned, however, was that the emerging groups typically were not organized in this fashion, and attempts to categorize them as such were not only fallacious but also unreliable. Thus, the course of the research was altered to understand the structural nature of East European organized crime and the types of enterprises in which these groups were interested.

METHODS

This study relied predominantly on qualitative research methods, including interviews with law enforcement officials, intelligence analysts, government officials, investigators, and corporate security directors, all of whom work with international organized crime. The interviews, in most cases, followed a consistent protocol that documented the interviewees' experience with organized crime and observations on current trends, including motivations and compounding factors. The exceptions were interviews done under incidental situations, typically at a conference where the interview time was limited. Even in these cases, I was able to ask and record primary questions from the protocol.

Most persons interviewed were from the United States and Europe (both Eastern and Western), although four interviewees were from the Pacific Rim.[3] Persons were selected for the interviews on the basis of their knowledge and experience in the light of the positions they hold with their organizations. Corporate security directors were included in the research because of the increasing involvement of organized crime in cargo theft, theft of intellectual property,

manufacture and distribution of counterfeit commodities, and industrial espionage.

In addition, I was given access to a wide range of investigative reports and documents. A content analysis was completed with these materials to the extent possible. In a few cases, I was permitted to read and take notes from the documents, but not copy them.[4]

An analysis matrix was designed to document the interviewees' responses to key questions. In addition, on selected variables the interviewees were asked to give their perceptions on a 5-point scale. On the basis of these responses and the collective observations documented in the interviews, the information was integrated for analysis in this chapter.

The reader is cautioned that the findings have limitations that should be considered. Most important is the threat of maturation, given that the interviews for this project were conducted over an 18-month period. Moreover, the rapidity of drastic change in Eastern Europe over a comparatively short time is having an impact on organized crime there. To help control for this threat, I conducted some follow-up interviews with critical individuals who deal with these issues. Although the follow-up interviews were comparatively brief, they attempted to address the concerns posed by the threat. A second limitation, which is inherently applicable to this methodology, is that findings will be influenced by the biases and interests of those interviewed. To balance this threat, I interviewed people not only in law enforcement but also in government, who had a broader view of the issues, and in private industry, who view the issues from a different perspective. Interrater reliability was not a threat because all interviews were conducted through the same protocol. Moreover, the use of consistent "control questions" helped control for any biases of the researcher.

With respect to reporting results, because of the critical nature of information involved in this study—frequently of a "classified" or "confidential" nature—interviewees were guaranteed confidentiality in their specific responses to control questions. In some cases, the persons interviewed permitted use of their comments; in other cases, comments were stated in an open forum. In these instances, the comments were attributed by position and affiliation. Although I was given access to classified information, that information was used as background and to give direction for further study, but not included in this chapter.

RATIONALE FOR EAST EUROPEAN ORGANIZED CRIME

A 1992 United Nations report from the Commission on Crime Prevention and Criminal Justice observed that "transnational crime, which until very recently had been virtually unknown, was becoming a problem for the countries of Eastern Europe" (United Nations, 1992c, p. 9). An interesting finding from the same report stated, "Transborder criminality was, in a sense, the price of increased freedom and technical progress in communication, travel and transportation" (p. 9).

The need to understand East European organized crime and its trends centers on several critical factors. Among them are the following:

> East European organized crime has not been studied nearly to the extent of other organized crime networks, such as "traditional" organized crime (Mafia/Cosa Nostra); the Asian triads, tongs, and Yakuza; the South American drug cartels; and Jamaican posses.

> "Western" researchers, law enforcement personnel, and intelligence specialists had limited access to people and officials behind the Iron Curtain. When access was obtained, it typically was under rigidly controlled circumstances.

> Warsaw Pact countries tended to deny that organized crime—or any major crime problems, for that matter—existed.

Important changes that occurred in Europe over the past 3 years have significantly contributed to the growth of organized crime and its expanding influence. These include the following:

> Full implementation of the provisions of the EC via the Single European Act.[5]

> Dissolution of the Warsaw Pact and its sociopolitical ramifications.

> Movement of East European countries toward a market-based economy with relatively little experience and few controls that could inhibit organized crime.

> The reunification of Germany, which has provided a concentrated avenue linking Eastern and Western Europe.

> Government instability in many East European countries that contributes to fewer controls on crime, as well as a diminished effort to control crime.

There is evidence of not only growth in East European organized crime groups but also participation in organized crime by former members of the security (intelligence) services of these countries (e.g., the KGB, Stasi, Hungarian Security Service). This contributes to the sophistication and broader "reach" of these groups. Evidence already exists that these groups have appeared in the United States. Importantly, organized crime is profit oriented. Its inherent characteristic is economic expansion through illegitimate means. As such, organized crime seeks those areas where the greatest profits can be attained; the United States is obviously one of those areas and a target of the East European groups.

THE LITERATURE

We must be concerned in the United States about new and emerging crime trends. By all indications, the threats posed by East European organized crime clearly fall within this purview. Although the research is limited, particularly applying European organized crime trends to the United States (except for the Italian/Sicilian Mafia), compelling evidence supports the notion that the threat exists. Similarly, the federal government has not developed any type of comprehensive strategy to deal with this crime threat, nor have state and local agencies developed strategies to understand—or even antici-pate—the phenomenon. As sure as state and local law enforcement agencies across the United States have had to learn to cope with the violence, intimidation, and drug trafficking of Jamaican posses, and increasingly Asian groups, so will they have to address the *Chechen, Ostankinsky,* and other such groups emerging from Eastern Europe.

The impact and dynamics of organized crime in general on U.S. society are well documented in a wide range of sources (e.g., Abadinsky, 1985; Edelhertz, 1987; Fox, 1989; President's Commission on Law Enforcement and Admini-stration of Justice, 1967; President's Commis-sion on Organized Crime, 1986). As such, these elements are not discussed in this review. Rather, concern is focused on issues related to the problem emanating from Eastern Europe.

At the outset, it should be clear that organized crime is not new in Eastern Europe. For years, groups have been active in the former Soviet Union—notably Russia and the Ukraine—in-volved in drug trafficking and operating the black market, with its incidental effects on cor-ruption (Joutsen, 1993). Because of the omni-presence of the police state during the commu-nist regimes, it was difficult for these groups to operate outside the former U.S.S.R. and signifi-cantly more difficult to operate outside the War-saw Pact countries, even though some groups took advantage of official corruption, which was informally known as the "Party Mafia" (Serio, 1993). As the Iron Curtain opened, how-ever, among the first to rush through were loosely organized crime cartels that saw the opportunity to grow in the West. In this regard, Lee and MacDonald (1993) stated,

The demise of communist totalitarianism in the East, the transition from socialist to free market economies, and access to the global economy have kindled new incentives and opportunities for or-ganized crime. . . . [Similarly,] uncertain eco-nomic conditions, weak law enforcement, . . . un-protected frontiers, and porous financial systems further bolster the rapid rise of a vast new [crime] industry. (p. 90)

In a comparatively short time, these groups have established criminal connections, trade routes, and banking arrangements in the West (see Serio, 1992). As one intelligence analyst observed,

We are witnessing an explosion in organized crime. . . . To make matters worse, we expect new Russian and Afghan mafias will emerge shortly. The early part has already begun. (Perry, 1992, p. 1)

Orenstein (1992), in quoting a Hungarian police official, observed.

The major problem today is . . . the growing in-volvement by significant numbers of specialized and organized international criminals in . . . crimi-nal activities. (p. 15)

In a similar vein, a British criminal intelligence official told the researcher,

Organized crime groups from the Balkan states who previously were involved in minor thefts and drug trafficking are now involved in grand schemes of theft and black marketing. Buyers can order what they want—a Mercedes, a gun, a heli-copter—and have it delivered.

An Istanbul police official expressed the same concerns to the researcher, adding,

Our petty thieves have broadened their trade and increased their intensity. We can neither keep up with who is involved nor adequately investigate their activities. International borders are water for criminals and stone for the police.

The movement of criminals through Europe has become increasingly apparent. A Berlin po-lice commander told me,

We are seeing large numbers of new criminals from the East. They are bold, violent, and very entrepreneurial. They appear to have affiliations, but we do not have enough information about them—just speculation.

More forthrightly, a British Chief Constable stated,

> With the changes on the continent, I fear Europe is like a sieve with the international criminal becoming the norm. They [criminals] are far more adept at amalgamation than the EC governments.

The chief constable went on to say,

> If anybody in the United States thinks that Eastern European organized crime is only a problem for Western Europe, think again.

Inquiries by the U.N. Commission on Crime Prevention and Criminal Justice concluded that international organized crime

> . . . could become powerful enough to inhibit social and economic development, threaten the stability of governments, and reduce their capacity to meet the legitimate aspirations of their citizens. (1992a, p. 5)

The same report goes on to note,

> Organized crime had expanded its scope, exploiting the transition to market economies and infiltrating into legal activities under the cover of . . . its huge profits. (p. 5)

Certainly, this factor is most prevalent in Eastern Europe, where the broadest number of countries are attempting, in a relatively short time, to change their economic structure.[6]

From investigations in New York, California, Pennsylvania, and Massachusetts, it is clear that "with the dismantling of the Soviet Union and the subsequent lax emigration policies, Russian criminals have begun to carve out a niche in the United States" (Serio, 1992, p. 5). The extent of East European organized crime activity in the United States is simply not known. Similarly, our knowledge about the types of criminal enterprises, commodities, and best means to investigate (and infiltrate) these groups is limited, as is our knowledge about the true systemic impact this has on the United States.

Orenstein (1992) stresses the need for criminal justice agencies to prepare for the problem:

> As organized crime, internationally financed, secures its foothold there [in Eastern Europe], the gap between crime and law enforcement will continue, for the present, at an alarming rate. (p. 36)

Looking at one element of organized crime, drug trafficking, Lee and MacDonald (1993) offer an ominous forecast:

> Drug traffickers' escalating infiltration of fledgling Eastern [European] financial systems threatens the integrity of Western commercial institutions, including U.S. banks and corporations operating in the region. (p. 105)

They go on to note the dramatic impact these groups may have and warn, "the United States cannot ignore the geo-strategic implications" of these groups.

Although the literature is limited and largely anecdotal, it clearly illustrates that East European organized crime exists and is a threat to North America. Unfortunately, there has been virtually no analysis of information to define parameters of the problem and to articulate potential responses from a strategic perspective.

DEFINING ORGANIZED CRIME

It was noted earlier that changes in European organized crime are indicative of an evolution of organized crime on a global scale. Historically, organized crime has been viewed in terms of the "traditional" or "familial" crime syndicates broadly known as Cosa Nostra or the Mafia. In the past decade, the perspective of organized has been broadened, largely as a result of drug trafficking, to include the South American drug trafficking groups (e.g., Medellin and Cali cartels) and Asian crime groups (e.g., triads, tongs, Yakuza). As we look toward the future, it is increasingly evident that organized crime must be viewed from an even broader context.

Many definitions and descriptions of organized crime exist. Regardless of the definition, several consistent characteristics emerge:

An accumulation of profit

Longevity

A structure to further the groups' crimes

Use of violence to help in attaining goals

Ability to corrupt government officials, police officials, and/or corporate officials

Noted organized crime researcher Howard Abadinsky (1985) defines organized crime:

A non-ideological enterprise that involves a number of persons in close social interaction, organized on a hierarchical basis for the purpose of securing profit and power by engaging in illegal and legal activities. Positions in the hierarchy and positions involving functional specialization may be assigned on the basis of kinship or friendship, or rationally assigned according to skill. . . . Permanency is assumed by the members who strive to keep the enterprise integral and active in pursuit of goals. It eschews competition and strives for monopoly over particular activities on an industry or territorial basis. There is a willingness to use violence and/or bribery to achieve ends or maintain discipline. Membership is restricted, although non-members may be involved on a contingency basis. (p. 7)

Increasingly, however, it appears that the nature of organized crime is changing and that this traditional vision, which we have long held, may need to be revised. Recently revised perspectives serve as illustrations. For example, Interpol defines organized crime as "any enterprise or group of persons engaged in a continuing illegal activity which has as its primary purpose the generation of profits and continuance of the enterprise regardless of national boundaries." From another perspective, the German Bundeskriminalamt (BKA) operationalizes organized crime as "the planned commission of criminal offenses, determined by the pursuit of profit and power, involving more than two persons over a prolonged or indefinite period of time, using a commercial or business license scheme, violence, and/or intimidation."

The Dutch intelligence service, Centrale Recherche Informatiedienst (CRI), takes a unique approach by viewing organized crime as having eight progressive elements:

1. Any hierarchical structure
2. Internal support and sanctions
3. Money laundering
4. Corruption and bribery of legal system officials
5. Involvement in more than one illegal activity
6. Organizations that hide behind front companies
7. Criminal activities that cover a long period of time
8. Members who act violently against competitors

Using these eight elements, the Dutch developed an ordinal hierarchy to rate the level of "intensity" or degree of sophistication for a criminal enterprise's involvement in organized crime activities. This process serves as one means to develop a law enforcement response to organized crime threats by considering seriousness as related to available resources to deal with the problem.

Numbers 1 and 2 = a low level of organized crime

Numbers 3, 4, and 5 = a moderate level of organized crime

Numbers 6, 7, and 8 = a high level of organized crime

Although some variance exists in these definitions, clearly the trend among international law enforcement organizations is away from the "familial" view and toward a more "entrepreneurial" perspective.

The View of Organized Crime as "Entrepreneurial Crime"

The movement toward viewing organized crime as "enterprise crime" came about because of its market-driven nature: Any commodity for which a profit can be earned is open to organized crime. As noted by a British detective inspector, "Legitimate business never travels without criminal company."

Entrepreneurial groups appear to develop through an evolutionary process. If on a time line, the developmental stages would be (a) loosely organized, (b) refined networks, (c) refined structure, (d) more sophisticated operation, and (e) maturation of the enterprise. Individuals and perhaps small groups who have common criminal interests tend to amalgamate loosely for certain criminal purposes. Just as in the case of many new business initiatives, if the crime amalgamation seems to work—that is, generate profits—then the enterprise takes on more structured characteristics. Some groups may be short-term alliances with minimal structure; others become quite sophisticated organizations. Clearly, however, levels of structure and sophistication vary widely on a continuum, with a notable degree of ebb and flow between crime groups. This fluid nature makes it difficult to develop a clear picture of these enterprises, as well as to give an accurate assessment of their activities. Diversity and change in organized crime activities have occurred because, as noted by a Dutch Ministry of Justice official, the dollar amounts in organized crime earned from commercial crime exceed that earned in drug trafficking. The "enterprise" of OC can reach into many areas:

Counterfeit currency

Drug-related crime

Arms-related crime

Vice-related crime

    Prostitution

    Slave trade

    Illegal gambling

Offenses against property

    Motor vehicle theft

    Burglary rings

    Thefts from warehouses

    Receiving stolen property

    Cargo theft

Violent crime

    Racketeering

    Robbery

    Extortion

White-collar crime

    Theft of trade secrets

    Counterfeit merchandise

    Investment fraud

    Illegal employment

    Blackmail

    Corruption

EVOLUTION OF INTERNATIONAL ORGANIZED CRIME

Radical changes occurring around the world are having a notable influence on organized crime. Solidification of the 12-member EC; Hong Kong's change to Chinese rule in 1997; the breakup of the Soviet Union and dissolution of the Warsaw Pact; movement of East European countries toward market-based economies; growing numbers of people immigrating to Western Europe and North America; and the impact of technology on swift communications and bank fund transfers are all among the radical changes affecting the "new world order." Ironically, the same factors that promise greater human rights and a better quality of life for many in the world also bring increasing criminal activity and creative illegal initiatives from organized crime groups.

Organized crime's growth can be viewed in an "ink spot" analogy: Organized crime is like an ink spot, starting with concentration in one area and slowing spreading out, encompassing more area and frequently crossing international borders. The Dutch CRI breaks organized groups into three categories:

Traditional Organized Crime

    Italian Mafia

    Chinese, Japanese, and Vietnamese crime syndicates

Drug-Specific Organized Crime

    South American cartels (35 cartels)

    West Indian organized crime (yardees, posses)

Turkish clans (feeding the Balkan route)

Indian subcontinent crime syndicates

Foreign and Others (involved in any kind of commodity)

West African

Russian

Ukrainian

East European conglomerates

My interviews with police officials from both hemispheres confirmed that the level of organized crime was increasing in their respective countries. Moreover, the character of organized crime groups was changing with regard to structure, membership, and commodities toward the enterprise model. Officials from 15 countries agreed that many traditional perspectives of organized crime, hence approaches to deal with the problem, had to be rethought if law enforcement methods were to address the problem effectively. Several key factors have emerged that warrant further study by both academicians and policymakers.

Globalization

Although organized crime has always been multijurisdictional in nature, it is becoming increasingly so. On the basis of the information from this research, global criminality may be classified into two categories. Criminals who commit *transnational crime* are "based" in one country but cross international borders to commit their crimes and then return home. As one illustration, this has long occurred along the U.S.-Mexico border, notably related to auto thefts and burglary; however, it is now occurring on a large scale in Europe. This is particularly true since the internal EC border controls have been virtually eliminated and the East European borders have opened for easy passage. According to those interviewed, the most common transnational organized crimes have been auto theft and thefts of consumer goods (especially electronic items) from warehouses and shipments.

The second category is *international crime*. This occurs when an ongoing criminal organization has established its enterprise in two or more countries. Drug trafficking, money laundering, counterfeiting, and black markets are among the crimes occurring in this venue. The Italian Mafia, South American drug cartels, Japanese Yakuza, and Russian Chechen groups are illustrations of this type. Although factors associated with the transnational and international crime groups obviously overlap, the basic characteristics of each influences the law enforcement strategies used to deal with the problem.

The Nature of Organized Crime

As noted previously, the basic nature of organized crime seems to have shifted somewhat. Increasingly, groups have emerged that interact much more like entrepreneurs; essentially, the term *organized crime* is more of a euphemism for a broader problem. Whereas organized crime has always been profit-oriented, it has traditionally involved a narrowly defined collective of members, most of whom were drawn to the group as a result of the unifying factor of heritage, kinship, or other common ground. Moreover, members typically stayed with the organization as career criminals, either with one specific crime group or with a recognized "companion" organization.

Entrepreneurial crime, in contrast, has a relatively small core of people who are permanent members of the enterprise. Others are brought into the enterprise as needed to deal with specific issues—for example, theft from shipments, auto theft, drug trafficking, and theft of intellectual property. The entrepreneurial criminal organization seeks a targeted commodity and amalgamates with other groups that best serve the profitable interest of the enterprise. In many ways, this approach is similar to an "adhocracy" or "task force management" found in many businesses.

Fewer long-term associations take place in entrepreneurial criminal enterprises, even in an ongoing market arena such as drug trafficking. As one British detective chief inspector observed, "Today's diverse organized crime groups are operationally more like corporate raiders; only the criminals use violence and illegal methods to solidify their market and profit." Just as businesses today seek to increase profits through diversification of investments and greater efficiency and effectiveness of operations, so are organized crime groups. This is particularly true of the newer generations of crime cartels.

Basis for Amalgamation

One may reasonably ask what glue binds together the diverse organized crime groups. On the basis of the collective experiences of international law enforcement officials, organized crime groups appear to be bound by one or more of four factors. First is *ethnicity*. The sharing of a common language and cultural norms not only brings together people who have similar beliefs but also engenders greater levels of trust. A good illustration in this category is the Asian triads and Yakuza. This commonality makes communications more effective, expectations more clearly defined, and penetration of the enterprise significantly more difficult for law enforcement officials.

The second factor is *geography*. Out of convenience and a belief that proximity contributes to security, many organized crime groups tend to amalgamate on the basis of geographic location. For example, the Italian and Sicilian Mafia groups are basically structured around different geographic regions where they are "based," although their reach is international in scope. Similarly, many East European groups have amalgamated, largely by accident rather than intent, on the basis of geography. This is notably true within Russia, where the geographic area is so vast (and membership is reinforced by ethnic homogeneity).

A unique example of geographic organized crime found during the course of this research deals with piracy on the high seas. Notably off the coasts of Southeast Asia, West Africa, and Northeastern South America, organized crime groups have been involved in major thefts by piracy. Typically, freighters are attacked, with portions of the cargo stolen along with the contents of the ship's safe (which frequently holds

substantial amounts of cash intended to pay the crew and meet incidental expenses while under way). In some instances, the ships are steamed to another location, perhaps for several days, until the cargo can be off-loaded. Not only is there a direct loss of goods and cash, but also an indirect loss of an estimated £6,000 ($9,900 U.S.) per day in costs of operating the ship.

Third, some crime groups, notably the most entrepreneurial of those, were amalgamated on the basis of their ability to obtain, distribute, and merchandise a *commodity*. Because of convenience, expertise, availability, or other similar factor, organized crime groups amalgamate to traffic in a given item or substance. Most apparent is drug trafficking; however, counterfeit money, counterfeit goods, and stolen cars are also examples of commodities around which organized groups have come together to secure profits in a limited-commodity arena.

The fourth category might be called *social-political commonality*. Groups amalgamate on the basis of a sense of common bonds related to lifestyles and social characteristics. Although their primary intent remains profit generation, other factors influence their motivation. Outlaw motorcycle gangs, which are growing throughout Europe (including a chapter of Hell's Angels in Moscow), represent one illustration. Certainly, income is important to members; however, subscribing to the values and social systems of the "biker culture" is an important dynamic in the perpetuation of the groups. A similar phenomenon, with a significantly different social structure, can be found in organized crime groups that contribute their profits to the Provisional Irish Republican Army (PIRA). At the outset, these groups developed schemes simply to fund PIRA; however, money was increasingly filtered to the groups' members for personal profits. Although the commonality of their political beliefs remains an important binding link, some evidence suggests that these groups now exist with a primary purpose of developing wealth for the members of the group while at the same time contributing funds to support PIRA's activities.[7]

The binding ties of organized crime group members typically involve a variety of factors. Yet, one of these four characteristics appears to permeate the relationship as the linchpin that holds all aspects of the group together. These bonds are important factors for the police to understand in developing their investigative and enforcement strategies.

RUSSIA

In a candid discussion with the first deputy head of the Organized Crime Control Department of the Russian Ministry of Interior, a remarkable observation was made. The general stated,

> Criminality has become the most important factor threatening the change toward [democratization] in Russia. In particular, organized crime is undermining the economy, safety, and security of the Russian people.

Russian organized crime is pervasively involved in corrupting foreign trade officials, industry leaders, politicians, and law enforcement officials. Frequently, organized crime groups have better intelligence than the police, with many crime principals becoming "decision makers" in small towns. The Russian crime syndicates are involved in such things as drug trafficking, stealing shipments of consumer goods, stealing intellectual property, trafficking in stolen nuclear materials, and racketeering. Russian organized crime also includes a violent group of criminals who readily kill their competitors and brazenly traffic their cargoes in armed convoys across the republic.

The Russian police have had limited successes in dealing with these crime cartels for several reasons. The extent of bribery the criminals use, the resources they have to avoid the police, and the government's competing needs to stabilize the country's economic and political system are among those reasons. Another problem is establishing effective lines of communication with law enforcement organizations in other countries. Some Western countries still are hesitant to have completely open communications with Russian authorities; consequently, the sharing of intelligence is limited, leading to growth of the criminal enterprise.

According to one official, Russia is experiencing unprecedented bank fraud. In addition, there are virtually no bank robberies; banks are paying extortion money to be protected from robberies. There is widespread bribery, killing of competitors in criminal enterprises, and extortion of business leaders. Forged licenses and documents have become a widespread business, as has corruption and stealing anything that can earn a profit. As one unique example, Estonia is having a major organized crime problem related to stolen and illegally obtained nonferrous metals.

Another problem is that 19% of Russia's police officers left the police service in 1992; many became involved in organized crime. The same is true of former KGB personnel who suddenly found themselves out of work. Arms trading at all levels has also been extraordinarily high. There have been attacks on police officers to steal their guns, widespread thefts of guns from armories, and a growth in "cottage factories" making guns for sale.

It is estimated that up to 4,000 organized crime groups operate in Russia, many ethnically related, others being of both a geographic and ethnic amalgamation. The sizes of these groups range from 30 members to more than 1,000 members. Most of the larger organized crime groups in Russia have "connections" with organized crime in other countries, notably Poland, Hungary, Germany, Israel, and the United States. One Russian official estimated that "Russian criminals have $25 billion [U.S.] in foreign banks worldwide."

OTHER ISSUES OF INTEREST

Among those interviewed, discussions consistently turned toward drug trafficking in various forms. One factor that became apparent was that the "Balkan route" for smuggling drugs from both the Golden Triangle and the Golden Crescent has shifted north to avoid the political conflagrations between Yugoslavia, Croatia, and Bosnia Herzegovina. It is interesting to note that although political strife upsets many elements of life, organized criminals quickly adapt to these changes in order to maintain their "business."

Beyond drugs, other interesting trends in illegal commodities trading were discovered. The most active commodities being trafficked by both East and West European organized crime groups appear to be consumer goods and cars. Conversations with corporate security directors of various international companies disclosed that they have had their own problems with organized crime. Increasing numbers of corporations have experienced industrial espionage and counterfeiting of their products. Their experiences indicate that specialized criminal groups with wide expertise are among those attempting to steal the various corporate "crown jewels."

Somewhat surprisingly, there was comparatively little discussion of terrorism among the officials interviewed. Two reasons appear to be the basis for this reserve. First, although terrorist groups and organized crime share some common interests (particularly with respect to arms trading), they nonetheless have separate motivations. Similarly, separate investigative bodies deal with each type of group. A second reason, which appeared to be of greater influence, was that the overall threats posed by terrorism were deemed to be significantly less than those posed by organized crime.

As a final point, concern about computer-related crime and its use by organized crime groups was growing. The agencies of most interviewees had little experience in computer crime investigations, yet they viewed this as an area already beginning to plague most countries. It was also recognized that, as a result of the vast profit potential associated with computer-related crime, it would only be a matter of time before organized crime groups aggressively pursued high-tech targets.

Illustrating the diversity of organized crime targets, a representative of the Hungarian National Central Bureau (Interpol) told me,

Smuggling and black market alcohol, tobacco, and electronics are a foundation economy for organized crime in Hungary. It is hard to control because these are items people want. It's also hard to control because, with the country's poor economic conditions, even an illegal economy adds jobs.

A German BKA official expressed his concerns to me, noting,

The political changes in Eastern Europe have clearly had an impact on the Federal Republic of Germany. We feel that Germany is becoming the new center for organized crime because of its growth here. This change is absolutely revolutionary.

The emerging organized crime groups are creative in their endeavors. For example, the British Immigration Service has found increased numbers of forged passports that are of high quality. The passports are used for a range of purposes, including illegal immigration, the defrauding of social services, credit card fraud, use by terrorists for international travel, and virtually any other criminal enterprise for which a false identification would be useful.

According to one British official, French identity cards are most frequently found. Of all forged passports, 24.1% come from EC countries; 34.7% come from Africa. The forged passports are of excellent quality; many forgeries cannot be determined without forensic analysis. Frequently, people who have been identified as members of organized crime groups travel on forged passports, usually from their native country. Similarly, a Dutch official told me that women involved in prostitution rings in the Netherlands and Germany are frequently found traveling on high-quality forged passports from Russia.

A German BKA official stated, "We know [Russian organized crime members] are here, but we have a considerable deficiency of information about who they are and how they work." Criminal activities of these groups include fraud, counterfeiting money, and trafficking stolen precious metals, stocks, titles, licenses, and documents. Many of these groups developed their criminal expertise during the Cold War, when controls were rigid; thus, they became proficient in profiteering in the shadow economy. Moreover, in Germany, the organized crime groups have blackmailed Russian exiles to participate in their enterprises. East European organized criminals, which appear to be most prominent in Germany, are from the Georgian Republic, Russia, the Czech Republic, and Ukraine. The BKA's estimated profit of Russian organized crime in Germany in 1992 was 1.7 million deutsche marks ($1,063,000 U.S.).

Stolen cars are among the popular organized crime commodities. In 1987, Germany had 49,460 reported stolen cars. In 1992, that number jumped to 131,329 reported stolen cars, many of which were expensive automobiles such as Mercedes Benz, BMW, Porsche, and Jaguar. The most sophisticated East European organized crime process begins when the organized crime group receives an "order" for a car (usually something like, "We are looking for "X" cars). Thieves steal targeted cars in Western Europe that are then immediately driven to Poland, where border guards have been corrupted, to a location around Gdansk. The cars are then shipped to North Africa, where forged certificates of origin, bills of sale, and authorizations for shipment are issued (Morocco appears to be a primary location). The newly "retitled" cars are then sold primarily throughout the Mideast and Japan. Needless to say, a criminal organization that follows this modus operandi is highly sophisticated, organized, and well financed.

When asked about their attitudes and experiences, not surprisingly interviewees from European law enforcement and intelligence agencies had greater experiences with East European organized crime than those in either the United States or the Pacific Rim. Despite this, *all* saw the threat of organized crime growing to become a more serious problem and, with complete unanimity, believed that the probability of the United States being an East European organized crime target was high (see Tables 11.1 and 11.2). This agreement was supported by the responses of corporate security directors. Interestingly, although both the government and private sectors see threats as high, comparatively little has been done to develop effective countermeasures to the problem. Common responses from government officials were something to the effect that "We have other priorities," "Our budget won't permit new programming," or "We don't yet know enough about the threat." Corporate security directors, however, tended to say their primary problem was convincing corporate executives that threats posed by these (and other) groups were realistic problems for which they must plan.

One might speculate that an underlying, yet important, reason for the inattention is that threats from East European organized crime are not "politically expedient." Drug trafficking, South American drug cartels, violent crime, and gangs are among the politically popular crime issues. Consequently, these problems receive the greatest funding, research, and policy attention. This observation is not meant to undermine these problems; rather, it illustrates how priorities are established. Unfortunately, U.S. history shows that institutionalized responses to problems tend to wait until the problem is overwhelming, rather than plan ahead to develop intervention strategies.

With respect to violence and East European organized crime, results were mixed. European government officials who had the greatest contact with East European organized crime rated the violence threat notably higher than officials from the United States, the Pacific Rim, and the private sector. This finding suggests that more needs to be learned about the violence of these groups.

Given the history of organized crime globally, the pervasiveness of organized crime in the United States, and the findings of this research project, it appears clear that the probability of

TABLE 11.1 Responses of Government Interviewees

Government Interview Source	Experience With EEOC* A	Threat of EEOC Growth B	Threat of EEOC Violence C	Former Security Service Involved D	Probability U.S. Is Target of EEOC E	Developed Effective Countermeasure F
Dutch 1	1	1	3	3	1	3
Dutch 2	1	1	2	2	1	2
Dutch 3	1	1	1	3	3	3
Britain 1	1	1	1	2	1	2
Britain 2	1	1	3	3	1	3
Britain 3	1	1	1	4	1	4
N. Ireland 1	4	1	3	4	1	4
German 1	1	1	1	2	1	1
Belgium 1	1	1	1	3	3	3
Italy 1	3	1	2	3	1	2
Norway 1	2	1	1	2	1	2
Russia 1	1	1	1	1	1	3
Russia 2	1	1	1	1	1	2
Russia 3	1	1	3	1	1	3
Hungary 1	1	1	2	2	1	3
Hong Kong 1	3	2	4	3	1	3
Malaysia 1	3	2	4	4	1	4
S. Korea 1	4	2	4	4	1	4
Singapore 1	3	1	2	3	1	3
U.S. Federal 1	3	1	2	3	1	2
U.S. Federal 2	2	2	3	3	1	4
U.S. Federal 3	2	2	4	2	1	3
U.S. Federal 4	2	2	4	2	1	3
U.S. State 1	3	3	3	5	1	3

NOTE: *East European organized crime.
Scale (5-point Likert)
A   1 = A Great Deal   to   5 = None
B   1 = Very Serious   to   5 = Not Serious
C   1 = Very Serious   to   5 = Not Serious
D   1 = Very Frequently   to   5 = Never
E   1 = High Probability   to   5 = Not Probable
F   1 = Extensive   to   5 = None

East European organized crime becoming a major factor in North America is high. As such, initiatives must be taken to better understand these groups, identify key players, understand their methods, and develop countermeasures for prevention, disruption, and prosecution.

RESPONSES TO THE PROBLEM

Law enforcement has recognized that new initiatives must be taken to deal with global organized crime. Consequently, some efforts have been made in this regard.

National Criminal Intelligence Service

In 1992, Britain changed the National Drugs Intelligence Unit to the National Criminal Intelligence Service (NCIS) to meet the broadening trends of organized crime. As implied by the name, the responsibilities of the service have significantly expanded in recognition of both the globalization of crime and the involvement of organized crime groups in activities that go far beyond drug trafficking. Strategic intelligence has been incorporated into the NCIS responsibility, as has specific attention directed toward Eastern Europe.

TABLE 11.2 Responses of Corporate Interviewees

Government Interview Source	Experience With EEOC* A	Threat of EEOC Growth B	Threat of EEOC Violence C	Former Security Service Involved D	Probability U.S. Is Target of EEOC E	Developed Effective Countermeasure F
Foreign 1	1	1	1	2	1	3
Foreign 2	1	1	3	3	1	3
Foreign 3	2	1	3	2	1	2
Foreign 4	2	2	4	2	1	1
Foreign 5	3	2	2	3	1	2
Foreign 6	2	1	3	2	1	2
U.S. 1	5	3	4	4	1	4
U.S. 2	5	4	4	5	1	4
U.S. 3	2	3	4	3	1	2
U.S. 4	4	3	4	4	1	3
U.S. 5	4	2	4	4	1	3
U.S. 6	3	1	4	2	1	1
U.S. 7	3	2	4	2	1	1
U.S. 8	3	2	4	3	1	3
U.S. 9	3	2	4	3	1	3
U.S. 10	4	2	3	2	1	2
U.S. 11	2	2	3	3	1	3
U.S. 12	3	1	3	2	1	2
U.S. 13	2	1	2	2	1	2

NOTE: *East European organized crime
Scale (5-point Likert)
A   1 = A Great Deal   to   5 = None
B   1 = Very Serious   to   5 = Not Serious
C   1 = Very Serious   to   5 = Not Serious
D   1 = Very Frequently   to   5 = Never
E   1 = High Probability   to   5 = Not Probable
F   1 = Extensive   to   5 = None

Europol

Interviewees discussed the EC's creation of Europol with respect to its role in law enforcement and relationship to Interpol. Europol was conceived as an EC-wide intelligence clearinghouse to deal with all aspects of criminality affecting the 12 EC member states. It is still in its development stage, with no permanent site yet selected (it appears that its headquarters will be in the Netherlands, Germany, or France). Problems with Europol's full implementation remain. For example, convention ratification must occur before information can be shared outside the EC, and a decision must be made whether Europol members will have any operational responsibilities. Despite these and other concerns, hope is held high that Europol will serve as an important resource in dealing with global organized crime.

Interpol

The International Criminal Police Organization (Interpol), an international clearinghouse for information on criminals and crime commodities, has long provided information to member law enforcement agencies worldwide. As a broader approach, Interpol has revisited its work on organized crime to provide a more effective worldwide service of intelligence and information. For example, Interpol has created the Analytical Criminal Intelligence Unit at its headquarters in Ste. Cloud, France, with newly added personnel explicitly trained in intelligence and crime analysis. In addition, four new organized crime group projects have been established to target explicit concerns: (a) OCSA deals with organized criminal gangs of South American origin; (b) MACANDRA targets the Italian Mafia groups; (c) ROCKERS is an initiative directed toward outlaw motorcycle gangs in Europe; and (d) EASTWIND develops intelligence on all types of Asian organized crime groups. These group projects serve as a foundation for Interpol's new organized crime initiatives, with additional group projects likely to be developed in the future.

Law Enforcement Organizations

Some countries have either created new organizations or established new responsibilities in existing organizations in order to deal with global organized crime. For example, in 1991, Italy created the Direzione Investigativa Antimafia (DIA) to explicitly investigate and enforce creative new anti-Mafia laws. As another illustration, because of established funding links between organized crime and the Provisional Irish Republican Army (PIRA), the Terrorist Financial Unit (TFU) for Northern Ireland was created to attack organized crime cartels from a financial crimes investigation perspective, similar to the Financial Crimes Enforcement Network (FinCEN) in the United States.

Other law enforcement organizations—such as Germany's Bundeskriminalamt (BKA), the Dutch Centrale Recherche Informatiedienst (CRI), Australia's National Crime Authority, the Royal Canadian Mounted Police (RCMP), the Organized Crime Unit of the Russian Federation, and both the U.S. Drug Enforcement Administration (DEA) and Federal Bureau of Investigation (FBI)—have renewed initiatives and programming directed toward global investigation and information sharing related to the control of organized crime. Unfortunately, some efforts are being met with resistance.

National Security

An emerging concern encircling the international organized crime issue is that the line between international law enforcement and national security is becoming increasingly blurred. This is particularly true since the nuclear threat has significantly diminished while economic competition between countries has increased and social stability within countries has been threatened by the effects of the worldwide drug market. Consequently, greater cooperation and closer working ties are needed between the law enforcement community and the intelligence community.

The new world order has ushered in a new spirit of optimism for global peace; at the same time, it has opened the door to limitless opportunities for global organized crime groups. Increasingly, issues of global crime are the new genre of national security threats. When, in the mid-1980s, President Reagan declared drugs to be a national security threat to the United States, a new era was beginning to bring national security and law enforcement more closely together. This situation is prompting new questions about the relationship between law enforcement agencies and the intelligence community (notably, the Central Intelligence Agency, National Security Agency, and Defense Intelligence Agency). Moreover, given the executive order declaration that a national security threat encompasses economic threats to the United States, the crime-related national security threat is expanding beyond drugs and includes such things as theft of intellectual property, industrial espionage, black marketeering, counterfeiting of goods, and computer-related crime.

Perhaps the weakest link in the law enforcement chain is the poor relationship and communications between Western governments and those of the former Warsaw Pact. This problem can be corrected with relative ease and should receive a high priority in any future initiatives.

SUMMARY

This chapter was intended to provide a wide-ranging discussion on changes in global organized crime. The observations and conclusions are the product of an initial analysis of two broader research projects. Among the key points that may be considered for further research are the following:

- Organized crime is increasingly entrepreneurial in nature, with a "structure" that best suits that goal.

- Organized crime is increasingly global, being of both an international and transnational character.

- East European organized crime is rapidly growing in scope and influence; it is a significant threat about which more must be learned.

- East European organized crime has demonstrated that it is extremely violent.

- North America, and the United States in particular, are targets of the East European criminal enterprises.

- Law enforcement (and intelligence) organizations must prepare to intervene in the growth of East European organized crime now, not play "catch up" as they have traditionally done.

NOTES

1. Several East European countries are actually "Eurasian" when considered geographically. The traditional characterization of "East" and "West" is an oversimplification of the region and its social-political environment. Politically, East European countries can be classified as the former Soviet Bloc countries and non-Soviet East European countries. The former Soviet Bloc countries include Bulgaria, Czechoslovakia (now the Czech Republic and Slovakia,) the former German Democratic Republic or East Germany, Hungary, Poland, and Romania. Of course, a portion of the former U.S.S.R. is included in this grouping, which consists of Ukraine, Russia, and the Balkan states (Belorussia, Estonia, Latvia, Lithuania, and Moldavia). The remaining former Soviet republics are geographically in Asia.

Non-Soviet East European countries are Albania, Macedonia, and the former Yugoslavia (now Serbia, Croatia, and Bosnia Herzegovina). Turkey was also considered East European for this research although it geographically transgresses both Europe and Asia.

Because of the change occurring in Eastern Europe, conventions of generality are made to clearly identify the regions. Moreover, distinguishing between the former Soviet Bloc and non-Soviet East European countries is an important element in the analysis of issues in this study.

2. The five Italian and Sicilian Mafia groups are the Calabrian 'Ndrangheta, the Neapolitan Camorra, the Sacra Corona Unita, N.S.C.U., and the Stidde.

3. The interviewees were from the following organizations: Dutch Ministry of Justice, Dutch Centrale Recherche Informatiedienst (CRI), British National Criminal Intelligence Service, British Home Office, London Metropolitan Police, Belgium Gendarmerie, Russian Ministry of Interior, Moscow Police, Terrorist Financial Unit of Northern Ireland, Hungarian Interpol National Central Bureau, Royal Hong Kong Police, Malaysian Police, South Korean Police, Italian Direzione Investigativa Antimafia (DIA), Germany's Bundeskriminalamt (BKA), the Oslo (Norway) Police, the Istanbul (Turkey) Police, FBI, DEA, CIA, Department of Defense, (DOD), Florida Department of Law Enforcement (FDLE), and the corporate security directors of 19 corporations from the United States, United Kingdom, France, Spain, and Norway.

4. Generally, copies of the documents were available in English. In four cases, documents were translated by experienced linguists from either the police organization or Michigan State University (two German documents, one Italian, and one Spanish). In addition, I obtained access to a wide range of United Nations documents.

5. The European Community is a coalition of West European countries that, through parliamentary cooperation among the member states, ratified the Single European Act to create an economic (and subsequently social) common market "without frontiers" (see Owen & Dynes, 1992). The 12 European Community member countries are Belgium, Denmark, France, Germany, Greece, Ireland, Italy, Luxembourg, the Netherlands, Portugal, Spain, and the United Kingdom. West European countries that are not EC members were divided into two categories for this project. The primary non-EC West European countries are Austria, Finland, Norway, Sweden, and Switzerland. Secondary non-EC countries are so designated because their location or size has limited organized crime involvement. Although some were addressed in the research, their role was limited. These include Andorra, Liechtenstein, Malta, Monaco, San Marino, and Vatican City. For this research, Cyprus was considered West European because of its location as a Mediterranean island that has strong political, social, and economic ties to Europe, although some geographic sources classify it as Asian. Iceland is geographically considered part of the European continent; however, because of its small population and geographic

distance from "the continent," it had little role in the current research.

6. In an interesting related note, intelligence sources in Europe have learned that representatives from South American drug cartels have made overtures to several East and West European countries. The offer is that the cartel will pay the country's national debt in exchange for "safe haven." The amounts of money are truly mind-boggling.

7. Interestingly, some officials interviewed stated that organized crime profits from PIRA activities were becoming so vast that PIRA leaders had no desire to bring peace to Northern Ireland. Instead, they fueled the conflict in order to keep profits coming into the enterprise. Although the situation in Northern Ireland does not appear to be that dichotomous, some evidence supports this notion as related to some PIRA leaders.

PART V

COMMENTARY

In Russia, do we spell it Mafia or Mafiya? Does it matter? Despite what the Great Bard had to say about roses, when looking at organized crime we prefer the adage that if it walks like a duck, talks like a duck, and smells like a duck, it's a duck. In Chapter 14, you'll find *Mafiya* used to mean essentially the same thing as *Mafia*. Chapter 12 is a rather lengthy one, as it should be, because it deals with the history, structure, and function of Russian organized crime. Three of the six authors are native Russians and experts on the criminal justice system there. Note that Joseph Albini (lead author of Chapter 12) has apparently revised his research agenda from American to Russian organized crime.

Again, the social climate is crucial to drawing a conclusion that it enables organized crime to flourish and also to the research context. You cannot study organized crime in Russia, say the authors, unless you understand the rapid and intense social changes that have taken place in that country since the breakup. This notion drives home the point made throughout this text that organized crime is not an insulated event. It does not operate in a vacuum. It must be fed; and it most commonly feeds on those who look to it for goods and services. The feed trough is

seemingly bottomless, for no matter the damage to individuals and businesses done by organized crime, replacement victims are apparently always on hand. Regardless of what part of the world is in focus, organized crime needs a nurturing social environment to succeed.

The systematic classification of types that have characteristics or traits in common is called a *typology*. Typologies are clarifying aids that provide the skeletal basis for knowledge. In Chapter 12, Joseph Albini, Roy E. Rogers, Victor Shabalin, Valery Kutushev, Vladimir Moiseev, and Julie Anderson suggest that organized crime in Russia can be divided into four "major" forms: (a) political-social, (b) mercenary, (c) in-group, and (d) syndicated. That said, the authors return to the debate about what is the Mafia, saying that Mafia is a method, rather than a thing, that the broad use of the term has incorrectly made the Mafia synonymous with organized crime. If understood as a method of criminality, organized crime can then exist anywhere the social and cultural environment exists to foster it. The authors say it is "criminals that migrate," not criminal organizations. They ask why the emigrants from Sicily who settled in the United States entered into a criminal life while their cousins who went to Brazil and

Argentina did not. Regardless of their individual predisposition toward crime, Albini et al. say the national cultural and social conditions in North and South America were different and hence can be found differential tolerances for organized criminality.

Criminality, or deviance, is in the eyes of the beholder. What you think untoward or criminal may not be considered so by the next person. This cultural acceptance of certain behaviors, seen by some as criminal but by others as not, is nicely demonstrated by an anecdote from the New York Police Department. For the last two decades, many immigrants from Russia settled in the Brighton Beach section of Brooklyn. Largely noncriminal, they went about their way as did any predecessor group trying to make a living in a new country. They bought cars and inevitably went through red lights or for any of a thousand reasons were pulled over by the police for traffic infractions. These Russian folk "knew" how to deal with the police. When the police stop you for a traffic violation in Moscow, the most expedient way to handle the matter is pay the cop. Well, that doesn't sit too well with the NYPD, and a fair number of Russians found themselves arrested for bribery. A clash of cultures, for sure, yet illustrative of the power of cultural norms to define deviance. (The resolution of the problem was to offer the police cultural sensitivity training and the immigrants an introduction to the laws of New York and how best to deal with the police.)

J. Michael Waller and Victor Yasmann, in Chapter 14, describe the institutionalized corruption in Russia, albeit at a higher level. According to Waller and Yasmann, those people charged with arresting organized crime are themselves a large part of the problem. Far different from the mundane example above, this chapter documents corruption and coverups at the highest levels of the Russian government. As do the authors of Chapter 12, these authors also discuss the historical antecedents of current conditions, positing that the suppression of private business, market activity, and property rights during the earliest year of Soviet rule has laid the groundwork for today's malfeasance. At the root of it all is a parasitic attachment to the means of controlling and transferring wealth. The Ministry of Internal Affairs (MVD), indeed the entire government in Russia, is seen as a kleptocracy. How such greed and corruption could develop under the watchful eye and iron hand of the KGB is the gravamen of this piece of research. Ubiquitous corruption and nepotistic political protectionism are the clues to the "how" the current state of affairs came about. None less than President Boris Yeltsin describes Russia as a "superpower of crime," mainly because of the innately corrupt nature of its law enforcement agencies, including those charged with national security and intelligence gathering.

The way the United States and other Western countries are helping Russian authorities fight organized crime is based "on an assumption that Moscow has the political will or sincere interest" to carry on such a battle. Waller and Yasmann tell us that such an assumption is false. Interspiced with verbatim accounts of investigators, businessmen, and politicians, this chapter makes excellent reading for its portrayal of the Russian political machinery, which is vastly different from the portrayal the popular media give us. The account by Waller and Yasmann is credible and should be taken at more than face value. Their writing is not hyperbole. This is solid research, and the claims of widespread corruption and political machinations should be treated as facts. However distasteful or incredible your first reaction to this chapter might be, it certainly is supported by Chapter 13.

Like Albini, Robert Kelly has moved his research agenda to Russia, this time bringing along Rufus Schatzberg and Patrick Ryan. In Chapter 13, they analogize the function and structure of Sicilian institutions to the Russian experience with organized crime. Again, a quote from President Boris Yeltsin highlights Chapter 13's subject matter: "We have become a mafia state on a world scale. Everyone thinks that political issues could lead to an explosion but crime could as easily blow us asunder" (cited in Handelman, 1995). These authors describe the political machine of Russia, the Communist Party itself, as a mafia, and proceed to provide cogent evidence in support: "The Communist Party was never a political party in the Western sense." Rather, the entire economic mechanism of a vast empire was "appropriated" by a ruling elite (the party) using intimidation and terror tactics. Repeating part of the message in the two chapters that sandwich it, Kelly et al. note the legacy of early Soviet days in which the most successful entrepreneurs were those who knew best how to grant favors, place payoffs, and line their own pockets. They quickly move to the 1990s, but not without frequent references to Sicily and the collusive arrangements between the politicians and Mafia of that country. Warning is given that as the colusive social and political arrangements exploded (literally) in the death of Magistrates Falcone and Borsellino (the primary anti-Mafia jurists in Italy), Russia might well face a like destruction. Whereas in Sicily the accommodations made by politicians to the Mafia are no longer an open secret, in Russia the very environment that allows organized crime to grow unabated might toll its own death knell.

Pay particular attention to the passage describing the rise of the Mafia in Sicily as a response to a societal need to manage private property rights during the transition from a feudal to a capitalistic economy. Understand how the Mafia provided a service that the state could not provide (protection) and when that task was in hand, branched out into other areas where "violence and extortion were their defining behavior." Kelly et al. contend, "A parallel set of conditions exists today in Russia" and "the past of Sicily may be Russia's future."

Before running to the psychiatrist's couch for help with the feeling that organized crime is devouring the world, reread the concluding portion of Chapter 12. During the era of corrupt government, Russia has been able to produce some of the world's most beautiful music, sculpture, and art; Nobel Prize winners; and a space program that rivals that of the United States. All is not dark. Waller and Yasmann (Chapter 14) say that there are indeed capable and honest professionals in law enforcement, security, and intelligence services. And, somewhat warily, Kelly et al. (Chapter 13) offer a palatable outcome if Russian organized crime, now an *in vivo* embryo, will imitatively develop into an entity somewhat resembling its Western counterparts that *will be thereby containable.*

Using the suggested readings below, can you support the argument made by Kelly et al. that there are real similarities between Sicily and Russia in social structure? All three chapters in Part 5 have a common theme; what is it? A similar conclusion is reached by Alan Block (1983)—that for organized crime to exist, there must be in place a triumvirate of criminals, clients, and politicians (p. 57). Block, a historian, was examining organized crime in New York. Given the material presented in these three chapters, is Block's definition of organized crime applicable to Russia?

SELECTED READINGS

Arlacchi, P. (1986). *Mafia business: The Mafia ethic and the spirit of capitalism.* London: Verso.

Blok, A. (1974). *The Mafia of a Sicilian village, 1860-1960: A study of violent peasant entrepreneurs.* New York: Harper & Row.

Hess, H. (1973). *Mafia and Mafiosi: The structure of power.* Lexington, MA: D. C. Heath.

Mori, C. (1933). *The last struggle with the Mafia.* New York: G. P. Putnam.

Pantaleone, M. (1966). *The Mafia and politics.* New York: Coward & McCann.

Sterling, C. (1990). *Octopus: The long reach of the Sicilian Mafia.* New York: Norton.

12 RUSSIAN ORGANIZED CRIME

Its History, Structure, and Function

JOSEPH L. ALBINI   VALERY KUTUSHEV

ROY E. ROGERS   VLADIMIR MOISEEV

VICTOR SHABALIN   JULIE ANDERSON

In analyzing Russian organized crime, the authors describe and classify the four major forms of organized crime: (a) political-social, (b) mercenary, (c) in-group, and (d) syndicated. Although the first three classifications existed throughout Soviet history, the syndicated form began to emerge in the late 1950s, expanding during the corrupt Brezhnev years (1964-82), exploding during *perestroika,* and reaching pandemic levels after the demise of the Soviet Union in 1991. The abrupt transformation of Russian society from a centralized command economy to one driven by the forces of market capitalism created the sociopathological conditions for the malignant spread of mercenary and especially syndicated organized crime. New criminal syndicates were created by an alliance of criminal gangs/groups and former members of the Soviet Union's communist *nomenklatura* (bureaucracy), and the consequence was the criminalization of much of the Russian economy. The social structure of these syndicates is based on a loose association of patron-client relationships, rather than a centralized hierarchical system; their function is to provide illicit goods/services desired by the people. The authors conclude their study by emphasizing that what has taken place in Russia is not peculiar to the Russian people, but rather exemplifies what can happen to societies that experience rapid and intense social change.

THE PROBLEM OF DEFINING ORGANIZED CRIME

The study of Russian organized crime encompasses the challenge and acknowledgment of all the facets of human behavior, of historical and social change, the many forms that political and economic development can take, and the complexity of the psychology and creativity of the criminal mind that seeks money and power. The Russian experience with organized crime has many lessons—economic, social, and political—from which the discipline of criminology and, indeed, nations and governments can benefit and learn. The Russian experience with organized crime is a lesson in reality. Absent here are the romance and mythology that have surrounded the image of organized crime in the United States as one originated, controlled, and centrally organized by the "Mafia," or "Cosa Nostra." To expect that the American public will finally begin to read the scholarly works on the subject to show that a belief in Mafia and Cosa Nostra has only served to excite readers and visually stimulate movie audiences is too much to ask because mythologies die only with much difficulty. They die hard because they serve a purpose; they excite, entertain, and construct social reality. But history has taught us that mythological constructs are mythology, not reality. And this is true of organized crime in America and the American public's conception of it. The study of Russian organized crime should serve as a laboratory within which the basic features of organized crime reveal themselves. These features and characteristics are basic to its nature, and although historical and cultural factors exert their influence and create some differences in the countries in which organized crime exists, the essence or basic characteristics of organized crime are inherent to its nature.

As we read the literature on organized crime in Russia, both scholars and journalists seem to agree that Russian organized crime is not like the Mafia in the United States. What this comparison means precisely is hard to discern, particularly when some authors refer to organized criminals in Russia as "the Russian Mafia." But this usage is at the core of our discussion; that is, the term *Mafia* has become a synonym for *organized crime*. This confusion emerged as a result of the indiscriminate use of the term *Mafia* among American scholars and journalists. In Albini's pioneering work *The American Mafia* (1971), the argument was made that there never was a secret criminal society called "Mafia," either in Sicily (its supposed country of origin) or in the United States (the country of its supposed exportation). If we correctly understand its origin in Sicily, the Mafia was not and is not one organization, but rather, the term is better understood as a method or modus operandi of a criminal endeavor that has the following three components (Albini, 1971, p. 88):

1. The use of force, intimidation, or threats of such
2. The structure of a group whose purpose is that of providing illicit services through the use of secrecy on the part of its associates
3. The assurance of political protection from the legal structure that is necessary for its continuous operation

As a method, then, Mafia can exist anywhere. As for its being exported or imported, we should understand that organized criminals migrate; the system and the criminals' ability to employ it in any given country, by contrast, depends on the social conditions and social system of that country, which may either foster its use or stifle its development. Thus, as has been noted (Albini, 1992, p. 87), it is argued that the Sicilian Mafia migrated to the United States during 1870 to 1920. During the same time, an equally large migration of Italians to Brazil and Argentina took place; yet, Della Cava (1977, p. 197) notes, "not only are Italians and their descendants rarely associated with professional criminality, in either country, but also 'organized crime' itself exists on a greatly reduced scale." So, too, as Albini (1986) has noted in his study of organized crime in Great Britain, Italians are virtually nonexistent as a major force in organized crime activity.

Contrary to popular Mafia lore, specific ethnic groups do not create or determine whether Mafia will exist; rather, the existence of social, economic, and historical factors in each society set the stage for its emergence and success. Thus, in the history of the United States, virtually every ethic group has been found to have had members that participated in organized crime. Their method has always been the same. Yet, because of a need for mythological belief, the Sicilian Mafia has caused the word *Mafia* to become a synonym; it can be a synonym, but not one for referring to a secret criminal organization—rather, for what is a *method* of organized criminal activity.

So, as we move toward understanding the nature of organized crime in Russia, the Russian experience allows us and forces us, if we truly wish to understand its reality and the reality of organized crime in any other country, to apply clear and useful distinctions to the term *organized crime*.

THE NEED FOR
A SPECIFIC DEFINITION

As one reads the scant literature (Abadinsky, 1992, pp. 264-165; Kenny & Finckenauer, 1995, p. 276) on Russian organized crime, particularly that in the United States, one immediately notes confusion regarding whether Russian organized crime is, in fact, organized crime, whether it is a form of Mafia, how it is structured, and a variety of other elements. By contrast, Lydia Rosner (1986) presents a more useful portrait of the Russian immigrant and Russian organized crime in the United States by examining this immigrant group's value system regarding how it relates to crime in Russia and then by examining the adaptations these immigrants have made regarding criminal activity in the United States.

Once again, we stress that Mafia as a method is dependent for its effective development on the social setting in which it exists far more than it is on the structure or organization of the groups that engage in it. We can stress the logic behind this observation by simply asking, "Has any ethnic, racial, or other type of group, irrespective of its organizational structure, not been successful in its involvement with organized criminal activity in the United States?" The Irish, Poles, Germans, Japanese, Chinese, motorcycle gangs, Jamaicans, prison gangs, Cubans, Colombians, Mexicans, the Black Guerrilla "family," and the Aryan Brotherhood are just a few we mention, but the list goes on. Why does it go on? Because the United States is the land of opportunity for success in organized crime. U.S. society, with its historically changing but ever-present needs and demands for illicit goods and a public that has hidden under a guise of morality, has set up a system in which great financial wealth can be made. This wealth can be acquired, providing that one wishes to

take the risk of possible imprisonment or death or both and has the ingenuity by which to provide some form of political protection for one's criminal enterprise through favors for their protectors or by simply giving them direct payoffs.

This is the American way of crime. The mythology of the "Sicilian Mafia" has been just that—a mythology.

The Sicilians have been no different from any other group in their modus operandi or structure in terms of achieving success at organized criminal ventures in America. For the past three decades, they simply became the show that America watched in an effort to convince itself that the real threat of organized crime lies from outside its boundaries in the form of an invasion of foreigners and their mystical secret society. Social and political systems allow for the creation of organized crime. That is a fact. And so the Russian social system in the past and particularly since the collapse of the Berlin Wall has laid the breeding grounds for organized crime to flourish in Russia. That, too, is a fact. As we demonstrate, the Russians are no more or less moral than Americans. In fact, as we show, American and Russian patterns of organized crime are, in many respects, similar. Their differences emerge only as those influenced by such factors as historical development and the rapidity of the economic, political, and social changes that occurred in Russia at the turn of this decade. Along with those found in America, there are similarities between the Russian patterns and structure of organized crime and those found in the history and development of organized crime in Sicily.

DEFINITION AND STRUCTURE

The basic problem with the literature that grapples with the question of whether Russian organized crime in America and Russia is really organized crime, we believe, comes from the mistaken need for writers to continue to emphasize the structure of criminal groups more than their function. No one makes this point more succinctly than Southerland and Potter (1993, p. 264). Speaking to the structure and function of criminal groups, they conclude:

> The empirical evidence suggests that criminal enterprises are small, centralized organizations with short hierarchies, little specialization, and unwritten formalization based on socialization. The logic of the situation based on organization structure theory demonstrates how unlikely it is that a very large tightly controlled and organized criminal conspiracy could function in operational reality.
>
> A monopolistic syndicate by definition would have an extremely large number of employees and numerous functional specialties such as drugs, prostitution, gambling and loansharking. To achieve its goals, the syndicate would have to provide constant instruction and information to street-level purveyors. It would have to monitor employee performance, keep careful records, and engage in considerable discussion about specific plans. These behaviors would imperil the very existence of the organization. If such a conspiracy existed, removing its leadership would cripple the enterprise. Experience demonstrates that this has not happened despite extensive successful prosecutions of prominent organized crime figures.

We are in agreement with Southerland and Potter and think it would be more productive to study the functions of organized crime groups because the structure is assuredly based on that function. Many writers, it seems, are so influenced by a belief in a conspiratorial model of criminal enterprises that they go searching for large, complexly structured groups of participants. In doing so, they miss the trees for the forest. As we observe Russian organized crime, we find that, like American organized crime, the function—that is, what the criminals are trying to accomplish in terms of goals—definitely influences the structure. Therefore, in our search and discussion, we find it productive to employ Albini's (1971, chap. 2) classification of the four major forms of organized crime:

1. *Political-social organized crime:* The goal is not direct financial profit or the changing or maintaining of the existing political-social structure. An example of this is terrorism or the Ku Klux Klan.

2. *Mercenary organized crime:* The goal is the attainment of direct financial profit. Included are racketeering, extortion, organized theft of goods, confidence games, and other forms of profit-oriented crimes.

3. *In-group organized crime:* Financial gain is not the direct goal, but instead the purpose lies in the individual's psychological and social gratification of belonging to a group that engages in deviant and criminal activity. Included here are the hedonistic or violent gangs that engage in thrills or violence but do so for the adventure itself. Examples of this are the adolescent and street-corner gangs, found in most cities, that frequently engage in street fights over territory, or "rumbles."

4. *Syndicated organized crime:* The goal is to attain direct financial gain by providing illicit goods or services or both through the use of threats or violence and by attaining forms of police or political "protection" that will safeguard the criminal from legal interference. Examples are gambling, prostitution, and drug syndicates.

The reader will note that each of these forms of criminal activity has a different goal and that the structures and size of the group will vary, depending on the structural and personnel differences required in the achievement of each goal. The confusion that so often occurs in the literature arises from the fact that many authors use the term *Mafia* to describe organized criminal activity that is mercenary or political-social in nature. The term *Mafia,* if it is used properly to describe a method, is really correctly used only when it refers to syndicated crime. But even here, because the term has become so indiscriminately, erroneously, and randomly used, we advocate that it not be used (because of the misunderstanding its use creates). Instead, we prefer and use the term *syndicated crime.*

RUSSIAN ORGANIZED CRIME: A TRADITION

As we move now to the analysis and description of Russian organized crime, we do so within a theoretical background that views its development from a historical and social perspective.

To argue that Russian organized crime is a current phenomenon is to miss its existence within Soviet society in the past.

To say, however, that it is not a current phenomenon is to fail to understand that the breakdown and breakup of the Soviet Union in 1991 opened new roads and new opportunities for organized criminal ventures to develop within Russia itself and to reach out across international boundaries. This phenomenon has become so pronounced that the Russian government has appealed for international help from legal agencies in its fight against organized crime (*Las Vegas Review Journal*, 1994). So, too, because Russian organized crime is now viewed both by the American public and by American law enforcement agencies as part of America's growing crime problem, we present our discussion in the context of comparing the Russian and American experience. Also, as we noted earlier, because Russian organized crime manifests a profile of emerging from the rapidity and abruptness of swift historical and societal change, it serves as a laboratory of social-scientific research. Also, we believe that because of the confusion concerning the nature of the Mafia in Sicily, it will be of heuristic value to the international study of organized crime to compare the similarities and differences of syndicated criminal development in Russia and Sicily. Indeed, there are many similarities along with drastic differences.

Let's move on, then, to the investigation and understanding of this complex, multivariable, social-cultural phenomenon known as organized crime.

As we stated before, to say that Russian organized crime is a new phenomenon is to miss a major lesson learned from the Russian experience—mainly, that although totalitarian political systems can control most aspects of social life, they cannot totally control all of them. So as V. L. Dedenkov (cited in Shabalin, Albini, & Rogers, 1990, pp. 5-6) notes, following the Russian Revolution, a variety of criminal groups or organizations appeared that have been given the name "thieves within the code." These groups varied in size, had a leader, and had rules of behavior for their members, one of the major

rules being that members not become involved in politics. It is difficult to construct an accurate profile of these organizations because one of their major features was secrecy. Sterling (1994b, p. 47), citing the work of the Russian poet and ex-thief Mikhail Dyomin, notes that such organizations date back to the 1600s. However, Sterling seems to agree with Dyomin that these were organized on the model of the Sicilian Mafia. At this point, we should note that both Sterling's and Dyomin's arguments are based on an erroneous confusion: that of viewing Mafia, the so-called Sicilian secret society, with other Sicilian criminal groups known as "Frattellanze" or "brotherhoods." Mafia, as we define it as a method, could not and did not emerge in Sicily until 1860, when the institution of universal suffrage provided the third component of what constitutes syndicated crime or Mafia as method—political protection (Albini, 1971, p. 127).

These brotherhoods arose in the 1700s to fight the Bourbons, whose rule began in 1738. The frequent mythological and erroneous belief that the Mafia in Sicily began as a benevolent organization to fight the French oppressive government is born here. These brotherhoods, as Antonino Cutrera (cited in Albini, 1971, p. 114) states, though they stressed secrecy and each was organized and had a leader, were organized, not for noble purposes, but instead to make profits from theft and extortion. As such, they seem to have had the same structure and function as the thieves within the code. We argue, then, that the thieves within the code in Russia, from the scant information we have regarding them, were, at least during the early years of Soviet Security Police and later Stalinist repression from 1920 until 1950, at most, criminal organizations that engaged in mercenary, not syndicated, crime. Later, particularly after the breakup of the Soviet Union, some of these thieves-within-the-code groups did begin engaging in forms of syndicated crime.

The 1920s saw a struggle for power among different factions in the Communist Party; it was especially intense after the death of Lenin in 1924. By 1928, Stalin had eliminated the opposition and ruled with an iron fist until his death in March 1953. The Stalinist era was from 1928 to 1953.

In reference to the organized criminality of the thieves within the code and of organized crime in general in Russia during the communist era, officially the Soviet government took the position that such activity was a product of a capitalistic system and therefore could not exist in a socialist society (Shabalin et al., 1990, p. 1). Hence, any information regarding evidence or allegations of its existence was flagrantly suppressed to the point that when KGB and military personnel themselves reported such activities, they were simply told, "There is no organized crime in the Soviet Union." We should also add that, during this era, the majority of crimes for which people were arrested, such as those arrests resulting from the purges of the 1930s, were politically motivated and viewed as crimes against the state (Shabalin et al., 1990, p. 6).

Although there is nebulousness about the nature of organized crime groups in Russia before the revolution and in the postrevolutionary 1920s and Stalinist era, this nebulousness begins to clear as we move into the 1950s. The current, mistaken, but prevalent belief is that, in Russia, organized crime in its contemporary forms did not exist until the tearing down of the Iron Curtain or, put another way, that Russian organized crime first appeared as a result of *glasnost* and *perestroika*.

Rosner (1993) is quick to counter this point of view, and we agree with her that various forms of Russian mercenary and syndicated crime were in existence even though they were being hidden by the Iron Curtain. In fact, we would argue that the current forms of mercenary and some forms of syndicated crime began appearing and evolving in complexity by the end of the 1950s and flourished during the period of stagnation—the label given to the period of rule of the Communist Party leader Leonid Brezhnev (1964-82) (Shabalin et al., 1990, p. 7). This period is important to our later discussion of the development of various forms of organized crime. During this time, the breeding grounds for the development of organized crime

emerged when capital investment was allocated to the military in an effort to gain missile parity with the United States, all at the expense and sacrifice to the Soviet people's standard of living (Shabalin et al., 1990, p. 7).

Konstantin Simis, writing in 1982, had already labeled the U.S.S.R. the "corrupt society" and stated then that both "the Soviet state and society alike [were] rotten with corruption from top to bottom" (p. 179). To say that organized crime in Russia is a new phenomenon, then, is to miss the role of its historical development since the 1950s and the changes in the political, economic, and social system of Russia and its republics during the era of stagnation.

Nonetheless, we must make an important distinction between the era before and the era after the breakdown and breakup of the Soviet Union between 1989 and 1991: That is, prior to this period, organized crime in the Soviet Union focused primarily on enterprises within its political and territorial boundaries; after the fall, it extended its enterprises and boundaries to international markets and territories.

When Eastern Europe broke away from communist control in 1989, it had a profound effect on the Soviet Union. Many nationalists wanted independence for their republics. During that same year, the Communist Party competed with other parties for seats in the new Duma (Parliament). When the military and the KGB failed in the August 19-21, 1991, coup, Boris Yeltsin dissolved the Soviet Union and created the Commonwealth of Independent States (C.I.S.). He also outlawed the Communist Party (it later became legal under a different name) and seized its assets of more than 3 billion rubles.

To understand organized crime in Russia during both periods, we must examine the nature of its origins within the cultural and historical development of the Soviet Union itself. For within the values of this culture juxtaposed and in conjunction with the economic, political, and other aspects of Soviet society, this form of criminality took root. After its various types had developed and its various groups formed, its exportation into other countries and the nature of these exported forms of criminality became dependent on the social, economic, and political environment of those countries into which they were exported and on the demand for illegal goods and services that existed in the global marketplace. We are here trying to emphasize the distinction between the phenomenon of a criminal system that develops within a society generated by individuals born and raised in that society and their individual participation in similar forms of that criminality outside that system. Thus, although Mafia as a method developed and exists in Sicily, it is a composite of the Sicilian life and culture of Sicily. If Sicilians who participated in that system came to the United States, as some of them did, it is not the Mafia that is transported. A cultural system, as such, cannot be transported; instead, individuals migrate and bring with them their criminal values and techniques. Ultimately, however, whether such criminals are successful in effectively instituting these criminal enterprises in their country of destination depends on the amenability of the social system of that country to foster such development.

By contrast, criminal groups or criminal secret societies with a particular modus operandi could migrate to a foreign country as a group. If their style of criminality is new to that country, then we can speak of these groups as having exported a new form of crime. If, however, that form of criminality already exists within the country they enter, we can hardly refer to these criminals as having exported it into that country. In either respect, as we noted, whether these groups are successful in implementing their criminal operation depends on the social, economic, political, and other conditions of the country into which they migrate.

We make the above distinctions because, in the literature concerning organized crime, particularly that of Russian organized crime, we so often note the use of the term *export* in the discussion of what are described as new forms of organized crime in the United States and other countries. A major illustration of this is witnessed in the argument that has become a part of U.S. folklore—mainly, that the Sicilians "exported" the Mafia to the United States. History shows us that Mafia as a method existed in America as early as the time of the Civil War, long before the conditions surrounding the Prohibition Era in the 1920s allowed the Sicilians and many other ethnic groups to take their turn at engaging in a pattern of crime—syndicated crime—that is as American in origin as apple pie.

RUSSIAN ORGANIZED CRIME: AFTER THE BREAKUP

It is true that many changes in the types of organized criminal enterprises and the organizations of the groups operating them took place after the fall of communism in 1989-1991. But to argue that the fall created this surge in Russian criminality is to miss the realities of what was occurring in Russia before the coming of *glasnost* and *perestroika*. Rosner (1993) makes this point succinctly in the title of her article— "Crime and Corruption in Russia Are Nothing New." We agree with her that the seeds of what has grown to become the formulation of criminal groups that now threaten international peace and safety through the terror of the potential sale of nuclear material (*Time,* 1994b) were sown in the very system of communism and its inherent and absolute policy of the state owning all goods and services. In the reports of recent conferences and seminars held in Russia, Professor V. Shabalin and A. I. Dolgova and various other social scientists, government representatives, and lawyers have noted that the current practice of bribery and corruption certainly existed during the time of the czars and historically have been an embedded part of the very nature of Russian society. Indeed, N. G. Chemyskevsky speaks of Russia as a land "rich in bribe takers . . . since time immemorial" (Shabalin et al., 1990, p. 18).

Our purpose here is not to degrade or pass judgment on Russian society or its people; most Russians are honest citizens. Instead, we wish to observe, analyze, and discuss a way of life that Rosner (1986) refers to in the title of her book as *The Soviet Way of Crime.* This system incorporates a cultural way of social interaction, brought about by political and economic restrictions, that has come to constitute the arena of life in Russia for most of the 20th century.

THE PATRON-CLIENT RELATIONSHIP

It is a way of life and crime that arises out of needs, values, and social interaction patterns that can be understood only within the web of a historical development and social structure unique to Russia. This does not mean that there are no similarities to other cultures. Indeed, one could argue that, in the way of crime, Russia has several historical-social patterns that are similar to those of Sicily. But history and social forces do not form societies so that they are identical; hence, the differences far exceed the similarities. Yet, in the social potential for the development of syndicated crime, the people of Russia and of Sicily definitely have one feature in common: They both have a distrust of government and governmental power. Sicilians developed this distrust because of the many and rapid foreign invasions during which the conquerors took over the land, took what they needed, and either left or were forced to leave by cultural revolutions or other foreign invaders. Under such conditions, one learns to rely on family and communal ties as resources for sustaining life and human relationships, as opposed to relying on the typically unfulfilled promises of central governments. In Russia, governments under both the rule of the czar and that of the communist state represented totalitarianism in one form or another where individual freedom was suppressed. As such, like the invading foreigners of Sicily, the internal governmental system of Russia has made the Russians, like the Sicilians, distrustful of government. This common historical inheritance in both Sicily and Russia has produced a method of social interaction in which patrons and clients become the basic social format for interaction.

The terms *patron* and *client* describe power relationships that gain their meaning only within the context of social interaction. This power is not formalized in the legal system, nor is it established by conventionally prescribed rules. Yet, it lies at the basis of interaction, both legal and illegal, in both Russian and Sicilian society. To describe these terms, we turn to the work of Jeremy Boissevain (1966, p. 18), who defines a *patron* as any person in a position of power and influence and who thereby can help or protect others not in that position. The *client,* by contrast, is the person who seeks and receives the assistance and protection for which he or she, in return, offers services to the patron. Eric Wolf (1966, pp. 16-17) further elaborates on the description by noting that no two functionaries in a patron-client relationship are equal. He also notes that patrons and clients can engage in both legal and illegal actions in which the patron provides assistance and protection, with the client returning the favor by being loyal to the patron, giving political support, and providing the patron with information that is vital to his or her personal and social welfare.

Patron-client relationships are not governed by legal norms, but instead are based on social norms in which there is an accepted faith between the two participants that each will carry out his or her end of the bargain. Most important, the power relations between patrons and clients are constantly in a state of change so that a patron at one time or in one situation may later become the client of his or her original client. So, too, a patron, while serving as such to a client, may him- or herself simultaneously serve as a client to another patron. Thus, the patron-client relationship must be understood as a system of interaction taking place at and between various levels of social strata and involving constantly changing power positions. The nature of patron-client relationships varies from society to society, but in Sicily and Russia, the system operates to form networks of relationships in which the more clients a patron has, the more power the patron gains from favors he or she can request. This power is enhanced further by the vital information the patron obtains; in turn, the more patrons a client has, the more power he or she obtains from the protection and service the client can receive. As such, it is a mutually reinforcing system in which, in terms of cost-benefit analysis, it serves both parties to cooperate and help one another. As such, both parties can gain and retain power.

Because of the distrust of government in both Sicily and Russia and the development of the patron-client system of interaction, the breeding grounds for syndicated organized crime were entrenched in both social systems. In Sicily, the catalyst for the development of Mafia as a method resulted from ownership of land in the *gabel-lotto*, or landlord system, which developed following the abolition and breakdown of the feudal system in 1812 (see Albini, 1971, chap. 4). These landlords slowly established themselves in the social structure by developing patron-client relationships in which they could offer services, legal and illegal, to a variety of clients. In time, they hired men skilled in the use of violence, and through time, the landlords threatened and employed violence against those who opposed them. Finally, when Italy obtained universal suffrage, the landlord could now provide votes for government officials who, in turn, if elected, would be in a position to offer the landlord and all his clients protection from the law.

In Russia, the catalyst was not land as land, and its tenure under the czars never had or took the format of Sicily's *gabellotto*. Hence, the criminal activity described during that era and following the early days of communist rule as thieves within the code or bands of thieves organized around the major element of secrecy was primarily that constituting forms of mercenary crime. These groups stole for financial gain or profit but had no political protection. It remained to the days of the full development of the communist state, to the development of the political and economic system of the 1960s Soviet society, for syndicated crime to emerge as a pattern that took hold and continues today. There is no doubt that *perestroika* and *glasnost* exerted their influence in the direction and volume of syndicated crime, but the system of the

patron-client way of crime in the Soviet Union was already alive and doing well before these political programs were introduced.

What land was to the spawning of syndicated crime in Sicily in the 1860s, state-owned goods and services were to become in the Russia of the 1960s, the bartering ingredient that generated the development of Russian syndicated crime. By contrast with Russia and Sicily, in the United States, where syndicated crime has existed as early as the 1860s, it was and continues to be Americans' desire for illegal goods and services that historically has created the many criminal syndicates that procure political protection and threaten and use violence to make such goods available.

Organized crime, then, particularly syndicated crime, is a complex phenomenon. The structure of the groups that engage in it reveals many variations; thus, ethnicity, kinship, business, and other bases for organization and cooperation appear and vary in the societies in which syndicated crime exists. Indeed, in contrast with the belief in a large, centralized, bureaucratic format of syndicate structure, research reveals the opposite: Structures small in the number of functionaries, with continually changing involvement of personnel and power relationships and constantly changing webs of networks and enterprises, are the features that make this form of criminality the menace that it is. It is not the secrecy in which these groups conduct those enterprises, for the practice of secrecy is a natural ingredient to all criminal enterprises. Nor is it the largeness of the group that sustains such enterprises, for largeness would hamper rather than aid their effective functioning. Instead, the existence of many small syndicates, with their multitude of network patron-client relationships and the demand for their goods and services, gives syndicated criminals their strength and persistence in societies that allow them to function. At the end of the argument concerning its existence lies the reality that societies, not individuals, create the basis for syndicated organized crime.

SYNDICATE CRIME IN A
STATE-CONTROLLED ECONOMY

The basic source of syndicated crime in Russia arises, as Rosner (1993) explains, in the fact that, in the Soviet Union, all goods and services were owned by the state. As such, theoretically, there could be no private enterprise. We say "theoretically" because, in reality, there was a way, the Soviet way of crime: That way was to steal goods from the state or illegally barter for the performance of services in a manner that, like theft, would have been considered a crime against the state.

The state, of course, was caught in a dilemma: It needed to provide goods and services to its populace, but it was also concerned about developing and keeping its military strength equal, if not superior, to that of its then adversary the United States. In the 1960s, particularly under the rule of Leonid Brezhnev, most capital investment was diverted into the science and military establishment in an effort to counteract the new U.S. threat of missile development. In doing so, the state seriously reduced the production and supply of goods and services that constituted the basic necessities for life and comfort among the general population. As a result, a black market for all goods and services emerged.

This condition was further complicated by the political reality of what Simis (1982, pp. 2, 27) calls "the dual system of government" that existed at that time—that is, the bodies of government such as the Council of Ministers and other agencies empowered to govern by the constitution, alongside the Communist Party, which is not even mentioned in the constitution, yet became the real ruling body of the Soviet Union. As Simis further explains, because the state, which owned all goods and services and was the sole employer of the population, was subject to the Communist Party's decisions, this translated into the party really being the sole controller of all aspects of Soviet life.

And so, it seems that when shortages in goods and services were created by the state's allocations of money for military purposes in the 1960s, the Soviet citizens at all levels began to create their own manner of obtaining the goods and services that often constituted the basic necessities of life or that made living easier and more pleasant.

Lev Timofeyev (1990, p. 58), a Russian critic of the Soviet regime, puts this reaction on the part of Soviet citizens very succinctly when he observes: "No violence or brainwashing, however intensive, could make man forego the basic relations of supply and demand. Apparently, nature has not provided any other mechanism for supporting the social life of *Homo sapiens.*"

And so the shortage brought into action the use of patron-client relationship. As Rosner (1993, p. 1) describes it,

> Thus a state employee could find work doing private repair jobs for those who could pay him with meat or clothing stolen from their jobs. The state employee had to obtain his supplies from a network of "friends" whose favors he rewarded with favors of his own. A state cement truck driver would exchange some cement, delivered to a private job, for some coats for his children. A state clerk in an automobile licensing agency would exchange the right to drive a motor vehicle for gasoline for his own use or sale.

As Lev Timofeyev (1990, p. 58) notes further, "Everything is bought and sold in this country. Everything including the official positions in the Communist Party."

And Rosner (1993, p. 1) adds to Timofeyev's observation by noting that further alienation from the central government took place as the national organization in the republics themselves became totally corrupt, the people in charge staying in power and increasing their power by granting and exchanging political favors as well as employing private procurers in order to obtain all types of goods and services.

Syndicated crime, as a form, existed at this time because it is difficult to distinguish the criminals from the political protectors. Because many people, if they could, were stealing goods from the state and wheeling and dealing in the game of exchanging goods and services, it is ludicrous to argue that criminal syndicates were established to provide illicit goods to those who desired them. Why? Because this entire system of citizens and government agents obtaining goods and services was so widespread as to have become itself the social norm. So, too, violence, though it seems to have occurred in the form that Rosner (1986, p. 9) mentions as the use of violent force by "thugs" working for corrupt district party members, was not, during this time period, a pronounced feature of this system or the Soviet way of crime. Ironically, and further confusing the issue of the existence of syndicated crime, during this era of communist rule, as Timofeyev (1990, pp. 56-57) notes, any entrepreneurial activity, whether engaged in by criminal groups or honest businesspeople, was by definition considered illegal and punishable by law. But because so many government officials were themselves engaging in corrupt practices, it is difficult not to argue that the government itself consisted of a form of organized crime. For if the corrupter is simultaneously the corrupted, where are the boundaries for establishing the definition and essence of the legal system?

It seems, then, that the period prior to the fall of communism and the breakup of the Soviet Union became the training and breeding ground for the development of syndicated crime in contemporary Russia. Up to that time, the criminality—if one can call it that, considering the fact that stealing from the state and the rampant exchanging of goods and services among Soviet citizens had become the social norm—was, for the most part, contained within the Soviet Union. But with the breakup of the Soviet Union and the movement toward the development of a market economy and the privatization of business and industry, the former Soviet Union experienced one of the most rapid and tumultuous changes in the history of social change. The breeding and training grounds now having been established, Russia and its republics were a ripe market for the development of an international market of criminal ventures. And so, in the late 1980s and early 1990s, this Soviet way of crime extended its boundaries and developed its various forms of contemporary organized crime, including the clear development of syndicated organized crime.

The picture of the contemporary scene in Russia is best painted by the 1993 *U.S. News & World Report* article most timely entitled "Focus on Change" (1994, p. 17). The report reads:

> The former Soviet Union is a cauldron of contrasts. It is now 15 separate countries, the sum of the new parts much less than the old whole. Russia dominates, undeniably weakened; its military is dispirited and underfunded, its economy in a steepening plunge, its political reform stalemated. But it is also strong. Its arsenal of 30,000 nuclear weapons is intact; it has vast reserves of natural resources, a solid labor base and a growing entrepreneurial class. In Russia and the other new states, many younger leaders haven't abandoned hopes of radically reforming political systems.

This report then describes the current process of converting the military and defense industry into civilian production by using the Russian term *konvulsiya* ("convulsion"; p. 17); and, indeed, *convulsion* is probably the best word for describing the entire current social system of Russia and the federation. In a state of convulsion, the human body loses equilibrium. Convulsing political units do the same.

ECONOMIC DISEQUILIBRIUM AND ORGANIZED CRIME

We use the analogy of disequilibrium because Russia and its former republics are caught in a web of contradictory and conflicting political and social forces often serving to frustrate and block the desperately needed move toward a unified and cooperative approach toward the resolution of economic and other problems. This situation is a perfect setting for the proliferation of crime, particularly organized crime. As the movement and changes geared toward privatization began to emerge slowly in 1989 and 1990, the forces—business, political, and criminal—of the old and the new power groups began to clash. Young entrepreneurs who honestly believed that a private and free economy was the new mode of doing business did, in fact, begin creating business enterprises. At first, it seems that the old-time Communist bureaucrats simply expected these young businesspeople to fail because these bureaucrats believed that any capitalistic venture, by its very nature, could not succeed. When these bureaucrats saw that these entrepreneurs could and were becoming successful, however, they either used their legal power and the law itself to arrest them, often as Timofeyev (1990, pp. 58-59) notes, labeling them as "Mafia-profiteers" or, recognizing that there was gold in those capitalistic hills, decided to join them and allow the capitalistic system to work for them.

And so privatization, definitely established as an economic program in 1992, became, as Rosner (1993, p. 2) puts it, "the ultimate shakeout of a bureaucratically corrupt system." But with privatization, the world, not just Russia and its federation, became the stage on which the current drama of Russian organized crime would be enacted.

Internally, the breakdown of the Soviet Union sounded the bell for various republics to demand or fight or both for independence. A look at the military operations of the Russian special forces reveals that, since 1989, political-social organized crime became a major concern for the new Russia. In 1989, political unrest demanded military intervention in Uzbekistan. In the spring of 1990, ethnic unrest in the trans-Caucasian republics demanded Russia's military action. Indeed, May and June 1992 saw political upheavals in the form of riots, protests, civil war, terrorism, and other forms of political-social criminality in Kazakhstan, Uzbekistan, Georgia, and Dagestan. These and the continued conflict between Azerbaijan and Armenia over Nogorno-Karabakh created a continuing sequence of criminal acts of a political-social nature. Jim Shortt (1993), who has trained KGB personnel and police and security forces in the Baltic states before, as well as after, independence, cites numerous cases of terrorism and other forms of social-political organized crime. What is interesting about Shortt's description and analysis of these political-social actions is his mention of the involvement of Russian "Mafia" functionaries. Quick to note that, in Russia, *Mafia* is a generic term for racketeers, black marketeers, and gangsters (p. 39), Shortt mentions that these criminal gangs were frequently employed to help the cause of interior ministers in various former republics. As such, Shortt notes, in Latvia, in March 1992, a criminal group went to the extent of disguising themselves as members of a military unit by wearing the Russian military red beret and camouflage. These groups, as Shortt observes (p. 27), disguised as official Russian special units, were actually paid criminals whose task was to protect and facilitate the escape of other criminals in the event of attack by authentic Russian forces.

MERCENARY CRIME: THE NEW ROBBER BARONS

Probably the most voluminous form of organized criminality ushered in by the breakup of the U.S.S.R. and the movement toward privatization lies in the category of mercenary crime. For here, the goal is not the seeking or retaining of political power, but outright profit itself.

Russian research (Shabalin et al., 1990, p. 7) finds a direct relationship between the growth of contemporary organized crime and the improvement of the economic system. Russian students of the topic agree that "the level of organized crime is closely associated with the state of the economy" and that "within the economy is hidden the nucleus of the criminal corporation."

We note once again that the breeding grounds for the growth of organized crime and the accompanying patron-client system of social interaction necessary for its development were already intact prior to the coming of privatization; one, then, can readily understand that when the economic gates were open, a flood of criminal ventures began to flow through Russia, its former republics, and the world. This growth has brought to the foreground a term that has come to be widely used in the discussion of contemporary Russian organized crime—"the shadow economy"—and rightly so, for within the context of this economic system, organized crime seems to have increased in both types and number of enterprises, as well as its extension into international markets.

But we must note that the shadow economy and its frequently employed synonym, "the black market," has its roots in the past social patterns of Soviet society. Its evolution into contemporary forms spawned by criminals must be viewed from the perspective of a system where, formally, all goods and services were owned by the state to one slowly trying to change to a system of individual entrepreneurs. We define *shadow economy* as "the entire complex of non-accounted, non-regulated and illegal types of economic activities (different from normative documents and rules of the economy)" (Shabalin et al., 1990, p. 12).

But, in offering this definition, we heed the words of Lev Timofeyev (1990, p. 59), who reminds us that the entire Soviet economy has been nothing else but an "enormous 'black market' of goods, services, official positions and privileges." Timofeyev also answers the question of why the black market nonetheless has helped create the current growth and expansion of organized criminality. He explains:

> The chief drawback of the Soviet black market in comparison to the free market is that in the former the profit is not genuine capital, it cannot be used for investment, for expanding production and improving productivity. Untaxed cash acquired in this market is typically used for personal consumption or converted into gold and valuables which in the recent period are increasingly apt to be taken out of the country via illegal routes. (p. 56)

This practice casts the shadow of criminality across Russia, and the shadow it casts takes many forms.

Paul Klebnikov, writing in *Forbes* magazine (1994a, pp. 74-84), compares current Russia

with that era of the robber barons in America during which the robber barons dominated American capitalism. Men like Cornelius Vanderbilt, John D. Rockefeller, and others gained control of huge assets, not through theft, but through their organizational skills and financial leverage. Klebnikov then describes several Russian businessmen who have become wealthy. It is here worthwhile, for the purpose of our discussion, to note briefly the description of how one of these men became successful because it illustrates our point that the old political-economic system in Russia has blended with the new. Klebnikov writes about Mikhail Khodorkovsky, chairman of Menatep Bank, a Russian bank with close to $1 billion:

> His first financial backing came from one of the communist-controlled district councils of Moscow. Later, Khodorkovsky apparently bought out the district council. Now this swarthy young man runs a vast conglomerate. It includes Menatep Bank, a dozen other banks, Moscow real estate, a steel mill, one of Russia's largest producers of titanium as well as food processing and chemical companies. (p. 74)

His article goes on to tell how Khodorkovsky lives in luxury but is surrounded by a host of private security guards.

The web of patron-client relationships, apart from allowing for the creation of robber barons, has also allowed for the old and the new to come together in the establishment of a variety of new mercenary organized criminal adventures.

ORGANIZED CRIME ACTIVITIES

The fear of nuclear war, spawned by the threat of nuclear missiles falling into the hands of terrorists, has caused concern over organized crime and its involvement in the sale of plutonium, as well as nuclear missiles themselves. It is difficult to estimate the extent of such ventures, but the fact that two attempted illegal sales of radioactive materials were thwarted by Russian police in 1994 and that, since 1991, close to 440 cases of the attempted smuggling of nuclear material into Germany, most being rendered ineffective by sting operations (*Time*, 1994b, pp. 46-51), makes the possibility of such sales loom as real threats.

In his discussion of the sale of nuclear material, William Burrows (1994, pp. 54-55) states the reality surrounding this issue by reminding us that Iraq, Iran, Libya, and other countries would be interested in purchasing plutonium. With such a demand, the possibility always exists that both lone freelancers and criminal syndicates in Russia or one of its former republics may serve as the avenue for establishing and facilitating these connections. Obviously, the sale could come from some scientist or official who has access to such material, or organized criminals could bribe the source of access to obtain the nuclear material and arrange for its sale.

A great danger is posed by the conversion of the Russian army as an object of the activities of criminal associations. These associations have the following aims:

Procurement of valuable raw materials

Acquisition of technology for next to nothing

Control over the sale of military technology abroad

Use of army transportation capabilities for illegal conveyance

Seizure of various types of weapons

Recruitment of discharged servicemen into subunits for guarding criminal structures

So, too, organized crime leaders attempt to corrupt and infiltrate special military detachments such as the Russian Cossacks and other elite units entrusted with guarding military supply depots in an effort to attain weapons and nuclear and other valuable materials.

In contrast with the questionable sale of nuclear material, Louise Shelley (1994), testifying before the Commission on Security and Cooperation in Europe, alerts us to the large illicit trade in military equipment, which is alarming because it is helping support armed conflicts within the former Soviet Union and other parts of the world. This information that Shelley cites is given credence by the recent scandal and accusations against Russian Defense Minister Paval Grachev (*Time*, 1994c, pp. 80-81), who, in answering accusations from the Russian Parliament, accused the Parliament of being the real culprit because it controls the purse strings. In either respect, the scandal surrounds the illegal sale of military property in Germany.

According to an article by Seymour Hersh (1994, p. 75), 60 kg of highly enriched uranium were seized by the Russian Ministry of Security in April 1994 at Izhevala, Russia; 20 people were arrested and charged with smuggling. Hersh also argues the possibility (p. 76) that Russian scientists, because of the loss of the basic necessities of life—housing, health care, and regular paychecks—may be leaving the country and trading not only their scientific knowledge but also high-tech weapons components. Hersh does note that the Department of Energy believes there is no evidence that nuclear weapons or materials have been exported from the Soviet Union (p. 75). However, there is always the possibility, as Claire Sterling (1994b, p. 215) suggests, that nuclear sales outside Russia and its republics have been made, but the reason the world does not know about such sales is that "a solid wall of secret agents . . . blocks the view." It does appear that there is a legitimate concern in Russia and one of its republics—Kazakhstan—over the control and export of nuclear weapons into the hands of terrorists when we saw recently that 1,300 lb of uranium stored in Kazakhstan, which evidently Saddam Hussein was desperately trying to obtain, went instead to the United States and is now safely stored in Oak Ridge, Tennessee (*Time*, 1994c, pp. 38-39).

We should note that, legitimately, Russia, to the tune of $2.2 billion in 1992 alone, has been aggressively selling weapons to India, China, Syria, Iran, and other countries in its effort to convert industrial defense production into civilian production. Unfortunately, the fact that the Russian government cannot offer long-term support and service for its technologically complex weapons has not made this the effective conversion finance-raising solution it was intended to be ("Focus on Change," 1994). No doubt, however, the demand for these weapons will allow criminal groups to continue the illicit sale of such weapons to those countries or groups that, even though the continued servicing of such weapons cannot be guaranteed, will nonetheless purchase them out of dire need.

Along with these ventures in Russia and its former republics are other types of mercenary crime. One example is the scams concerning credit and banking violations in which capital made from illicit activities is used in establishing businesses that serve as fronts for illegal transactions. In a sophisticated version of the "long-firm fraud" scheme developed and practiced widely by British criminals (Albini, 1986, pp. 103-104), a Russian criminal group stole $200 million from the Russian state in 1992. This scheme, described by Sterling (1994b, pp. 108-109), entailed the creation of a straw bank in the small republic of Chechnya, which sent Russia's central bank fraudulent or phony "credit advisories" for $200 million, which the directors of the straw bank indicated they had on deposit. The straw bank then asked Moscow for a credit line to import computers. The central bank sent the money to a dozen commercial banks in Moscow. When informed that the computer deal had not gone through, these 12 commercial banks simply allowed the cash to be withdrawn and sent back to the straw bank, no questions asked, and minus their cut. Sterling (1994b, chap. 5) also cites numerous other cases of fraudulent business ventures, sometimes involving Americans and other foreigners working in conjunction with Russians, in which petroleum and other goods and materials resulted in the increase of the wealth of these individuals and the depletion of the Russian economy. In Moscow, in January 1994, a seminar entitled "For Honest Business" was sponsored by the Russian Criminological Association. Here, as Shabalin (1995) notes in his summary of the seminar, material and discussions showed that Russia today has a fast-growing network of commercial banks and stock and currency exchanges that, through illegal investment of

funds, are literally running rampant simply because state control over such activities has been seriously weakened. This weakness is a result of criminal associations lobbying to influence political decisions and the legislative process itself. According to the Analytical Center of the Academy of Sciences of Russia, 35% of capital and 80% of election shares today are transferred into the hands of criminal and foreign capital.

Along with enterprises involving the use of fraud, other organized mercenary criminal enterprises exist in Russia. These typically function as they do in other countries. An example is the enterprise of counterfeiting. With the increasing use of sophisticated photocopiers, counterfeiters in many countries are producing bills and transporting them across international boundaries. Some of these bills have already made their way from Iran to the former Soviet Union (*U.S. News & World Report,* 1994b, p. 79). The widespread use and flow of counterfeit bills in Russia is demonstrated by the case involving the kidnapping, in 1993, of a teacher, bus driver, and schoolchildren by criminals in Rostov, Russia. After demanding and receiving the ransom money paid in U.S. currency, the kidnappers made a final demand—that they receive a machine that could distinguish between real and counterfeit bills (*U.S. News & World Report,* 1994b, p. 73). As we move now into our discussion of the organized protection and extortion forms of organized crime, those typically referred to as "rackets," we use this topic to lead us into our discussion of syndicated crime in Russia. We do this because these forms of rackets, depending on the format they take, can be of the mercenary or syndicated type.

In one type, the organized perpetrators have no political or police protection. For the most part, the "Black Hand" in the United States, for example, because it typically did not have political protection, used fear and intimidation by sending letters to Italian immigrants in an effort to extort money from them (Pitkin & Cordasco, 1977). So, too, currently in New York and other cities, as Kelly et al. (1993) have found, Chinese street gangs in the Chinese communities extort money from Chinese businesspeople. As

Kelly et al. note (p. 226), these activities persist, not because the criminals have political or police protection, but rather because, out of fear, the victims refuse to file charges or testify against these criminals. Hence, in Russia, we find criminal gangs that, simply because they are adept at using intimidation and force, work the protection and extortion schemes without police or political protection. Like the Italian and Chinese criminals in the United States, these groups rely on the fact that their victims are too fearful to report the crime or to serve as witnesses in any legal action taken by the authorities. Typically, when they sell protection to businesses, such protection is based on an agreement. Thus, as Arthur Fisher (1994, p. 24) reports, thugs who guard the multitude of street kiosks that sell everything from imported camcorders to video games in Moscow usually offer their services for 20% of the sales.

The protection operation, both in Russia and other countries where it is practiced, often originates out of a symbiotic need created by social conditions. Thus, often, it is not the criminal who forces protection on the businessperson, but instead the businessperson who, recognizing the need for protection in an environment where theft is so rampant, seeks and agrees to be protected for a price.

In many contemporary protection and extortion schemes in Russia, however, the reality is that many of these rackets have the backing and protection of political or police alliances or both. Recently, organized criminal associations have been subsidizing the education of young criminal participants studying law, with the goal of having them later assume positions of power within this legal system, thus further ensuring protection to their criminal enterprises.

Political protection is obtained from either a powerful patron in the legal system who grants it in return for money or favors or a political protector who is part of the criminal enterprise itself. Thus, a minister or high government official can become the protector for a criminal venture or, in many cases, create the criminal venture itself and then offer protection to those who operate it. In this respect, it would be like

the case of John Morrissey (Albini, 1971, pp. 186-189) in the United States, who because of his patronage to Tammany Hall and his support from fellow Irish voters, was elected as a New York state senator, as well as a representative in the U.S. Congress. As such, he was able to offer political protection for his own criminal syndicate operations.

LAW ENFORCEMENT
AND ORGANIZED CRIME

At this point, we must note the role played by the KGB, police, and other government officials in the Russian saga of organized crime. Typically referred to as "state rackets" (Shabalin et al., 1990, p. 22), these subsume those types of criminal enterprises in which official position and power are used to extort or protect the victims. Rosner (1993, p. 3) tells us how party officials, with the backing of the law, imprisoned more than 200,000 entrepreneurs and then often took over their enterprises. The growth and proliferation of these criminal types of organizations, as Timofeyev (1990, p. 60) observes, have come to control large regions, as has been demonstrated in Uzbekistan, and have come to serve the interests of the Communist Party, the armed forces, and the secret police. Rosner (1993, pp. 1-2) notes that in the quest for wealth and power, KGB leaders and other officials of the state looted state-run industries and turned these positions into vehicles for increasing their own personal wealth. Indeed, some KGB officers added to their personal wealth by confiscating the personal property of those arrested for state crimes, often burglarizing the homes or apartments of those incarcerated and then either keeping the goods for their own use or turning them over for sale in the black market.

The KGB was reorganized in May 1991 and became known as the Ministry of Security of the Russian Federation. As such, it became, for the first time, a "union-republic" agency. The belief is that the new KGB has the intent of repenting for its past political misdeeds (Azreal

& Rahr, 1993, p. 5); however, many believe that the organization changed only in the upper echelons and that the basic membership of the organization remains the same. For this reason, as Stephen Handelman (1994, p. 15), testifying in June 1994 before the Commission of Security and Cooperation in Europe, stated, U.S. police are reluctant to get involved not only with the KGB but also with most police forces in Russia because they suspect that these organizations continue to be generally corrupt.

The severity of the status of state rackets operating in Russia is revealed in Handelman's testimony when he notes (1994, p. 11) that, in 1993 alone, no fewer than 1,500 Russian government officials were charged with serious corruption, and another 4,500 cases of bribery went to trial. These statistics, as Handelman observes, hardly begin to match the real volume of corruption that continues to go on undetected.

Added to this level of corruption is that found among the police and the military. The chief of Moscow's police force estimates that, on his force alone, 95% of his men are on the take ("Russia's Mafia," 1994, p. 22). Those who are honest have to work under the most dire conditions, with no equipment or antiquated equipment. As Handelman states (1994, p. 11), detectives in some cities literally are forced to chase their suspects by using taxis or bus services.

Speaking to the issue of police problems in Russia in 1992, V. Kutushev noted that, in the United States, with the exception of inner-city residents, there typically is respect for the police and friendly interaction between citizens and police. In Russia, this is not the case. When police in Russia attempt to arrest a citizen, they are most likely to meet with resistance. The number of policemen killed in 1991 was 140, and each year the number increases.

As for the military, in February 1993, Russian defense officials stated that they planed to discipline 3,000 army officers for questionable business enterprises, and 46 general officers faced court martial proceedings regarding corruption charges (Hersh, 1994, pp. 67-68). Such corruption and the delving into criminal enter-

prises by military personnel no doubt have been spawned by the deplorable living and fighting conditions that military personnel have been subjected to in recent years. The extreme state of these conditions is revealed in the fact that Russian soldiers and their families have recently been forced to go without the basic necessities of water, heat, and food to the point that four recruits died of malnutrition (*Time,* 1994c, p. 81).

And so, the protection and extortion groups, those with political or police protection and those without, have established themselves on the streets of Russia and its independent states. And violence has become a common part of these ventures. In Nizhni Tagil, a city in the Ural Mountains, the extreme form that this violence can take was illustrated when a group of Russian criminals hijacked a T-90 tank, drove it to the local market, and fired at a criminal group of Muslims who were trying to wrestle protection money from the vendors (*U.S. News & World Report,* 1994a). The Russians, in doing so, let the Muslim criminals know that this would continue to be solely their enterprise.

THE EVOLUTION OF CONTEMPORARY SYNDICATES

The evolution and growth of syndicated crime in Russia and the former republics are evidenced in the development of criminal ventures in which the three elements of syndicated crime are fully established—that is, (a) the rendering of illegal goods and services, (b) the use of violence or the threat of it, and (c) the assurance of protection from legal interference.

Here we see the establishment and functioning of syndicates that involve and evolve from a variety of ethnic, social class, and other backgrounds. Their major enterprises are prostitution and the smuggling of drugs and other goods. Because both of these enterprises necessitate that the public seeking the illicit service and the criminals who deliver them interact or make contact with one another, political protection is necessary for their continued operation.

Thus, in prostitution, women, homosexual men, and other individuals whose services can be sold for profit are made available in certain areas of the cities or are "on call" for the customer who seeks more privacy in the encounter. If necessary, the women or men are transported to various regions or even into other countries, depending on trade demands and profits. Reminiscent of the Prohibition Era in the United States, these women and homosexual men often are subject to physical and other abuse if they disobey those who oversee their work.

Although the smuggling into Russia of automobiles stolen in the United States and used cars from Japan, along with the smuggling of antique artworks out of the country, constitute a form of high profit for criminal syndicates, drug smuggling is the venture that reaps the largest profits. By its very nature, as Albini (1992, chap. 4) explains, drug syndicates typically involve functionaries from various countries interacting with one another. Because, as Sterling (1994b, p. 105) notes, the Russian former republics produce 25 times more hashish than the rest of the world and opium poppies flourish in abundance in Afghanistan, Uzbekistan, and other territories of the former U.S.S.R., the drug trade in contemporary Russia is alive and well. Drug traffic flows both within and outside Russia and its federated states. As such, it has attracted smugglers from all parts of the world, and the ties between Russian syndicates and those in other countries literally encircle the globe. This has created what Phil Williams (1995b, pp. 60-61) calls "strategic alliances," alliances in which the functionaries of criminal syndicates in various countries, like the functionaries of businesses that engage in legitimate ventures, seek and form associations that are mutually beneficial to their operations.

Sterling (1994b) speaks repeatedly of "the Pax Mafiosi," giving the impression that syndicates, particularly those in Sicily, have now established and made an everlasting peace with one another because of their realization that cooperation, rather than conflict, will more effectively divide the spoils for all. This, we believe, is an uneasy conceptualization describing an uneasy form of peace treaty. So, too, Sterling seems to give the impression that such peace treaties are new to the world of drug smuggling and exist primarily among and between large, well-established syndicates. Williams (1995b) shows us, however, that such alliances exist among many small syndicates as well. But we believe that Sterling's Pax Mafiosi can be misleading because of the impression that it has now become a new, continuing and lasting form of interaction. If we draw from simulation or game theory, the n-person, non-zero-sum-game model, theoretically, would explain why such cooperation takes place: mainly, because both or all parties stand to gain in the venture. This assumes a rationality of action that may appear valid in theory, but in the reality of life, all too often human behavior manifests a logic predicated on emotion, culture, and attributes other than logic. Thus, as Williams (1995b, pp. 68-69) illustrates in regard to the interaction of the Medellin and Cali cartels in Colombia, although in the early 1980s they began in a state of alliance and cooperation, by the end of the 1980s, they were, in effect, at war with one another. Speaking to the point of the cooperation and conflict that typically occur among functionaries of criminal syndicates, Handelman (1994, p. 22) makes our point succinctly when he states:

> Criminals are just like governments. . . . I mean . . . governments . . . can't get it together, criminals can't either.

The contemporary syndicates operating in Russia and its federation, primarily those involved in drug smuggling and other organized syndicated crimes, have evolved from various social-cultural origins. Thus, many thieves-within-the-code gangs, having the brotherhood structure that they manifested during the era of the Soviet Union, have increasingly provided themselves with political and police protection; in so doing, they have moved into syndicated forms of organized crime such as drug smuggling and prostitution. Others continue to operate primarily in mercenary forms of organized crime. Thus, according to one source ("Russia's Mafia," 1994, p. 20), when Russia moved toward privatization, these thieves-within-the-code gangs, because they had amassed large sums of capital, proceeded "to buy a state that was in the process of being rebuilt."

According to Handelman (1994, p. 13), these thieves within the code generated further wealth after the fall of the Soviet Union through their participation in the black market. Many of these "thieves," Handelman notes, are functionaries on both upper and lower levels in both syndicated and mercenary types of organized criminal enterprises in contemporary Russia.

As is true of many organized crime groups in Russia and other countries, ethnicity is a factor in the origin and development of such groups. Ethnicity often serves as a basis from which organized criminals draw membership in gangs and for trust among gang members. Hence, the Chechen syndicate has an ethnic and historical base (Serio, 1992, pp. 6-7). The Chechens are largely a Muslim group that were deported from their homeland in the Caucasus region of Russia by Stalin in 1944 on charges of collaborating with the Nazis. They returned in 1957. According to Serio, the Chechens are different from many other criminal syndicates operating in Russia today in that they draw their membership exclusively from their ethnic ranks and have a hierarchical arrangement based on clan relationships. This group is involved in a variety of mercenary and syndicated crime activities, including smuggling automobiles and the sale of narcotics. A group known for its use of extreme violence, it operates not only in Russia but also in Germany, Austria, Hungary, and other European countries. The Chechens supposedly have recently sent members to New York to set up operations in the United States.

Although it is difficult to assess the full extent and ramifications of Russian organized crime in the United States, Rosner (1986, chap. 4) discusses its presence in Brighton Beach, New York, and Kenny and Finckenauer (1995, pp. 275-280) mention its presence in New York City, Los Angeles, and Philadelphia. These groups, it seems, are involved in extortion, drug trafficking, medical fraud, and a variety of other enterprises. It is still too early to determine the full extent of their criminality and what directions they will take. Their patterns and enterprises, however, suggest that they engage in organized criminal ventures similar to those of other American syndicates currently functioning in American society.

CONCLUSION

This, then, is the nature of organized crime in Russia. We have presented a portrait of its history, structure, and function to lay a foundation for future study. We hope that our description and classifications will become the basis for comparisons with organized crime in other countries and cultures because there are many lessons to learn from the Russian experience.

But we end our discussion with an understanding that what has taken place in Russia exemplifies what can happen to societies that experience rapid and intense social change. The portrait we have painted should not be viewed as one of Russian society or the Russian people as being totally morally corrupt. If such were the case, there would not be so many voices in Russia seeking solutions and turning to other countries for help. By comparison, the United States has not been without its own forms of corruption. Watergate and the savings-and-loan scandals have affected U.S. society and serve as reminders that the United States, when it comes to morality, is not without moral weaknesses. Indeed, because of its moral hypocrisy concerning illicit drug use, syndicated crime in America is doing so well.

As we take a parting look at our portrait of Russian organized crime, let's depart with an understanding that what has occurred and is occurring in Russia and its federation has its basic roots in the social upheaval that results from rapid social change. The roots lie in the nature of the destructive forces that accompany a nation that has truly experienced "convulsion" resulting from a series of intense shock waves that have politically, economically, and socially battered Russia and the Soviet Union during this century. First came the Russian Revolution, which appeared to be a movement geared toward freedom for the proletariat, but was it really freedom that resulted when, in fact, as Shortt reminds us, "Lenin maintained himself in power by force of arms" (1993, p. 3)? Then, in 1941 came the Nazi invasion and the Soviet struggle for survival against this oppressor. Then, in the 1950s came the Cold War and the potential threat of conflict with the United States. Then, in 1989-1991 came the breakdown and breakup of the Soviet Union and its republics.

When human beings undergo such rapid changes and stress, it is referred to as "trauma." Although we do not usually use the term to apply to societies, "trauma" is what Russian society has repeatedly experienced during this century. As the wall of communism came down, various sectors of Russian society and its republics began their own attempts at effecting or resisting further change. Indeed, as Shortt (1993, p. 39) points out, the Russian organized criminals at the time opposed the breakup because they feared the breakup would create, as it did, new national borders, thus making the payment of bribes a requirement for transporting their illegal goods across these borders. Political officials, serving as patrons to their sympathizing clients, purposefully attempted to create political upheaval; these upheavals produced many forms of political-social organized crime. During the same time period, however, many of these political officials, while engaging in their efforts to create social disturbances, continued to receive money for services rendered, sold ranks, and protected one another by participating in the criminal enterprises of a shadow economy (Shabalin et al., 1990, p. 26).

This social trauma reached the point where President Boris Yeltsin, on June 14, 1994, issued a decree, "On the Urgent Measures to Defend the Population Against Gangsterism and Other Kinds of Organized Crimes." The decree introduced strict legal measures that could be used against organized crime groups.

Whether these measures will be applied successfully remains to be seen. Rosner (1993), writing long before this decree was issued, had already addressed the issue and expressed the opinion that a crackdown on the newly formed criminal groups "would be an arbitrary act in the battle for power, under the guise of a crime control solution" (p. 3).

And so, we end our discussion with the awareness that Russia and its former republics are at that stage of social change where it is difficult to predict with accuracy in which direction they will go. Some critics fear a return to a complete state of communist rule; others fear that Russia will become a dictatorship if Vladimir Zhirinovsky (*Time,* 1994a, pp. 39-45) were to come to power. Others, like Vladimir Kvint (1994), suggest that Yeltsin could restore the Russian monarchy and make himself a regent for life.

Although public opinion polls in Russia show that Russians are in favor of conversion to a free enterprise system, Pipes (1990) warns that this may be merely a reflection of a panacea and that "it will take a long time to reorient the psyche of the people in a direction conducive to genuine economic freedom" (pp. ix-x). Paul Klebnikov (1994b, p. 228), in contrast, believes it is a strong possibility that Russians, by swapping foreign bank credit for shares in Russian oil and gas companies, will put their economy back together again. If what Klebnikov suggests does happen, this would serve as a motivating factor to strengthen what some see as a strong desire on the part of the Russian people to move toward privatization and democracy.

Oddly enough, the social upheaval that has taken place in Russian society in the past century is reflected once again in the current plans to reconstruct the Cathedral of Christ the Savior in Moscow (*U.S. News & World Report,* 1994b, pp. 67-68). This cathedral is a dynamic symbolic reminder of Russia's century of trauma. In 1812, Czar Alexander I ordered its construction in gratitude to God for Russia's victory over Napoleon. It took 70 years to build. In 1931, Stalin ordered it destroyed to obtain the copper and marble from its structure and to make way for a monument to communism, a building that was to be taller than the Empire State Building and an accompanying statue of Lenin bigger than the Statue of Liberty. This palace of Soviets, however, never materialized. Today, there are plans to reconstruct the cathedral, making it identical to the one destroyed by Stalin.

Despite its major problems, Russia has produced, during this century of conflict, some of the world's most beautiful music and art, Nobel Prize winners, the awe-inspiring sculptures of Vadin Sidur (Daniloff, 1994), and one of the world's most successful space programs. Indeed, it is to Russians that American astronomers are turning for help in a menace to the earth more far-reaching than organized crime—mainly, the potential dangers from destructive, near-earth asteroid collisions (L. Friedman, Executive Director of the Planetary Society, personal communication to senior author, 1994). It is believed that between 1,000 and 2,000 objects—asteroids and husks of old comets—now orbit the sun in the earth's immediate neighborhood. Any of these, scientists hypothesize, if they were to collide with the earth, could potentially put an end to human civilization. We hope that Russian and American scientists, working together and studying this phenomenon, can avert it, because if one of these objects of sufficient size strikes the earth, there will no longer be any reason to worry about or study the phenomenon of organized crime.

13 PRIMITIVE CAPITALIST ACCUMULATION

Russia as a Racket

ROBERT J. KELLY

RUFUS SCHATZBERG

PATRICK J. RYAN

The function and structure of Sicilian institutions provide a historical lesson in how and why the Mafia flourished to the extent that attempts to imprison its leadership have threatened the stability of the very government that is tolling its death knell. Extrapolating from that experience, the work of Follain, Joutsen, Varese, and others provides the authors with a theoretical framework for understanding the dependency between the liberal democratic system being introduced in Russia today and the current Mafia activity in that country. Crime, be it "organized" or not, is not new to Russia. Until the breakup of the republics, Western researchers knew little of its nature or its scope. Should the violence associated with Russian crime continue, it may overwhelm the entire society, or we may see an alliance of wealthy elites and multilayered criminal conspiracies juxtaposed but miles apart from the noncriminal, "ordinary" citizens. The authors proffer from their experience in and with Russia several predictions for the future of this new Mafia, indeed, for the future of Russian society.

We have become a mafia state on a world scale. Everyone thinks that political issues could lead to an explosion but crime could as easily blow us asunder. (Boris Yeltsin, cited in Handelman, 1995, p. 117)

Organized crime is destroying the economy, interfering in politics, undermining public morals, threatening individual citizens and the entire Russian nation. . . . our country is already considered a great mafia power. (Boris Yeltsin, cited in Sterling, 1994a, p. 3)

Sterling and Handelman, the writers who quote Boris Yeltsin, warn continually and clearly that the Russian "Mafia" (the Italian term has been appropriated into the Russian language *tout court*) has so deeply penetrated government, business, and state security forces that it has virtually transformed and reconstituted the entire post-*perestroika* society into a criminal formation. Yeltsin, the political maestro who, astride a tank, not long ago defied a communist *putsch,* now admits unabashedly—not in cautionary tones, but as matter-of-fact—that the state has been hijacked by hit men, racketeers, and extortionists, that its corrupted politicians have brazenly amassed huge fortunes in bribes, and that military men have shamelessly peddled weapons—from Kalashnikovs to nuclear missiles—for the right price.

As we argue below, two major crime waves appear to have ensnared the Soviet state and now hold Russia and the independent republics making up the amorphous Confederation of States in a stranglehold. Actually, the former state structure in the Soviet Union could itself have been identified as a Mafia. The Communist Party was never a political party in the Western sense, but rather a ruling elite that used terror and intimidation to appropriate the entire economic mechanism of a vast empire. Its rulers paid no more mind to the principle of political legitimacy than did the Dons of Castellammare and Palermo. Although the analogy is imperfect, the Soviet Communist Party was more akin to Cosa Nostra than Il Partito Communista Italiano, and its dispensations of power and wealth were unchallenged by either election or law. Party chiefs ruled the republics just as surely as John Gotti and crime "family" Bosses ran their fiefdoms in New York. According to Vaksberg (1991), in Azerbaijan, a southern republic, the Caspian Sea caviar Mafia, the Sumgait oil Mafia, and the fruits, vegetables, cotton, customs, and transport Mafias all reported to the party chief and enriched him in return for his turning a blind eye to their rackets. To carry the analogy further, one might say that when Mikhail Gorbachev achieved power in 1985, he became "boss of bosses," the leader of a Communist Party Politburo, most of whose members were sultans of crime and corruption. The Central Committee too was filled with hacks whose principal purpose was the protection of the party as a privileged caste by turning Leninist ideology to their advantage. In a state in which property theoretically belonged to

all—in other words, to no one—the Communist Party owned everything, from the docks of Odessa to the citrus groves of Georgia. Before Gorbachev and the semblance of reform, party chieftains in the Leonid Brezhnev era understood that the imperative of stability obliged them to pay homage to and grease the Moscow Don.

In Brezhnev's days, the political environment encouraged the growth of crime and thrived under the direct patronage of party leaders in Central Asia, the Transcaucasus, and the Black Sea coast. These were remote areas and provinces, distant from Moscow, where local wealth and clan loyalties existed even before the hectic ascendancy of communism and allowed the growth of a second economy and second power, albeit one restrained by the need to display a proletarian rather than a czarist propriety. To be fair to the Soviet rulers, the system they inherited from Leninism could only survive with a large black market that counterbalanced the effects of suffocating bureaucracies filled with greedy officials. Those engaged in trade as either entrepreneurs or managers had to know how to operate within that system: whom to pay off, whom to grant favors, and how to line their own pockets.

The collapse of the party apparatus was the death knell of the greatest Mafia the world has ever known. From dissidents within the *nomenklatura* and officials in satellite countries making up the Warsaw Pact, the wholesale corruption and social brutalities of party *apparatchiks* were revealed after the breakup (Dijilas, 1992; Simis, 1982). In these portraits, the party functioned as the equivalent of a large criminal syndicate whose defining, essential aspects were the acquisition and exploitation of personal power through extralegal means.

Corruption in the Soviet system was not merely a matter of exceptions and lone deviants—the "rotten apple" theory used routinely by embarrassed police officials in the West to exonerate their departments—but of systemic, pervasive malfeasance and misfeasance, which lead to the inescapable conclusion that the structural criminal character of the party apparatus and the whole political system facilitated crime and protected criminals from exposure. And in other ways, Stalin's terror mirrored Mafia tactics; he used intimidation and credible threats of violence as instruments of coercion and discipline that fostered an atmosphere of secrecy and widespread suspicion. As the Stalinist terror faded under Nikita Khrushchev and then Leonid Brezhnev, the Communist Party's business became "business" in the sense of the word when describing organized criminality.

In the Khrushchev era, a penitential mood took hold temporarily with the acknowledgment of Stalinist excesses. (We are tempted to see the period as one not unlike the obsessional war preparations in the fictional Corleone family, during which the veteran boss Clemenza tells Michael that a major gang war from time to time is a healthy purgative usually followed by an Arcadian period of cooperative relations and alliances that are profitable, stable, and safe.) Still, despite the meltdown and loosening of the ideological rigidities of the Stalinist era, we believe that the failure of the Khrushchev experiment was not only disastrous for the Soviet Union but also somehow fundamentally crucial for the rest of global history and, not least, for the future of socialism. Indeed, it appears that the Khrushchev generation was the last to believe in the possibility of the renewal of Marxism, let alone socialism; rather, it was the other way around, that the failure of egalitarianism generally now determines the utter indifference to Marxism and socialism seen in several generations of younger intellectuals. But we think this failure was a determinant of the most basic development in other countries as well.

Although we do not want the Russian comrades to bear all the responsibility for global history, there seems to be some similarity between what the Soviet Revolution meant for the rest of the world positively and the negative effects of the last, missed opportunity to restore that revolution. Both the anarchism of the 1960s in the West and the Cultural Revolution in China are to be attributed to that failure, whose ago-

nizing prolongation, long after the end of both, explains the universal triumph of cynicism in the omnipresent consumerism of the postmodern contemporary era. It is therefore no wonder that such profound disillusionment with political praxis should result in the popularity of the rhetoric of market abnegation and the surrender of freedom to a now lavish invisible hand.[1]

Only in the post-Stalin time after the violence of collectivization and industrialization was over did the party's Mafia structure take shape. In the 1960s, a trade Mafia developed that was a pyramid of payoffs originating in the top ministries and the Central Committee and trickling down to shopkeepers where everyone "got a piece." The scams and bribes were tributes to the human imagination, matching the guile and adroit styles of the best con men and professional criminals anywhere in the world. And this swamp of corruption was not a secret to the Soviet people any more than the existence of the Mafia is a mystery to Palermo's retail merchants forced to pay protection money. Like their Sicilian counterparts, the Soviet Mafiosi made themselves known at every turn.

PERESTROIKA AND GLASNOST: THE GRAND MACHINERY OF VARIOUS APOCALYPSES

In 1992, one of the authors traveled through two major urban centers of Russia and then south through the Ukraine, the Donets region, and across the Black Sea to Istanbul. Short of a calamity, the politics of a foreign country are ordinarily of meager interest to a traveler, and were it not for the locals' cloying interest in organized crime and its reverberations, this trip would have been no different. Surprisingly, the foreign visitor's imagination was exercised by *Road Warrior* visions of catastrophe and dystopia. Some of the simplest questions about Russian politics and organized crime remain almost beyond objective analysis, clouded as they are by the rather generalized acceptance by the populace of organized crime as an ordinary way of doing business, indeed of life. As the legitimating myths of the former political system slip away, will the state fail and implode into anarchy and banditry? Has it already collapsed?

The organized crime problem may actually be more apparent than real if it is remembered that law enforcement agencies are busy coping with daily survival themselves and so their capacity and initiative to enforce the law are somewhat blunted. Informal market-related producers—or in less euphemistic language, the black markets—are openly tolerated and, in some instances, explicitly authorized. In Moscow, St. Petersburg, and throughout the republics, many ordinary citizens and government officials agree that competitive forces, processes, and economic incentives were sorely needed to overcome the clogged state allocation systems. Also evident from the trip across the southern tier was little overt expression of political criticism of the government's handling of crime control; the voices of opposition, clearly disgusted with the organized crime problem, seemed muted more, we suspect, out of inertia and nostalgia than from a sense of fear and censorship. Of course, some members of Parliament who were aggressively anti-Mafia paid with their lives, so a general sense of anxiety and intimidation also hung in the air. But the tentative impression was that the law enforcement agencies were anxious about resorting to wholesale repression, which would only awaken popular resistance. With the exceptions of the die-hard Communists, the young, and the insane, the Russian people now seem to avoid politics altogether. Generally, one could say that Russians have, by and large, no sympathy left for communism (although most feel a strong sense of nationalism) and that the democratization that has occurred in terms of a rapid transition from an administrative command system to a market economy constituted the genesis of a process resulting in the wholesale criminalization of the economy by new sets of actors. That the changeover is still under way only bolsters the criminals' efforts. The criminalization is no

less real for the fact that the transition is ongoing; in fact, it enables it.

The outcomes of *perestroika* and *glasnost* enabled the private sector to achieve legal status during Gorbachev's regime. Unlike capitalism in China, where corruption is also massive, its major support comes from the *nomenklatura*, the upper echelons of the Communist Party, and even their approval is ambiguous; cadres in regional and local party committees were hostile or demanded a large cut of private profits or both. The first private businesses, known as "cooperatives," were obliged to bribe and lie to authorities and hire goon squads in order to stay in business, even if they wished to work honestly, which most did not (Kampfner, 1994). These cooperatives were regarded by most citizens as criminal enterprises. Today, according to Handelman (1995) and Sterling (1994a), virtually every small business across Russia pays protection money to some gang; former party commissars appropriate lucrative businesses for themselves; most fortunes in raw materials are smuggled out through the porous borders of former Soviet republics; and ministers and government officials peddle property and favors (Shabalin, 1995). Moscow has become a sort of frontier town reminiscent of Dodge City in 19th-century America. Almost all new commercial space is controlled by Russia's gangsters.

Thus, it is possible to conceive of two "Mafias" or two waves of organized crime, with the latter, the post-*perestroika* version, connected with and indelibly stamped by its predecessor. In the West (United States), the Mob historically moved in where no legal economy existed—in drugs, gambling, and vice in general—creating an informal "shadow economy." Occasionally, where it could compromise or reach a politician, the Western Mafia meddled in government contracts and operated protection schemes. But in the Soviet Union, as we learn now, no economic transaction was untainted. It was as if the entire Soviet Union were ruled by a great crime family known as the Communist Party. The party's intricate bureaucratic layers offered countless opportunities for mischief, and no one could afford to avoid a certain amount of complicity. In short, it was impossible to be honest, and as if to deepen the gloom, the mighty Aleksandr Solzhenitsyn (1991) wrote,

> The corrupt ruling class—the many millions of men in the party/state *nomenklatura*—is not capable of voluntarily renouncing any of the privileges they have seized. They have lived shamelessly for decades at the people's expense—and would like to continue doing so. (pp. 75-76)

With Gorbachev's purges of party Mafiosi in the Politburo amounting to little, Solzhenitsyn's jeremiads seem retrospectively prophetic indeed. After aborted coups by party officials and conspirators from the army, state collectives, party security organs, and the military-industrial complex, ideology was hardly the point any longer.[2] With the party in ruins, remnants of its structures actively collaborated with new illegal clans that emerged in the post-Gorbachev period.

As in Eastern Europe, party apparatuses often remain in power because so few outsiders are competent enough to run factories and administer huge bureaucracies. Consequently, former party executives, collective enterprise chairpersons, factory bosses, and security chiefs remain in firm control. Party men cling to their properties with a death grip, perhaps in the vain hope of a resurgence of the old regime amid the anarchy of the current situation. At the same time, a sense of lawlessness prevails in many cities and towns out in the peripheries of the great conurbations of Moscow, St. Petersburg, Kiev, Odessa, Kharkov, Rostov, and geographically proximate Siberian communities; a second wave of Mafia emerged with new sets of mobsters—independent of the communist party structures. They, too, are called Mafia, which they resemble, but many are more like the unscrupulous figures of primitive capitalism: the robber barons, the Vanderbilts and Rockefellers with their attendant thugs and stooges. Whereas the early century capitalists were not labeled criminal because their activities were not yet entered in the penal law, the activities of their Russian cousins are legally criminal, and the gang's structure clearly denotes organization.

The new Russian Mafia gets rich in a number of ways, with drugs being among the most lucrative of illicit businesses. According to Sterling (1994a), the former Soviet Union produces 25 times more hashish than the rest of the world—another example of the Almighty's enigmatic generosity in seeing that the country has so many valuable raw materials. Drug production and dealing were not unknown in Soviet times, but they were limited.

> When Soviet controls fell apart, . . . things changed. By 1992, family-sized poppy fields yielding two crops a year materialized and were put under heavy armed guard. New plantations in Uzbekistan increased by 1,000%. Around 200,000 acres were planted with poppies in Kyrgyzstan. Plantations were springing up in Tajikistan. Others were spreading over a thousand square kilometers of empty radioactive terrain around Chernobyl . . . underground laboratories started to produce synthetic drugs such as Crokodil and Chort, a thousand times stronger than heroin. Russia had the rare distinction of being at once a user country, a transit country and a producer country, all on its customary extravagant scale. (Sterling, 1994a, p. 106)

The newer, even more ominous trade (if that is conceivable) that is possibly unique to the former Soviet Union is in fissionable nuclear materials. Little has been written about it, and what is available says nothing really definitive, probably because no one knows the extent of this "emerging" black market. It is known that Russia is the world's largest or second largest producer of such materials. Handelman (1995) speculates, persuasively in our opinion, that few of the more than 150 mining and manufacturing sites in Russia for nuclear raw materials are secure and serve equally as centers of smuggling and thievery as they do as mining sites. It would be hard to believe that the administrators and security managers of these sites and stockpiles of uranium and weapons materiel are immune to the temptation of sudden wealth in a political climate of lawlessness.

With all the turbulence since 1991, one can imagine a quasi-Italian scenario, with another "revolution" in a decade or so when a more enfranchised, civically conscious generation of Russian middle-class, law-abiding citizens—similar to that which rose in Sicily after the Mafia murders of Falcone and Borsellino, and many others, who were appalled by decades of elite accommodation with organized crime—will forcefully demand an end to it. Perhaps Russians will have more luck than the Italians have had at interdiction.

We can extrapolate from Italy's experience with organized crime and tentatively formulate a theory of criminal development in Russia. Follain (1995), for example, suggests, on the basis of his analysis of Italian organized crime, that the malevolent relation between the liberal democratic system that Russia is attempting to introduce and the current Mafia activities is inevitable. His argument is that when the Mafia gains a political purchase, the appearance of free choice will serve only to consolidate organized crime's position in the society. The dilemma in Russia would then be that parliamentary elections might do no more than place power in the hands of those forces with the determination and wealth to pack the Duma with compliant stooges. Characteristically, such dependencies are mutually parasitical, of tenuous loyalties, and fleeting in the face of serious challenge. The opposite, of course, might occur in the form of counterinstitutional developments among those in religion, business, and education that just may become powerful enough to resist the criminal forces and push the government into taking strong anticrime measures. Significantly, the experience in Italy barred the "fair weather friend" nature of the criminal/political associations as intergang violence intensifies that bespeaks the domination of both upper- and underworlds by the Russian criminals and the elimination of the cozy partnerships evident today.

In Italy's case, when drug trafficking became the most profitable criminal activity by far, and when the struggle to centralize its operation in one Cosa Nostra group, the Corleonesi, precipi-

tated viciously fierce infighting among Mafiosi, the historic collusive symbiosis between organized criminal activists and members of the government began to dissolve. The Italian Mafia and the government were on a collision course in the 1980s that led to violence and murder against the former silent partners and protectors of the underworld (Stille, 1995). Similarly, to the extent that Russia moves along criminal pathways, the associated violence may eventually overwhelm the entire society.

In contrast with the power of a *nomenklatura* Mafia of pre-*perestroika* times, post-*perestroika* Russia exhibits an uncanny resemblance to Sicilian Mafia dynamics in Italy before the great benchmark events of 1992 involving the murders of Falcone and Borsellino, the crusading anti-Mafia magistrates. Until recently, many Sicilian politicians, out of a misguided sense of local patriotism or self-protection, pretended the Mafia was largely mythical, a scare created by northern politicians and economic interests to discredit southern Italy (Kelly, 1994). Subsequent events culminating in a rash of brutal murders exposed the dreadful results of the failure to face obvious facts. This is another explanation that is germane to theories of organized crime in Russia. In defiance of the traditional code of *omerta* (silence), many Sicilian journalists and law enforcement officials demonstrated the extent of the Mafia's deep penetration and collusion with successive governments in Rome that guaranteed the Mafia's own immunity from prosecution (di Argentine, 1993; Tarormina, 1993). Mafiosi were employed by the government as tax collectors and were recipients of government building contracts; hundreds of politicians in Rome and Palermo worked with Mafia leaders. In Italy, the Mafia flourished when it was linked to the political hegemony of the Christian Democrats.

Similarly, organized crime and its "first wave" flourished in the former Soviet Union under the predominant influence of the Communist Party.[3] Finckenauer (1994) sums up the political-economic conditions that resulted in the "second wave" of organized crime:

The *perestroika* reforms of the late 1980s, outlawing the Communist Party, and the demise of the USSR itself in 1991—followed by the horrendous economic problems of the past several years— have all fed an enormous growth of new forms of organized crime. Under the conditions, some of the traditional staples of western organized crime (mostly unknown in the old Soviet Union) such as drug trafficking and prostitution, but especially extortion of new companies, businesses, and restaurants, have become among the more prevalent forms of current criminal enterprises in Moscow and other former Soviet cities. (p. 249)

Changes in the structure of crime have prompted some interesting efforts at theoretical explanation. In looking at this phenomenon from a perspective that is broader and more encompassing than in the former Soviet Union, Joutsen (1995) sees the growth of the second wave, of organized criminality as affected by at least three factors: (a) the expansion of crime opportunities, (b) a substantial increase in the numbers of actual and potential offenders, and (c) the lack of available control and containment capacities within law enforcement agencies.

The later descriptive factor may not be as empirically accurate as we might wish when applied to Russia in its pre- and post-*perestroika* phases. The Soviet police function was not sensitive to entrepreneurial crime conducted on an individual basis as occurs in Western societies where corrupt ties do exist between law enforcement and professional criminals but where a significant amount of enterprise crime is initiated by nongovernmental actors. That qualification aside, Joutsen (1995) appropriates the theoretical perspective of Cohen and Felson (1979), very persuasively in attempting to understand the growth of organized crime occasioned by *perestroika* in Central and Eastern Europe. The first of the three master variables making up the model, the expansion of crime opportunities, reflects a structural change in the nature of the economy from a state-controlled system to one guided by market forces, and this means the amount of goods available increases considerably. In addition, as state controls slacken, the security crusts around borders break down, thus

expanding the opportunities for criminal smuggling to develop. Second, the existence of a shadow economy as a consequence of an unrelentingly poor standard of living, unemployment, and inflation means that people often turn to the black market and crime as a way of supplementing income. The numbers of actual and potential offenders increase as the Gulag (prison system) is dismantled. Compared with the West, prison populations in former Warsaw Pact and Soviet republic countries have always been greater. Where little was done to rehabilitate inmates, prisons became a recruiting pool for criminal enterprises that include organized crime. Third, according to Joutsen (1995), Russia lacks the available control and containment capacities with law enforcement agencies; there are shortages in adequate personnel, facilities, training of personnel, and equipment and inadequate legal tools to help police and prosecutors. Lacking the experts and tools—such as RICO laws, electronic surveillance equipment, and Witness Protection Programs—organized crime will probably grow before serious efforts are introduced to control it. In the West, the fear is that organized criminals will migrate and cross borders (Finckenauer, 1994).

In an approach that complements Joutsen (1995), Varese (1994) adapts an analytic framework that attempts to understand the genesis of the Mafia in Sicily and applies it to the social structural conditions in post-*perestroika* Russia. Varese takes Gambetta's theory of the emergence of Mafia in Sicily and examines the extent to which it can be applied in Russia. Gambetta (1993) sees the Sicilian experience as a response to a massive structural change in its political economy during the transitional phases from feudalism to capitalism when property was privatized and made an exchangeable commodity in a system of market relations. According to Gambetta, the state, during this extraordinary period, lacked the resources and skills to protect private property rights that became salable through market forces. Historically, the *latifundia* (large estates) were guarded by private security forces known as *gabellotti* (proto-Mafia) who functioned as agents and landlords for the landed gentry and aristocracy that owned much of the arable acreage in Sicily's agricultural economy (Blok, 1974). With economic changes and the breakup of land monopolies, property was redefined as an exchangeable commodity, and entrepreneurs and owners needed protection that the state could not provide. Thus, the Mafia emerged to satisfy the demands of the new landowners. The Mafiosi were prepared to use violence in their roles as land agents and regulators. Over time, Mafiosi ventured into other activities where violence and extortion were their defining behavior. A parallel set of conditions exists today in Russia, where the reappearance of private property and its exchange value, according to Varese (1994), has meant the emergence of extralegal groups prepared to provide protection services that state agencies cannot offer.

The privatization reforms brought to an end the Soviet monopoly over property and created a market condition in property and enterprise businesses in which the state law enforcement apparatus could not or would not serve. Because criminal justice agencies were themselves implicated in extortion rackets or were too incompetent to confront them, nonstate groups and individuals (often the very perpetrators of criminal acts against property and businesses) appeared, ready and able to supply that protection. The conclusion is obvious: Until Russia realigns its criminal justice system to control extortionate predation against the commercial sector of the emergent market economy, the past of Sicily may be Russia's future.

It is doubtful that anyone who has tried to do business or lived in Russia in recent years has not broken one of its laws. A legal system deliberately constructed for a socialist police state has proved hopelessly inadequate for modern commerce. In reality, Russia's market economy provides the milieu for Mafia-type activities. Simply put, Russia lacks a network of statutes in its enforcement apparatus to capably facilitate lawful operations of private and state-owned enterprises.

Noteworthy and somewhat amazing is that the system has not collapsed into utter anarchy,

given the levels of crime, chaos, and dismay, and it being terribly vulnerable to what Yeltsin ruefully and laconically describes as a "Mafia State" where major portions of the nation's economic activity are relegated to gray zones of violence, corruption, black markets, shortages, and inefficiencies. It is a frightening image of Russia that shows a giant of a nation in economic chaos, threatened by civil war, lurching toward fascism, and hijacked by organized crime. It seems that "bad" money is being pumped into the upperworld's legitimate economy so fast that a logical (and intriguing) question is whether Russia will survive its dealings with the robber baron climate of business, culturally and socially intact and with sufficient resources and energy to mature into a real market economy.

Despite the models having been developed in different contexts, the logical possibilities linking the two theoretical models of Joutsen and Varese plausibly describe changes in the nature of Russian organized crime. Doubtlessly, the temptation is strong to see "family resemblances" inherent in the structures of otherwise culturally and politically heterogeneous societies. The structural debate goes back to Ianni/Albini, who detected the genesis of organized crime in the dynamics of the social institutions and the ethos of society—not necessarily in the cultural artifacts of particular subcultural and ethnic minorities. What appears to be happening in Russia, with the collapse of the Soviet Union and the repudiation of its institutional setup, is the emergence of new progressive forces forming a new sense of "the political," "the economic," "privacy," "business," "lifestyle," and that crucial psychological sensibility, "success." For the committed Communists, the historical lessons of 1991 must be especially bitter because it has often been said that every age is dominated by a privileged form, or genre, that seems by its structure the fittest to express its secret truths; that function is now gone for the hardliners. The period of capitalism in Russia drove the ideologically sacred sense of *partinost* to extinction; the deep, underlying materiality of all things has finally risen, dripping convulsively into the light of day; and it is clear that the political culture itself is one of those things whose fundamental materiality is now not merely evident to Russians, but quite inescapable. *Politics* in Russia now means simply the care and feeding of the economic apparatus (in this case, the market rather than the collectively owned and organized means of production). And crime—organized crime—is no longer limited to colorful rural bandits and comparatively small vice gangs in some cities; it is an appendage and expression of "primitive capitalist accumulation."[4]

What is to be done? That famous question of Lenin's could not be more pertinent today as Russia reels from crisis to crisis. Organized crime in Russia, much like its counterparts elsewhere, is not part of one gigantic organization. There is a multitude of gangs in addition to criminal groups with origins in the former Communist Party, the state-owned industries, the military, and the KGB.

It seems evident that the Russian government has been incapable of containing the frenzied criminal conspiracies and behavior unleashed when the party system was overthrown and the country moved toward capitalism. A reasonable conclusion from the available research, commentaries, writings, and analyses of events would have to lay most of the blame for the anarchy and crime at the doorstep of the government when it hastily abandoned most economic controls before attempting to devise, develop, and deploy institutions essential for a market economy. Instead of doing the latter, the government behaved in ways that stimulated criminal instincts and opportunities, for example, by installing confiscatory tax rates that invited tax evasion and by implementing artificially low domestic energy prices that created incentives for vast corruption in the energy export trade. Even more fundamentally, however, in large part the failure to control crime has occurred because many elements in the government became partners in criminal enterprises. Lacking any meaningful conflict-of-interest laws, and with many ministries managed by greedy bureaucrats more concerned with self-aggrandizement than performing their duties, it

is no surprise that the Russian government itself appears to be a major source of the problem of organized criminality. Although President Yeltsin has repeatedly declared war on crime and has made it one of his top priorities, law enforcement agencies have only meager results to show despite periodic anticrime campaigns.[5] Gangsters are arrested from time to time, yet the arrests often seem as much the result of intergang warfare whose publicity demands a police response than of police efficiency.

Were it not for the widespread violence connected with criminal activity, many might consider the ugly scramble for the acquisition of commercial assets regrettable but no more than an essential prelude to a capitalist economy. After all, the "buccaneers" of American capitalism—Rockefeller, Carnegie, the Vanderbilts, and the Mellons—were not squeamish in hiring professional thugs to do their bidding in labor disputes or in destroying competition without regard for the personal devastation that ensued. Added to this clambering is the lack of legitimate private capital in the Soviet Union, so aggressive and extralegal attempts by officials and managers to secure a place in the new economic system are to be expected and should not be considered a uniquely Russian development.

Unfortunately, the surge of crime in Russia has not been just a matter of cunning bureaucrats cutting corners to cull as much personal benefit as possible from privatized state assets. It is additionally associated with more dangerous criminal activities in drug trafficking and abuse, gang wars, and the illicit trade in everything imaginable, including fissionable material. The Proudhonist formula "property is theft" has been modified and converted for bureaucrats and gangsters in the protocapitalist world of Russia to "power becomes property." This is quite different from the American saw "money is power." In Russia, the power to do crime yields property (wealth). In the United States, at least on the surface and idealistically, one legitimately amasses the wealth and then wields power.

In quantitative terms, it is impossible to measure the power of organized crime, but there are some estimates: For instance, Handelman (1994) says that Russian law enforcement officials believe organized crime accounts for 30% to 40% of the national turnover in goods and services. But even if we take such an estimate as approximately correct, it is difficult to determine just what it means. Here, problems of definition plague inquiry. Is a businessperson forced to pay 20% of his or her earnings to a gang for "security services" thereby a part of organized crime? The extortion fees help sustain the criminal, but the businessperson is obviously a victim who doubtless would be quite willing to save the money if local police could provide adequate protection. As in the Sicilian experience, absent government services, someone, usually a bad guy, will step in to provide "protection." How, too, does one distinguish between victims and perpetrators, between those who hire assassins and traffic in drugs and those who occasionally bribe an official for a favor? All are involved in criminal activity that tends to increase the power of criminal syndicates and enterprises, but the effects on society are vastly different.

As the struggle for Russia intensifies, it may begin to resemble the Mafia-infested island of Sicily and southern Italy in more ways than even Varese envisions. Should current trends continue, Russian society could be sharply polarized, with wealthy elites and multilayered criminal conspiracies forming out of a deft use of the incoherent tax system and a lack of controls on international capital market flows on the one side, and on the other, everyone else. As they do in Italy, criminally assisted elites, living side by side with impoverished masses of people in the cities, towns, and countryside, could further fracture Russian society to a point where it devolves into a plutocracy, with the powerful, the criminal, and the wealthy arranging matters so that they live in a different country from their ostensibly fellow citizens. They, like their Mafiosi counterparts in Italy, will have their own schools, banks, resorts, and information networks; their own private police and security systems; and their own politicians and government officials. Communism is over, but organ-

ized crime could become the perfect tool for reinstalling another Machiavellian power elite thriving on the formula of divide and rule.

Shelley (1995) does not think the post-Soviet phase will necessarily lead to democracy and the installation of an effective anti-organized crime control apparatus. Indeed, she says,

> The existence and pervasiveness of organized crime may preclude the transition to democracy, limit personal freedom, and thwart legitimate foreign investment and open market economies. Since organized crime has already partially supplanted many of the governments of the successor states, the citizens may be trading one form of control for another; domination by the Communist Party may be replaced by the controls of organized crime. (p. 7)

A democratic capitalist economy may be no more than a pipe dream in the post-Soviet states where Mafias are deeply entrenched; more likely, a parasitic politics, a type of political clientelism that cripples local markets in capital, commodities, industrial, and consumer goods, seems like a natural consequence of a subculture of extortion and intimidation where criminal groups have deeply penetrated the institutional structure of the society.

CONCLUSIONS: EMPIRE AND CRIME

In terms of criminal phenomena, the collapse of the Soviet Union should not be a celebration of hope for the renewal of history—that may be illusory; *perestroika* merely serves as host for the metastases of empire crime. Our hypothesis is that we are dealing here, not with a disappearance, but with a dispersal of the Soviet empire and its attendant criminality from closeted centrality into all the local, provincial, and territorial micro-empires. The dismantled systems (and the process is not over yet) find the means to perpetrate themselves in other ways—not by dynastic filiation with the Communist Party as in the past, but by something like fractal division, by scission. We now find micro-autarhies, micro-criminal activities, bearing within themselves, in miniature, all the vices of the past. Thus, crime, like politics, is perpetuated in other forms—fragmented, peripheral, and new, infecting all phases of social and economic life; and like politics, which becomes transpolitical, crime is transnational and governed by a single passion: recycling lucrative criminal enterprises that worked in the past and inventing accommodations for new criminal opportunities and actors.

It was observed above that Russia resembles Sicily as a structure of political expediency that generates Mafia. But Sicily has also recently given birth to a strategy of Mafia dissolution. Can the same kind of energy be harnessed by Russia? In Italy and Sicily, anti-Mafia policies emerged as forms of repentance and revenge captured by the concept and figure of the *pentito,* which appeared in the 1980s among Red Brigade terrorists (Kelly, 1991). To achieve this, Italy used some American law enforcement techniques—RICO, electronic surveillance, Witness Protection Programs—that helped bring about the conversions and cooperation that were previously unthinkable. Involved in the moral housekeeping (prodded by outrageous assassinations and acts of outlaw defiance that enraged the public) were not only Mafiosi but also politicians and government officials. As if to buttress the purgation was the willingness of the Italian government to expose its own collusive transgressions with the Mafia—a spectacle, incidentally, not likely to occur in the United States, where the anti-organized crime policy has been one of "control and containment" (Edelhertz, 1987).

Many Red Brigade terrorists experienced a self-abnegation, a disenchantment, as they told it. In the confessional mode, they engaged in a psychology of self-dispossession, giving up their predilection to destroy, murder, and create mayhem in the name of some structures of power for which the public had shown some sympathy; and they began to increasingly and implacably oppose such terrorist methods of implementation. Repentance passed first from the ultra-Left Brigades, to communism, to the whole revolutionary movement, and then to the Mafia. It affected the avant-garde, then, like a contagion, washed back into collective ideologies and practices of crime and corruption. The rather astonishing ease with which it occurred in Italy was an obvious sign that the country was tumbling down the slopes of history. Was this the energy of a corpse? The *pentiti,* in seeking redemption, suddenly went back on all their previous beliefs and came to serve Italian society as a vaccine against all radical temptation. The same with the Mafiosi: After several "confessions" and expurgations from contrite and remorseful murderers, there was a drop in the voltage of public interest, and these individuals became pathetic as persons but powerful as witnesses, as antidote to the societal-level plague of which they were a part.

Glasnost in Russia has meant an opening up of modernity, but not just the area of human rights evinces change; economic catastrophes, political upheavals, and crime all increased with the liberalization of the regime in the former U.S.S.R. Before, all these things had been repressed, and now they are returning. The consequences of the destabilization and demolition of institutions have not only meant the dismantling of the "Evil Empire" (which at least was visible, however much opaque and localized in the Eastern Bloc countries) but also its insidious metamorphosis into something more fluid and elusive, more able to metabolically infect the West. Some law enforcement officials openly worry about the threat of the now recognized organized crime entities in Russia.

Russia's great weapon is not its arsenal of nuclear weapons (which it is selling off), but a reciprocal crime contamination between East and West—not so much through aggressive actions against criminals as by the disintegration of the walls separating and shielding the two former antagonists. As Russia comes out of its deep freeze and as economic and social structures become more and more porous, flexible, international, and progressive, it will be interesting to see whether in its defrosted form its organized criminality is imitative of the West and thereby containable, or a emission of new, frightening energies that lay trapped for more than a half century by the great experiment called communism.

NOTES

1. Communism and Marxism were extinct dogmas in the Soviet Union and Eastern Europe long before the disillusionment occurred in the West. Although not especially relevant to the themes of this chapter, there is the oddity of influence where the message of Marxism and Communism exercises a spell on Western intellectuals long after their rejection among Soviet workers, citizens, and even party officials. One wonders how this can be: Why Marxism haunts the air, lingers, and virtually mesmerizes a significant number of Western social scientists. Radical and mainstream criminologists in the United States have always been respectful of Marxism as a body of ideas and have resorted to Marxist-inspired explanations of crime with great conviction and enthusiasm. It is very likely that, for many of the same reasons why individuals are attracted to the social sciences, they find Marxism interesting; its leading questions go to the core of the social science enterprise, and at the same time that it offers an analysis of social organizations, it suggests a diagnosis for redressing social flaws and defects. Marxism's "historical inevitability" is, in a way, emotionally uplifting. The Marxist analysis offers a way out of the pessimism of inevitability through the notion of planned human intervention (communism) into social processes to raise the welfare of people. Criminology has also been affected by the implications of the analysis of problems that Marxism initiated. For example, organized crime analysis has moved from a Lombrosian focus on the criminal as a deviant and defective to institutional flaws in social structure as a precipitant and progenitor of criminal behavior.

2. Daniel Bell's premature announcement of the "end of Ideology" some four decades ago has a new and unexpected plausibility in Russia and Eastern Europe. But ideology is now over, not because class struggle has ended and no one has anything to fight about, but rather because the fate of ideology can be understood to mean that conscious ideologies and political opinions have ceased to perpetuate and reproduce the system. In the great Communist Manifesto, Marx urges us to do the impossible, to think about economic development and its social expressions positively and negatively all at once—to achieve, in other words, a type of thinking (dialectical) that would be capable of grasping the demonstrably baleful features of capitalism along with its extraordinary and liberating dynamism simultaneously, within single thoughts, and without attenuating any of the force of either judgment. We are expected somehow to lift our minds to a point at which it is possible to understand that capitalism is at one and the same time the best thing that has ever happened to the human race, and the worst. Central to the 19th-century debate and now in Russia and other former communist societies is the rhetoric of the "market," which amounts to a fundamental struggle for the legitimation or delegitimation of communist/socialist discourse on the nature and purpose of social institutions. The surrender to the various forms of market ideology—on the Left, not to mention everybody else—has been perceptible and universal. Everyone is now willing to grant that no society can function efficiently without the market and that government planning is obviously impossible. More boldly, the proposition of anticommunism comes to this: The market is in human nature. In terms of the "end of ideology" thesis, *politics* now means simply the care and feeding of the economic apparatus—or, the market. Needless to say, the classical notion of the market (which conservative ideologies conveniently ignore) is meaningless in the realm of multinational corporations and giant oligopolies. As Galbraith suggested long ago, oligopolies are an imperfect substitute for planning of the socialist type.

3. This is not to say that organized crime did not exist before the Communists came to power. On the contrary, in parts of Russia, the Ukraine, Georgia, and elsewhere, traditions of organized crime preceded the Bolsheviks but were never more than parochial ventures by comparison with the communist era (see Amir, 1986; Finckenauer, 1994; Kenny & Finckenauer, 1995, chap. 10).

4. Here we project some conception and hypotheses about conditions and factors and their reproductions making up the milieu of organized criminality. This is perhaps the moment to say something about contemporary discussions on organized crime theory and of efforts to stigmatize various models as merely descriptive and ad hoc. Reuter (1994) complains that there is no significant organized crime theory. His sketch of an acceptable theory amounts to little more than a formalization within the frameworks of industrial organization theory. Reuter's recommendations are an attempt to think about a specific phenomenon, organized crime, within the large paradigmatic structures of economic theory. One is left with the impression that a complex, multifaceted phenomenon like organized crime is reducible to axiomatic statements within the calculus of industrial organizational theory. We think such strictures are damaging and ultimately self-defeating when theory is construed as the elite language of privileged scientific discourses and idioms. Organized crime is simply too complex and too vulnerable to historical exigencies to be confined to any particular paradigm, and

when it is, its insularity becomes apparent. It is not as if an ethnographic account of organized criminal activity is short on theory, whereas an essay on the businesslike parameters of a vice activity becomes the exemplary model of scientific work on the phenomenon. They are both forms of discourse, and to that extent they produce, rather than just reflect, their objects of reference. The difference between them may lie in their operational qualities. The ethnographic account is more expository, temporally bound to events it describes; econometric analyses of vice make their contribution by informing and edifying about "businesslike" characteristics of some types of organized criminality. The latter does not invalidate the former; nor does it necessarily precede it. They exist side by side—the one as an enabling part of the other, ideally speaking—like the recto and verso of a sheet of paper. For an elegant piece of theorizing still in its formative stages, see Albanese (1995).

5. Private communications among the authors and Russian law enforcement officials, June 1994. Russian law enforcement experts clearly recognize the threat of rampant crime and its impact on the possibilities of a democratic society. The seriousness of the problem is also acknowledged by the U.S. Congress. In a rare move, the Senate Select Committee on Intelligence invited James F. Collins, the State Department's senior coordinator for Russia and other former Soviet States, to testify on the subject of organized crime. Before outlining government policies designed to protect U.S. citizens and to assist the Russian government in coping with the problem, Collins (1995) observed: "Crime now poses—some three-plus years after the end of the Soviet Union—a major challenge to the government and the citizens of the NIS (New Independent States) as they pursue the uncharted road from communist totalitarianism authority to democracy and market economies" (p. 270).

14 RUSSIA'S GREAT CRIMINAL REVOLUTION

The Role of the Security Services

J. MICHAEL WALLER

VICTOR J. YASMANN

Russian law enforcement agencies, security organs, and intelligence services, far from being reliable instruments in the fight against organized crime and corruption, are institutionally part of the problem because of not only their co-optation and penetration by criminal elements but also their own absence of a legal bureaucratic culture and their use of crime as an instrument of state policy.

The approach of the United States and other Western countries to helping Russian authorities fight organized crime has been based on an assumption that Moscow has the political will or sincere interest to wage such a battle. When analyzing the Russian government's approach to fighting organized crime and the institutional bureaucratic corruption that has allowed the so-called Mafiya to flourish, it becomes apparent that the country's political, economic, security, and law enforcement elites fundamentally are part of the problem. It is no accident that the Russian government readily has adopted the Western model of organized crime as a phenomenon at the fringes of political and economic society.

In the Russian federation, the opposite of the Western models is true. The country's ultrabureaucratized administrative system, its lack of adequate laws, and its lawless sovietized culture have combined to merge rampant government corruption not only with organized fringe criminal groups but also with highly organized, regimented, and disciplined structures at the core of the system. The individuals who headed and ran these structures suddenly found themselves in possession of vast human material and administrative resources. They attached themselves as parasites to legitimate entrepreneurship as the Soviet system collapsed and market structures developed.

This parasitism finds its roots in the earliest years of the Soviet state, when the Bolshevik secret police, the All-Russian Extraordinary Commission for Combating Counterrevolution and Sabotage (VChK, or Cheka), smashed private business, market activity, and property rights by confiscating citizens' private property, arresting and murdering tens of thousands of people for conducting any form of trade or barter, and helping the Communist Party collect and catalogue the spoils for the use of the new ruling elites or for exportation for hard currency abroad. As the Cheka developed into what became known as the Committee for State Security, the organization increasingly served the systematically corrupt Communist Party *nomenklatura* (Simis, 1982; Voslensky, 1984). The Soviet collapse did not break the Cheka-KGB continuum. Today's Russian security organs have carefully maintained the "Chekist" legacy, glorifying the Cheka in the country's history, continuing institutional reverence to Cheka founder Felix Dzerzhinsky, preserving the Cheka's sword-and-shield crest and other symbols as their own (as has the federal State Procuracy), and pointedly referring to their own officers as "Chekists" (Waller, 1994, pp. 9-34).

THE GREATEST THREAT TO RUSSIAN SECURITY

Russian leaders have begun to acknowledge that the greatest clear and present danger to the security of society and of the Russian state itself is internal corruption and crime. Ironically, the services responsible for "state security" are more a part of the problem than the solution. The Ministry of Internal Affairs (MVD) and the successor agencies to the KGB not only have allowed themselves to become corrupted within every level of their bureaucracies but as matters of policy have deliberately taken on economic and business roles that place the services in positions that invite large-scale manipulation of wealth that runs counter to their legal obligations to fight crime. Furthermore, impunity is endemic to Chekist bureaucratic culture. A Russian parliamentary investigator (Ryabov, 1991, p. 25) found after interviewing state security officers throughout the ranks, "They have no understanding in their minds that they are serving the constitution or the law; they have no reverence for the rule of law and citizens'

rights." How a kleptocracy could develop as quickly and broadly as it has in Russia, under the watchful eye of as all-powerful a punitive organization as the KGB and its successors, becomes apparent when examining the Chekists' ties with legitimate business, government corruption, and organized crime.

Over the past 2 years, leading politicians, including President Boris Yeltsin and the heads of each house of Parliament, State Duma Chairman Ivan Rybkin and Federation Council Chairman Vladimir Shumeiko, repeatedly postulated that the criminalization of the Russian government and society poses the principal threat to the country's national security. The MVD and other institutions published numerous analytic reports. One of the most recent, "Economic Crime and the Security of Citizens, Society, and the State" (1995), was prepared by Federation Council Deputy Chairman Aleksandr Dolgoplatev, Committee on Security and Defense Chairman Petr Shirshov and Deputy Chairman Petr Premyak, and Aleksandr Gerasimov, chief of the Department of Administrative and Criminal Legislation of the chamber's Legal Administration.

The report is based on information submitted to the Federation Council by the Presidential Security Council, the Ministry of Foreign Economic Relations, the Ministry of Finance, the Ministry of Economics, the Ministry of Justice, the State Committee for Anti-Monopoly Policy, the Federal Service for Export and Currency Control, the Central Bank, the Academy of Sciences, and practically all Russian security and law enforcement agencies, as well as Interpol and the U.S. Federal Bureau of Investigation (FBI). Summarizing the material, the authors of the report presented the following parameters of what President Yeltsin once called the "superpower of crime":

> Corruption in government is rated as a greater threat to Russia's economic security than is the sharp decline of industrial output and the explosive growth of organized crime.
>
> In 1993 and 1994, federal officials and bureaucrats took bribes and other forms of illegal

income to misappropriate licensing export quotas, registration of commercial enterprises, and easement of real estate, the value of such fraud liberally estimated at $100 billion.

Despite its third-place ranking as a threat to economic security, organized crime currently controls about 40% of Russian gross domestic product.

Overall, organized crime encompasses 41,000 economic entities, including 1,500 state enterprises, 4,000 share-holding societies, 500 joint ventures, and 550 banks.

Approximately 700 legal financial and commercial institutions have been created by criminal entities for the purpose of money laundering.

The authors of the report admit they do not know of effective countermeasures to confront the menacing problem they describe. Neither do the Western powers whose aid policies are intended to promote democratic market reforms. Journalists and scholars (Sterling, 1994b; Vaksberg, 1991) have described Western-style organized crime in the former Soviet Union and its new global reach, and some have recognized that the old Communist Party *nomenklatura,* bureaucracy, and the so-called power ministries of Defense, Internal Affairs, and various former KGB security organs have emerged as Russia's largest corrupt and criminal class. Journalist Stephen Handelman (1995) depicts today's organized crime situation most stunningly in his book *Comrade Criminal: The Theft of the Second Russian Revolution.* He also presents the ruined morale of the honest Russian law enforcement officers who tried to combat post-Soviet organized crime as soon as the Communist Party collapsed, but were denied the legal and material tools, both by the Yeltsin government and by Western assistance programs. Handelman's lengthy investigation shows that Russia's most serious organized crime problem is not as much the Sicilian-style Mafia "families" with which the United States is familiar, as it is the government bureaucrats and officials and the institutions they privatized to themselves. Using different methodology and sources, the 1995 Federation Council report appears to support Handelman's findings, which were first published in London the year before. Handelman's quote (1994) from a frustrated former Moscow prosecutor summarizes the problem: "The main way the mafiya penetrates into the economy is via the bureaucrats. They are our main enemy. The mafiosi are only the second enemy" (p. 000).

Several books published in the former Soviet Union also tend to confirm Handelman's evidence and conclusions. *Mafiya: Unannounced Visit,* by MVD Colonel Vladimir Ovchinsky (1993), demonstrates the knotting of the corrupt state bureaucracy and the criminal underworld. The book contains several anti-Western passages but in general provides an adequate view of the criminalization process in the last years of Communist Party rule. Renowned film director and Democratic Party of Russia leader Stanislav Govorukhin, in his book *Country of Thieves* (1994), reveals the consolidation of the old *nomenklatura* and young, upscale "New Russians" into a powerful criminal class and discusses the global dimension of their activities. Govorukhin made a name for himself in 1993 after releasing his film *The Great Criminal Revolution,* about the economic transition from communism. Significantly, neither his film nor his book has found its way to a broad audience in Russia. The film was effectively banned from cinema and television screening, and the book was published in Estonia.

The structure of the Russian criminal world and its penetration into law enforcement agencies are demonstrated in *Red Mafiya,* by MVD Major General Aleksandr Gurov (1995). Gurov, who founded and led the MVD Administration for Combating Organized Crime, was squeezed out of the MVD and later from the Federal Security Service (FSB), which comprises most of the KGB's internal security units. The reason for his forced retirement, he says with irony, is that his attitude toward organized crime "hampered economic reforms." Finally, Georgy Podlesskikh and Andrei Tereshonok prove in *Thieves in Law* (1994) that organized crime in the Soviet Union and Russia was and remains to a great extent under the control of both the

MVD and the KGB and its successor services. Using internal KGB documents, the authors show that the MVD and KGB, for different purposes, "supervised" and influenced organized crime and directed its activity and channels far beyond the borders of the former Soviet Union.

Like the works of Handelman and the late American investigative journalist Claire Sterling, the new Russian publications show how the West and most U.S. officials, at best, have failed to comprehend and, at worst, are ignoring two important phenomena. First, the powerful surge of corrupt and criminal activity, which Govorukhin aptly calls the "Great Criminal Revolution," is not just a new dimension of organized crime. In the words of Aleksandr Solzhenitsyn (1992), the revolution is "an amalgam of former Party functionaries, quasi-democrats, KGB officers, and black-market wheeler-dealers, who are standing in power now [and have] represented a dirty hybrid unseen in world history" (pp. 75-76). By its scale, global reach, and devastating potential, the Great Criminal Revolution not only poses a menace to what remains of economic and political reforms in Russia and other former Soviet republics but also presents a strategic threat to the interests of the United States and the other industrialized democracies.

The second phenomenon, what is often seen as a "spontaneous" development of Russian organized crime, in many instances is a process unleashed by the communist/state security oligarchy and in important respects is guided by them. The greatest growth of organized crime and corruption in Russia is produced by the financial and banking sector. As we attempt to demonstrate in this chapter, the business sector contains a deep concentration of former high-ranking KGB officers who steered its creation and development in the late 1980s and early 1990s and merged large portions into the criminal underworld.

Security Organs Become Corrupted by Organized Crime

Lack of accountability has allowed the near-thorough corruption of the law enforcement and secret services as they penetrated traditional organized criminal groups. The MVD had primary responsibility in the decades through the Brezhnev regime, but it had become so corrupt that longtime KGB Chairman Yuri Andropov, who succeeded Brezhnev as Communist Party general secretary in 1982, directed the KGB to reimpose direct control over the MVD the following year. Podlesskikh and Tereshonok (1994) find that Andropov created a new directorate called "V" within the KGB Third Chief Directorate to supervise and control the MVD. Although the KGB historically controlled the MVD in overt and covert form, the scale of corruption in the early 1980s prompted a strictness of control not seen since the early Bolshevik period when the *militsiya* was run by the Cheka and its successor, the OGPU. At the same time, according to Podlesskikh and Tereshonok, who cite internal KGB documents as sources, the KGB had renewed its old practice of directly working with and recruiting criminal chieftains, a practice the KGB had relegated for decades to the MVD. Penetrating more deeply within the corrupt MVD structure and the criminal underworld, the KGB concluded that the degree of corruption within the MVD exceeded the threat posed by organized crime. As a result, the KGB restored the old Cheka tradition of "relying on criminals in combat" against "enemies of the people," which in the eyes of the Chekists were corrupt MVD officers, Communist Party officials, and state administrators.

To this end, the KGB First Chief Directorate, responsible for foreign intelligence, trained special units for covert penetration of the leadership of organized criminal groups. In one cited example that took place in 1988, it dispatched four such units, called "Vulkan," "Bizan," "Vera," and "Taya" (Podlesskikh & Tereshonok, 1994, pp. 117-123). The task of these and other units was to channel the violent activity and, if needed, to direct the terror of organized crime against the MVD and others considered "enemies of the people." KGB guidance virtually transformed the Russian Mafiya, which only a decade ago looked underdeveloped and provincial, at best. KGB officers provided the criminal chiefs with their institutional and organizational experience, professional intelligence, and tradecraft and later shared their contacts, first domestically, and later internationally. Podlesskikh and Tereshonok (1994) remark,

> Striving for total control on all dissent and deviating behavior, the KGB simply could not have missed paying attention to Russian organized crime. By putting organized crime at its service, the KGB gained tactically, but lost strategically, by advancing and consolidating the "horrible mutant," the modern professional underworld. . . . And in contrast to the "world proletariat," about whom the Kremlin's adventurists dreamed, the criminal clans of all countries are indeed moving to the quickest unification. (p. 233)

Until the late *perestroika* period, the MVD was primarily responsible for combating common economic crimes and had the largest caseload of any agency in the Soviet Union. The most authoritative individual to have seen the situation firsthand was Vadim Bakatin, the reform Communist who headed the U.S.S.R. MVD from 1988 to late 1990 and who was tapped to lead and attempt to dismantle the U.S.S.R. KGB after the 1991 coup attempt. Bakatin (1992, p. 46) noted in retrospect that the lavishly funded and bloated KGB was often a "waste of time and personnel," whereas the poorly equipped MVD was severely overburdened. He found that, in the KGB Investigation Department, each investigator had a caseload of 0.5 cases per year, whereas the average investigator in the analogous MVD department had more than 60 cases per year. Whereas the MVD bore the brunt of attacks for its inability to fight crime, the KGB suffered from no such image problem.

The KGB did, however, have official authority to investigate certain economic crimes, particularly theft of state property. When whitecollar crime became a public problem in the late Gorbachev era, the KGB was not blamed for the crisis, but instead was given new organized crime-fighting functions (Knight, 1990, p. 98). The move provided the KGB, after the abolition of the Communist Party's monopoly of power, with a new *raison d'être* to protect "democratization" by leading the war against the "Mafiya."

Russian Federation MVD Minister Viktor Barannikov (1991) commented, "Why did the KGB get involved in (fighting crime] at all? Its leaders simply felt that sooner or later they would be asked for concrete results, for something real done in the state's interests. . . . and so crime was needed." Despite the vast legal, extra-legal, and technological tools the former KGB has at its disposal, it has done virtually nothing to dent organized crime except in selective instances involving political opponents, certain ethnic groups, and "unauthorized" criminals. Fighting organized crime is one major, new public relations theme begun by KGB Chairman Vladimir Kryuchkov that its successor services maintain today (Waller, 1994, pp. 221-276).

The KGB Role in Mass Pilferage, Illegal Privatization, Money Laundering, and Drug Smuggling

Mass Pilferage and Illegal Privatization

At the same time the Communist Party leadership gave the KGB responsibility for fighting organized crime, it was embarking on a *perestroika* campaign of mass pilferage of state property and natural resources and commissioned the KGB to dump rubles abroad, illegally sell vast quantities of raw materials for hard currency, and launder the hard currency proceeds in the West. Sterling (1994b) and Handelman (1995) describe some of these activities, as do revelations by Russian investigative journalists. Weeks after the Soviet collapse, a parliamentary investigative commission (Ponomarev & Surkov, 1992) reported the following:

> Realizing as irrevocable the loss of then-authoritative and ideological priorities in society, the Politburo of the CPSU CC [Central Committee] made several secret resolutions toward direct concealment in commercial structures of property and

monetary resources actually accumulated at the expense of the nation. Based on this, at all levels of the party hierarchy, there was a mass founding of party banks, joint enterprises, and joint stock companies in 1990 and 1991.

A Central Committee resolution titled "On Emergency Measures to Organize Commercial and Foreign Economic Activity of the Party," passed in 1990, details how the party intended from the start to conceal its holdings in the embryonic market economy. The resolution (Ligachev, 1991) called for numerous actions, including the following:

Preparation of proposals to create some new "interim" economic structures (e.g., foundations, associations), with minimum "visible" ties to the Central Committee, that could become focal points of the "invisible" party economy; immediate preparation of plans for using anonymous organizations to mask direct links to the party when launching commercial and foreign economic party activity; in particular, consideration of the possibility of merging with already functioning joint ventures, international consortiums, and so forth through capital investment

Consideration of ways and means of establishing a bank controlled by the Central Committee, with the right to conduct hard currency operations, the investment of the party's hard currency reserves in international firms controlled by friends of the party

Creation of a consulting firm with the status of a legal entity, but without direct links to the Central Committee *apparat,* for the practical organization of economic cooperation and the provision of brokerage services for foreign economic activity of various party organizations and the commercial firms of fraternal parties

Russian State Procuracy investigators found that, from such directives, party officials founded more than 100 banks and commercial enterprises in Moscow and 600 in the Russian federation, as well as companies based in the West (Timofeyev, 1992, pp. 119-120). Former KGB Colonel Viktor Kichikhin (1991), who served in the Fifth Chief Directorate responsible for ideological enforcement, witnessed the process firsthand: "In 1989-1990 most of the Soviet-Western joint venture enterprises were created by our directorate, except those which were established directly by the Central Committee of the CPSU." The process was so integrated that one former KGB general (Timofeyev, 1992, pp. 108-109) commented,

The market will be occupied by the ruling apparat and the KGB, because they have the opportunities to control the process of privatization and the creation of new enterprises. They have the licenses, they have the influence. . . . This is not so much for the party's sake as it is for self preservation. . . . There is undoubtedly an element here of an organized retreat . . . under which the retreating force tries to maintain some element of order and the possibility of preserving a nucleus, and then perhaps, in time, returning to the past.

Money Laundering

Parliamentary investigators admitted only scratching the surface with their aborted 1991-1992 probe. They found that the External Intelligence Service (SYR) played a major role in large-scale money laundering between 1989 and 1991, when it was known as the KGB First Chief Directorate, and that the SYR covered up the entire operation since that time. Describing phony agreements in Italy to transfer cash to Swiss and British banks and to defraud the governments of Italy, Greece, and Portugal, investigator A. P. Surkov (1992) stated:

The party moved abroad at least 60 tonnes of gold, eight tonnes of platinum, 150 tonnes of silver, and in the safes of Western banks are stored resources of the Communist Party amounting to from 15 to 50 billion dollars. There are significant violations with valuable metals which have shown up in the State Repository for Precious Metals. Gold bullion, for example, was provided to the KGB. On October 30 [of 1990], the KGB was given 502 kilograms of valuables. Among this were gold bullion, gold American dollars [*sic*] stored for some special operations, and they were not returned in time, a gold brooch with 31 diamonds, a gold ring with 20 diamonds, a gold brooch with 12 diamonds and two emeralds, a gold necklace with 104 diamonds, a gold brooch with 60 diamonds, and so on. They received, by the way . . . and there is a basis to think that the Moscow Special Alloys Plant did not fall outside the KGB's attention, and naturally, that of party functionaries. There is an opinion that in 1990, a contract was made between the Glavalmazzoloto [Main Industrial Association for Gold and Diamonds] and the South African DeBeers Company for sale of 59 percent of the diamonds mined through 1995, and this was done with the intent of hiding the transfer of hard currency through third parties into secret party accounts. . . . There were flagrant violations in the State Repository for Precious Metals, and yet the same people are retained in their posts under the Russian structure.

Parliamentary commission members (Ponomarev & Maksimov, 1992) thought they knew where much of the stolen cash and bullion was located, but they lacked specific account numbers in the possession of the Ministry of Finance and other bureaucracies and lacked resources to conduct a full investigation on their own. They met active resistance within the KGB even though they found that the state security chief at the time, Vadim Bakatin, honestly did what he could to help the commission. When the probe focused on the son of former Soviet Prime Minister Valentin Pavlov, who worked at a Luxembourg bank, and on the son of former KGB Chairman Vladimir Kryuchkov, who was KGB station chief in Switzerland, SVR Director General Primakov blocked the investigation (*TASS*, 1992; L. Ponomarev & G. Yakunin, personal communication, March 27, 1992).

One commission member (Surkov, 1992) said in the report to Parliament, "We have already emphasized it in the previous hearings, we had to get help . . . primarily from Yevgeniy Maksimovich Primakov and his service. He should have all this in his archives, where all this is scrupulously recorded." Auditors found that Primakov's service actively managed "valuable everyday objects," including liquor and perfume, not only for intelligence purposes but also for corruption, according to a commission investigator (Surkov, 1992): "That's what our distinguished Yevgeniy Maksimovich has. He has [the records]. He actually has that so we would not need to be hollering to the entire world for help. He has that stuff here." The internal security ministry, now called the Federal Security Service (FSB), also had records, the investigator said, noting that the security chief had tightened secrecy "of all archival materials."

The commission (Ponomarev & Surkov, 1992) proposed that President Yeltsin instruct the SYR, Ministry of Defense, and Presidential Apparatus to

> provide an investigative crew and its experts direct access to the archives of the USSR KGB, the General Secretary of the CPSU CC, the Presidium of the USSR, and other archival material, having tasked the colleagues of these authorities to provide the investigators and their experts with all possible help and support in seeking out the documents concerning the financial activity of the CPSU.

Yeltsin failed to comply. Primakov persuaded Supreme Soviet Chairman Ruslan Khasbulatov to terminate the investigation and disband the commission. Yeltsin, meanwhile, had gone public with requests for the West to help Russia recover the lost billions, hiring the New York-based Kroll Associates to track down the funds. But he would not countermand Primakov, and Kroll, after meeting dead ends, quit in early 1994. A Kroll investigator told the press that the firm's findings raised suspicions about certain players and institutions in the former Soviet Union. "Our problem is that when we sent it to Moscow, it was never followed up" (Radio Free Europe/Radio Liberty, 1994).

Drug Smuggling

Persistent Western allegations and investigative reports of drug smuggling by the KGB and organizations under its control, long dismissed or unappreciated in the West (Douglass, 1990; Ehrenfeld, 1990; Somer, 1984), were raised from a far different source in 1995, when a group of former KGB and GRU officers concerned with corruption issued a report accusing several former KGB generals of creating and operating an international drug trafficking ring in collaboration with Moscow city officials and banks. The anticorruption group, which calls itself "Felix," after Cheka founder Felix Dzerzhinsky, was set up just before the disintegration of the Soviet Union in 1991 to investigate economic crimes and first went public in December 1993. It claims to consist of approximately 60 professional KGB and military intelligence veterans with experience abroad and trained for special operations and terror. Felix members claim not to serve in the current security services but in other government agencies, united by common purpose and determination to reverse Russia's free fall into corruption and crime.

Since going public, Felix has provided several of its "research reports" to various Russian newspapers. Usually, the reports are signed with the pseudonym "Ivan Ivanov, intelligence officer," and many contain patently false, inflammatory material of a nationalist bent. Some Felix reports contain "revelations" about the October 1993 attack on the Russian Parliament building, allegedly in conjunction with Israeli special units, or about Western plots to destroy Russia's nuclear potential. Rhetoric is also aggressive; a paper on NATO expansion called for Russian reoccupation of the Baltic states, and a Felix member openly proposed assassinating Prime Minister Viktor Chernomyrdin and former KGB First Deputy Chairman Filipp Bobkov for their allegedly corrupt activities that he blamed for destroying the country.

Nevertheless, much of the material put out under the Felix name appears to have been prepared with sensitive information from the security and intelligence services. One such example is a report ("Felix," 1995) published by two diametrically opposed newspapers, the proimperial and ultranationalist *Zavtra* and the liberal *Segodnya,* and cited in 17 other Russian publications. The report directly accused former KGB generals of creating and running an international narcotics trafficking operation and

cast General Bobkov with the central role. This particular Felix report was taken seriously by independent Russian journalists who managed to corroborate enough facts to convince them of its general validity, and some of its authors were invited to present a book about international drug trafficking at the Center for Defense Studies of King's College at London University (Vetrov, 1995). Bobkov, until recently, was a key adviser to Most Financial Group Chairman Vladimir Gussinsky and is reported to have been behind many other financial institutions linked to Moscow Mayor Yuri Luzhkov and Prime Minister Chernomyrdin. Bobkov was, for many years, the second-ranking official in the KGB and was reputed to be its chief ideologue.

Under KGB Chairman Andropov, Bobkov created the notorious Fifth Chief Directorate, responsible for persecution of dissidents. He was also known as the grand master of political surveillance, who during his 40 years in the service directed an enormous secret informer network among the intelligentsia and the media. He left the KGB in 1991 after being blamed for the bloody crackdown in Vilnius, Lithuania, and joined the Most Group as chief of its advisory council. Very soon, the mid-size bank appeared in the limelight, and its young chairman, a Komsomol organizer, was recognized as one of Russia's most influential bankers.

According to the Felix report (1995), however, Bobkov and a group of other former KGB generals joined several newly created banks and stock exchanges to keep them under control. Using their organizational and analytic abilities, their experiences and foreign agent networks abroad, and the internal resources at their disposal, Bobkov and the other KGB "bankers," which Felix calls the "Moscow narco group," soon established their financial positions internally and extended their activities abroad. The Felix report states:

> The officers who joined this group had extensive experience in intelligence, combat, and analytical covert work, as well as purely personal connections in many countries of both the near and far

abroad. In addition, at the time they already had fairly good contacts with their former colleagues who had gone into business and banking, including dealing with foreign countries. As a result, the group's founders had ample opportunities to organize international channels for moving drugs, using in this regard legal business mechanisms, access to the banking systems of other countries (especially Great Britain, Luxembourg, Switzerland, Gibraltar, Cyprus, the Bahamas, and the Antilles), as well as money laundering and income-hiding.

At the same time, other KGB officers took the Russian banking system under their "protection." According to Vitaly Sidorov, director of security of the Association of Russian Banks, about half of the private security chiefs in the country's banks are former KGB officers, another quarter are from the MVD, and the remainder are military and GRU military intelligence officers. Sidorov himself is a former KGB general.

Felix (1995) alleges that Bobkov and his comrades began manipulating the banks they penetrated to launder money from narcotics trafficking in an enterprise with former KGB officers who had worked in Burma, Cambodia, Laos, and Korea in the 1970s and 1980s. Today, the operations are reported to center mainly at the Russian naval base at Cam Ranh Bay, Vietnam. At the final stage, according to Felix, the Moscow narco group, as a new entity, set up connections with Italian, Rumanian, Colombian, Peruvian, and Cuban trafficking networks. As with narcotics production in Southeast Asia, the Moscow narco group paved the way for drug trafficking from Afghanistan via Chechnya and Russia to the West, according to Felix, which describes how warring factions were used in the smuggling and laundering processes through early 1995. Some Moscow narco group members "were still active service officers of the security services of Russia and the CIS," as they moved large quantities of narcotics to North Africa, Europe, and the United States.

The Felix report appears to combine genuine facts with intentionally planted disinformation. It is clear that the report's authors would like to project the misdeeds of former KGB generals-turned-liberals on all Russian reformers. One member of the Felix group said in an interview (Baranov & Lyashko, 1995) that the report was prepared because "it became simply impossible to act in the usual way inside the organs" and that the problem had to be made public to "influence decision making." If corrupt politicians, businesspeople, and journalists were not prosecuted and convicted through such revelations, he explained, the Felix group would follow by assassinating suspected culprits, including top government officials.

The Felix drug report appears to provide some answers to questions being asked in Russia: What is behind the many strange twists and turns of the Chechnya war? Why has no one from the scores of professional assassinations of journalists, businessmen, and bankers been arrested and tried? Why has the government's fight against organized crime been so feeble, and the Russian elite so tolerant of the problem? And why, as some liberal mass media in Moscow maintain, must organized crime be used in combat against other forms of crime and against a rise in fascism? The Felix document, despite its many faults, leaves little doubt that current and former top KGB officers in Moscow still play important political and criminal roles in society, and not just among the revanchists.

Continued Theft of Western Business and Financial Information

Regarding theft of Western business and financial information, the Russian government is continuing the Soviets' business and financial espionage offensive against the West. Because of the lack of checks and balances, the lack of distinction between the security and intelligence services and private business, and the widespread corruption and criminality within the services, this espionage offensive is particularly dangerous to both Russian reform and Western security because it is completely vulnerable to exploitation by organized crime. It also blurs the distinction between Russian intelligence threats and criminal threats to the West.

The Soviet espionage offensive redoubled in 1989, as the CPSU increased the establishment of front companies, joint-stock enterprises, and joint ventures and as KGB officers began ensconcing themselves in the leaderships of these firms. A secret KGB training and operations manual published that year noted that "active reserve" or "operational reserve" officers no longer needed to mask their identities when approaching foreigners; indeed, it was becoming an asset to announce one's "former" career in the KGB because foreign businesses thought it attractive; Chekists could provide security and get things done like no one else. The manual stated,

> Sometimes, the fact that an officer has been identified [as KGB] does not have to represent an obstacle to his work in an agency, if he really is a competent specialist whose area of expertise corresponds with the mission of the specific agency, and is therefore capable of exploiting the trust of foreign colleagues. (KGB, 1989, p. 17)

Western firms wishing to do business were required to form a joint venture with Soviet companies. By 1992, according to one report (Rahr, 1994, p. 28), about 80% of all joint ventures in the Russian federation involved KGB officers; some American businessmen estimate from their own experience that approximately three fourths of Russian joint ventures include KGB officials. Russia has continued the Soviet custom of placing a ranking KGB officer in top positions, usually at the deputy director level, in medium and large state and semi-state enterprises (Yasmann, 1994, pp. 10-11). Penetration of private companies has already been described. Some KGB businessmen interviewed acknowledge that they receive support from their active duty colleagues (Kryshtanovskaya, 1993, p. 8). The reliance of Western businesses on KGB officers in the former Soviet Union is so strong that some business organizations are reluctant to warn their members, for fear of alienating the Chekists. The editor of *Russia Business Watch,* the official newsletter of the U.S.-Russia Business Council, commissioned one of the authors to write an article about Russian espionage threats to American business for publication. After the article was edited and accepted for publication in the June 1994 newsletter, however, higher-ups in the council pulled the story just as it was going to press. The author was told it was "not in the interests of our trade council to run a piece on industrial espionage." The reason, U.S.-Russia Business Council staffers and officials privately acknowledged, was because the article might provoke Chekists involved with council patrons.

With the influx of foreigners under *perestroika,* KGB foreign intelligence found an intelligence boon, enabling expanded espionage on the cheap. Foreigners could be cultivated, recruited, and handled safely and inexpensively on home territory, away from the eyes of Western counterintelligence. The KGB stated in its manual (1989, p. 24):

> Businessmen, and specialists in the areas of economics and finance who dispose of important political, economic and scientific technical information are of significant interest. Operational cultivation of such individuals on the territory of the Soviet Union is facilitated to a certain extent, because they regularly visit the Soviet Union, and are interested in the development of commercial relations with Soviet agencies and organizations.

The espionage targets would be relatively soft, according to the manual (KGB, 1989, p. 43), because they had "an interest in concluding favorable deals with Soviet foreign trade organizations or joint projects with Soviet scientific organizations, especially for the purpose of ultimately achieving a material advantage." The intelligence objective is not only political or military but also to help preserve old markets from Western encroachment (Kalugin, 1994) and benefit Russian industries and businesses tied to the established *nomenklatura* agricultural, energy, and military-industrial sectors.

Signals and communications intelligence facilities are also used for business purposes. The former KGB Eighth Chief Directorate and Sixteenth Directorate, now known as the Federal

Agency for Government Communications and Information (FAPSI), controls Russia's physical communications systems, including government telephone lines, high-frequency communications, and cryptography services. FAPSI announced its intentions to offer and solicit entrepreneurial ventures and would lease closed communications channels to financial and business groups (*Rossiyskaya Gazeta,* 1991). In 1995, President Yeltsin signed decrees giving FAPSI the authority to monitor, register, and record all electronic financial transactions in the country and to compel banks and other financial institutions to pay for the service. The money FAPSI raises is divided between FAPSI and a special Fund of the President's Programs (*Moskovsky komsomolets,* 1995). The Russian electronic intelligence base near Lourdes, Cuba, also performs a much greater business and economic role than in the past. When Moscow renewed an agreement with Havana in November 1992 to continue using the facility, the Kremlin sent not a security or military official to sign the pact, but Deputy Prime Minister for Foreign Economic Affairs Aleksandr Shokhin (Fletcher, 1992).

High Stakes Spoils System

The law enforcement, security, and intelligence bodies have had a huge stake in dividing up the spoils of the Soviet system. Notes business leader Konstantin Borovoi (1994, p. 83), who in 1989 created the Russian Commodities and Raw Materials Exchange, an ideological battle is being waged over the post-Soviet economy. This battle, he says,

> is connected not only with control over the activity of commercial organizations, but also with the problem of the struggle against organized crime. This is a struggle against those who call the KGB an organized crime [group], which means that this is a struggle against independent market instruments. This is the same instrument, the same principle of the old economy which today simply destroys new instruments and creates a rather criminal environment in the economy. The new

KGB structures, as in the past, are trying to take newly created structures under their invisible control.

Through his personal experience as a businessman who got his start in the late 1980s, and his conversations with many colleagues, Borovoi (1994, pp. 83-84) found a pattern between *perestroika*-era entrepreneurs and the KGB:

> First, the racket; strong pressure, then a KGB proposal to help. After that there are two schemes. On the one hand, it is either penetration of KGB officers into the top leadership of the company, or the leadership of the company got in close contact with the KGB, and the company ceased to exist as an independent commercial organization. Since then, its activity was not controlled by economic laws. As a rule, at first these companies run into some economic difficulties, and then such a commercial organization suddenly begins to receive absolutely fantastic benefits or licenses—for aluminum, zinc, copper, or tomato paste—and begins a strong development. This is the scheme according to which some commercial organizations developed, the scheme of "engagement" of independent enterprises and cooperatives. There are lots of examples, and they are very visible in the market. The insiders immediately know that this organization has become a part of the financial structure of the KGB.

The ideological dimension of the battle, in Borovoi's view, is between "producers and profiteers," or more aptly, between genuine entrepreneurs who wish to thrive in a market economy and those who latch on to entrepreneurs as parasites. In this environment, Borovoi (1994, p. 84) observes "a very close interaction between criminal groups and law enforcement agencies."

Security and intelligence officers, as well as the services themselves, exploit and abuse their authority in order to obtain unfair business advantages. The same is true for military personnel. The murky status of thousands of former KGB officers in the "operational reserve" or of "active reserve" officers who work in government ministries or the private sector in a legitimate capacity while simultaneously fulfilling a security or intelligence function does not permit one to know whether or not officers engaged in criminal activity are doing so at the behest of the service or are freelancing (Albats, 1994, pp. 57, 120-149; Rahr, 1994, p. 28; Waller, 1996).

Although the Russian government has lodged criminal charges against senior MVD and military officers for alleged corruption and criminal activity, most prosecutions were delayed, and few were actually tried (Jamestown Foundation, 1994, p. 9). No effective legislative, judicial, or other civilian oversight exists over Russia's law enforcement, security, and intelligence services (Waller, 1994, pp. 181-220).

Moscow's Political Approach to Fighting Organized Crime and Corruption

President Yeltsin's commitment to fighting crime and corruption has been selective and often politically motivated. As Soviet leaders did previously, Yeltsin tolerates crime and corruption when it suits him, and he fights them when it is politically expedient. Since 1991, he or his immediate subordinates have announced no fewer than six major anticrime initiatives, all of which emerged not as legal, but as political, campaigns. Handelman (1994, p. 14) observes, "This was not really a war against crime; it was a war against wild democracy, wild capitalism. The actual mafiya lords, the godfathers of crime, were not touched. Particularly the Russian gangs, the Slavic gangs, who saw it as a way of getting rid of their rivals." Even more to the point, the "war" was—and is—against the political opponents of Yeltsin and his inner circle of former party bureaucrats and officers from the armed forces, MVD, and KGB. At the street level, it is predominantly a war between those who would become part of the racket and those who would not.

Meanwhile, the state and presidential bureaucracies, including the "law enforcement" agencies, have continued to grow. By early 1995, personnel levels in the government bureaucracy reached 1.66 million, or 1.7 times larger than it was in 1989 (*Segodnya,* 1995a).

This figure excludes the so-called power ministries of Defense, Internal Affairs, and the former KGB components. Despite the reshuffling and reorganization of individual ministries and departments, their aggregate sum has experienced numerical growth. By mid-1995, Russia had 14 internal intelligence, security, and law enforcement agencies (Economic Crime, 1995; Sherr, 1995), with an estimated strength of 1.8 million servicemen. To this number must be added more than 25,000 private security and detective services that employ more than 100,000 security officers (Yasmann, 1995). In the last 10 years, every Soviet, and later Russian, minister of internal affairs has requested and received additional budgetary means for strengthening the MVD to fight organized crime. From 15.9 trillion rubles allotted in the 1995 budget for the security and law enforcement community, the MVD and its Internal Troops (who fought much of the war in Chechnya) received about 30%, whereas the FSB and SVR received about 12% (*Segodnya,* 1995b; *Sovetskaya Rossiya,* 1995). Paralleling the swelling of the security bureaucracy was an unprecedented growth of all types of organized crime. The average officially reported level of criminality has increased 10 times the level of 1991. The bulk of these statistics constitute so-called economic crime, which reportedly increased 30 times over the same period. According to the MVD Administration on Economic Crime, whose figures can be used only as a benchmark, crime related to the financial-banking sector increased 42% in 1994, with import-export-related crime increasing 50% and corruption and misuse of public office growing 59% (*Nezavisimaya Gazeta,* 1995).

The following examples illustrate the Russian government's selective approach to fighting organized crime and corruption:

The 1991-92 parliamentary investigation of organized mass theft of property and financial fraud estimated that billions of dollars were illegally laundered and held abroad in bank accounts for Communist Party and KGB officials. Law makers concluded that all detailed records rested with the

External Intelligence Service (SYR), formerly the KGB First Chief Directorate, and other agencies, and called on Yeltsin to instruct the SVR to cooperate and track down the funds. Yeltsin declined. SVR Director General Primakov asked Supreme Soviet Chairman Khasbulatov to shut down the investigative commission. As noted earlier, Khasbulatov complied.

Russian officials also refused State Procuracy requests in late 1991 and early 1992 for SYR files on mass property theft, money laundering, and financial fraud. The money was never recovered (Lisov, 1992).

When internal security chief Viktor Ivanenko, a KGB general, informed Yeltsin in early 1992 of criminal activity within the president's inner circle, Yeltsin fired him (Albats, 1994, p. 305; Kalugin, 1994).

Ivanenko was replaced in early 1992 by longtime Yeltsin crony Viktor Barannikov, a general in the MVD, who made a show of fighting certain organized crime groups but did little objectively to combat the problem or root out corruption within the government bureaucracy and the security services. Barannikov gradually began siding with Yeltsin's main adversaries, Khasbulatov and Vice President Alexander Rutskoi. When the political break was irreconcilable, Yeltsin fired Barannikov in July 1993, using corruption as an excuse. Despite Barannikov's lavish display of ill-gotten wealth, the government never prosecuted him (Filipov, 1994; Yasmann, 1993, p. 18). He died 2 years later.

In early 1992, Yeltsin placed his increasingly hostile Vice President Rutskoi in charge of agricultural reform—a responsibility designed to doom Rutskoi's political career—and later that year named him to lead a state commission to coordinate government anticrime activity. Commission staff included 50 senior MVD, Defense Ministry, internal security, and foreign intelligence officers and was empowered to investigate any public official suspected of illegal activity. Yeltsin named Rutskoi's hostile archrival, State Counselor Gennadiy Burbulis, to the commission, leading to strong suspicions that

the president intended that it be a dysfunctional body (Yasmann, 1993).

Yeltsin appointed Yuri Boldyrev as state inspector in March 1992 to lead a government anticorruption campaign. Boldyrev remained politically loyal to Yeltsin, but his probes, as those of Ivanenko, led to members of Yeltsin's inner circle. Yeltsin fired him within 12 months (Albats, 1994; Filipov, 1994). Boldyrev's replacement, Alexei Ilyushenko, directed attention away from Yeltsin's inner circle to investigate alleged corruption of the president's chief opponents, including "anticrime" leaders Rutskoi, Barannikov, and former MVD Deputy Minister Andrei Dunayev (Filipov, 1994).

Boldyrev (and his predecessor Valeriy Makharadze) had charged the commanders of the Western Group of Forces in Germany with corruption and illegal weapons sales. Ilyushenko cleared the commanders. Yeltsin later named Ilyushenko as procurator general, but Parliament refused to confirm the nomination, citing cronyism and political behavior unbefitting a prosecutor (Filipov, 1994).

Moscow mobster Otari Kvantrishvili ingratiated himself with authorities by funding MVD sports teams, a charity to aid disabled Moscow police officers and slain officers' widows and orphans, and other activities. After he was murdered in early 1994, top MVD generals attended his funeral (Baranovsky, 1994, p. 15; Erlanger, 1994; Hughes, 1994).

Reformist Finance Minister Boris Fyodorov, after being squeezed out of office in early 1994 by *nomenklatura* interests, warned the West that economic aid and loans were being "manipulated" to undermine reform and that therefore they amounted to Western "compensation" for government corruption (Fyodorov, 1994).

Less than 1 year after Fyodorov was forced out, Vladimir Panskov was appointed finance minister. In the interim, federal prosecutors investigated Panskov, then first deputy chief of the State Tax Committee, for alleged misuse of public office, large-scale bribe taking, and forgery of official government documents as part of an effort to grant illegal tax exemptions for his client companies. Boris Uvarov, the chief investigator at the Federal State Procuracy, opened the case against Panskov and issued a warrant under which Panskov was arrested in March 1993. Four months later, however, Uvarov was removed from the investigation. The case was suspended, and Panskov was released from custody and received a position in the presidential administration. The new investigator appointed by Acting Procurator General Ilyushenko found no wrongdoing on the part of Panskov. In May 1994, Uvarov obtained new testimonies of Panskov's alleged misdeeds and unsuccessfully tried to renew the case. In December 1994, President Yeltsin unexpectedly named Vladimir Panskov as finance minister and incorporated the position into the Russian Security Council. All legal procedures against him were withheld on Ilyushenko's orders. In June 1995, Uvarov was sent into retirement (*Izvestiya*, 1993; *Komsomolskaya Pravda*, 1995; *Rossiyskaya Gazeta*, 1993; *Vek*, 1995). In October, President Yeltsin fired Ilyushenko after months of public outcry against the chief prosecutor's use of the Procuracy to attack political opponents, his alleged protection of corrupt family members, and his failure to prosecute mobsters and corrupt officials

CONCLUSION

Russia has become what President Yeltsin termed a "superpower of crime," not merely because of the absence of adequate laws or the supposed robber baron period through which some apologists say is a natural stage of economic development, but because of the inherently corrupt nature of its law enforcement, security organs, and intelligence services. Paradoxically, it is those very organizations on which the Russian government, the Russian people, and the West are relying to fight corruption and organized crime. The Mafiya is flourishing on the vast resources of the former KGB. Indeed, those services do contain capable and honest professionals, as shown by those whose careers and even lives have been sacrificed. These individuals, however, do not control the services today, and without political will at home and pressure from abroad, they are unlikely to for the foreseeable future.

Interviews

Vadim V. Bakatin, last chairman of U.S.S.R. KGB, 1992.

Konstantin Borovoi, businessman, 1993.

Maj. Gen. Oleg D. Kalugin, former chief of KGB foreign counterintelligence, 1992, 1993, 1994.

Lev Ponomarev, Chairman, Russian Federation Supreme Soviet Commission Concerning the Events Associated With the Attempted Coup d'état of 19-21 August 1991, 1992, 1993, 1994.

Rev. Gleb P. Yakunin, member, Russian Federation Supreme Soviet Commission Concerning the Events Associated With the Attempted Coup d'état of 19-21 August 1991, 1992, 1993.

PART VI

COMMENTARY

Our global examination of organized crime now finds us in Asia. No, this is not an "if it's Tuesday, this must be Belgium" type of excursion. By now, you should be under the impression that the study of "our thing" is a serious matter indeed. The authors of Chapters 13 and 14, in Part V, warn of the possible collapse of one of the world's greatest countries because of organized crime activities. Yet, given what you have read thus far about the social-cultural environment that allows organized crime to work its predations, would you expect anything else when examining the rest of the world? Hong Kong is the focus here. In mid 1997, Hong Kong once more came politically under the direction of the People's Republic of China, and many people have speculated about changes in the offing. Criminologists have been especially attuned for any expansion of organized crime groups to the mainland or, in the light of that country's intolerance for all types of crime, a movement east to North America, south to Australia, or west to Russia and Europe. Will the return of Hong Kong to mainland China herald the globalization of triad-sponsored criminal activity?

In Chapter 15, James McKenna describes organized crime in Hong Kong. Data were obtained from senior officials in agencies responsible for combating crime in the Pacific Rim nations. The interview data were then examined within the context of a review of the historical and contemporary literature on Hong Kong's organized crime. The print media were not ignored in compiling the data. The result is an outline of the structure and makeup of criminal groups operating in or from the Royal Colony. Another typology categorizes this brand of organized crime as (a) triads and affiliated groups, (b) street gangs, (c) criminal gangs, (d) multilevel crime syndicates, and (e) criminal enterprises. You'll find these categories defined in the chapter.

The immersion of criminal activities in the larger social activity is seen in McKenna's comments about the triads. Only a small "splinter" faction of triad members are involved, but note the variety of activities in which they are involved. In areas as diverse as car parking, interior decorating, building construction, prisons, and the vice trade, McKenna found evidence of organized crime's involvement. Three case studies provide evidence of the ability of triad leaders to co-opt the police. Organized crime's "well known" influence on law enforcement, says McKenna, has been, is now, and will continue into the next century, to be "great, lengthy, and legendary." In conclusion, McKenna dispels fears that with the return of Hong Kong to mainland China this year, triad leaders will flee to North America and Europe to take up their criminal activities anew. "Contemporary evidence does not support" the concern. Instead, McKenna discerns a "gold rush mentality" among triad leaders toward the People's Republic. His prediction for post-1997 Hong Kong is a movement north and west into China, rather than east (United States) and south (Australia).

The authors of Chapter 16 are a bit more specific regarding the threat of triad expansionism. John Dombrink and John Song say there is some doubt that Asian organized crime "would ever fill the same role" as its American counterpart because there is no empirical evidence that triads are even remotely interested in "penetrating labor unions, the garment industry, construction, and waste management." And as has been said about the Mafia in Sicily and the United States, these authors emphasize that triads are not the sum total of Asian organized crime. As for emigration, Dombrink and Song offer reason why triad leaders may leave Hong Kong, and more reasons why they may not. What happens remains to be seen, but one thing is certain: The organized crime groups of the Far East are more loosely structured and diverse in outlook and membership than the more commonly known groups. A de-emphasis on hierarchical structure gives the triads a "resiliency" of structure that rapidly flexes and adapts to challenges from the law enforcement community. Changes worldwide in commerce and industry have affected organized crime as well. The authors see a qualitative change in the gangs' ability to move persons, goods, and money across borders (citing Williams, 1995a).

Chapter 16 is "archival" research in that it examines the available literature or already published research and astutely organizes the selected material to make a point. This methodology allows the authors to make predictions about what we can expect post-1997 in terms of the criminal threat from Asia. One is given above, that organized crime is not the exclusive domain of the triads. Drugs distribution by the

Asian groups will continue to be a problem, but "it is our observation that triads are not coming [to America] in large droves." Dombrink and Song have more to say, but we'll leave it to you to discover their findings.

Chapter 17 moves us into Vietnam and environs for a historical look at the beginnings of Vietnamese criminal groups. Ken Sanz and Ira Silverman describe the organization and membership of Vietnamese gangs in this country. You might have a problem with calling what Sanz and Silverman describe "organized" crime. Many of the activities outlined are those of street gangs, much akin to the criminality of American street gangs. Don't dismiss this piece out of hand. Read on to discover that, as slow as change has been, evidence now suggests quite sophisticated and skilled criminal organizations peopled only by Vietnamese are operating in this country. Key to this chapter is the suggestion that as political relations between the United States and Vietnam, Laos, and Cambodia normalize, there will be increased opportunities for Southeast Asian crime groups. On the one hand, cooperative pacts, an increased flow of contraband, and easier travel for criminals will bridge the United States to Southeast Asia. On the other hand, already-established crime groups in Japan and Korea (and probably Russia) will look on Vietnam as a "new zone of opportunity." The authors make predictions about changes in the organization chart to a more hierarchical version, but one that is malleable enough to go outside the organization when a special expertise is needed.

Sanz and Silverman say change is coming. Economic trends, political developments, and technological advances have, in the first instance, made intercontinental deals a fact of everyday life, and the criminals of Southeast Asia have fully taken advantage of it all. In this country, these groups have moved "away from high-risk, street-level crimes" toward more sophisticated and profitable criminal activities. Improved communications capability has enabled criminals to more easily put long-range ventures together. Counterfeiters keep up with changes in the technology of reproduction devices, and this crime is not beyond the purview of the Vietnamese groups. Counterfeiting is not limited to currency. Improvements in metallography spawn fake watches. The demand for "big name" fashions, and the big price such labels demand, has created an industry devoted exclusively to copying the latest clothing fashions. Medical advances have created a demand for donor organs; that demand is being met by Asian mobsters who either force donations or pay such a relatively ridiculous low price for body parts that smuggling them internationally becomes profitable. The authors connect this chapter to those in Part 5, with the observation that the black market in nuclear-grade weapons might find a ready market in Southeast Asia.

The rapid-fire changes described in this final research makes it a fitting closure. It segues to your editors' admonition that the study of organized crime never ends. For most of J. Edgar Hoover's leadership tenure at the FBI, organized crime was not an enemy. As we learned more about it, it seemed to grow in threatening stature. More likely, it had remained the same size, in both membership and gross product, but our reaction to it gave it dimension and body. So, too, with Asian groups and even the Russian groups. So long as we remain blissfully un-aware of something's existence, it is not a force for reckoning. You are cordially invited to continue your excursion into the study of organized crime, without editorial guidance, but with our best wishes that you will never be disheartened by its threat. On balance, most of the world's people are not directly affected by gangsters and remain blissfully unaware. If you have read this work cover to cover, your happy un-awareness is forever gone, and for that your editors apologize.

As part of the apologia, please note the absence of questions ending this section. If you are a student reader, the professor will take care of questions. For all others, good journey.

SELECTED READINGS

Booth, W. (1991). *Triads: The growing global threat from the Chinese criminal societies.* New York: St. Martin's.

Chin, K. (1990). *Chinese subculture and criminality: Nontraditional crime groups in America.* Westport, CT: Greenwood.

Kaplan, D., & Dubro, A. (1988). *Yakuza: The explosive account of Japan's criminal underworld.* Reading, MA: Addison-Wesley.

Posner, G. C. (1988). *Warlords of crime: Chinese secret societies—The new Mafia.* New York: McGraw-Hill.

15 ORGANIZED CRIME IN THE FORMER ROYAL COLONY OF HONG KONG

JAMES J. McKENNA, JR.

Given the social dynamics, social change, and criminogenesis immanent in contemporary China and Hong Kong as presented by this author, it appears that, for the post-1997 period, the triads will flourish in China and there will be no substantial immigration of triad members to North America, Western Europe, and Australia. Criminologists will continually have the opportunity to apply anomie theory, strain theory, cultural deviance theories, opportunity theory, conflict theory, and radical theories in explaining crime and criminal behavior in China and Hong Kong.

This report on organized crime in the Royal Colony of Hong Kong is part of a larger research project on the international or transnational activities of Asian organized crime groups that was funded by the Office of Research and Sponsored Projects of Villanova University. Information and data for this research project were obtained through the cooperation of the Interpol-General Secretariat, the Interpol-U.S. National Central Bureau, the Royal Hong Kong Police Force, the Hong Kong Customs Service, the Federal Bureau of Investigation (FBI), the Drug Enforcement Administration (DEA) of the U.S. Department of Justice, and the U.S. Customs Service of the U.S. Department of the Treasury. Senior command officers or agents of these law enforcement agencies in Hong Kong were interviewed as part of this research. Other information and data were obtained from the reports and monographs of these agencies and a review of the historical and contemporary literature on Hong Kong's organized crime that was printed in English. Additional information was obtained from a

AUTHOR'S NOTE: I wish to acknowledge the extraordinary support given this project by Dr. Walter C. Zacharias, Jr., Assistant Vice-President, Villanova University, and his staff at the Office of Research and Sponsored Projects.

This work first appeared in the *Journal of Contemporary Criminal Justice, 12*(4), November 1996, and was revised for this edition.

content analysis of selected print media, including *Asiaweek, South China Morning Post, Eastern Express, Hong Kong Standard,* and the *New York Times.* I conducted the field aspects of this research during April, May, and June of 1994 and September, October, and November of 1996 while on sabbatical from Villanova University and a visiting academic at the University of Hong Kong. The primary focus of this chapter is the local activities of organized crime groups in Hong Kong during the past 5 years.

CRIME IN HONG KONG

In regard to economic crime, Hong Kong is highly criminogenic. Some of the crime-producing factors in Hong Kong are similar to those in the United States—for example, materialism, entrepreneurial initiative, wealth as a goal, competitiveness, the profit motive, success at all costs, significant wealth differentials or gaps among various social groups and categories, pragmatism, urbanization, and corruption. Some criminogenic factors, however, are unique to Hong Kong: its geographic location, topography, and history. Hong Kong also shares some criminogenic factors with other Asian countries: secret societies, drug use, drug trafficking, and colonial exploitation, to name a few. Hong Kong is also similar to most other countries in that organized crime accounts for only a small percentage of the crime recorded annually. The Royal Hong Kong Police (RHKP) reported that organized crime was linked to less than 5% of crimes recorded for 1991, 1992, and 1993 (Ng, 1994). Yet, popular opinion and some evidence tends to support the view that organized crime pervades all sectors and segments of the colony to the extent that it is an essential part of the fabric of the society (CBS News, 1993; Sung & Lee, 1991). On the basis of their research on organized crime, Dombrink and Song (1992) claim that 1 out of every 20 residents of Hong Kong may be a member or affiliate of an organized crime group. These organized crime groups are overwhelmingly identified as triad societies or triads to the point that *triad* has

become synonymous with *organized crime* in Hong Kong. Even though Donnelly (1986) correctly states that triads are not the only organized criminal groups in Hong Kong and the RHKP (1988, p. 10) report that the majority of the members of any identifiable youth gang will not be triads (Hodson, 1995, p. 6), the interchangeable use of *triad* and *organized crime* persists in official records and reports, in the media, and in public opinion. Furthermore, this research was able to identify only a very small number of organized crime groups that were not triads. The major nontriad group was the Big Circle; the rest were small, localized, independent crime groups that tended not to be involved in the traditional rackets of organized crime. With this being the case, the research focused on the activities of identifiable triads and the Big Circle.

Whereas the RHKP and the government know about organized crime and triads in Hong Kong and the police readily identify triad activity, both have difficulty defining them. Hong Kong law defines a *triad society* as an illegal Chinese secret society that uses triad ritual and nomenclature. It is illegal because it has been neither registered with, nor exempted by, the government. The first anti-triad law, passed in 1842, 1 year after the founding of the colony, made it unlawful for a person to belong to a triad. With the near elimination of triad ritual and nomenclature in contemporary Hong Kong and with an urgent need to update the legal definitions of organized crime and triads, the Legislative Council debated these definitions in their deliberations on the Organized and Serious Crimes Bill from 1991 (Secretary of Security, 1991) until its passage on October 12, 1994. The law became effective in 1995. Twenty years earlier, however, the RHKP (1974) had no great difficulty defining *triad*. The RHKP answered the question, What are triads? as follows:

> Whatever the triads might have been in the past and notwithstanding their original objectives the Triad Society is today simply a gang of vicious criminals. They deliberately exploit the fear and mysticism generated by the name triad in order to

bind themselves together and by similar means hold in fear a large and susceptible section of the public. (p. 4)

Today, the RHKP defines organized crime by its illegal activities and the groups that are engaged in these activities as triads if they use any of the following: triad names, triad jargon, and triad rank, structure, and paraphernalia (Hodson, 1995). With this approach, the RHKP currently lists 57 known triad societies, a shown in Table 15.1.

The Sun Yee On, part of the Chiu Chow groups, with an estimated membership of 56,000, has the most active gangs. Next in rank order of gang activity are the Wo groups and the 14K triads (Ng, 1994; RHKP, 1992). An analysis of the triad-related crime in 1992 shows that 38% involved assault; 25%, threat/intimidation; 14%, triad; 13%, damage; 5%, public order; and 5%, robbery. The nearly two thirds of the total triad-related crime (63%) that consists of assault and threat/intimidation are most likely a reflection of the triads' major activities—extortion and protection (RHKP, 1992).

STRUCTURE AND ORGANIZATION OF THE TRIADS AND THEIR AFFILIATED GROUPS

The structure of the triads and affiliated groups tends to be nonhierarchical, task oriented, and bonded together by informal relationships. The organizational types of these groups include youth gangs, street gangs, criminal groups, multicrime syndicates, and criminal enterprises. *Youth gangs* usually have members who are 12 to 18 years old. They often wear distinctive clothing or symbols and gather or "hang out" in a specific place. Their major activity is having "fun," which may include delinquent behavior. The majority of gang members have no triad allegiance or links; these members are the most likely to leave the gang for various reasons (e.g., residential change, employment, maturation) and cease delinquent and criminal activities.

Those gang members who are in or join a triad will graduate into a street gang.

Members of *street gangs* are in the age cohort of 16 to 25. Triad membership is held by a majority of them. Leaders of the street gangs are usually triad office bearers. Triad gang members publicly present themselves within their claimed territory as belonging to triads by dress, language, and behavior. These public displays and confrontations with rival gangs give the impression that triad members completely dominate an area. Their values, norms, and behavior form a subculture and act as a role model. The activities of the gangs are organized and directed toward street-level crime, such as the extortion of shopkeepers and hawkers, the protection of premises within their territory, debt collection, and street-level drug dealing. The gangs readily use violence in their rackets, in the protection of their "turf," in retaliation or revenge against rival gangs, and in random assaults against strangers while usually under the influence of drugs or alcohol. The weapons most frequently used in gang violence are baseball bats, clubs, metal pipes, and choppers (knives and cleavers) because of the effective gun control policies of Hong Kong. As a result of their public displays and violence, street gangs receive more police attention and response than any other group.

The third type of organized gang identified by the RHKP is the *criminal gang*. These gangs operate in the tradition of career criminals and professional thieves. They specialize in pickpocketing, shoplifting, burglary, and armed robbery, especially the robbery of banks and jewelry stores. They have no defined physical area or limits. Members of these gangs may or may not be in a triad; they do, however, interact with triads and other criminal groups. These interactions involve the fencing of stolen goods and documents; the obtaining of counterfeit passports, identity cards, and driver licenses; the procuring of firearms; and the smuggling of robbers from another country.

Multicrime syndicates are involved in both diverse and overlapping criminal activities. Their activities range from the local level to the

TABLE 15.1 The Triads of Hong Kong

				The Major Triads				
14K *20 factions*	*Wo* *12 factions*	*Chiu Chow* *6 factions*	*Luen* *4 factions*	*Tung* *4 factions*	*Tung (East)* *3 factions*	*Kwong* *2 factions*	*Ching* *2 factions*	*Others*
14K Baailo	Wo Hop To	Chiu Kwong Sh'e	Luen Fei Ying	Luen Lok Tong	Tung Luen Sh'e	Kwong Hung	Ching Nin Sh'e	Chuen Yat Chi
14K Hau	Wo Kwan Lok	Fuk Yee Hing	Luen Hung Ying	Luen Kung Lok	Tung On	Kwong Luen Shing	Ching Wah Sh'e	Yuet Tong
14K Kim	Wo Kwan Ying	King Yee	Luen Shun Tong	Tung Kwan Ying	Tung On Wo			Chuk Luen Bong
14K Kin	Wo Lee Kwan	Sun Yee On	Luen To Ying	Tung San Wo				
14K Lai	Wo Lee Wo	Tai Ho Choi						
14K Lun	Wo On Lok	Yee Kwan						
14K Mui	Wo Shing Tong							
14K Ngai	Wo Shing Wo							
14K Sai Kong	Wo Shing Yee							
14K Sai Shing Tong	Wo Yee Tong							
	Wo Yung Yee							
14K Sat	Wo Hung Shing							
14K Shing								
14K Shun								
14K Tai Huen								
14K Tak								
14K Tung								
14K Yan								
14K Yee								
14K Yee Shing Tong								
14K Yung								

international level. Their organization is complex, combining legitimate and illegitimate activities and organizations. Legitimate businesses are used in a layered structure to conceal assets and to maintain control. Their criminal activities include drug trafficking, credit card fraud, arms and alien smuggling, and money laundering. Syndicate members may or may not be triads, and those who are triads may be from different triads. No one person or specific triad runs or controls the syndicate. In addition to triad members and nontriad criminals, syndicate members also include people who are viewed as participants in the legitimate business and professional sectors of Hong Kong.

The final organized criminal groups operating in Hong Kong according to the RHKP are the *criminal enterprises*. The criminal enterprise differs from the criminal syndicate mainly in that its members who have triad and nontriad criminal pasts have distanced themselves from triad identifications and hands-on crimes. They are fully accepted as being legitimate, law-abiding members of various Hong Kong communities. The subtle and complex organization of the enterprise manipulates and co-opts the political, law enforcement, commerce, media, and professional sectors. This is achieved through the compromising or corrupting or both of politicians, law enforcement personnel, lawyers, accountants, community activists, and the managers and executives of media, banking, and business corporations. The manipulating, co-opting, lobbying, compromising, and corrupting take place under the guises of legitimate interests in the free enterprise system of Hong Kong's capitalistic economy and in the individual and human rights activism that is present in Hong Kong's democracy movement (Hodson, 1995; RHKP, 1974, 1988).

TRIAD CRIME AND THE PERVASIVENESS OF ORGANIZED CRIME

The criminal activities of a specific triad do not involve the total triad or the triad leader, the Dragon Head. The criminal activities are carried out by a faction of the triad or a splinter segment of the faction. The area-boss, a big brother, directs the criminal activities with a high degree of independence and autonomy. The criminal activities that the area-boss directs include the traditional rackets of organized crime and the newer ones that are the products of the modern technological society. Triad extortion, protection, and blackmail rackets operate in regard to illegal gambling, public transportation, taxis, illegal passenger-goods vehicles, valet parking, the entertainment industry, clubs and bars, gymnasiums, street vendors, shops, fresh markets, hotels, restaurants, tea houses, recreational activities, public housing, interior decorating, building construction, manufacturing operations, schools, prisons, and the vice trades. Prostitution, pornography, loan-sharking, credit card fraud, and drug dealing on the local level are controlled by the triad area-bosses.

Examples of the pervasiveness of organized crime in Hong Kong in which the linkages that exist among the triads, the criminal syndicates, and criminal enterprises can be found are in the movie industry, law and politics, and law enforcement. For the movie industry, the claim has been made that triads control 80% to 90% of it ("Police Target," 1993). This control includes the scalping of movie tickets for alleged sold-out movies by triad street gangs through collusion with theater ushers and managers; triad extortion and protection for on-location filming; movie stars being coerced and starlets assaulted and raped; and film being destroyed (Cheng & Kwong, 1992; Lo, 1993). An example of the triad control of the movie industry is to be found in the destruction of film by armed men on January 8, 1992, because movie star Leslie Cheung refused to work for a triad film company. In response to this incident, actors and other workers in the movie industry held a public march on January 15, 1992, protesting triad control in their industry. The RHKP, however, reported that many of the marchers were triad members. The major organized crime groups having control in the movie industry are the Sun Yee On, the 14K, the Wo Hop To, and the Big Circle. The Sun Yee On is the largest group and the triad with the greatest control over the movie industry. The greatest competition to their control comes from the nontriad, the Big Circle, and the 14K triad who have joined forces for a takeover. This competition, as would be expected, has been marked by violence. In 1992, movie producer Choi A Chiming, who was suspected of being connected to an Amsterdam drug trafficking syndicate, was shot to death. Not long after this killing, film director Wong Long-wai, associated with the Hunnan Big Circle, was attacked, hospitalized for serious injuries, and shot to death while in the hospital. In 1993, Sun Yee On faction leader Andely Chan Yiung, the Tiger of Wan Chai, was the victim of a Mob hit while participating as a race-car driver in the Macau Grand Prix. Chan's participation in the race was under the sponsorship of movie producer Steven Lo Kit-shing, who was with Chan when he was killed. On October 19, 1995, Steven Lo Kit-shing was the victim of a chop attack. While hospitalized for his injuries, he had 10 personal body guards (Lo & Gilbert, 1995; Mosher, 1992b).

In all the conflict among the triads and the Big Circle for dominant control of the movie industry, a certain irony exists that has the makings of a movie. The scenario includes *The Oriental Daily,* the Chinese language newspaper with the largest circulation, doing a big exposé of organized crime's control of the movie industry. This crime-fighting newspaper was founded in 1969 by Ma Sik-chun, who jumped bail and fled to Taiwan in 1978 after being charged with drug-related offenses by the Hong Kong authorities. In Taiwan, he joined his brother, the infamous "White Powder" Ma Sik-yo, another fugitive from Hong Kong. With the founder's departure to a safe refuge, the operations of *The Oriental Daily* were placed in the hands of Ma Sik-chun's eldest son, Ma Ching-Kwan. Under his leadership, *The Oriental Daily* in recent years has taken exception to the films on the "gangsters Ma." Many of these films were produced by Heung Wah-sing, whose father founded the Sun Yee On society in 1921 (Cheng & Kwong, 1992; Mosher, 1992b).

The pervasive influence of the triads in law, law enforcement, and politics is also quite evident. The Independent Commission Against Corruption (ICAC) reported that the triad infiltration of the legal profession includes bribery, kickbacks, corruption, and touting. The key triad players within the legal profession are the law clerks. The Canadian Consulate in Hong Kong reported that 95% of law clerks have links to the triads. The law clerks compromise, co-opt, and corrupt lawyers and lawmakers. Many lawyers know of the profession's corruption by the triads, especially in criminal law, but take little action ("ICAC Links," 1993; Lo, 1993; Luk, 1995; Sung & Lee, 1991). In addition, the alleged leader of the Sun Yee On is a retired legal practitioner who has ties to the disciplined services (police, fire, and corrections), the Legislative Council, and the Regional and Urban Councils, as well as the legal profession (Sun Yee On, 1993). The 1990 case of Warwick Reid, a deputy director of public prosecution and head of the Commercial Crimes Unit, also showed the linkages that exist among triads, crime syndicates, and crime enterprises, as well as the pervasiveness of organized crime. Reid, when charged with corruption, fled and was arrested 4 months later in Manila. Subsequently, he pled guilty to having obtained approximately $1,459,950 through corrupt practices and was sentenced to prison for 8 years. In a plea bargain attempt, his defense counsel offered to have Reid testify in six trials involving wealthy people, triad gangsters, and former police officers in relation to drug and arms smuggling, fraud, and extortion (Lo, 1993).

In regard to organized crime's well-known influence on law enforcement and politics in Hong Kong, it is sufficient and succinct to say that it has been great, lengthy, and legendary and that the legacy continues today and will continue into the next century. One incident, the "white glove" confrontation with police, shows that organized criminal groups avail themselves of modern public practices to gain support for their cause and to embarrass the police. In this incident, 1,000 men wearing white gloves on their right hands arrived in hired buses at a new housing estate in Laguna City. Their intent was to put down deposits on flats and then resell them at an inflated profit and to protest against the sale being rigged. The white-gloved men were members of the Kum Tong triad. When they broke up the queue of waiting applicants, they were chased by 100 well-armed police. The next day, the Boss of the Kum Tong held a press conference to complain that six of his men had been beaten by the police and that the police were in collusion with the 14K, the Sun Yee On, and the Lo Dan to give disproportionately fewer places to the Kum Tong. The Kum Tong were only seeking justice and fairness (Lau, 1990; Wong & Cheng, 1990). In two more recent cases, triad linkages with police officers were more direct and evident. In the first case, the Organized Crime and Triad Bureau of the RHKP arrested two sergeants, three constables, and 27 members of the Fuk Yee Hing triad for operating extortion rackets involving housing estate decorating companies (Goodsir, 1995b). In the second case, a judge stopped the trial of a man accused of murder and ordered that he be acquitted because of the "sinister" police-triad link that resulted in his arrest. The linkage involved two triad members and a police sergeant and a constable making a covert deal for the alleged murderer to be handed over to the police (Buddle, 1995).

Although the three cases that have been described illustrate specific linkages between the triads and the police at the community level, triads have been able to influence the People's Republic of China at all levels.

THE RUN-UP TO 1997 AND POST-1997

For at least the past 5 years, government leaders and law enforcement executives throughout the world have been debating the consequences of the return of Hong Kong to China on July 1, 1997. Many of those participating in the debate have expressed concern, if not fear, that during the run-up to the time that the People's Republic of China (P.R.C.) gains sovereignty over Hong Kong, an exodus of triad leaders from Hong Kong will take place. The emigrating triad leaders are expected to immigrate to Chinese communities in Western Europe, the United States, Canada, and Australia. Some of the expectation is based on Hong Kong triads being identified with drug trafficking in Japan, the Philippines, Taiwan, Korea, Singapore, Australia, the Netherlands; the Canadian cities of Vancouver, Montreal, Hamilton, and Ottawa; and the major cities of the United States (Chin, 1992, p. 2; Dobinson, 1992, pp. 1-7; Dombrink & Song, 1992; McKenzie, 1994). More recently, Flynn (1995) reported that many police forces around the world are known to be concerned that the 1997 change of sovereignty will lead to influxes of triad members in other countries. Although the concern over the expected invasion by triad Bosses to other countries persists, contemporary evidence does not support it. For example, it has been reported that, as of 1991, only 100 triad Bosses have emigrated from Hong Kong (Sung & Lee, 1991) and that some of the early émigrés are returning to Hong Kong, albeit with legal passports from their host countries. In addition, if large numbers of triad members have immigrated to other countries, they are certainly not getting arrested and imprisoned. The Hong Kong Security Branch reported that 12 Hong Kong residents were imprisoned in the United States, 10 in Australia, 5 in Canada, 4 in Germany, and 2 in the Netherlands (Bode, 1995). Furthermore, the triad involvement in the international or transnational trafficking of drugs has been going on for decades, and it has no relationship to Hong Kong's sovereignty. What the evidence does seem to show is that the Hong Kong triads now see the P.R.C. as the new "Golden Mountain." This has resulted in the triads having for some time a gold rush mentality toward China, and they have either already staked their claims or are ready to stake their claims (Law, 1995).

Australia, a nation that continually had expressed fear of an influx of triad members from

Hong Kong in the run-up to 1997, had a parliamentary committee present a paper on the threat of a triad exodus to Australia. The authors of the paper said that the economic boom in China and greater economic freedom there had provided attractive opportunities for Hong Kong-based triads and that Australia should not fear a triad exodus ("Triad Exodus," 1995). The same is true for North America and Western Europe. It is far easier for the triads to exploit the criminal opportunities of China and Hong Kong than to cope with foreign cultures and languages and with racial and ethnic minority statuses and to compete with the indigenous organized crime groups in various nations for power and economic success. It also must be recognized that Paramount Leader Deng's economic reform and open-door policy have resulted in the P.R.C. experiencing a great increase in crime, graft, and corruption.

At the 1995 Interpol annual assembly in Beijing, President Jiang Zemin of the P.R.C. said in his keynote address that the 16-year-old policy has opened the door to international crime, which was now "seriously endangering the safety of the Chinese people and hindering sound social development" ("Global Economic Links," 1995, p. 12). What President Jiang failed to recognize in his speech was the indigenous organized crime and triad activities that have been taking place in his country for years. Groups within the People's Liberation Army (PLA) have had smuggling, counterfeiting, embezzlement, and bribery as their main illegal activities. Because the PLA can only be investigated with the approval of the Beijing government, these organized crime groups have licenses for crime ("China's Market Reforms," 1994). Moreover, the Public Security Bureau of the P.R.C. is alleged to be involved in large-scale smuggling between Guangdong Province and Hong Kong (Wong & Cheng, 1990). Another example of the activities of these groups was the Royal Navy patrol craft HMS *Peacock*'s intervention in the attempted hijack of a cargo ship in Hong Kong waters by an armed Chinese marine patrol that had boarded the ship. The uniformed Chinese personnel who boarded

the ship were believed to be border security guards (Ball, 1994). In addition to these uniformed organized crime groups, the P.R.C. has more traditional organized crime groups smuggling drugs from the Golden Triangle by overland routes through China, mainly through Yunnan Province (Dombrink & Song, 1992). There are also the organized crime groups in the P.R.C. who, with their "snakeheads" smuggle mainland Chinese from Fujian Province throughout the world. The most established and entrenched organized crime group in China, however, is the Big Circle, with its members consisting mainly of former Red Guards. The Big Circle has a reputation for committing crimes through armed violence in both the P.R.C. and Hong Kong. Despite this reputation or because of it, the Big Circle has been viewed as the only organized crime group able to move rather freely in the P.R.C. (Davis, 1995, p. 43).

The presence of organized crime in the P.R.C. for at least two decades provides a certain perspective to the 1992 statement of Public Security Minister Tao Siju: "Triad members are not all cut out of the same cloth. Some are patriotic to China and Hong Kong" (Mosher, 1992a, p. 16). Moreover, Tao also claimed that his statement had the support of Deng and other top P.R.C. politicians. It also should be noted that Tao's statement would have been most likely supported by Chairman Mao Tse-tung if he were still alive. Such support is found in Mao's public appeal on July 15, 1936, to the Elder Brethren, a triadlike secret society with many bandits and thieves as members, for their help in fighting the Japanese invaders of China, with the promise to forget past discord and to accept them in the union to save China (Robertson, 1977). In his continuing remarks, Tao commented that Hong Kong gang members would be allowed to visit and establish businesses on the mainland. The alarm and questions raised by Tao's comments among the people of Hong Kong increased when it was subsequently learned that the P.R.C. had made contacts with the Sun Yee On, Hong Kong's largest and wealthiest triad, as early as 1988, that the Beijing government had been soliciting the Sun Yee

On to invest in its entertainment industry, that Tao had met with the leaders of the triad several days before his public statement, and that the Sun Yee On and other triads have provided protection to P.R.C. leaders when they traveled abroad. In response to the ongoing solicitation of the P.R.C., the Sun Yee On is well established in Shenzhen and Shanghai (CBS News, 1993; Davis, 1995).

Although President Jiang failed to comment on the indigenous organized crime groups and his government's solicitation and encouragement of triad investment, he did express concern in regard to graft and corruption. His concern over corruption manifested itself in his removal from office of Beijing Party Chief Chen Xitong and his subsequent purge from the Politburo for corruption ("Former Party Chief," 1995; Gilley, 1995). Unfortunately, the fate of Chen Xitong has not served as a lesson. Despite the authorities' attempts at control, graft and corruption continue to be significant factors in the growth of organized crime in all levels of the P.R.C., especially the Public Security Bureau (Crothall, 1995; Davis, 1995). A similar concern exists in Hong Kong in regard to the RHKP and corruption. Secretary for Security Pete Lzi Hing-ling has stated that corruption among police officers has "surged" (No, 1995). Moreover, there has been alarm over lax management and a slip in police standards that has increased the potential for graft and corruption (Goodsir, 1995a). With a study showing that 40% of senior officers of the RHKP above the rank of superintendent plan to leave the force before 1997, the control of graft and corruption is critical (Law, 1995). A veteran Southeast Asian law enforcement administrator with extensive experience in Hong Kong and China commented that, in the post-1997 period, corruption will increase among the political leaders of the P.R.C. and the top people of the P.R.C. and the friends of China will be protected. He also predicted an increase in corruption for the PLA, the RHKP, and the political leaders of Hong Kong (personal interview, 1995).

CONCLUSION

Given the social dynamics, social change, and criminogenesis imminent in contemporary China and Hong Kong that have been presented, it may be concluded for the post-1997 period that the triads will flourish in China; that there will be no substantial immigration of triad members to North America, Western Europe, and Australia; and that criminologists will continually have the opportunity to apply anomie theory, strain theory, cultural deviance theories, opportunity theory, conflict theory, and radical theories in explaining crime and criminal behavior in China and Hong Kong.

16 HONG KONG AFTER 1997

Transnational Organized Crime
in a Shrinking World

JOHN DOMBRINK

JOHN HUEY-LONG SONG

The authors of this chapter examine the transnational nature of organized crime in Hong Kong and its impact on other countries under the reversion of Hong Kong to China in 1997. The "push" and "pull" factors are offered to explain the dilemma that triads and organized crime in Hong Kong face in determining whether they will stay or leave. The speculation that Chinese triads and organized crime will fill the same role as traditional organized crime in the United States is disputed.

In this chapter, we make several points: (a) There are competing hypotheses about the effect of the reversion of Hong Kong to the People's Republic of China (P.R.C.), and it is not clear which of those can be upheld from available data; (b) Hong Kong's role as an important place in the context of certain multinational crimes committed by some multinational crime groups has been significant, and growing as world finance and communications is more connected; (c) evidence suggests Hong Kong triad and organized crime activity in many

AUTHORS' NOTES: We thank Robin Neal of Buffalo State College for her assistance in summarizing news stories for this chapter, and Darius Bagahi of the University of California at Irvine for his research assistance. Portions of the chapter were presented at the 1995 Annual Meeting of the American Society of Criminology in Boston and at the Annual Meeting of the Academy of Criminal Justice Sciences, Las Vegas, Nevada, March 15, 1996.

We also thank the Pacific Rim Research Program at the University of California at Irvine for funds for a 1989 research trip by John Dombrink. Interviews were conducted in Hong Kong in 1989 by coauthor Dombrink with officials of the Royal Hong Kong Police, of other Hong Kong legal system officials, and of other countries. We acknowledge the National Institute of Justice and Lois Felson Mock for an invitation to present a paper describing some findings from NIJ 88-IJ-CX-0049 at the Multinational Asian Organized Crime Conference in San Francisco, September 1991. Interviews were conducted with more than 200 police and prosecutors and Asian community leaders in New York, San Francisco, Los Angeles, and Washington, D.C., as part of that research project. Some interviews were conducted in San Francisco with U.S. and P.R.C. officials connected to a heroin-importing case involving a citizen suspect from the People's Republic of China, which also involved Hong Kong.

countries around the world in recent years; and (d) within Hong Kong itself is a range of criminal organization structure and function, and these groups have reacted to the changeover in different ways.

HONG KONG APPROACHING 1997

Triads, which are Chinese in origin, are significantly represented in Hong Kong (e.g., Wo Group, 14K) (Booth, 1990; Lau, 1991; U.S. Department of Justice, 1988). They may have members who are connected to American criminal groups and gangs or who serve as partners and intermediaries, including some who relocated to the United States before the July 1, 1997, transition of Hong Kong to the P.R.C. Nonetheless, much debate is occurring, and will occur, whether the triad influence will be large scale and redirect the interests of the American groups, will cause competition and violence among the American groups, or will provide emerging leaders within the American context.

The purpose of the formation of triads in China historically was political at its outset. The British colonization of Hong Kong helped the triads develop under a foreign system that most colonized Chinese did not trust. After the Chinese nationalists defeated the Manchus and established the Republic of China in 1911, the triad movement continued, not as the politically inspired, patriotic movement it once was, but as a shell for the pursuit of organized criminal activities.

The Communist Revolution in mainland China drove many triad members into Hong Kong in 1949. The Hong Kong government's crackdown in the late 1950s pushed the triads either underground or into a low profile for the next decade, until 1967, when the police were fully occupied in maintaining order on the streets during a period of civil unrest and riots. Hong Kong's economic success during the 1960s provided ever-increased opportunities in the traditional areas of triad influence of vice, gambling, and narcotics. As Roger (1989a) points out, however, triads today

continue to be involved in the criminal activities with which they have traditionally been associated, such as gambling, prostitution, extortion, protection, loansharking and narcotics. While these activities fall within the "typical organized crime" area, today's triad societies are not the large organized crime syndicates that they once were. Today, the degree of a triad's involvement in criminal activity will vary dependent on [a member's] age, motivation and ability.

Experts in both the Royal Hong Kong Police (RHKP) and the U.S. Federal Bureau of Investigation (FBI) have indicated that the triad affiliation becomes secondary when it comes to Chinese organized crime. Some significant overlap of membership may occur between triads and organized crime, but triads are not necessarily organized crime. Roger (1989b), a ranking officer of the RHKP, estimated about 50 triad societies, of which about 15 regularly come to police attention. He estimates 300,000 individual triad members and affiliates in Hong Kong.

Chin (1995b) suggests some factors that might influence the movement of Hong Kong-based triad members and their operations and capital to other countries, including the United States.

Some (B. Merritt, personal communication, September 1989) have argued that it is in the interest of the Hong Kong triads to concentrate on Hong Kong, at least until the 1997 issues are resolved, or at least hedging their bets by staying in part. Chin suggests that impending competition from P.R.C. criminal groups, such as the Big Circle gang, might force the Hong Kong-based triads away. The ruthlessness of the latter, along with whatever connections they have with some corrupted P.R.C. officials, argue in their favor in such a competition. Chin also suggests that younger generations of triad members are more willing than their more conservative elders to be involved in activities, such as drug trafficking, that necessitate multinational presence. Another point by Chin is that some triad members and groups feel the strain of successful and energetic police prosecution of them in Hong Kong and are looking to diversify in countries where it is easier to evade law enforcement. At the same time, Chin concludes that recent events, including political instability, have created new opportunities for Hong Kong triads that compel them to stay, at least as long as possible to maximize revenues.

Although some law enforcement authorities assume that triads will move most of their criminal operations out of Hong Kong, others predict that the movement will be small scale and limited to senior members only (Chin, 1995b, p. 61).

Several competing hypotheses have been proposed regarding the role of triads in Hong Kong after 1997. From one perspective, the fragmentation of triad societies in Hong Kong may prohibit triad control of gangs in North America (Roger, 1989a). Mutual business interests of Chinese organized crime groups, however, may expand the scope of influence of the criminal gangs in the United States and other countries. From another perspective, the reversion to the P.R.C., which still operates under a different legal system, will still be problematic, even with the continuity of the Hong Kong legal system beyond 1997.

The years since the hearings held by the President's Commission on Organized Crime in 1984, which raised questions about Chinese triad relocation of their operations from Hong Kong to the United States, have witnessed different forms of population movement. In the first few years after the treaty was signed in 1984, out-migration of Hong Kong residents to other countries surged; once many of the out-migrants secured a foreign visa or citizenship, they returned to Hong Kong. Still, trust in China's promise of "one country, two systems" has been wavering because of several known incidents in the recent past.

According to some observers, the factors that might "push" the triad members to go abroad are (a) the P.R.C.'s intolerance of organized crime, which in many cases serves as a reminder of the corrupting nationalist government before the Communist Revolution in late 1940s; and (b) the alleged tolerance of some organized crime operations by some Chinese communities

in the United States. In contrast, the "exodus theory" suffers when other observers believe that (a) it is easier for triads to do business in Hong Kong than in the United States; (b) corruption in the P.R.C. may provide an opportunity for triads to thrive in Hong Kong and maybe in China; (c) the disunity of Chinese communities in the United States may not offer an effective cover for organized crime; (d) the diversification of triad activities in different regions of the world may reduce the impact on the United States and U.S. law enforcement; and (e) U.S. success in prosecution of several Asian crime groups in New York City and other metropolitan areas makes Hong Kong triads think twice before moving their operations to the United States.

One Chinese community leader in New York City indicated that when the United States authorized investment visas, triad members might come here directly. Although it would be unfair to imply that applicants for investment visas or immigration to the United States are coming from a less than legitimate background, triad members who would otherwise have any legal means to come to the United States may now take on this opportunity. The requirements for investment visas may be too strict, however, for any sizable numbers of triad members to migrate.

But it is also true that it doesn't take too many influential triad members to overwhelm the already understaffed law enforcement. It took only one Eddie Chan—a notorious former Hong Kong police officer and triad power (B. Merritt, personal communication, September 1989)—to raise havoc for law enforcement in Chinese communities in New York City in the early 1980s.

THE MULTINATIONAL CRIMINAL

The discussion of Hong Kong takes place in the context of international discussion of the impact of multinational organized crime. The criminology, law enforcement, and international affairs communities have increased their focus on the operations of multinational organized crime in the past 5 years.

Williams (1995a) observes several features of these groups. First is *resilience.* There are several features of this, but foremost is their nonhierarchical nature:

> Transnational criminal organizations are diverse in structure, outlook and membership, but all of them pose formidable challenges for law enforcement at both the national and international levels. One reason for this is their emphasis on loose network structures rather than excessively formal and structured hierarchies. (Williams, 1995a, pp. 14-15)

He references Lupsha's depiction of even the most hierarchical groups as having "networks of affiliation, a point echoed by American Drug Enforcement Agency (DEA) and FBI officials charged with monitoring the international heroin trade" (Williams, 1995a, p. 15). These groups are thus both *flexible* and *adaptable;* they are highly fluid and can respond rapidly to law enforcement challenges, characteristics that describe the Hong Kong drug-selling organizations. Williams also emphasizes growing *sophistication,* which also describes the diversification and economic entrenchment of the Hong Kong triads and organized crime groups.

At a 1991 conference in San Francisco on Multinational Asian Organized Crime, U.S. Assistant Attorney General Robert S. Mueller (1991) spoke before representatives of the attending countries (United States, Canada, Australia, New Zealand, the Netherlands, Korea, Japan, Malaysia, Hong Kong, and Thailand) about the emergence of a new phenomenon— the "multinational criminal." Criminologists and law enforcement officials had for many years studied and tracked those criminals who moved from country to country or those who used the bank secrecy laws of some countries, such as Switzerland, Panama, the Cayman Islands, the Turks and Caicos Islands, and others. Mueller was referring to a qualitative change in the rapidity with which the multinational criminals of the 1990s could move persons, goods, and money across borders, factors that describe the Hong Kong crime groups.

HONG KONG AND OTHER COUNTRIES

United States

When triad members have left Hong Kong for a haven in a foreign country, many have chosen countries with established ethnic communities. In the United States, San Francisco, with increasing Wo Hop To presence since the late 1980s, and New York have seen an increase in Hong Kong triad-related incidents.

In the United States, triad members need to integrate into existing criminal structures. Criminological analyses of Chinese organized crime in the United States have distinguished among the role of criminal gangs, more fluid criminal groups, tongs, triad heroin-importing groups, and organized crime (Chin, 1990b, 1995a; Song & Dombrink, 1994).

Because of the proximity of Hong Kong to the Golden Triangle, Hong Kong has, for some time, served as a transshipment center for heroin exported to other countries. In addition, the minimal control on the movement of money into and out of Hong Kong makes it an ideal place for money laundering operations (Gaylord, 1990; Kaplan, Goldberg, & Jue, 1986; Kerr, 1988).

One feature that some have noted is that most of the criminal gang members in New York City are foreign-born (Chin, 1990b; Kifner, 1991). In New York City, trouble has arisen among the Cantonese and Fukienese tongs. The Cantonese tongs, such as the On Leong and Hip Sing tongs, have been established in Chinatown for many years. In recent years, Fukienese tong members and criminal gang members associated with them have established themselves in New York City. Police believe that the shift in the rivalries among the tongs in New York reflects the shifting political balance overseas, with the growth of P.R.C. influence (Dobson, 1993, p. 2).

The relationship between the tongs and the Chinese youth gangs today is one of symbiosis, rather than of hierarchy. The historic respect for the elderly in the Chinese community has weakened at the same time as the independence of the youth gangs has grown. This new relationship seems to take away the structural characteristics for the tongs to be considered organized crime, and at the same time reinforces the perception that the Chinese youth crime groups are no longer beholden to a larger organized crime "family." It has become more difficult for tongs to effectively assert control over youth gang members. It is also becoming more common for triads from Hong Kong to network with both tongs and youth gangs and to enlarge their criminal influence. One effect of this new trend may be the decrease in power of the tong-gang combined crime groups, but the rise of a more internationally experienced and integrated crime group.

The U.S. government, however, has successfully completed many criminal prosecutions of Chinese triad members in the last few years. The charges have included extortion, gambling, murder, drug trafficking, prostitution, and the smuggling of illegal immigrants. Since July 1987, 77 defendants facing drug-related charges have been extradited to the United States or are awaiting extradition from Hong Kong. Many of these defendants are drug barons from Hong Kong who have been caught smuggling drugs into the United States. Although the police have said that this crackdown has put a dent in the organized crime in the Chinese community, they are concerned with others who may try to replace the prison-bound leaders.

Other Countries

During the years leading up to the reversion of Hong Kong to the P.R.C., triad involvement in many countries has been noted. For example, Chinese gangs in Russia have caused concern, leading President Boris Yeltsin to claim the presence of several thousand Chinese gangs amid a general growth of criminal gang presence and even dominance of the emerging economy there (Dobson, 1994, p. 3).

The P.R.C. has its own issues—including that of heroin being transshipped across its boundaries. Other reports have documented stolen container vehicles being driven from Hong Kong to the P.R.C., and Hong Kong triads providing money, expertise, and connections to Yunnan drug traders (Szeto, 1995, p. 4). Triads have reportedly invested in karaoke bars in Beijing and formed alliances with local clans and underground gangs (Lam, 1995, p. 6). Triads also controlled a majority of karaoke bars in Shenzhen and run gambling dens in Guangzhou (Szeto, 1995, p. 4).

Hong Kong triads ran a narcotics trafficking and kidnapping gang that involved senior Philippine police officers in their kidnapping of a Taiwanese businessman near Manila in May 1993 (Dobson, 1993, p. 2).

In Japan, Chinese gangs control 60% of Japan's heroin trade and are involved in activities as diverse as robbery, gambling, extortion, and drug trafficking. In 1994, Chinese mainlanders were responsible for almost 4,500 criminal cases, or 40% of crime committed by foreigners in Japan (Kohut, 1995).

In Spain, the police believe that triad-based groups are involved in illegal immigration, near-slave labor, extortion, prostitution, drugs, and gambling.

In South Africa, the triads are believed to be involved in the smuggling of illegal immigrants, poached ivory and rhino horn, and abalone and other seafood delicacies. The Hong Kong police have cooperated with South African officials by alerting them when important triad members may be heading toward South Africa (Van Heerden, 1995, p. 7).

In Australia, 40 separate raids have indicated that the triads may not be selling drugs at the street level but that they are responsible for the importation of heroin from Hong Kong to Australia (McKenzie, 1994, p. 5). In New Zealand, the police believe that 18 triad members currently living in New Zealand have links to the 14K and Sun Yee On triads (Ambler, 1993, p. 4).

In Canada, triad groups such as the Kung Lok, 14K, Wo Hop To, and Sun Yee On have established links through lawyers to smuggle drugs by using tours of big-name entertainers of Canada (Yu, 1993, p. 2).

HONG KONG
CONTROL OF TRIADS

According to some reports, within Hong Kong, as 1997 approached, career criminals—including triad members—were getting away with more crime. Witnesses and victims were extorted by the triads. Under existing law, they are not obligated to give information and cooperate with the police. This makes the evidence seized by the police in a crackdown useless because there is no corroborating evidence to back up the seized evidence (Tam & Wong, 1993, p. 1).

In addition, triad involvement with organized crime has been on the increase. There has been a 20% increase of triad-related drug trafficking and bookmaking cases, and a 30% increase in triad-related gambling cases. Officials stated that a new law may help the situation for the police. The Organized and Serious Crimes Bill would make it necessary for witnesses to help in the investigation and would provide tougher sentencing.

The P.R.C. has been asked to issue a stronger message that Hong Kong triads will not be tolerated after 1997. Beijing has noted that they are concerned with the "threat of the triads to the social order and political stability of Hong Kong." One concern is that the P.R.C. may allow triad members to make investments on the mainland (Chan, 1993, p. 5).

The P.R.C. is reported to be readying an anti-triad law to break up triads that have been setting up their syndicates in that country. Officials have stated that triads have been linked to the increase in fraud, drug trafficking, and smuggling in recent years, particularly in Southern China. Beijing has noted the rapid expansion of triad-related groups in China and has said that

overseas organizations have come to China to create gangs and encourage people to become members. The new law would attempt to keep the triads' activities in check and reeducate the police in the history of triads and their development over the years (Cheung, 1994, p. 1).

CONCLUSION:
HONG KONG TRIADS AND 1997

Hong Kong Commissioner of Police Li Kwan-ha openly disputed the theme running through the 1993 International Asian Organized Crime Conference that triads were behind all Asian organized crime. He said, "It is true that Hong Kong's organized crime fraternity has amongst its ranks members of triad societies, but I cannot over-stress the fact that organized crime is not the exclusive domain of the triad, just as it is not the exclusive domain of the Mafia in America or, indeed, Italy" (Dobson, 1993, p. 2).

Even if there were to be an exodus of triad members of a significant size, some knowledgeable observers have expressed doubt that Asian organized crime would ever fill the same role as traditional organized crime in the United States, unable or uninterested in penetrating labor unions, the garment industry, construction, and waste management (Chin, 1990b; Goldstock, 1984). Still, the impact on the Chinese community and the role in heroin and immigrant smuggling portends a high profile for these issues in many countries over the next few years.

Given the pluralization of Chinese immigrant communities in the United States and the possibility and opportunity to corrupt public officials in the P.R.C., triad members may hold a wait-and-see attitude while seeking a niche in other countries, including the United States. It is our observation that triads are not coming in large droves. Capital can move many places. Although it is not invasion, triads have already acted on some opportunities in the United States.

17

THE EVOLUTION AND FUTURE DIRECTION OF SOUTHEAST ASIAN CRIMINAL ORGANIZATIONS

KEN SANZ

IRA SILVERMAN

Many Southeast Asians immigrated to the United States after the collapse of South Vietnam in 1975. Slowly assimilating, this group is now an established part of the American way of life, and Asian communities, as with any immigrant group, are differentially identifiable only by ethnicity. Unfortunately, as with other immigrant groups, organized crime has been a component of these communities from the outset. The authors examine the structure and operations of Asian organized crime groups to conclude that we can expect to see enhanced cooperation between these Americanized groups and other organized crime groups on the international level. The untapped markets of Southeast Asia will be the focus of the cooperatives, and travel by criminals from country to country will increase. We can expect to face new, Asian-originated types of criminal activity, including opium and hashish trafficking, immigration schemes, international extortion, corporate kidnappings, and threats of disruption of corporate operations.

With the collapse of South Vietnam in 1975, many Southeast Asians immigrated to the United States. The first wave of refugees consisted of the merchant and professional classes and included military and political figures. They were not accepted by most Americans and had difficulty fitting into Western society. Most refugees overcame these adversities, however, and founded businesses in the communities where they settled. Unfortunately, organized crime has been a component of these newly developed and prosperous ethnic communities from the outset. This has occurred because a significant number of those airlifted from Vietnam were associated with the old Saigon regime or the South Vietnamese Army, both of which had long legacies

AUTHORS' NOTE: Much of the material for this chapter is drawn from Sanz, K., & Francisco, P. (1995). *Southeast Asian Criminality*. Tampa, FL: S. M. & C. Sciences.

of brutality and corruption. These military and political leaders, who had long taken advantage of their fellow Vietnamese, saw little reason to change their ways on arrival in the United States. Beginning with various extortion schemes, from which the proceeds were ostensibly directed toward patriotic causes to fund and arm Vietnamese rebels, they progressed to more traditional crimes such as robberies and burglaries. These crimes were likewise justified as securing funds for patriotic reasons.

In the 1980s, a second wave of immigrants emerged. They were referred to as "boat people" because they left their country on anything that would float in order to flee the repressive conditions of Communist Vietnam. More desperate and impoverished than their predecessors, they often spent years in "squalid resettlement camps where crowding and boredom bred mental illness, juvenile delinquency and riots" (Kleinknecht, 1996, p. 183). Many were ethnic Chinese who had long been repressed by the North Vietnamese Communists and were forced to flee their country because of a military clash between China and Vietnam in 1979. Also present were Amerasian children who had been outcasts in their home country. More than half of these refugees were under age 16 and alone, having been put on boats by their parents, who wanted better lives for their children. With little to do, many of these youths joined together in gangs that terrorized their already tormented countrymen.

When these youths arrived in the United States, they had already experienced the ravages of war and had been separated from their families and treated like "human garbage" in the Hong Kong refugee camps (Kleinknecht, 1996, p. 185). They needed help to deal with the heavy emotional baggage they brought with them, but were instead greeted with hostility by Americans to whom they represented an ugly reminder of a lost war. Even within their own communities, they failed to receive assistance. Many were placed with foster families, friends, or relatives who could barely provide for the survival of their own families. Most of the

placement parents had little time to nurture another parent's troubled child. Lacking emotional support and experiencing ridicule in school, it is not surprising that many of the youths dropped out and left their foster homes (Kleinknecht, 1996). Facing a depressed job market, unable to speak the language, and unwilling to work the grueling hours required by the fishing industry, most youths were unable to find employment. On the street, the gang became their family and source of income. Their rough appearance and lack of skill in committing crimes often drew the attention of local patrol officers. These officers were, however, unaware of the threat posed by such gangs. Police were content to ignore the petty criminal activity of the gangs, justifying their inaction on the grounds that only other Asians were being victimized.

LOCATION OF VIETNAMESE COMMUNITIES

Originally, the Ford administration's plan for resettlement of the South Vietnamese involved a strategy of spreading the refugees across the country. In this way, no single community would be unduly burdened. This plan, however, failed to consider the role of climate, locale, and a desire to live within homogeneous ethnic enclaves. This combination of factors initially resulted in the migration of Vietnamese to several communities in California and later to communities in Texas and Florida. Other communities in which they settled were close to the sea and included such areas as New Orleans, Portland, and New York City. Eventually, large Southeast Asian enclaves developed in interior states such as Colorado, Illinois, Missouri, and Oklahoma.

Initially, many refugees lived in government-assisted housing. They later moved to low-income housing and then to the suburbs during the mid 1980s. This movement reduced cloistered housing syndrome and concomitantly the size of inner-city "Little Saigons."

CHARACTERISTICS OF
VIETNAMESE CRIMINAL ENTERPRISES

The nature of Vietnamese criminal activity typically takes three forms: casual gangs, mobile gangs, and senior criminals. Two additional characteristics worthy of note are recruitment patterns and the role of females.

Casual Gangs

Casual gangs are composed of neighborhood youths bound together by a common ethnic and cultural background and past experiences, including shared refugee camp stays and negative experiences as newly arrived immigrants. Their relationships are further cemented by rejection, joblessness, and lack of family ties. For such youths, the gang becomes their family unit. Found principally in government-assisted housing and inner-city neighborhoods, these groups are characteristically leaderless and have fluctuating membership. In contrast with the mobile gangs discussed later, their criminal acts are limited to their home communities. These typically include sporadic, unsophisticated criminal endeavors such as petty burglaries, shoplifting, and "snatch and grab" retail thefts. Further, as a result of exposure to violence and rejection and the lack of appropriate socialization, these youths engage in indiscriminate acts of violence during the commission of crimes.

Mobile Gangs

Mobile gangs are unaffiliated and less organized Vietnamese gangs that typically vary in size from 10 to 20 members, but at times number as few as 3. Members generally range in age from 12 to 25. Changing in structure and membership as they travel, these transitory groups have few rules and no rites of initiation or penalties for leaving. Further, leaders may change from town to town and from one criminal venture to another.

Members often view themselves as social outcasts and flaunt an "outlaw" image as an indication of their rebellion. They frequently adopt a mental attitude characterized as "my crazy life." This attitude is typical of many other ethnic gangs and serves as a means to instill fear in their Asian victims of the possible consequences of cooperating with law enforcement authorities. With no family or jobs to tie them to any single community, they generally commit crimes in one city and then quickly relocate to another. Here, "brothers" assist them by providing safe houses or "crash pads," which allow them an opportunity to "cool off" and select new targets. These brothers not only supply intelligence on local conditions and potential targets but also train younger gang members in criminal endeavors. Additionally, they provide tools and equipment and supplement the capabilities of the gang by providing "local talent."

Mobile gangs have a preference for criminal acts that include extortion of legitimate Asian businesses, protection scams, drug trafficking, home and auto burglaries, auto theft, and home invasion robberies. Moreover, although all gangs exhibit varying degrees of violence in the commission of crimes, mobile gangs are more likely to engage in extreme acts of violence. Murders and serious assaults, which often occur during home invasions and acts of extortion, do not correlate with the degree of victim resistance. This phenomenon has been explained by some experts as a normal reaction of people who have witnessed brutality over an extended period of time.

Intelligence officers tracking these groups indicate that they follow a fairly distinctive itinerary. Their trek usually begins in British Columbia or Seattle and continues on into southern California or Texas. The gangs then move east to Louisiana, Mississippi, Alabama, and into Florida. From there, some continue northward, traveling through Georgia, the Carolinas, and on to Virginia, New Jersey, and New York. The gangs then routinely travel back to the West Coast by the same routes as they came. The gangs often stop in favored cities along the way to peddle contraband, recruit new members, and perpetrate new crimes. In the early 1990s, the gangs expanded their target areas, traveling via major highway routes to Colorado, Kansas, Indiana, and Illinois.

Senior Criminals

Senior criminals were initially older, displaced arrivals who lacked family ties, skills, education, and jobs. Forming groups with changing leadership and members, they committed random, opportunistic crimes in their home neighborhoods and other communities. Their criminal activities typically lacked sophistication and included such crimes as street-level prostitution, small-scale gambling parlors, protection schemes, petty larceny, burglary, fencing, and street-level drug trafficking.

By the 1990s, the role of older offenders in criminal endeavors had changed. Many youths who had previously participated in either casual or mobile gangs had grown older. That lifestyle no longer appealed to them because they were now married, had children, owned their own homes, and often had at least part-time jobs. At this point, they also appeared to be respectable members of community. These individuals continued to maintain ties with younger gang members but were no longer apt to hang out with their younger counterparts on the street corner or in the pool halls. Thus, their role in the traditional criminal endeavors of the gang changed from direct participation to oversight. Now they choose the targets, plan the crimes, and dispose of stolen property but leave the operational aspects of such endeavors to the casual or mobile gang members. They also provide safe houses for traveling groups. They continue to be involved in crimes in which they develop expertise or control or exclusively dominate the market. Such crimes include operating Asian gaming parlors; counterfeiting identification and business documents such as checks; making or selling clothing and watches; and running houses of prostitution. The operation of massage parlors and the control of street hookers are also popular criminal endeavors. Moreover, they occasionally form "entrepreneurial task forces,"[1] which are or-

ganizations developed specifically for more sophisticated criminal ventures.

Other Features

One unique feature of Vietnamese criminal activity is the role of females. In the 1980s, female gangs emerged on the West Coast in a pattern similar to that of their male counterparts. A second and more widespread feature is the involvement of females with mobile gangs. These females attach themselves to the groups because they are disenchanted with their former traditional lifestyle or are attempting to escape an untenable home situation. Their functions include acting as sex partners for male gang members and playing minor roles in criminal ventures, such as "lookouts" in retail diversion thefts and commercial or home invasion robberies. They may also serve as prostitutes and gambling house hostesses. In addition, they frequently hold contraband and weapons, knowing the reluctance of police to pat-down a young, nonthreatening "China doll." Following a traditional gang pattern, these females may also hang out with local neighborhood gangs and occasionally provide them with the same services as those provided to the mobile gangs.

Finally, the recruitment of new members is essential to the perpetuation of gang activities. As seasoned offenders become less willing to directly involve themselves in certain high-risk criminal endeavors, the need for young recruits increases. "New blood" is recruited from the ranks of newly arrived immigrants, neighborhood gang youths, and school grounds. These new recruits are immediately used as "muscle" while being trained by experienced gang members for more complex criminal endeavors.

EVOLUTION OF VIETNAMESE CRIMINAL ACTIVITY

The past 20 years have seen a slow but noticeable change in Vietnamese criminal activity. This change has been related, in part, to the youthfulness and basic needs of gang members. More important, it is rooted in Asian culture, which is steeped in tradition and slow to change. Change was only slight during the first 15 years; however, as the gang members became "Westernized," a more sophisticated criminal emerged. Figure 17.1 shows the evolution of Vietnamese criminal endeavors from low-level street crime to less risky and more sophisticated and profitable activities. The movement to increasingly sophisticated criminality has been greatly influenced by the assimilation of gang members into Western culture. Other contributing factors include increased knowledge and understanding of the demands for goods and services and the identification of vulnerable targets in their neighborhoods. An additional factor is the tolerance level for such activities within the Asian community. A better grasp of the dynamics of the American criminal justice system and its greater tolerance of certain crimes must also be factored into this equation. In this regard, a shift has occurred away from drug trafficking and toward the establishment of gambling parlors and neighborhood and commercial businesses. Increased involvement in all levels of prostitution has also been observed. Likewise, a shift has occurred from extortion assaults, commercial robberies, and home invasions to counterfeiting and fraud, including the production of identification papers, business licenses, and checks and money. Continued involvement in certain activities has increased the gangs' level of skill, expertise, and sophistication. For example, a shift from random car thefts to theft of cars "to order" greatly reduces the risk associated with holding stolen property while a buyer/fence or retail outlet is found.

Gambling operations have also grown. Lottery operations have expanded as salespeople develop regular clientele. Parlor gambling has expanded to houses and commercial establishments, including warehouses and storefronts. These new establishments now offer complete opportunities for all types of gambling, such as sports betting, cards, dice, and lottery sales. There has also been greater involvement in joint ventures, or what we have termed "en-

trepreneurial task force"-related activity, as senior criminals have recognized the benefits of such ventures. These advantages include expanded markets, reduced conflict, and higher profits. Finally, the move to more sophisticated criminal endeavors has required the recruitment of "specialists" for certain ventures, such as counterfeiting.

WHAT CAN WE EXPECT IN THE FUTURE?

Cultural Factors

Several major factors have enabled Asian crime groups to pursue their criminal activities with fewer restrictions than more traditional criminal groups. These include a lack of awareness by the law enforcement community because of language and cultural barriers and the fact that few police agencies employ Asian officers. Consequently, infiltration of these groups has proved extremely difficult. Added to this is a prevailing lack of concern for Asian victims and the known reluctance of Vietnamese to report crime to the police. This reluctance stems from a fear of reprisal and a general distrust of government officials.

Factors That Can Influence the "Near" Future

A few trends provide some indication of the nature and direction of future Asian and Vietnamese criminal endeavors. These trends are further defined as follows:

Economic Trends

In the past two decades, communist countries throughout Asia and the Pacific Rim have moved toward a more capitalistic economic system. The business communities in these countries have embraced capitalism because it provides more opportunities for entrepreneurs to achieve greater independence and a better life. This economic shift has received support and

1976–Early 1980s	Mid-1980s–Early 1990s	1992–1996
1. Burglary of homes	B & E commercial	B & E's by order—Commercial targets
2. Auto burglaries	Auto burglaries	Auto burglaries—air bags, stereos, CDs, computer electronics
3. Auto theft—Joy rides	Theft of auto parts	Theft of autos by order
4. Pool hall gambling	Gambling houses	Sport bookmaking operations/loan-sharking
5. Street-level prostitution	Houses of prostitution	Massage parlors, lingerie shops, escort services
6. Shoplifting	Diversion thefts	Diversion theft teams, theft by order
7. Counterfeit ID & INS documents	Counterfeit food stamps, commercial checks, cassette tapes	Counterfeit occupational licenses, CDs, videos, credit cards, clothing, cellular phones, money orders, and computer software
8. Strong-arm robberies	Home invasions & commercial robberies	Protection and extortion schemes
9. Aid to illegal immigrants	Finance illegal immigration schemes	"Operate" illegal immigration operations
10. Minor drug usage	Minor drug trafficking	"Mules" for larger drug operations

Figure 17.1. Evolution of Southeast Asian Crime 1976-1996

impetus from foreign investors. Moreover, the general public in these countries has embraced the capitalist system because it provides new goods and services. The movement toward capitalism is consistent with occurrences in other undeveloped countries and in those previously under Soviet domination. Such changes bring us closer to a global economy that will open new markets and expand opportunities for both legitimate and criminal entrepreneurs.

Political Developments

Negotiations among Vietnam and Cambodia and the United States and other Western countries have resulted in a gradual normalization of relations. The United States has appointed its first ambassador to Vietnam since the fall of Saigon, and travel restrictions have been eased to the point that travel to Vietnam by Westerners is increasingly common. In addition, movement toward the gradual normalization of trade will be followed by the establishment of immigration procedures. Although the impact of the 1997 takeover of Hong Kong by China is yet undetermined, there is little doubt that the more relaxed and democratic governments of Vietnam and Southeast Asia will undoubtedly "invite" Chinese and other Asian criminal entre-

preneurs to establish new markets within their countries. Concomitant with this will be the corruption of government officials at all levels, which will adversely affect the integrity of the political structure.

Technology

Advancements in transportation have brought Southeast Asia closer to Western markets and provide a quick and relatively safe method of moving contraband. Global criminal ventures are now facilitated by the ease of catching a flight and quickly traveling to a country in which one is virtually unknown to the authorities. Faster and more accessible communications systems facilitate contacts between criminal organizations and allow joint criminal ventures to be more easily planned and accomplished. Technological advancements also make it easy to counterfeit nearly anything, such as currency, clothing, and watches. Technology has also made it relatively easy to obtain a new identity. Medical advances have created a growing demand for human organs, whereas technological growth has created a market for trade secrets and information about new product research. Finally, the breakup of the Soviet Union has resulted in the development of a black market in high-tech and nuclear-grade weapons. Southeast Asia promises to be another emerging market for power brokers seeking the weapons "edge."

Future of Southeast Asian Crime

Between 1993 and 1995, five separate groups of criminal justice employees from Mississippi, Alabama, Georgia, Louisiana, and Florida participated in future research study panels addressing possible changes in Southeast Asian crime. Using a modified Delphi technique (Limstone, 1975) and the nominal group technique (Delbercq, Van de Ven, & Gustafason, 1975), each dealt with the following question: What changes will occur with Southeast Asian criminal groups, both domestically and in Southeast Asia, in the next decade? The consistency of the answers provided by these groups was remarkable.

Drawing from these deliberations and the anticipated developments discussed in the previous section, we can hypothesize that the following will occur. We can expect to see cooperative pacts between Southeast Asian criminal groups in Vietnam and those in the United States and Europe. These criminal groups will establish pacts with other ethnic criminal groups operating in various parts of the world. The opening of Southeast Asia will provide new markets for these criminal groups, and an increased flow of contraband between Asia and North America will be observed. This opening will facilitate the travel of criminals from country to country and contribute to the easy operation of the international slave trade and the baby/child adoption industry. Another lucrative market that is likely to develop as a result of medical advancements in the West is the trafficking of human organs and body parts. Southeast Asia provides a ready source for these biological components because of the abject poverty and generally low regard for the value of human life. In regard to the global vice mar-

kets, both the Koreans (who currently dominate the international Asian prostitution industry) and the Japanese (who control the manufacture of methamphetamine) will undoubtedly view the more open Vietnam as a new zone of opportunity.

In the United States, Vietnamese groups are expected to develop a more well defined leadership structure (hierarchical); however, membership is likely to be more fluid, with specialists being recruited for certain types of criminal endeavors. These groups will also take over markets controlled by smaller and less powerful groups. They will continue to move away from high-risk, street-level crimes to less risky and more sophisticated and profitable criminal endeavors. Expansion into newly developed international markets will also occur. More specifically, these criminal ventures will include opium, hashish, and heroin trafficking; immigration schemes and the counterfeiting of identification documents, currency, technological components, and entertainment items. These ventures will also include international extortion schemes, such as the extortion of money from family members (in the United States and other countries) who have relatives in Vietnam. Corporate and business schemes, such as kidnapping and threats of disruption of corporate operation, will also be observed. Such schemes are similar to the Sokaiya activities of the Yakuza.

NOTE

1. "Entrepreneurial task forces" are transitory organizations composed of nonaligned criminal specialists who associate for the purpose of achieving a common, usually more sophisticated, criminal objective. This pattern of activity can be found among many of the newly emerging ethnic criminals. These endeavors can include counterfeiting currency, fraudulent diversion of funds by electronic transfer, and theft of intellectual material (corporate espionage). This concept was initially proposed by David L. Carter in an article regarding international organized crime in 1995.

REFERENCES

Abadinsky, H. (1983). *The criminal elite: Professional and organized crime.* Westport, CT: Greenwood.

Abadinsky, H. (1985). *Organized crime* (2nd ed.). Chicago: Nelson-Hall.

Abadinsky, H. (1992). *Organized crime* (3rd ed.). Chicago: Nelson-Hall.

ABC News. (1992, February 20). *Primetime live.*

Adams, J. R., & Franz, D. (1992). *A full service bank: How BCCI stole billions around the world.* New York: Pocket Books.

Albanese, J. (1983). God and the Mafia revisited: From Valachi to Fratianno. In G. Waldo (Ed.), *Career criminals.* Beverly Hills, CA: Sage.

Albanese, J. (1985). *Organized crime in America.* Cincinnati: Anderson.

Albanese, J. (1989). *Organized crime in America* (2nd ed.). Cincinnati: Anderson.

Albanese, J. (Ed.). (1995). *Contemporary issues in organized crime.* Monsey, NY: Willow Tree.

Albats, Y. (1994). *The state within a state: The KGB and its hold on Russia past, present, and future.* New York: Farrar, Straus & Giroux.

Albini, J. (1971). *The American Mafia: Genesis of a legend.* New York: Appleton, Crofts.

Albini, J. L. (1975). Mafia as method: A comparison between Great Britain and U.S.A. regarding the existence and structure of types of organized crime. *International Journal of Crime and Penology, 3,* 295-305.

Albini, J. L. (1976). Syndicated crime: Its structure, function, and modus operandi. In F. A. J. Ianni & E. R. Reuss-Ianni, *The crime society: Organized crime and corruption in America.* New York: New American Library.

Albini, J. L. (1986). Organized crime in Great Britain and the Caribbean. In R. Kelly (Ed.), *Organized crime: A global perspective* (pp. 95-122). Lanham, MD: Rowman & Littlefield.

Albini, J. L. (1988, July). Donald Cressey's contribution to the study of organized crime: An evaluation. *Crime and Delinquency, 34*(3), 338-351.

Albini, J. L. (1992). The distribution of drugs: Models of organized criminal organizations and their integration. In T. Mieczkowski (Ed.), *Drugs, crime, and social policy* (pp. 79-108). Needham Heights, MA: Allyn & Bacon.

Albini, J. L., & Bajon, B. J. (1978). Witches, Mafia, mental illness, and social reality: A study of the power of mythical belief. *International Journal of Criminal Law and Criminology, 6,* 285-294.

Alexander, S. (1988). *The pizza connection.* New York: Weidenfeld & Nicholson.

Ambler, C. (1993, June 15). New Zealand warns triads of deportation. *South China Morning Post,* p. 4.

Amir, M. (1986). Organized crime and organized criminality among Georgian Jews in Israel. In R. J. Kelly (Ed.), *Organized crime: A global perspective* (pp. 172-191). Lanham, MD: Rowman & Littlefield.

Anastasia, G. (1991). *Blood and honor: Inside the Scarfo Mob—The Mafia's most violent family.* New York: William Morrow.

Anderson, A. G. (1979). *The business of crime: A Cosa Nostra family.* Stanford, CA: Hoover Institute Press.

Azreal, J., & Rahr, A. (1993). *The formation and development of the Russian KGB, 1991-1994.* Report prepared for the Under Secretary of Defense for Policy, National Defense Institute. Santa Monica, CA: RAND.

Bakatin, V. (1992). *Izbavleniye ot KGB.* Moscow: Novosti.

Ball, S. (1994, May 23). Uniformed raiders in attempt to hijack ship. *South China Morning Post,* p. 3.

Barannikov, V. (1991, December 31). *Izvestiya,* union edition. (Trans. BBC Summary of World Broadcasts, January 1, 1992, SU/1267/BI1).

Baranov, A., & Lyashko, A. (1995, July 7-14). *Komsomolskaya Pravda* (Trans. FBIS-SOV-95-131, July 10, 1995, pp. 18-21).

Baranovsky, I. (1994, April 15-21). Several versions of an assassination. *Moscow News,* p. 15.

Bell, D. (1960). Crime as an American way of life: A queer ladder of social mobility. In *The end of ideology.* New York: Free Press.

Bell, D. (1962). *The end of ideology.* New York: P. F. Collier.

Bergman, L. (Producer). (1990). Dragon head. *Sixty minutes.* New York: Columbia Broadcasting System.

Best, J., & Luckenbill, D. S. (1982). *Organizing deviance.* Upper Saddle River, NJ: Prentice Hall.

Blakley, G. R. (1967). *Task force report: Organized crime, Appendix C, Aspects of the evidence gathering process in organized crime cases.* Washington, DC: Government Printing Office.

Blakley, G. R., & Billings, R. (1981). *The plot to kill the president.* New York: Times Publishing.

Blau, P. M., & Scott, W. R. (1962). *Formal organizations.* San Francisco: Chandler.

Block, A. (1978, January). History and the study of organized crime. *Urban Life,* p. 6.

Block, A. (1983). *East side-west side: Organized crime in New York, 1930-1950.* New Brunswick, NJ: Transaction.

Block, A., & Chambliss, W. (1981). *Organized crime.* New York: Elsevier.

Blok, A. (1966, January). Land reform in a West Sicilian Latifondo village. *Anthropological Quarterly, 39.*

Blok, A. (1974). *The Mafia of a Sicilian village, 1860-1960: A study of violent peasant entrepreneurs.* New York: Harper & Row.

Blumenthal, R. (1988). *Last days of the Sicilians.* New York: Times Publishing.

Blumenthal, R., & Miller, J. (1992). *The Gotti tapes: Including the testimony of Salvatore "Sammy the Bull" Gravano.* New York: Random House.

Blumer, H. (1969). *Symbolic interactionism: Perspective and method.* Upper Saddle River, NJ: Prentice Hall.

Bode, M. (1995, July 16). Triads doing time in Japan. *Hong Kong Standard.*

Boissevain, J. (1966, March). Patronage in Sicily. *Man, 1,* 16-27.

Bonanno, J. (with Lalli, S.). (1983). *A man of honor: The autobiography of Joseph Bonanno.* New York: Simon & Schuster.

Booth, M. (1990). *The triads.* New York: St. Martin's.

Borovoi, K. (1994). KGB i pynochnaya ekonomika. KGB: Vchera, Segodnya, Zavtra, III. *Mezhdunarodnaya Konferentsiya, Doklady i diskussii.* Moscow: Glasnost Public Foundation.

Breakthrough in 9-year riddle of God's banker. (1991, August 14). *Daily Mail.*

Buddle, C. (1995, November 10). Murder charge thrown out. *South China Morning Star,* p. 1.

Burrows, W. (1994, August). Nuclear chaos. *Popular Science,* pp. 54-76.

Butterfield, F. (1985, January 13). Chinese organized crime said to rise in U.S. New York Times, p. 2.

Cantalupo, J., & Renner, T. C. (1990). *Body Mike: The deadly double life of a Mob informer.* New York: Villard.

Carlson, G. G. (1940). *Numbers gambling: A study of a culture complex.* Unpublished doctoral dissertation, University of Michigan, Ann Arbor.

Carlson, S., & Larue, G. A. (1990, Summer). Giving the Devil much more than his due. *Free Inquiry, 10,* 3.

CBS News. (1993, April 18). *60 Minutes: Dragon head* [TV Transcript]. Livingston, NJ: Burrelle's Transcripts.

Chambliss, W. (1971, November). Vice, corruption, bureaucracy, and power. *Wisconsin Law Review, 4.*

Chambliss, W. (1975, August). On the paucity of original research on organized crime: A footnote to Galliher and Cain. *American Sociologist, 10,* 36-39.

Chan, C. (1993, April 16). Call for forceful message to triads. *South China Morning Post,* p. 5.

Cheng, J. Y. S., & Kwong, P. C. K. (Eds.). (1992). *The other Hong Kong report 1992.* Hong Kong: Chinese University Press.

Cheung, J. Y. S. (1994, November 22). Beijing acts to stamp out organized crime. *South China Morning Post,* p. 1.

Chicago Crime Commission. (1990). *Organized crime in Chicago.* Chicago: Author.

Chin, K. (1990a). Chinese gangs and extortion. In C. R. Huff (Ed.), *Gangs in America* (pp. 129-145). Newbury Park, CA: Sage.

Chin, K. (1990b). *Chinese subculture and criminality: Nontraditional crime groups in America.* Westport, CT: Greenwood.

Chin, K. (1992). *Triad societies in Hong Kong.* Manuscript submitted for publication.

Chin, K. (1995a). *Chinatown gangs.* New York: Oxford University Press.

Chin, K. (1995b). Triad societies in Hong Kong. *Transnational Organized Crime, 1*(1), 47-64.

China's market reforms have exposed its troops to the forces of corruption. (1994, April 24). *South China Morning Post,* p. 1.

Clark, R. (1970). *Crime in America.* New York: Simon & Shuster.

Clark, R. C. (1986). *Corporate law.* Boston: Little, Brown.

Cohen, L., & Felson, M. (1979). Social changes and crime rate trends: A routine active approach. *Criminology, 25,* 933-947.

Collins, J. F. (1995, April 3). *Crime in the new independent states: The United States response.* U.S. Department of State Dispatch: 269-273.

Conklin, J. E. (Ed.). (1973). *The crime establishment: Organized crime in American society.* Englewood Cliffs, NJ: Prentice Hall.

Cooney, T. (1987a, April 23). The Mob chronicles. *Philadelphia Daily News,* pp. 3, 26, 27.

Cooney, T. (1987b, April 24). The Mob chronicles. *Philadelphia Daily News,* pp. 3, 36, 37, 38.

Cornwell, R. (1984). *God's banker: An account of the life and death of Roberto Calvi.* London: Unwin.

Cressey, D. R. (1958). Achievement of an unstated organizational goal: An observation on prisons. *Pacific Sociological Review, 1*(2), 43-49.

Cressey, D. R. (1959). Contradictory directives in complex organizations: The case of the prison. *Administrative Science Quarterly, 4*(1), 1-19.

Cressey, D. R. (1965). Prison organizations. In J. A. G. March (Ed.), *Handbook on organizations.* Chicago: Rand McNally.

Cressey, D. R. (1967a). The functions and structure of criminal syndicates. President's Commission on Law Enforcement and Administration of Justice: *Task force report: Organized crime.* Washington, DC: Government Printing Office.

Cressey, D. R. (1967b, November). Methodological problems in the study of organized crime. *The Annals, 374,* 107-112.

Cressey, D. R. (1969). *Theft of the nation: The structure and operations of organized crime in America.* New York: Harper & Row.

Cressey, D. R. (1972). *Criminal organization: Its elementary forms.* New York: Harper & Row.

Cressey, D. R., & Krassowski, W. (1957). Inmate organization and anomie in American prisons and Soviet labor camps. *Social Problems, 5*(3), 217-230.

Crothall, G. (1995, October 4). Graft penalty fails to stop cadres. *South China Morning Post,* p. 8.

Daniloff, R. (1994, December). An artist who faced down suffering with his eyes wide open. *Smithsonian,* pp. 119-126.

Davis, A. (1995, August 25). Law and disorder. *Asiaweek,* pp. 36-43.

Davis, J. (1939, August 19). Things I couldn't tell till now. *Colliers,* pp. 35-36.

Delbercq, A. L., Van de Ven, A. H., & Gustafason, D. H. (1975). *Group techniques for program planning.* Glenview, IL: Scott, Foresman.

Della Cava, R. (1977). The Italian immigrant experience: Views of a Latin-Americanist. In S. M. Tomasi (Ed.), *Perspectives in Italian immigration and ethnicity.* New York: Center for Immigration Studies.

DeMaris, O. (with Fratianno, J.). (1981). *The last Mafioso: The treacherous world of Jimmy Fratianno.* New York: Bantam.

di Argentine, A. B. (1993, August). The Mafias in Italy. In E. U. Savona (Ed.), *Mafia issues* (pp. 120-124). Milan: International Scientific and Professional Advisory Council of the United Nations Crime Prevention and Criminal Justice Program.

Dijilas, M. (1982). *The new class.* Orlando, FL: Harcourt, Brace.

Dintino, J. (1986, November). Paper presented at the Conference on Organized Crime and the Media, sponsored by the Media Institute of the National Italian-American Foundation, New York.

Dintino, J., & Martens. F. T. (1983). *Police intelligence in crime control.* Springfield, IL: Charles C Thomas.

Dobinson, I. (1992). The Chinese connection: Heroin trafficking between Australia and Southeast Asia. *Criminal Organizations, 7*(2), 1-7.

Dobson, C. (1993, October 3). Kidnap gang suspect hiding in Hong Kong. *South China Morning Post,* p. 2.

Dobson, C. (1994, June 15). "Global Mafiya" poses most serious threat to security. *South China Morning Post,* p. 3.

Dombrink, J., & Song, J. K. (1992). *Asian racketeering in America: Emerging groups, organized crime, and legal control* (Grant 88-IJ-CX0049). Washington, DC: National Institute of Justice.

Donnelly, T. (1986). Chinese triad societies. *International Criminal Police Review, 41*(401), 198-206.

Donnerstein, E. (1987, April). *Social science research and the pornography commission: Findings vs. conclusions.* Keynote address, Eastern Meetings, Society for the Scientific Study of Sex, Philadelphia.

Douglass, J. D., Jr. (1990). *Red cocaine: The drugging of America.* Atlanta: Iarion House.

Duggan, C. (1989). *Fascism and the Mafia.* New Haven, CT: Yale University Press.

Economic Crime and the Security of Citizens, Society, and the State. (1995). *Bisnes i bezopasnosti V Rossii, 1.*

Edelhertz, H. (Ed.). (1987). *Major issues in organized crime control: Proceedings of a symposium on organized crime sponsored by the National Institute of Justice, 1986.* Washington, DC: Government Printing Office.

Ehrenfeld, R. (1990). *Narco-terrorism.* New York: Basic Books.

Eichenwald, K. (1988, December 23). Untested victors. *New York Times,* p. D4.

Erlanger, S. (1994, April 15). In Moscow, the high life flowers at gangland funeral. *International Herald Tribune.*

Feder, S., & Turkus, B. (1952). *Murder, Inc.* New York: Permabooks.

Federal Bureau of Investigation (FBI). (1988). [Debriefing of Gerald H. Scarpelli, Investigative File #CG183B-2272.]

"Felix." (1995). *Segodnya,* April 11 and May 24; *Zavtra,* Nos. 12, 13, and 14.

Filipov, D. (1994, April 15). Same old swan song. *Moscow Times.*

Finckenauer, J. (1994). Russian organized crime in America. In R. J. Kelly, R. Schatzberg, & K. Chin (Eds.), *Handbook of organized crime in the United States* (pp. 245-268). Westport, CT: Greenwood.

Fisher, A. (1994, August). Moscow rules. *Popular Science,* pp. 24-79.

Fisher, D. (1973). *Killer: Autobiography of a hit man for the Mafia.* Chicago: Playboy.

Fletcher, P. (1992, November 4). Moscow, Havana ink pact. *Reuters.*

Flynn, K. (1995, October 5). Triads play key role in heroin surge. *Eastern Express.*

Focus on change. (1994). *U.S. News & World Report,* pp. 17-20.

Follain, J. (1995). *A dishonored society.* Boston: Little, Brown.

Former party chief in $16.65 billion probe. (1995, October 5). *South China Morning Post,* p. 12.

Fox, S. (1989). *Blood and power: Organized crime in 20th-century America.* New York: William Morrow.

Franzese, M., & Matera, D. (1992). *Quitting the Mob.* New York: HarperCollins.

Fyodorov, B. (1994, April 1). Moscow without mirrors. *New York Times.*

Galliher, J. F., & Cain, J. A. (1974, May). Citation support for the Mafia myth in criminology textbooks. *American Sociologist, 9.*

Gambetta, D. (1993). *The Sicilian Mafia: The business of private protection.* Cambridge, MA: Harvard University Press.

Gardiner, J. A. (with Olson, D. J.). (1967). *Task force report: Organized crime, Appendix B, Wincanton: The politics of corruption.* Washington, DC: Government Printing Office.

Gaylord, M. (1990). The Chinese laundry: International drug trafficking and Hong Kong's banking industry. *Contemporary Crises, 14*(1), 23-37.

Gerth, H. H., & Mills, C. W. (Eds.). (1946). *From Max Weber: Essays in sociology* (pp. 196-244). New York: Oxford University Press.

Giancana, S., & Giancana, C. (1992). *Double cross.* New York: Warner.

Gilley, B. (1995, October 12). Fall from grace. *Far East Economic Review,* p. 17.

Glaser, B. G., & Strauss, A. L. (1967). *The discovery of grounded theory.* Hawthorne, NY: Aldine.

Global economic links spur crime. (1995, October 5). *South China Morning Post,* p. 12.

Goldsmith, M. (1988, May). RICO and enterprise criminality: A response to Gerard E. Lynch, *Columbia Law Review, 88,* 774-801.

Goldstock, R. (1984). Statement before the President's Commission on Organized Crime, October 23-25. (Reprinted in *Organized crime of Asian origin.* Washington, DC: Government Printing Office)

Goldstock, R. (n.d.). *Some ruminations on the current and future status of organized crime in the United States and on efforts to control illicit syndicates and enterprises.* Unpublished manuscript.

Goodman, M. (1983a, February 20). Spilotro graduates to the Mob: "Tough grows into vicious." *Los Angeles Times.*

Goodman, M. (1983b, February 28). Spilotro slips up, makes war with cop. *Los Angeles Times.*

Goodsir, D. (1995a, October 6). Alarm over slip in police standards. *South China Morning Post,* p. 27.

Goodsir, D. (1995b, August 22). Officers arrested in triad flat scam. *South China Morning Post.*

Gouldner, A. (1976). *The dialectic of ideology and technology.* New York: Oxford University Press.

Govorukhin, S. (1994). *Strana voroy* [Country of thieves]. Narva, Estonia: Shans.

Grant, A. (1992). Rising gang violence result of "turf wars." Chicago Gang Connections [On-line]. Available: http://www.emergency.com/gangturf.htm.gang war

Gurov, A. (1995). *Krasnaya Mafiya* [Red Mafiya]. Moscow: Samozvel.

Gurwin, L. (1984). *The Calvi affair: Death of a banker.* London: Pan.

Haller, M. H. (1990, May). Illegal enterprise: A theoretical and historical interpretation. *Criminology, 28,* 207-235.

Haller, M. H. (1991). *Life under Bruno: The economics of an organized crime family.* Philadelphia: Pennsylvania Crime Commission.

Handelman, S. (1994, June). *Crime and corruption in Russia.* Briefing of the Commission on Security and Cooperation in Europe, Washington, DC.

Handelman, S. (1995). *Comrade criminal.* New Haven, CT: Yale University Press.

Hartsfield, L. (1985). *The American response to professional crime, 1870-1917.* Westport, CT: Greenwood.

Hawkins, G. (1969). God and the Mafia. *Public Interest, 14,* 24-51.

Hersh, S. (1994, June). The wild East. *Atlantic Monthly,* pp. 61-86.

Hess, H. (1973). *Mafia and Mafiosi.* Lexington, MA: D. C. Heath.

Hicks, R. D. (1990a, Spring). Police pursuit of satanic crime: Part I. *Skeptical Inquirer, 14*(3).

Hicks, R. D. (1990b, Spring). Police pursuit of satanic crime: Part II. *Skeptical Inquirer, 14*(3).

Hirschi, T. (1971). *Causes of delinquency.* Berkeley: University of California Press.

Hodson, D. (1995, June). *Organized criminal activity in Hong Kong.* Paper presented at the Fourth Asian Crime Workshop, Monterey Park, CA.

Hoffman, P. (1973). *Tiger in the court.* Chicago: Playboy Press.

Hoffman, W., & Headley, L. (1992). *Contract killer: The explosive story of the Mafia's most notorious hit man.* New York: Thunder's Mouth.

Hughes, C. (1994, June 7). Yeltsin: Russia a superpower of crime. *Associated Press* dispatch.

Ianni, F. A. J. (1974). *Black Mafia: Ethnic succession in organized crime.* New York: Simon & Schuster.

Ianni, F. A. J. (1976). The Mafia and the web of kinship. In F. A. J. Ianni & E. R. Reuss-Ianni, *The crime society: Organized crime and corruption in America.* New York: New American Library.

Ianni, F. A. J., & Reuss-Ianni, E. R. (1972). *A family business: Kinship and social control in organized crime.* New York: Russell Sage.

ICAC links legal profession to triads and bribery. (1993, January 16). *South China Morning Post.*

Irwin, J., & Cressey, D. (1962). Thieves, convicts, and the inmate culture. *Social Problems, 10,* 142-155.

Izvestiya. (1992, November 5). morning edition, p. 5 (Trans. FBIS-SOV-92-215, November 5, 1992, p. 16).

Izvestiya. (1993, March 12).

Jamestown Foundation. (1994, October 15). *Crossroads,* p. 9.

Johnson, D. (1983, October 6-19). God's godfather. *London Review of Books,* pp. 12-13.

Johnson, E., Jr. (1962). Organized crime: Challenge to the American legal system. *Journal of Criminal Law, Criminology and Police Science, 53,* 399-425.

Joutsen, M. (1993). Organized crime in Eastern Europe. *CJ International, 9*(2), 11-18.

Joutsen, M. (1995). Organized crime in Central and Eastern Europe. In J. S. Albanese (Ed.), *Contemporary issues in organized crime* (pp. 201-211). Monsey, NY: Willow Tree.

Jowitt, K. (1983, July). Soviet neo-traditionalism: The political concept of a Leninist regime. *Soviet Studies, 35,* 275-297.

Kahaner, L. (1988). *Cults that kill.* New York: Warner.

Kalugin, O. (1994, March 10). *Nepszabadsag.* Budapest. (Trans. FBIS -SOV94-048, March 11, 1994: pp. 14-15).

Kampfner, J. (1994). *Inside Yeltsin's Russia.* London: Cassell.

Kaplan, D. E., Goldberg, D., & Jue, L. (1986, December). Enter the dragon: How Hong Kong's notorious underworld syndicates are becoming the number one organized crime problem in California. *San Francisco Focus, 68*(84), 147-148.

Kelly, R. J. (Ed.). (1986). *Organized crime: A global perspective.* Lanham, MD: Rowman & Littlefield.

Kelly, R. J. (1987a, Fall). The evolution of criminal syndicates. *Law Enforcement Intelligence Analysis Digest, 2*(1), 1-32.

Kelly, R. J. (1987b). The nature of organized crime and its operations. In H. Edelhertz (Ed.), *Major issues in organized crime control* (pp. 5-50). Washington, DC: National Institute of Justice.

Kelly, R. J. (1990). Field research among deviants: A consideration of some methodological recommendations. In C. D. Bryant (Ed.), *Deviant behavior: Readings in the sociology of norm violations.* New York: Hemisphere.

Kelly, R. J. (1991). Terrorism and intrigue. *Italian Journal, 5,* 148-158.

Kelly, R. J. (1994, July). Breaking the seals of silence: Anti-Mafia uprising in Sicily. *USA Today,* pp. 72-76.

Kelly, R. J., Chin, K., & Fagan, J. (1993). The structure, activity, and control of Chinese gangs: Law enforcement perspectives. *Journal of Contemporary Criminal Justice, 9*(3), 221-239.

Kelly, R. J., & Schatzberg, R. (1987). *Black organized crime: Some considerations.* Paper presented at the annual ASC meetings, Montreal.

Kempton, M. (1969, September 11). Crime does not pay. *New York Review of Books, 13.*

Kenny, D. J., & Finckenauer, J. O. (1995). *Organized crime in America.* Belmont, CA: Wadsworth.

Kerr, P. (1988, January 4). Chinese criminals move to broaden role in U.S. *New York Times,* p. 1.

KGB. (1989). *Politicheskaya Razvedka s Territorii SSSR: Uchebnoye posobiye* [Political Intelligence from the Territory of the USSR: Training Text]. Moscow: Krasnoznamennyi Institut KGB CCCP imeni Yu. V. Andropov/NIRIO.

Kichikhin, V. (1991). *Novoye vremya, No. 43.*

Kifner, J. (1991, January 6). New immigrant wave from Asia gives the underworld new faces. *New York Times.*

Klebnikov, P. (1994a, November 21). Russia's robber barons. *Forbes,* pp. 74-84.

Klebnikov, P. (1994b, September 12). Sovereign junk. *Forbes,* p. 228.

Kleinknecht, W. (1996). *The new ethnic mobs: The changing face of organized crime in America.* New York: Free Press.

Knight, A. W. (1990). *The KGB: Police and politics in the Soviet Union.* Winchester, MA: Unwin Hyman.

Knox, G. W. (1994). *An introduction to gangs* (rev. ed.). Bristol, IN: Wyndham Hall.

Kochan, N., & Whittington, B. (1991). *Bankrupt: The BCCI fraud.* London: Gollanz.

Kohut, J. (1995, April 20). Police in Japan are facing a new challenge from a wave of violence by Chinese gangs. *South China Morning Post.*

Komsomolskaya Pravda. (1995, September 28).

Kryshtanovskaya, O. (1993, August). I'm tired of politics: Let's get down to business. *Nezavisimaya Gazeta.* (International edition in English, Vol. 4, Nos. 4-5, p. 8).

Kusche, L. (1983). The Bermuda Triangle. In G. O. Abell & B. Singer (Eds.), *Science and the paranormal.* New York: Scribner.

Kvint, V. (1994, December 5). Restoring the Romanovs. *Forbes,* pp. 145-152.

Lam, W. (1995, April 15). *South China Morning Post.*

Landesco, J. (1968). *Organized crime in Chicago.* Chicago: University of Chicago Press. (Original work published 1929)

Las Vegas Review Journal. (1994, November 22). p. 9A.

Latour, B., & Woolgar, S. (1986). *Laboratory life: The construction of scientific facts.* Princeton, NJ: Princeton University Press.

Lau, D. (1991, September). *A compendious history of triads.* Paper presented at the U.S. Department of Justice's Multinational Asian Organized Crime Conference, San Francisco.

Lau, E. (1990, May 31). Hand in glove: Triad Boss alleges police collusion. *Far Eastern Economic Review,* p. 11.

Law, S. L. (1995, September 29). Tough transition. *Asiaweek,* pp. 28-30, 32.

Lawrence, P. R., & Lorsch, J. W. (1967). *Organization and environment.* Boston: Harvard University Press.

Lee, R. W., & MacDonald, S. B. (1993, Spring). Drugs in the East. *Foreign Policy, 90,* 89-107.

Levin, P. (1983a, April 10). Mob informer Cullotta's early link-up with Spilotro. *Las Vegas Sun,* p. 1.

Levin, P. (1983b, April 11). At 17, Mob informer Cullotta was stealing $25,000 monthly. *Las Vegas Sun,* p. 1.

Levin, P. (1983c, April 12). Cullotta finally hits the "big time" with $500,000 jewelry heist. *Las Vegas Sun,* p. 1.

Ligachev, Y. (1991). Vospominaniya. *Argumeniy I fakty, No. 6.*

Limstone, H. A. (1975). *The Delphi method: Techniques and applications metechnique.* In H. A. Limstone & M. Turoff (Eds.), *The handbook of futures research.* Reading, MA: Addison-Wesley.

Lisov, Y. (1992). Testimony. Hearings of the Russian Federation Supreme Soviet Commission Concerning the Events Associated with the Attempted Coup d'état of 19-21 August, 1991. (Translated in *Demokratizatsiya: The Journal of Post-Soviet Democratization, 4*(3), Spring 1996)

Lo, G., & Gilbert, A. (1995, October 19). "Triad" ambush on film producer. *South China Morning Post,* p. 3.

Lo, T. W. (1993). *Corruption and politics in Hong Kong and China.* Buckingham, UK: Open University Press.

Lombardo, R. (1991, Fall). Organized crime: A control theory. *Criminal Organizations, 6*(2), 8-13.

Luk, M. (1995, September 14). Prove triad link: Legal group. *Eastern Express.*

Lupsha, P. A. (1981, May). Individual choice, material, culture, and organized crime. *Criminology, 19,* 3-24.

Lynch, G. E. (1987a). The crime of being a criminal, Parts I and II. *Columbia Law Review, 97*(3, 4), 661-764.

Lynch, G. E. (1987b). RICO: The crime of being criminal. *Columbia Law Review, 87,* 661-920.

Lyons, A. (1988). *Satan wants you.* New York: Warner.

Maas, P. (1968). *The Valachi papers.* New York: G. P. Putnam.

Mack, J. A. (1973). The "organized" and "professional" labels criticized. *International Journal of Crime and Penology, 1.*

Mack, J. A. (1975). *The crime industry.* Lexington, MA: D. C. Heath.

Mallowe, M. (1988, May). Arrivederci, Nicky. *Philadelphia Magazine, 79,* 106.

Maltz, M. (1976, July). On defining organized crime. *Crime and Delinquency,* 338-346.

Maltz, M. (1990, March). *Defining organized crime.* Paper presented to the Academy of Criminal Justice Sciences Conference on Organized Crime, Denver, CO.

March, J., & Simon, H. (1958). *Organizations.* New York: John Wiley.

Martens, F. T. (1983). Market analysis applied to the study of organized crime. *Federal Probation,* pp. 84-85.

Martens, F. T. (1985a, June). The Mafia and toxic waste disposal. *Federal Probation,* 78-79.

Martens, F. T. (1985b, September). Martens comments on Scarpitti and Block. *Today American Academy of Criminal Justice Science,* 3-5.

Martens, F. T. (1986, October). A counter-response to Scarpitti and Block. *Today American Academy of Criminal Justice Sciences,* 3.

Martens, F. T., & Longfellow, C. M. (1982, December). Shadows of substance: Organized crime reconsidered. *Federal Probation,* 3-9.

Martens, F. T., & Niederer, M. C. (1985, June). Media magic, Mafia mania. *Federal Probation,* 60-68.

Martin, J. D., & Romano, A. T. (1992). *Multinational crime: Terrorism, espionage, drug, and arms trafficking.* Newbury Park, CA: Sage.

McFadden, R. (1987, March 11). The Mafia of the 1980s: Divided and under siege. *New York Times.*

McIntosh, M. (1975). *The organization of crime.* London: Macmillan.

McKenzie, S. (1994, April 6). Australia targets HK triads in drug war. *South China Morning Post,* p. 5.

McWeeney, S. M. (1987, February). The Sicilian Mafia and its impact on the United States. *FBI Law Enforcement Bulletin, 56.*

Merriam-Webster, Inc. (1993). *Merriam-Webster's collegiate dictionary* (10th ed.). Springfield, MA: Author.

Merton, R. K. (1968). *Social theory and social structure.* New York: Free Press.

Meskil, P. S. (1976). *The Luparelli tapes.* Chicago: Playboy Press.

Mieczkowski, T. (1983). Syndicated crime in the Caribbean. In G. Waldo (Ed.), *Career criminals.* Beverly Hills, CA: Sage.

Mieczkowski, T., & Albini, J. L. (1987, February). The war on crime: Are social scientists effective in changing conceptions of organized crime? *Law Enforcement Intelligence Analysis Digest, 2.*

The Mob on trial: A special report on organized crime. (1986, September 7). *Newsday,* pp. 4-5, 26-28.

Moore, M. (1987). Organized crime as a business enterprise. In H. Edelhertz (Ed.), *Major issues in organized crime control* (pp. 153-168). Washington, DC: U.S. Department of Justice, National Institute of Justice.

Moore, W. H. (1974). *The Kefauver committee and the politics of crime: 1950-1952.* Columbia: University of Missouri Press.

Moorehead, C. (1984, February 2-15). Just good friends. *London Review of Books,* p. 19.

Mosher, S. (1992a, April 16). Patriotism is enough: Chinese statement on legal issues creates unease. *Far Eastern Economic Review,* 16.

Mosher, S. (1992b, January 30). Shot by the Mob. *Far Eastern Economic Review,* 28, 29.

Moskovsky komsomolets. (1995, July 8). p. 1. (Trans. in FBIS-SOV-95- 131, July 10, 1995, p. 24)

Mueller, R. S., III. (1991, November 6). *Statement before the Senate Permanent Subcommittee on Investigations.* Committee on Governmental Affairs, United States Senate.

Nadelson, E. A. (1992, March 14). Gotti. *The Independent,* p. 729.

Nelli, H. S. (1976). *The business of crime.* New York: Oxford University Press.

New York State Task Force on Organized Crime. (1988). *Corruption and racketeering industry* (Interim report). Ithaca, NY: Cornell University, New York State School of Industrial and Labor Relations.

Nezavisimaya Gazeta. (1995, February 2).

Ng, L. (1994, April 1). Sun Yee On heads list of 57 triads. *South China Morning Post,* pp. 1, 4.

No, K. (1995, October 15). Police graft inquiry. *South China Morning Post.*

Nobody today wants to run the Mob. (1970, August 9). *Chicago Today,* Sec. 1, pp. 4, 9.

NRC Handelsblad. (1991, July 27). Italie is geen serieus land [Italy is not a serious country].

O'Brien, J. F., & Kurins, A. (1991). *Boss of Bosses: The fall of the Godfather: The FBI and Paul Castellano.* New York: Dell.

Orenstein, H. S. (1992). Crime and punishment: Old problems and new dilemmas for an emerging Eastern and Central Europe. *Low Intensity Conflict, 1*(1), 1-41.

Ostrow, R. (1991, February 9). The Mob against the ropes: Prosecutors using new laws are cracking *omerta*—the code of silence—to jail hoodlums. *Los Angeles Times.*

Ovchinsky, V. (1993). *Mafiya: Meobya vlennyi vizit.* Moscow: Infra-M.

Owen, R., & Dynes, M. (1992). *The Times guide to 1992: Britain in a Europe without frontiers.* London: London Times.

Parsons, T. (Ed.). (1947). *M. Weber: The theory of social and economic organization.* New York: Free Press.

Perry, S. (1992). Western intelligence paints pessimistic world crime picture. *CJ International, 8*(6), 1, 4.

Pileggi, N. (with Hill, H.). (1985). *Wiseguy: Life in a Mafia family.* New York: Simon & Schuster.

Pipes, R. (1990). Foreword. In L. Timofeyev (Ed.), *The anticommunist manifesto.* Bellevue, WA: Free Enterprise.

Pistone, J., & Woodley, R. (1987). *Donnie Brasco: My undercover life in the Mafia.* New York: New American Library.

Pitkin, T., & Cordasco, F. (1977). *The Black Hand.* Totowa, NJ: Littlefield, Adams.

Podlesskikh, G., & Tereshonok, A. (1994). *Vory v Zakone: Brosok k Vlasti.* Moscow: Khudozhestvennaya literatura.

Police target movie extortion rackets. (1993, October 24). *Hong Kong Standard.*

Polsky, N. (1967). *Hustlers, beats, and others.* Chicago: Aldine.

Ponomarev, L. A., & Maksimov, A. (1992, February 4). [Interview]. *Federal News Service.*

Ponomarev, L. A., & Surkov, A. P. (1992, February 8). Conclusion. Hearings of the Russian Federation Supreme Soviet Commission Concerning the Events Associated with the Attempted Coup d'état of 19-21 August 1991. (Translated in *Demokratizatsiya: The Journal of Post-Soviet Democratization, 4*(3), Spring 1996)

Powers, R. G. (1987). *Secrecy and power: The life of J. Edgar Hoover.* New York: Free Press.

President's Commission on Law Enforcement and Administration of Justice. (1967). *Task force report: Organized crime.* Washington, DC: Government Printing Office.

President's Commission on Organized Crime. (1986, April). *The impact: Organized crime today.* Washington, DC: Government Printing Office.

Provost, G. (1989). *Across the border: The true story of the satanic cult killings.* New York: Pocket Books.

Radio Free Europe/Radio Liberty. (1994, February 7). *Daily Report, 25*(2).

Rahr, A. (1994, February 25). Reform of Russia's state security apparatus. *RFEIRL Research Report, 3*(8).

Reid, E. (1954). *Mafia.* New York: New American Library.

Renner, T., & Giancana, A. (1984). *Mafia princess.* New York: William Morrow.

Renner, T., & Kirby, C. (1987). *Mafia enforcer: A true story of life and death in the Mob.* New York: Villard.

Renner, T., & Teresa, V. (1973). *My life in the Mafia.* Garden City, NY: Doubleday.

Reuter, P. (1983). *Disorganized crime: The economics of the Visible Hand.* Cambridge: MIT Press.

Reuter, P. (1985). *The organization of illegal markets: An economic analysis." Washington, DC: U.S. Department of Justice, National Institute of Justice.*

Reuter, P. (1994). Research on American organized crime. In R. J. Kelly, R. Schatzberg, & K. Chin (Eds.), *Handbook of organized crime in the United States* (pp. 91-120). Westport, CT: Greenwood.

Robertson, F. (1977). *The inside story of the triads: The Chinese Mafia.* London: Routledge & Kegan Paul.

Roger, A. (1989a). *Organized crime in Hong Kong.* Unpublished manuscript, Organized and Serious Crime Group, Royal Hong Kong Police.

Roger, A. (1989b). *Triads in Hong Kong past and present.* Unpublished manuscript, Organized and Serious Crime Group, Royal Hong Kong Police.

Rogovin, C. (1990, March). *The invaluable contributions of Donald Cressey to the study of organized crime.* Paper presented to the Academy of Criminal Justice Sciences Conference on Organized Crime, Denver, CO.

Rosner, L. (1986). *The Soviet way of crime.* Cambridge, MA: Bergin & Garvey.

Rosner, L. (1993, March 15). Crime and corruption in Russia are nothing new. *Law Enforcement News, 19,* 1-3.

Rossiyskaya Gazeta. (1991, December 28). First edition, p. 2. (Trans. FBIS-SOV-92-001, January 2, 1992, p. 57)

Rossiyskaya Gazeta. (1993, March 13).

Rowan, R. (1986, November 10). The 50 biggest Mafia Bosses. *Fortune, 50.*

Royal Hong Kong Police (RHKP). (1974). *Triad societies in Hong Kong.* Hong Kong: Government Printer.

Royal Hong Kong Police (RHKP). (1988, July). *Triads in Hong Kong: Past and present.* Hong Kong: Criminal Intelligence Bureau.

Royal Hong Kong Police (RHKP). (1992). [Data on triad-related crime provided by the Organized Crime and Triad Bureau].

Russia's Mafia. (1994, July 9). *The Economist,* 19-22.

Ryabov, N. (1991, September 18). State commission to investigate the activity of state security organs. *Rossiyskaya Gazeta.* (Trans. FBIS-SOV91-181: 25)

Ryan, P. J. (1990). RICO, OCCA, defining organized crime: Organized crime is what organized crime does. *Criminal Organizations, 5*(2), 2-8.

Ryan, P. J., & Kelly, R. J. (1989). An analysis of RICO and OCCA: Federal and state legislative instruments against organized crime. *Violence, Aggression and Terrorism, 3*(1&2), 49-100.

Salerno, J., & Rincle, S. (1990). *The plumber.* New York: Knightsbridge.

Salerno, R., & Tompkins, J. S. (1969). *The crime confederation: Cosa Nostra and allied operations in organized crime.* Garden City, NY: Doubleday.

Scarpitti, F., & Block, A. (1985). *Poisoning for profit: The Mafia and toxic waste in America.* New York: William Morrow.

Schatzberg, R. (1990). *Black organized crime: The Harlem policy rackets, 1920-1930.* Unpublished doctoral dissertation, City University of New York.

Schelling, T. (1967). The economics of organized crime. *Task force report: Organized crime.* Washington, DC: Government Printing Office.

Schelling, T. (1971). What is the business of organized crime? *American Scholar,* pp. 175-184.

Schlegel, K. (1987). Violence in organized crime. In T. S. Bynum (Ed.), *Organized crime in America.* New York: Criminal Justice Press.

Schlesinger, A. M. (1978). *Robert Kennedy and his times.* New York: Ballantine.

Schoenberg, R. J. (1992). *Mr. Capone.* New York: William Morrow.

Scott, W. R. (1981). *Organizations.* Upper Saddle River, NJ: Prentice Hall.

Secretary of Security. (1991). *Explanatory notes on the organized crime bill.* Hong Kong: Government Printers.

Segodnya. (1995a, January 13).

Segodnya. (1995b, February 15).

Seidl, J. M. (1968). *"Upon the hip": A study of the criminal loan-shark industry.* Unpublished doctoral dissertation, Harvard University, Cambridge, MA.

Serio, J. (1992). Shunning tradition: Ethnic organized crime in the former Soviet Union. *CJ International, 8*(6), 5-6.

Serio, J. (1993). Organized crime in the former Soviet Union: Only the name is new. *CJ International, 9*(4), 11-17.

Shabalin, V. A. (1995). Organized crime and business: A report on the International Seminar for Honest Business. *Criminal Organizations, 7,* 23-25.

Shabalin, V. A., Albini, J. L., & Rogers, R. E. (Eds.). (1990). *Report No. 9: Organized crime.* Press Group Report V, Novosibirsk. Prepared by the Joint Russian-American Academic Committee to Promote the Study of Comparative Criminal Justice.

Shaw, C., & McKay, D. (1942). *Juvenile delinquency and urban areas.* Chicago: University of Chicago Press.

Shelley, L. (1994). *Crime and corruption in Russia.* Briefing to the Commission on Security and Cooperation in Europe, Washington, DC.

Shelley, L. I. (1995, Fall). Post-Soviet organized crime: Implications for economic, social, and political development. *Trends in Organized Crime, 1*(1). (Reprinted from *Demokratizatsiya, 2*(3), pp. 341-358, Summer, 1994)

Sherr, J. (1995, November-December). The new Russian intelligence empire. *Problems of Post-Communism, 42*(6).

Shortt, J. (1993). Preface. In *KGB: Alpha team training manual.* Boulder, CO: Paladin.

Simis, K. (1982). *U.S.S.R.: The corrupt society.* New York: Simon & Schuster.

Smith, D., Jr. (1971, Fall). Some things that may be more important to understand about organized crime than Cosa Nostra. *University of Florida Law Review, 24,* 1-30.

Smith, D., Jr. (1975). *The Mafia mystique.* New York: Basic Books.

Smith, S. (1967, September 1, 8, 29). *Life.*

Smith, S. (1968, March 15). *Life.*

Smith, S. (1969a, February 14). *Life.*

Smith, S. (1969b, May 30). *Life.*

Solzhenitsyn, A. (1991). *Rebuilding Russia* (A. Klimoff, Trans.). New York: Farrar, Strauss, & Giroux.

Solzhenitsyn, A. (1992, September 2). [Ostankino television interview, Moscow].

Somer, T. (Ed.). (1994). *International terrorism and the drug connection.* Ankara, Turkey: Ankara University.

Song, J. H. L., & Dombrink, J. (1994). Asian emerging crime groups: Examining the definition of organized crime. *Criminal Justice Review, 19*(2), 228-243.

Southerland, M., & Potter, G. (1993, August). Applying organization theory to organized crime. *Journal of Contemporary Criminal Justice, 9,* 251-267.

Sovetskaya Rossiya. (1995, March 28).

Steinberg, J. (1989, August 17). Capos and cardinals. *London Review of Books,* pp. 13-14.

Sterling, C. (1994a). *Crime without frontiers: The worldwide expansion of organized crime and the Pax Mafiosa.* Boston: Little, Brown.

Sterling, C. (1994b). *Thieves' world: The threat of the global network of organized crime.* New York: Simon & Schuster.

Stevens, P., Jr. (1990, Summer). The dangerous folklore of satanism. *Free Inquiry, 10*(3).

Stier, E., & Richards, P. (1987). Strategic decision making in organized crime control. In H. Edelhertz (Ed.), *Major issues in organized crime control* (pp. 65-80). Washington, DC: National Institute of Justice.

Stille, A. (1995). *Excellent cadavers: The Mafia and the death of the first Italian republic.* New York: Pantheon.

Stone, M. (1992, February 3). After Gotti. *New York.*

Sun Yee On. (1993, October 3). *South China Morning Post.*

Sung, Y., & Lee, M. K. (Eds.). (1991). *The other Hong Kong report 1991.* Hong Kong: Chinese University Press.

Surkov, A. P. (1992, February 10). Testimony. Hearings of the Russian Federation Supreme Soviet Commission Concerning the Events Associated with the Attempted Coup d'état of 19-21 August 1991. (Translated in *Demokratizatsiya: The Journal of Post-Soviet Democratization, 4*(3), Spring 1996)

Sutherland, E., & Cressey, D. (1966). *Principles of criminology.* Philadelphia: J. B. Lippincott.

Sutherland, E. H., & Cressey, D. R. (1974). *Principles of criminology* (9th ed.). Philadelphia: J. B. Lippincott.

Sykes, G., & Messinger, S. (1960). The inmate social system. In A. Cloward, D. Cressey, G. Grosser, R. McCleery, L. Ohlin, G. Sykes, & S. Messinger (Eds.), *Theoretical studies in social organization of the prison* (pp. 5-9). New York: Social Science Research Council.

Szeto, W. (1995, March 8). Stolen trucks moved across border daily. *South China Morning Post,* p. 4.

Talese, G. (1971). *Honor thy father.* New York: World.

A theory of organized crime control: A preliminary statement. (1966). Mimeographed paper prepared by the technical staff and consultants of the New York State Identification and Intelligence System.

Tam, L., & Wong, L. (1993, August 4). Law is protecting triads: Report. *South China Morning Post,* p. 1.

Tarormina, G. (1993, August). Organization and functions of the Direzione Investigativa Anti-Mafia—DIA (Anti-Mafia Investigative Board). In E. U. Savona (Ed.), *Mafia issues* (pp. 18-21). Milan: International Scientific and Professional Advisory Council of the United Nations Crime Prevention and Criminal Justice Program.

TASS [in English]. (1992, January 21). (1313 GMT, in FBIS-SOV-92-014, January 22, 1992, pp. 59-60)

Time. (1987, March 9). Behind the walls. p. 27.

Time. (1994a, July 11). pp. 39-45.

Time. (1994b, August 29). pp. 47-51.

Time. (1994c, December 5). pp. 38-39, 80-81.

Timofeyev, L. (1990). Some notes on the black market economy. In L. Timofeyev (Ed.), *The anticommunist manifesto.* Bellevue, WA: Free Enterprise.

Timofeyev, L. (Ed.). (1992). *Russia's secret rulers: How the government and criminal Mafia exercise their power.* New York: Knopf.

Triad exodus "is no threat" to Australia. (1995, February 4). *Eastern Express.*

Turner, W. (1983, June 12). Testimony details city underworld's control of a Las Vegas casino. *New York Times,* p. 30.

Tyler, G. (1962a). *Organized crime in America.* Ann Arbor: University of Michigan Press.

Tyler, G. (1962b). The roots of organized crime. *Crime and Delinquency, 8,* 325-338.

Tyre, P. (1991, December 1). These days, mobsters sing a different tune. *Newsday.*

United Nations. (1992a). Implementation of the conclusions and recommendations of the Ministerial Meeting on the Creation of an Effective United Nations Crime Prevention and Criminal Justice Programme. *Proceedings of the UN Commission on Crime Prevention and Criminal Justice.* Vienna, Austria.

United Nations. (1992b). Report of the Commission on Crime Prevention and Criminal Justice on its first session. *Substantive Session of the Economic and Social Council.* Vienna, Austria.

United Nations. (1992c). Strengthening existing international cooperation and crime prevention and criminal justice including technical cooperation in developing countries with special emphasis on organized crime. *Proceedings of the UN Commission on Crime Prevention and Criminal Justice.* Vienna, Austria.

U.S. Bureau of the Census. (1990). *1990 census report.* Washington, DC: Government Printing Office.

U.S. Congress. (1951). Senate Special Committee to Investigate Organized Crime in Interstate Commerce (Kefauver Committee). *Third Interim Report,* No. 307, 82nd Congress.

U.S. Congress. (1963). Senate Permanent Subcommittee on Investigations of the Committee on Government Operations (McClellan Committee). *Organized crime and illicit traffic in narcotics: Part I* (pp. 6-8).

U.S. Congress. (1983, February 16). Senate. Judiciary Committee, *Organized crime in the Northeast* (J-98-2. Part 1, pp. 105-299).

U.S. Congress. (1988, April 15). Permanent subcommittee on investigations. (Not available in published form)

U.S. Congress. (1990). *Joint hearing before the Committee on the Judiciary and the Caucus on International Narcotics Control. U.S. International drug policy—Asian gangs, heroin, and the drug trade. 101 Cong., 2d Sess.* Washington, DC: Government Printing Office.

U.S. Department of Justice, Criminal Division. (1988, February). *Report on Asian organized crime.* Washington, DC: Author.

United States ex. rel. Gerald Mayo v. Satan and His Staff. (1971, Dec. 3). Misc. No. 5357. United States District Court, W.D. Pennsylvania.

U.S. News and World Report. (1994a, March 7). pp. 3-7.

U.S. News and World Report. (1994b, December 5). pp. 73-82, 67-68.

Vaksberg, A. (1991). *The Soviet Mafia.* (J. Roberts & E. Roberts, Trans.). New York: St. Martin's.

Valiente, D. (1989). *The rebirth of witchcraft.* Custer, WA: Phoenix.

Van Heerden, B. (1995, April 1). *South China Morning Post,* p. 17.

Varese, F. (1994). Is Sicily the future of Russia? Private protection and the rise of the Russian Mafia. *Archives of European Sociology, 35,* 224-258.

Vek, No. 4, (1995).

Vetrov, A. (1995, April 11). *Segodnya*. (Trans. FBIS-SOV-95-076-S, April 20, 1995, pp. 20-25)

Victor, J. S. (1991, Spring). Satanic cult "survivor" stories. *Skeptical Inquirer, 15*(3).

De Volkskrant. (1987, July 18). Hoogste hof in Italie trekt arrestatiebevel tegen Marcinkus in [Highest court in Italy withdraws arrest warrant against Marcinkus].

De Volkskrant. (1990, May 19). Belangrijkste verdachte afwezig in proces over Banco Ambrosiano [Most important suspects missing from Banco Ambrosiano trials].

Voslensky, M. (1984). *Nomenklatura: The Soviet ruling class.* Garden City, NY: Doubleday.

Waller, J. M. (1994). *Secret empire: The KGB in Russia today.* Boulder, CO: Westview.

Waller, J. M. (1995, November-December). The KGB legacy in Russia. *Problems of Post-Communism, 42*(6).

Waller, J. M. (1996). Police, secret police, and civil authority. In J. Sachs (Ed.), *The rule of law and economic reform in Russia.* Cambridge, MA: Harvard University.

Wang, Z. (1996). Is the pattern of Asian gang affiliation different? A multiple regression analysis. *Journal of Crime and Justice, 29*(1), 113-128.

Wharton Econometrics Forecasting Associates. (1986). The income of organized crime. In *Report to the president and the attorney general: The impact—organized crime today* (pp. 423-425). Washington, DC: Government Printing Office.

Williams, P. (1995a, Summer). The new threat: Transnational criminal organizations and international security. *Criminal Organizations, 9*(3 & 4), 3-20.

Williams, P. (1995b, Winter). Transnational criminal organizations: Strategic alliances. *Washington Quarterly, 18,* 57-69.

Wolf, E. R. (1966). Kinship, friendship, and patron-client relations in complex societies. In M. Banton (Ed.), *The social anthropology of simple societies.* New York: Praeger.

Wolff, K. H. (Ed.). (1964). *The sociology of Georg Simmel.* New York: Free Press.

Wong, R. Y. C., & Cheng, J. Y. S. (Eds.). (1990). *The other Hong Kong report 1990.* Hong Kong: Chinese University Press.

Woolston, H. B. (1969). *Prostitution in the United States.* New York: Patterson Smith.

Yasmann, V. (1993, March 5). Corruption in Russia: A threat to democracy? *Radio Free Europe/Radio Liberty Research Report, 2*(10).

Yasmann, V. (1994, March 21-23). *Domestic aspects of the new Russian military doctrine.* Paper delivered at a conference of the Hanns-Seidel Stiftung, Wildbad Kreuth, Germany.

Yasmann, V. (1995). How many security services does Yeltsin have? *Prism, 4.*

Yu, K. (1993, March 27). Triads jump on Canto-pop bandwagon. *South China Morning Post,* p. 2.

INDEX

ABOUT THE EDITORS

Patrick J. Ryan retired from the New York City Police Department with the rank of Sergeant. He is Associate Professor in the Department of Criminal Justice at Long Island University, an Associate Editor of *Journal of Contemporary Criminal Justice,* and President of the International Association for the Study of Organized Crime. He is the author of *Organized Crime: A Reference Handbook* (1995), and a contributor to *The Handbook of Organized Crime* (1995), and has published numerous articles on the nexus of drugs and homicide and the problems of defining organized crime. He is a Judge in the New York State Criminal Court system for the Town of Stamford.

George E. Rush retired from the United States Air Force (Security Police) with the rank of Master Sergeant. He is Professor of Criminal Justice at California State University, Long Beach, Editor-in-Chief of *Journal of Contemporary Criminal Justice,* and a member of the International Association for the Study of Organized Crime. His major publications include *Police Supervision: Back to the Basics* (with P. M. Whisenand, 1991), *Police Supervision; The Fifteen Responsibilities* (1992); *Gangs, Graffiti, and Violence* (with D. A. Leet and A. M. Smith, 1997); *Policing in the Community* (with D. J. Champion, 1997); and *Inside American Prisons and Jails* (1997). His *Dictionary of Criminal Justice* (1994) is now in the fourth edition.

ABOUT THE CONTRIBUTORS

Joseph L. Albini is Professor of Criminal Justice at the University of Nevada, Las Vegas. His extensive writings on the Mafia and its proper definition include *The American Mafia* (1971). He is Co-Director of the Joint Russian-American Academic Committee for the Promotion of the Study of Comparative Criminal Justice and a member of the International Association for the Study of Organized Crime.

Julie Anderson is a graduate student in the Department of Criminal Justice at the University of Nevada, Las Vegas. She is a specialist in political science, and her current research includes nationalism, foreign and domestic affairs, and transnational conspiracies.

David L. Carter is Professor of Criminology at Michigan State University, East Lansing, and a Research Fellow, Police Executive Research Forum. He is former Secretary of the Academy of Criminal Justice Sciences and a member of the International Association for the Study of Organized Crime. He is widely published on issues of police, organized crime, and international criminal justice.

Donald R. Cressey (1919-1987) was, most notably, consultant to the President's Commission on Law Enforcement and Administration of Justice, 1967. Cressey's credits would, standing alone, fill a book. Anyone who studies organized crime has read Cressey.

Robert L. Davidson is Associate Professor in the Criminal Justice Department at Northern Michigan University, Marquette. His area of specialization is international crime and comparative criminal justice systems. He has co-translated, authored, and presented academic papers in both the People's Republic of China and the United States.

John Dombrink is Associate Professor in the Department of Criminology, Law, and Society in the School of Social Ecology at the University of California, Irvine. He has published numerous articles on criminal law and vice, including several on gambling, and is the author of *The Last Resort: Success and Failure in Campaigns for Casinos*. His current research is centered on analyzing the legalization of physician-assisted suicide in the United States.

Thomas A. Firestone is Associate Attorney in the firm of Fried, Frank, Harris, Shriver, and Jacobson in New York City. A graduate of Harvard Law School, he practices corporate litigation.

Mark H. Haller is Professor of History and Criminal Justice at Temple University, Philadelphia. His study of the Bruno crime family in Philadelphia is a classic monograph on entrepreneurial aspects of organized crime. He is a founding and current member of the International Association for the Study of Organized Crime.

Robert J. Kelly is Broeklundian Professor of Social Science at Brooklyn College; Professor of Criminal Justice at the Graduate School, City University of New York; President of the Edward Sagarin Institute for the Study of Deviance and Social Issues; and Past President of the International Association for the Study of Organized Crime. Among his major contributions to the field is *The Handbook of Organized Crime* (edited with K.-L. Chin and R. Schatzberg, 1995) and *Organized Crime: A Global Perspective* (1986).

Valery Kutushev is Rector of the Khabarovsk Graduate Military College in Khabarovsk, Russia. A lawyer, he has published numerous papers and monographs on the workings of the criminal justice system in Russia.

Robert M. Lombardo is Deputy Chief of the Cook County (Illinois) Sheriff's Department and Adjunct Professor at De Paul University, Chicago. He is former Commanding Officer of the Chicago Police Department's Asset Forfeiture Unit and has published on that topic in academic journals and for state and federal agencies. He is a contributor to *The Handbook of Organized Crime* (1995) and a Trustee of the International Association for the Study of Organized Crime.

Frederick T. Martens is Director of Security at Claridge Casino, Atlantic City, New Jersey, and former Executive Director of the Pennsylvania Crime Commission and Lieutenant Supervisor of the New Jersey State Police organized crime unit. His expertise on organized crime matters is widely sought, and his writings on organized crime issues appear in academic journals and publications of state and federal agencies. He is Past President of the International Association for the Study of Organized Crime.

James J. McKenna Jr. is Professor of Sociology and Director of Criminal Justice and Human Organization Science at Villanova University, Villanova, Pennsylvania. His professional interests include criminal typologies, sex offenders, drug offenders, custodial suicide, organized crime, and transnational criminal organizations. As an expert witness, he testifies in state and federal courts regarding police procedures and administration, the police use of force, false arrest and imprisonment, high-speed pursuit, suicides in custody, and prison procedures. A Past President of the Pennsylvania Prison Society and Chair of the International Association for the Study of Organized Crime's Election Committee, he has just completed a 6-month research project in Hong Kong, studying Asian organized crime.

Vladimir Moiseev is Professor of Philosophy and Chair of the Department of Philosophy at Irkutsk Graduate Militia College in Irkutsk, Russia. He is an expert on juvenile delinquency and the underclass in the Russian Far East and has published extensively on these topics.

Maurice Punch is Research Professor and Director of Faculty and Doctoral Research at Nijenrode University, the Netherlands, Business School. His current research includes corporate crime, deviant behavior, and regulation and control in business. He is an active member of the International Association for the Study of Organized Crime.

Roy E. Rogers is Assistant Professor of History and Psychology at St. Clair Community College, Port Huron, Michigan. He has held teaching posts at Eastern Michigan University, Ypsilanti; and the Khabarovsk Pedagogical University in Khabarovsk, Russia. He is Co-Director of the Joint Russian-American Academic Committee for the Promotion of the Study of Comparative Criminal Justice, is a member of the International Association for the Study of Organized Crime, and frequently serves as a consultant on the Russian criminal justice system.

Charles H. Rogovin is Professor of Law, Temple University School of Law, Philadelphia, and former Vice Chair of the Pennsylvania Crime Commission and President of the International Association for the Study of Organized Crime. A colleague of Donald R. Cressey, he is a recognized leader in the study of organized crime and expert on the subject.

Ken Sanz is a Special Agent for the Florida Department of Law Enforcement, with more than 24 years of professional experience. He has lectured to and consulted extensively with governmental agencies throughout North America on the topic of organized crime. His most recent research focuses on ethic crime and Asian criminal organizations.

Rufus Schatzberg retired from the New York City Police Department with the rank of First Grade Detective. He is Coeditor of *The Handbook of Organized Crime* (1995). An expert in black organized crime, his publications include *Black Organized Crime in Harlem: 1920-1930* (1994), *African American Organized Crime in the United States: A Social History* (with R. J. Kelly, in press), and numerous articles on terrorism, organized crime, and crime in the schools. He is also a member of the International Association for the Study of Organized Crime.

Victor Shabalin is a Colonel and Professor of Political Science at the Khabarovsk Graduate Militia College in Kahbarovsk, Russia. He is a member of the Criminological Association of

Russia and has participated in the drafting of new laws to combat organized crime in that country. His areas of specialization include the Russian Far East and Russian organized crime.

Ira Silverman is Professor of Criminology at the University of South Florida, Tampa. A founding member and past trustee of the International Association for the Study of Organized Crime, he has published extensively on the subject of organized crime and its workings and structure, and in the field of corrections. His most recent text is *Corrections: A Comprehensive View.*

John Huey-Long Song is Associate Professor in the Department of Criminal Justice at the State University College at Buffalo, New York. His research interests focus on adaptational issues of Asian immigrants to the American legal system. His most recent publications include research reports on the causes of Asian youth gangs, Asian victimization, and the policing of Asian racketeering.

J. Michael Waller is Vice President of the American Foreign Policy Council in Washington, D.C., and author of *Secret Empire: The KGB in Russia Today* (1994). An expert in international security affairs, he is Executive Editor of *Demokratizatsiya: The Journal of Post-Soviet Democratization,* a joint publication of the American University and Moscow State University.

Victor J. Yasmann is at the Jamestown Foundation in Washington, D.C., and was formerly an Analyst at the Radio Free Europe/Radio Liberty Research Institute in Munich, Germany. He is an Editor of the *Monitor* and *Prism* newsletters (Jamestown Foundation) and a Editorial Board Member of *Demokratizatsiya: The Journal of Post-Soviet Democratization.* He specializes in issues concerning mass media, security organs, and corruption in the former Soviet Union.